The Pelican History of the Church

GENERAL EDITOR: OWEN CHADWICK

Contents

Thanks for various kindness to R. W. Southern, Gordon Rupp, H. O. Evennett, H. C. Porter, Basil Hall, John Macauley, A. S. Bell, Martin Chadwick, Hugh Mead, and Edith Baker.

Part One

THE PROTEST

1

The Cry for Reformation

THE IDEA OF REFORMATION

At the beginning of the sixteenth century everyone that mattered in the Western Church was crying out for reformation.

For a century and more Western Europe had sought for reform of the Church 'in head and members' and had failed to find it.

If you asked the thinkers and publicists of the year 1500 what they meant when they proclaimed the Church to be in need of reform, they would not all have found it easy to be practical and definite. There might be excellent reasons for permitting an incumbent not to reside in his parish. The theoretical authority of the Pope might need practically to be diminished and confined within whatever bounds were considered expedient and legitimate. But in fact that authority was already limited, and limited drastically, by the rights of the governments in the various states; and its absolutism in theory was useful in practice as a dispensing agent, a necessary loophole by which princes and bishops might evade the rigorous working of canon law. Everyone confessed that the sale of benefices was deplorable. But the payment of legal fees in connexion with entry upon an ecclesiastical office might be justified as necessary to the running of the legal system. It was at first sight disgraceful that the Bishop of Worcester should be an Italian continuously resident at and engaged upon administrative duties in the court of Rome. But the King of England needed an ecclesiastical agent at the Vatican and thought it not unreasonable that an English ecclesiastical office should pay his stipend. What one honest man believed to be an abuse, another honest man defended.

Everyone wanted reform, or professed to want reform. How to reform and what to reform was not so clear. The energies of some reformers went to create new religious orders, or little groups of prayer and study. Bishops tried to be stricter against ordaining ignorant men, or to compel monks and canons to live according to their rule. But at the administrative level the quest for reform limped along like a lame man who does not know where he is going. From 1512 to 1517 a great Council of the Church, called Ecumenical (though few besides Italians were present), was sitting in the Lateran church at Rome. Its members listened to long and eloquent speeches, and sat for many hours. They agreed, amid much else, that schism and heresy should be suppressed; that the Turks were a danger to the Christian nations; that bishops should have more power over the monks, and that no one might preach except by lawful authority; that the Roman mobs must not sack the cardinals' houses on the Pope's death; that professors in their lectures must establish the truth of the soul's immortality; that the printing of unsound books should be stopped. The men of a reforming spirit might think these conclusions edifying. But some at least did not recognize in the decrees of the Council a fulfilment of the vague and elusive phrase, 'reform in head and members'.

The feeling, diffused through Europe, that the Church must be reformed was as diversified as possible. For Italian bishops it might mean that the constitutional machinery of the Vatican was top-heavy, that the power of the cardinals had increased and should be diminished. For preaching friars it might mean that the lives of their congregations were evil when judged by the ideals of Christian sanctity. For secular lawyers it might mean that the ecclesiastical courts and ecclesiastical exemptions were intolerable obstacles to effective administration. For churchmen it often meant that, amid the creaking and cumbersome mechanisms of clerical bureaucracy, the incidence of church taxation was efficient and burdensome; while a long history of papal warfare or politics or misgovernment had made men sceptical whether the kingdoms of God or of man were receiving any benefit from the revenue. Was it right that a dispensation from Scriptural decrees about marriage should be available, and if it was right, was it right that the dispensation should be so expensive to obtain? Was it not equivalent to one law for the rich and another for the poor? Was it right that a man with money could obtain permission to be married between Septuagesima and Ash Wednesday, and a man without money could not? Why should the centralized administration at Rome have the power to supersede the rights of local patrons in the appointment to benefices, and particularly when the administration seemed to use its power for the interest of its dependants? Was it justice that an ecclesiastic who committed a felony should be immune from the normal jurisdiction of the secular magistrates? When a government urgently needed money for the defence of the realm against Turkish invasion, was it expedient that churchmen should claim their vast endowments to be exempt from the duty of contributing? Was it worthy of the spiritual censures of the Church that the grievous weapon of excommunication should be wielded to collect debts and souls should be driven to desperation for trivial reasons? Why should the curate of a parish starve while his non-resident rector lived in comfort upon the stipend of the benefice? Were not too many of the clergy secularized – brawlers, drunken, adulterous, unworthy of their sacred office? Was not (if the critic was extreme, and perhaps in a pulpit) the modern Church a harlot, selling her beauty to anyone who could pay?

When churchmen spoke of reformation, they were almost always thinking of administrative, legal, or moral reformation; hardly ever of doctrinal reformation. They did not suppose the Pope's doctrine to be erroneous. They supposed the legal system and the bureaucracy to breed inefficiency, graft, injustice, worldliness, and immorality. If they were educated men, humanists of the Renaissance, these desires were sometimes mingled with a plea for intellectual improvement. They not only wanted popes and bishops to be less secularized, monks to practise their rule, parish clergy to be more instructed. They sometimes talked of a theology which should be less remote from human beings, more faithful to the Gospel, a faith which should be less external and more akin to the teaching of the Lord. But to gain this end they had neither desire nor expectation of anything which could be called a change in doctrine.

The sense that reformation was needed, though diffused and often vague, derived its strength from particular occasions. A priest who was observed to be publicly drunken in the taverns was allowed to continue his ministry without rebuke; the scandal was notorious; and it was hardly noticed that in some other cases of drunkenness pastoral discipline was enforced. A corporation engaged in a suit over property with a monastery found settlement to be impossible without such an expenditure of time and money as rendered the distant verdict futile. A cleric known to be guilty of homicide was seen to escape with a modest imprisonment on bread and water. A parish priest kept a concubine openly and was unrebuked. An illiterate devoid of any knowledge of the Latin tongue was ordained to the priesthood, and could be heard mumbling nonsensically through his prayers at the altar; and the parishioners knew nothing of learned and devout men whom elsewhere bishops might be ordaining. Too many scandals; too many inconveniences; too many injustices; too much inefficiency unremedied and apparently irremediable – these lent force to the cry of churchman and of politician for reformation.

The first question, then, in the public mind was not the question: 'Is the teaching of the Catholic Church true?' That teaching was believed to be unaltered through the long centuries of the past, unalterable into the future to eternity. In Bohemia there were Hussite heretics who exercised authority unrepressed. Hidden in the English countryside or in the Alpine valleys there were a few ignorant groups of Lollards or of Waldensians; in Germany a few strange meetings assembled to study the Bible and to frame, as men imagined, a wild medley of sedition and blasphemy. The cry for reformation meant the suppression, not the encouragement, of these secret discontents.

Many of the obvious abuses were abuses by the highest standards of churchmen but were useful to the sovereign of the state or his servants. Linacre, the physician of King Henry VIII, had been rector of four parishes, a canon of three cathedrals, and precentor of York Minster before he was ordained priest. He was receiving payment for his medical services by this variety of rectories and prebends.

These were rather corruptions of the State, perhaps, than of the Church. The king was more responsible than the Pope. The king must reward his servants richly if he were to be well served. Since the Church possessed a big part of the wealth of every country, he could reward many of them only if he placed them in ecclesiastical offices. The great French diplomat, Antoine du Prat, was elevated to the archbishopric of Sens and entered his cathedral for the first time in his funeral procession. Bishops were often more eminent as courtiers than as pastors. When King Louis XII of France entered Italy in 1509, he was accompanied by three French cardinals, two archbishops, five bishops, and the abbot of Fécamp; and the presence of this galaxy owed nothing to an unusual anxiety about the royal conscience. During the second quarter of the sixteenth century, there were twenty-two bishops in the province of Languedoc in southern France, and only five or six were resident in their sees. Graft was no less to be blamed upon the Church when it was royal graft; and yet abuses seemed worse when they were perpetrated by clergymen to the advantage of clergymen. The clergy were the keepers of the public conscience. It was their duty to restrain avarice, to sanctify poverty, to denounce the usurer and the simoniac and the adulterer, to excommunicate even kings if kings fell impenitent into mortal sin, to do justly and to love mercy,

and to walk humbly before God: To these purposes their
pulpits were sacred. If reform was needed, and everyone
was so agreed, it was the duty of the clergy to proclaim its
necessity and to demonstrate by deed and example that
this world was still subject to the Church. They looked upwards to the Pope, set (they believed) by Christ or by
Constantine over kings and princes, and expected that by
his word he could still bring peace and justice and integrity
to the peoples.

No Pope, not even a Hildebrand or an Innocent III,
could have satisfied these loose, uninformed aspirations. For
two hundred years the Pope's power had been sinking before the power of the kings. Though Christendom was still
an idea which could command armies, they were mean
little armies compared with the crusading hosts which once
had assembled to conquer Palestine from the infidel.
The conscience of Christendom was shocked when after
1525 the most Christian King of France was observed to
ally himself with the Turks; shocked when Pope Alexander
VI was among the first of Christian rulers to conduct
such a negotiation. And yet the shock was shallow. Though
men still believed in Christendom and still expected the
Pope to be the head of Christendom, they looked for political
leadership and security to their state and their prince. For
two hundred years the kings and governments had been
limiting the Pope's authority in their territories, restricting
his powers to the confines which suited their purposes, and
securing the effective right to appoint bishops. The authority
of the Pope was still far-flung. Every ruler of western Europe
must still reckon with it. The legal system of Latin Christendom continued to depend upon the papal courts. The
prestige of vicar of Christ and head of Christian society
continued to command a confused assent and respect
among the peoples. But the States of Europe were restricting
papal authority. To expect the Pope to reform the Church
was to expect a miracle which he had little power to perform. He might give impetus to reform by example, or by

influence, or by teaching; but the days were passing when he could command – supposing that he wished to command.

The Pope's prestige has often been moral as well as social and doctrinal. In the years 1500 to 1517 it was entirely social or doctrinal. Under Alexander VI Borgia, Julius II, and Leo X it appeared that the throne of St Peter, like other bishoprics, had become a remunerative if uncomfortable seat for worldly politicians. Not to see the contrast between precept and practice was to be blind. A ribald pamphleteer (perhaps Erasmus) described a dialogue at the gates of heaven when Pope Julius II sought to enter:

JULIUS: Open the door quick. If you had done your duty you would have met me with the full ceremonies of heaven.

ST PETER: You seem to like giving orders. Tell me who you are.

JULIUS: You recognize me, of course.

ST PETER: Do I? I've never seen you before, and at the moment I find the sight extraordinary.

JULIUS: You must be blind. Surely you recognize this silver key . . . Look at my triple crown and my jewelled pall.

ST PETER: I see a silver key. But it looks nothing like the keys which Christ, true Pastor of the Church, gave me . . .

Europe was astonished to see Pope Julius II put himself at the head of the papal armies in north Italy; to see the vicar of Christ, sword at side and helmet on head, climbing the breach in the fortress of Mirandola which his generalship had captured.* That he saved the Papal States from anarchy, that he caused the foundations of St Peter's to be laid (18 April 1506), that he employed Raphael to paint the *stanze* and Michelangelo the ceiling of the Sistine chapel – these were as nothing in the scale of moral judgement now being used. His work seemed that of an Italian, and of a great prince of the Renaissance, not that of an international and moral authority. At Tours in 1510 a commission of French doctors of divinity found itself anxiously debating the question: What is the value of excommunications pro-

---

* The Archbishop of York commanded one of the Pope's armies during part of this north Italian campaign.

nounced by the Pope against a king resisting aggression by the Pope's army?

For centuries men blasphemed in their cups and bawdy songs, and improvised anti-clerical ditties for their drinking friends. Now these amusements were no longer confined to the tavern. They were becoming public property, the reading and the commonplace of honourable and educated men.

The puritan of the Middle Ages saw in money the root of nearly all evil. And perhaps the most painful contrast between religious ideal and clerical practice lay at this point. Religious men, following St Francis of Assisi or Thomas a Kempis or countless others of the medieval Church, still believed poverty to be part of the highest moral endeavour. But they no longer revered poor men. The holy beggar was no longer the object of unqualified admiration; partly because experience had shown too high a proportion of frauds, but partly because the moral ideal was beginning to be modified in the presence of social and economic changes. Yet the devout men still assumed the ancient ideal of poverty and detachment. 'It is vanity to seek riches which shall perish and to trust in them. It is vanity to pursue office and climb to high rank. It is vanity to follow the desires of the flesh . . . vanity to wish for long life . . . vanity to love what passeth away so quickly, and not to hasten where abideth joy everlasting' (*Imitation of Christ I*, 1). The moral ideal was other-worldly; still monastic or quasi-monastic. But educated men, the middle class, the humanists, drinking deep from the springs of a rediscovered literature of Greece and Rome, filled with delight in this world, and finding themselves in a society of growing wealth, sensed incongruity and discrepancy between the ideal and the everyday life in which they found themselves. The old values inherited from the past were in conflict with the material and intellectual strivings of the present.

Money the root of evil – and yet ecclesiastical benefices seemed to the laity too often a mode of heaping gold upon gold. And in the realm of money, in the opportunities for ecclesiastical good living, it seemed to many observers that Rome was pre-eminent. Everything in the Church, said the critics with exaggeration, is sold for money – pardons, masses, candles, ceremonies, curacies, benefices, bishoprics, the Papacy itself. 'If Popes, the vicars of Christ, tried to imitate his life – that is his poverty, labour, doctrine, cross, and contempt of this world ... would they be like the Popes who nowadays buy their see with money and defend it with sword and poison?'

Erasmus was at Rome in 1509, Luther in 1511; and neither of them quite liked it. Much later, Luther said: 'I would not have missed seeing Rome for a hundred thousand florins, for then I might have been afraid of being unjust to the Pope.'

The word *reformation* (which, unlike the word *renaissance*, was used widely by contemporaries and had been used for two centuries and more) shows that this quest for better things was characteristically medieval in looking backwards for its model and its standard. All the writers of the later Middle Ages saw the primitive Church through rose-coloured glass. In the lives of the saints they read of heroism and apostolic zeal; and seeing the ordinary or worse than ordinary men around them, they looked back wistfully and uncritically. Once there was a golden age. There was devotion, fervour, religion, holy priests, purity of heart. But now that ancient age of gold has degenerated imperceptibly to silver, from silver to wood, from wood to iron. 'There is as much difference between us and the men of the primitive church as there is between muck and gold.' This was no new cry of the fifteenth century. Three hundred years before, St Bernard of Clairvaux wished before he died to see the Church as it was in ancient days, when the apostles cast their nets for souls, and not for gold and silver. It was one of the typical appeals of the medieval preacher. Many reformers thought that the Emperor Constantine caused the disaster by his donation (the gift of lands and secular authority to Pope Sylvester), that the golden age of Christendom had been ruined when the Pope acquired wealth. The new humanists of the fifteenth century were less naïve in their attitude to Constantine, and one of them, the papal secretary Valla, proved the legend of the donation to be a later forgery. But although the faint beginnings of a critical history made it less easy to think of a black present and a white past, a learned humanist like Erasmus still believed, if moderately, in a lost age of sanctity and purity. The Reformation always looked backwards.

A hundred years before, the claims of rival and competing popes forced churchmen to plan a reform of the Church in head and members. The Council of Constance (1414–18) and the Council of Basle (1431–9) met, passed many resolutions, and triumphantly ended the conflict in the Papacy. Their aspirations after reform in the administration and the piety of the Church were foiled by events, and by the weight of national and vested interests. But, while they had not done what they intended, they had sown dragons' teeth which by 1500 were springing up into armed warriors. Those Councils gave the idea of reformation such an airing that it could never be forgotten. They talked frankly, clamoured for change, advertised abuses, suggested remedies, evoked claims and an idealism which they had then failed to satisfy. They thereby multiplied discontent. If they failed in their practical aim, they left behind a state of public opinion which was restless, critical, disquieted, impatient, demanding reform in theory, and not always sensible of the practical consequences. In 1496 a Frenchman wrote that in men's conversation no topic was more frequent than that of reform.

Widespread, popular, and unsatisfied demands for reform are usually, in the end, revolutionary.

The demand grew by feeding on itself. Every bishop (and there were many) who attempted reforming measures in his diocese was liable not only to meet bitter resistance there but to raise further aspirations in neighbouring and neglected dioceses. Every monk who sought to persuade the monastery to a strict and regular life seemed to vilify other houses. To demand reform is to denounce abuse. To denounce abuse is to raise doubts in the public mind, to criticize officials, to hold them up to public opprobrium. To demand reform was to diminish the prestige of Pope, bishops, monks, friars, and parish priests, and to open the way to further criticism. The government of the hierarchy was being weakened by attacks upon the clerical order.

The word *anticlericalism* might be misleading, since it suggests the different bitternesses of the nineteenth century. But in 1502 Erasmus said that a layman was insulted unpardonably if he were called a cleric, priest, or a monk. In 1515 the Bishop of London, whose chancellor was reputed to have murdered a merchant tailor, told Cardinal Wolsey that in the circumstances a jury of any twelve men in London would condemn any cleric, though he were as innocent as Abel. Mr Skidmore of Isleworth said a few years later that 'Welshmen and priests' were sore disdained nowadays.

This cry for reformation, growing as a wind whips up the waves, was not a new standard of judgement and criticism. The demand had grown from the academic programme of a university into the clamour of a people. Yet it is needful to ask why the old desire was so much more potent now than a hundred years before. For reform seemed to have been frustrated. At the end of all the endeavours of the fifteenth century the Papacy had produced Pope Alexander VI Borgia. Reform had been tried, and had failed.

The tragedy of the Dominican friar Savonarola has given posterity this sense of failure in a dramatic form. When the French king Charles VIII passed through Florence in 1494, Savonarola begged him with passion to convene an ecumenical council at Rome and depose Pope Alexander VI. To the conquests of France the Pope was more useful upon his throne. Savonarola, burning with moral and prophetic power, persuaded the city of Florence to accept Christ as king, attacked luxury and simony and the papal curia, defied a papal suspension and then an excommunication, dispatched wild appeals to the sovereigns of Europe to convoke the reforming council, and, deserted at last by the Florentine mob, was burnt upon the piazza of the Signory on 23 May 1498. His was the medieval cry for reform, uttered in the old way, triumphant for a moment in the old way, suppressed in the old way. Most of his contemporaries saw little of importance in the tragedy. Less than twenty-five years later Erasmus, whose appeals for reform were half as passionate and twice as effective, thought Savonarola's defiance to be a sad example of the evils to be found among friars.

But what was it that made the call to reformation more potent and more revolutionary in the early sixteenth century than a hundred years before? Was it simply that the abuses were worse? That corruption so rotted the carcass that the hollow body collapsed in the moment when it was pushed?

The evidence upon this point, though hard to judge, suggests not. The Reformation came not so much because Europe was irreligious as because it was religious. The medieval Church begat repeated waves of fervent idealism, and was doing so again. The abuses now condemned were always abuses and always condemned at the bar of public opinion. A lot of parish priests were ignorant in 1500, a lot of parish priests were ignorant in every age. The reformers were under an illusion in looking back towards a golden age. The Church came to dominate western Europe in rough times, and the scars of that roughness could still be seen upon it. Most of the abuses were not so much worse. What was new was the extent of men's awareness of the defects in Church order and the possibility of remedy.

In certain areas, and in certain practices, there had been decline during the fifteenth century. The new world of credit afforded opportunities to the self-seeker beyond the

wilder dreams of his predecessors. There was a new blatancy
in non-residence, in piling up ecclesiastical offices, in keeping concubines, in drawing the pay of a priest without being
ordained as a priest. 'We Italians,' wrote Machiavelli,
'are more irreligious and corrupt than others ... because
the Church and its representatives set us the worst example,'
and there may be a truth somewhere in the complacent self-
accusation. But there was plenty of reforming idealism even
in the Italy of the later Renaissance.

What is undoubted is the extent of religious practice.
Henry VIII was said to hear three masses on days when he
was hunting and sometimes five on other days; and the
devout Margaret Beaufort heard six masses every day.
Medieval fervour threw up new modes of devotion, and the
later fifteenth century saw several new forms of piety.
Savonarola persuaded the Florentines to bring their
treasures and burn them; in 1507 Pope Julius II sanctioned
the cult of the holy house at Loreto, believed to be the
Lord's home miraculously transported by angels from
Nazareth; the Dominican Alain de la Roche (died 1475)
popularized the (much older) use of the rosary; in the
churches a characteristic monument was the Pietà, the
Virgin of pity with her dead Son; it was the age when the
Stations of the Cross began to be placed upon the walls of
churches; the union of a bell with a prayer of the Virgin,
known thereafter as the Angelus, is of the later fourteenth
century. A part of what is loosely known as 'Counter-
Reformation devotion' began to flower before the Reformation.

The strong and popular devotion to the Virgin was
accompanied by a marked growth in the cult of the saints
and their relics, and of pilgrimage to their shrines. Ill-
regulated fervour could be superstitious or even demonic.
In 1500 more witches were being tortured and burnt, more
Jews were being persecuted. But superstition was no innovation. Since the darkest ages peasants had consumed the
dust from saints' tombs or used the Host as an amulet or

collected pretended relics or believed incredible and un-edifying miracles or substituted the Virgin or a patron saint for the Saviour. In 1500 they were ardently doing these things. What was new was not so much the practice as the way in which the leaders of opinion were beginning to regard it.

In short, the perpetual gap between the religions of the literate and the illiterate was widening till it could hardly be bridged. While popular devotions, mingled with popular superstition, seemed to be almost uncontrollable by bishops or by theologians, while the ardour of the people was seeking the emotional cult, the printing press was at work publishing more than 100 editions of the Bible between 1457 and 1500.

We must therefore seek other explanations than the simple theory that the Church was too bad to continue, and consider two special circumstances: the increasing control of kings over their kingdoms, and the improved education of the intelligent minds of the western world.*

THE POWER OF GOVERNMENT

Kings Henry VII and Henry VIII were more powerful in England than any of their predecessors. King Ferdinand and Queen Isabella in Spain likewise; the kings of Portugal and Denmark, certain German princes, and even the German Emperor, were less weak than their recent predecessors. Government, though not modern, was becoming a little more modern. The pace varied from land to land. In England the private armies of the barons had been exhausted

* Some writers add a third circumstance – the discovery of America and the consequent widening of horizon and unsettlement of mind. There is little evidence to warrant so large a conclusion. The practical and social consequences became grave in the later sixteenth century, especially in the inflation of prices, but after the Protestant revolt. The theoretical consequences beset Christian thinkers only in the seventeenth century. There would have been Martin Luther if there had not been Christopher Columbus.

in the Wars of the Roses and the lords thereafter weakened by the Tudors; in France the feudal nobility remained great enough to divide the realm; in Poland the nobility was gaining control over the king. But the foundations of a civil service, of an improved machinery for administration and justice at the centre, the use of trained lawyers – these ingredients of a modern state marked the constitutional development of several realms during that age. And around these more effective governments was gathering the idea of the nation, the half-conscious and yet patriotic loyalty of their peoples.

The relation between this and the success of a Protestant revolt is undoubted but not easy to define. It might be said broadly that in England, and in Denmark, the Reformation came because limitation of the power of the Church was necessary to the further development of efficient government. Efficient government demanded restraint upon papal intervention, upon ecclesiastical privilege and exemptions, upon the legal right of an authority outside the country to levy taxes. In all the states of western Europe, and not only in the states which would later become Protestant, this began to happen before 1500.

But this connexion between constitutional development and the Protestant revolt, which looms so large in English history that it dwarfs every other consideration, was not a general rule throughout Europe. Before the Reformation began, the kings of Spain and France partially satisfied their need to control the Church. In 1478 the Pope granted to the Spanish sovereigns the right to set up and direct the Inquisition: a system of courts which effectively controlled the churchmen of the land and was under the immediate authority, not of the Pope or the bishops, but of the king. The inquisitors had power over all religious orders and (after 1531) over bishops, and there was no appeal to Rome from their verdicts. The kings of France, like the kings of England, but with more success, limited the interference of the Pope during the fifteenth century. In 1516, after long interviews between the Pope and King Francis I, was signed the Concordat of Bologna, which determined the legal relation of Pope and Crown until the French Revolution of 1789. The king secured the right of appointment to all the higher posts in the Church of France, and placed within narrow limits the right of appeal by the clergy to the see of Rome. He could now nominate to 10 archbishoprics, 82 bishoprics, 527 abbeys, and numerous priories and canonries, and as dispenser of these favours and their endowments he was indirectly in control of the property of the Church. When he wanted ecclesiastical money, his methods need not even be devious.

In the fifteenth century the kings of England were already controlling the appointments to bishoprics. Even the weak emperor Frederick III in Germany, even the weaker kings of Scotland, obtained this right of nomination to many sees. The Republic of Venice fought several battles with Rome to the same end. The Popes were slowly losing actual (not theoretical) authority over the churches in the different states, the appointments to higher posts, the right to levy contributions and to maintain the immunity of ecclesiastical estates from taxation, and the right to hear appeals without interference. But it is certain that the Popes had never before given away so much authority as by allowing the Spanish Inquisition and by granting the Concordat of Bologna to the French king. The Pope was becoming weaker because the governments were becoming stronger. And the stronger the government, the more helpless lay the vast wealth and possessions of the Church and the more dangerous to vested interests and to corruption was the cry for reform.

The Reformation was not always a means by which legitimate sovereigns strengthened their hold upon their states. The contrary is sometimes true. In many lands the Protestant revolt was associated with a political revolt against an external or foreign sovereign – as in Scotland, the Netherlands, Sweden, some of the Swiss cities, some of the

German princedoms seeking freedom from imperial supervision. Even the English political revolution against the Pope was a faint reflection of the discarding of a foreign master.

As the power of the prince was increasing and the power of the Pope decreasing, Church reformers looked to the government for effective power to reform. Reform needed a knife to cut through the legal knots which protected established abuse. In the tangle of rights and prescriptions, the conflict of legal systems secular and ecclesiastical, the rival jurisdiction of courts, the constant opportunity for delaying tactics, the powerlessness of the diocesan system, and the anarchy in some parts of the ecclesiastical administration, the idle and the vicious flourished comfortably. You wished to reform a monastery? If you went to the provincial of the order, or the bishop, or the Pope, you would probably end in years of frustrating litigation, at the end of which little good had been done; but if you went to the king, he might break rudely through the tangle and order the monks to behave or begone. The best of reformers, at least in Spain, England, France, Germany, wanted the sovereign to act. He alone possessed the power to act effectively.

The Cardinal d'Amboise, empowered by the king to conduct a reformation in France, needed fortifying for reform with a Bull (from Pope Alexander VI) giving him full authority as papal legate. Thus armed with weapons from the heads of Church and State, he conducted an admirable reformation of several monastic houses and congregations. In 1501 he determined to reform the Cordeliers at Paris, and commissioned two bishops to visit and reform the house. When the commission arrived, the friars hurried away to the chapel, exposed the blessed sacrament, and began singing psalms. The two bishops waited for four hours and then, frustrated, went away. Next day they came back with the Provost of Paris, a hundred archers, and a band of constables. Again the friars fell to their psalms. They were stopped, and the papal bulls and royal decrees were read to them. They replied by quoting extracts in a contrary sense from their charters and the canon law. After a prolonged deadlock, and a different commission composed of Cordeliers, the Cardinal at last secured a measure of reform in the house.

In the tangle of law, the reformer, though he needed papal power, needed royal powers also. He carried with him the decrees of the king as well as the bulls of the Pope, and he might need the king's guards. In modern language, though the State had always been necessary to the reform of the Church, it was becoming ever more necessary as its own power grew more effective, more sovereign.

The old ideal of a unity in Christendom was collapsing before the rise of the national states. The Vatican still trumpeted forth the claims of an Innocent III or Boniface VIII to world dominion. In 1493 Pope Alexander VI, as lord of the continents, divided the newly discovered world of America and the Indies between Spain and Portugal. In a European conflict Popes might still talk of deposing enemy kings from their kingdoms. Before a solemn audience of Alexander VI in St Peter's, Chieregato repeated the age-long interpretation of the two swords of power, the spiritual sword wielded by the Church and the temporal sword wielded by the State at the behest of the Pope. These vast pretensions corresponded to little enough in the cold reality of European politics. The Pope could sometimes secure what he wanted, but by diplomacy, no longer by decree. Bulls might thunder forth, and were still potent when they thundered, but behind the scenes there had been bargaining. To achieve anything important in France, Spain, Portugal, England, parts of Italy, parts of Germany, the Pope must secure the cooperation or the complaisance of the effective ruler. This was the age when the See of Rome first found it desirable to retain ambassadors (nuncios) in the European capitals. The first permanent nunciatures were set up at Venice in 1500 and at Paris in 1513. Men no longer bowed before the dread rebukes of the Church. They arranged them, compromised with them, argued about them, even bought them against their enemy – for in 1500 they were decidedly worth buying.

As the system of European states grew into manhood, the Italian needs and responsibility of the Papacy loomed larger relatively to the international responsibility. Like the other rulers of Europe, the ruler of the Papal States had to establish efficient control over his territories. The officials of the see needed to be Italian; popes were made to sign promises before election that all the Roman offices should go to Romans; the number of Italian cardinals steadily increased. To retain a majority of Italian cardinals was also to keep at a distance the pressure which kings might seek to exercise through their national cardinals. During the fifteenth century there were only two non-Italian popes, and one of them was Alexander VI Borgia. There was one more non-Italian pope, Adrian VI, who reigned briefly in 1522–3. There has not yet been another. It was hardly conceivable that a non-Italian could effectively perform the Italian duties of the Pope.

THE NEW LEARNING

The upper classes, the rulers, the merchants, were beginning to be better educated. The presses were working, the printers were multiplying, the libraries, though still tiny by later standards, were adding to the number and range of their books. The press made possible methods of study which were in embryo in the days of manuscripts. Texts could be compared, instruments of study acquired more cheaply, critical editions prepared, though the word 'critical' could not be used as it could in the seventeenth century, for the manuscripts still lay hidden in the library chests, and the methods of scholarship were not experienced. More people were reading books. Knowledge was increasing.

But the Renaissance was not only new information. It was a movement of the spirit as well as the mind. The idea of the Renaissance is irretrievably vague. Sometimes it has been supposed that the new atmosphere of individualism, of delight in the human being, of nature and art and the achievement of mankind, was a necessary and direct background to the religious revolution, as though man was rising like a Samson to cast off the withes which bound him to orthodoxy and the ascetic ideal. Stated thus baldly, the alleged connexion between Renaissance and Reformation is so obviously untrue that the most elementary knowledge of the age is sufficient to disprove it; so obviously untrue that opinions may be found to assert paradoxically that there was no connexion between Renaissance and Reformation. Sane historians do not doubt that the connexion, though not precisely that of cause and effect, was intimate. But it is much easier to be sure that the connexion exists than clearly to define it. Moral fervour like that of St Bernard was more responsible for the Reformation than critical freedom like that of Peter Abelard. It was more a movement of faith than of reason.

The humanists were as varied as possible. They had little in common except a love of classical antiquity. The humanists of Italy, where the revival of the classics was linked with the rising sense of nationalism and the glories of the Italian past, lived in an atmosphere markedly different from that of the humanists of the north, of Germany, France, and England. Italian humanism was literary, artistic, philosophical, whereas northern humanism was religious, even theological. This contrast, like many historical contrasts, diminishes on close inspection. It would be wrong to take seriously the affected paganisms of an eccentric like Pomponio Leto, who called himself High Priest, knelt every day in front of an altar dedicated to King Romulus, and every year celebrated the founding of the city of Rome. With a few marked exceptions, Italian humanism conformed to a religious spirit, and in the north there was an evident humanism of philosophy and literature. But the contrast remains. In France and Germany and England there was a movement taking a stimulus from the Italians and their renewed love of Greek and Latin antiquity, but transforming it into a decidedly religious context; the movement often known as Christian humanism, and represented at its best by John Colet and Sir Thomas More in England, by Lefèvre of Étaples in France, and above all by Erasmus of Rotterdam.

ERASMUS (*c.* 1466–1536)

Erasmus thought that in his boyhood northern Europe knew nothing of the new classical learning already flowering in Italy. He cannot be said without reservations to have devoted his life to any cause, for he loved his comforts dearly. But in so far as he undertook a cause, he intended to encourage the new studies by example and by precept and to remedy this state of northern 'barbarism'. Between 1498 and 1514 he lived in Paris, Oxford, and Italy, taught for two years at Cambridge, and thereafter settled at Basle, with intervals, until his death in 1536. Though his harmless vanity sometimes flattered him that he alone had educated the northern universities, the stream of learning was flowing more widely than he ever owned. But more than any other humanist, he wrote books which penetrated the homes and the studies of northern readers. The bookshops sold them in numbers prodigious for those days. A printer in Paris who heard a suggestion that the Sorbonne might soon condemn *The Colloquies* as heretical, hurried through the press an edition of 24,000 copies. Erasmus was more than a master of style and of scholarship. His natural wit was fed by a delicate and humorous and sometimes cynical observation of human beings. He could write to instruct and move as well as to amuse. But while he could not be dull, he was rarely superficial, his intellect was powerful as well as agile, he penetrated to the core of his subject.

As a satirist he poked fun, often gentle and sometimes bitter, at nearly all the various professions or classes of the state. His whimsical ridicule pricked or goaded kings, merchants, soldiers, tradesmen, scholars. Among all the targets, he aimed his most penetrating shafts at the abuses of the Church. It is a question whether he directed his thrusts at the Church more because worldly clergymen are easy prey for the satirist, or because he was offended in his moral sense and believed that ridicule gave a cutting edge to the plea for reform. The Netherlands was the home of those cells of reforming zeal and devotion known as the Brethren of the Common Life, the milieu from which had risen the peak of medieval devotional writing, *The Imitation of Christ*; and Erasmus received part of his education under their care. It is plain, at least, that he was not writing only to please, not writing only because he knew that criticism of ecclesiastics would multiply his sales. Erasmus was not fired by a reforming passion or zeal. But his sensible and scholarly nose was otherwise offended by the stink of corruption. He despised ignorance, superstition, obscurantism, and wished to cure them. Because his pen was able to portray those vices in the most entertaining light, he could communicate his own contempt to countless other minds. The diffused effect of writings like *The Praise of Folly* (1511) or *The Colloquies* (1518) cannot be calculated.

Educated men were mumbling all these things about the clergy, about monks and popes, corruption and graft, popular superstition and idolatrous practices. Erasmus expressed, and brilliantly, what they were barely articulating; and educated Europe laughed. Kings and bishops, scholars and merchants, anyone with a claim to be educated, hailed him at first with amusement and then with serious approval. By 1517 he had become part of the accepted order. Not so much in Italy, but in France and England and Spain and Germany, the new learning and Erasmian critique of the Church went hand in hand, especially among churchmen. More than any other single man, he lowered the European reputation of popes and clergy, monks and friars, and (above all) of the theologians.

Above all the theologians. He once described a contemporary as 'a scab of a fellow, theology incarnate'. He condemned them as pedants, logic-choppers, manipulators of meaningless notions, constructors of syllogisms, warriors over terms. 'A man might sooner find his way out of a labyrinth than the intellectual mazes of the Realists, Nominalists, Thomists, Albertists, Occamists, Scotists.'

This public scorn of the school-theologians weakened the bastions of traditional doctrine. It needs explanation. It is well known that the problems of logic and ethics and metaphysics can confuse the mind, but to despise them is not therefore inevitable.

The contempt for the schoolmen included a contempt for their 'crabbed' (that is, not Ciceronian) style or faulty grammar. But this was something deeper, stronger, more passionate than the contempt of a romantic poet or a neo-Gothic architect for his classical predecessors. It is more to be compared with the 'Battle between the Ancients and the Moderns' at the end of the seventeenth century, a battle wherein the literary disagreements rested upon a deeper discord of philosophy, the ancients thinking the moderns rash and perhaps heretical, the moderns thinking the ancients narrow and fanatical. 'I heard a camel preaching at Louvain,' said one of Erasmus's characters, 'that we should have nothing to do with anything that is new.'

First, the theologians were defending a creed by methods which seemed to be obsolete. Their theology was entangled with philosophical principles which many philosophers had ceased to believe.

For two hundred years the school of Nominalist philosophy*

* Nominalism: the axiom that only the individual is real. Therefore it is impossible to frame syllogisms with a universal premise, since the 'universal' is only a collection of unique individuals. Hence a strong scepticism about merely logical conclusions, as opposed to conclusions derived from observation or experience.

had been conquering the universities of northern Europe. The Nominalists were sceptical about the power of the human reason to reach true conclusions in the realm of metaphysics. They were known as 'the modern school' and were more or less dominant, by the year 1500, in many leading universities of Germany and France.

The Nominalists were orthodox by intention and were not overthrowing the doctrines of the Church. But they illustrated the helplessness of the reasoning faculty by displaying its inability to demonstrate the leading doctrines of Christianity. They were therefore sceptical about the great *Summae*, the medieval reconciliations between Christian doctrine and the natural philosophy of the Aristotelians. Many of these *Summae*, though written from diverse standpoints according to the school of the authors, constructed their reconciliations upon a confidence in the power of reason. The Nominalists believed that this ill-founded confidence undermined the massive structures of theology at their base and made them imposing piles of rubble. They did not think the doctrines of the Church to be untrue. They thought them to be known not by reason but by revelation – by the authority of the Bible or of the Church, indeed by the authority of both Bible and Church.

The attitude of theologians towards the doctrine of transubstantiation is a momentous illustration of the change in philosophy. St Thomas Aquinas, following his school of philosophy, distinguished between the 'substance' (or universal concept of the bread) and the 'accidents' (or external properties of the individual pieces of bread). He expounded the mystery of the Eucharist by proposing that the substance of the bread was changed into the substance of the Body of Christ, while the accidents, its appearance and colour and taste and shape, remained those of bread. The Nominalists could not believe, on rational grounds only, in the real existence of a universal or 'substance' of bread. Since the individual alone is 'real', they could only conceive a change of substance to mean a change of accidents at the same time. They believed the doctrine of transubstantiation to be true. The Church authenticated it and therefore it was true. Had we but the reason as a guide, we should think it untrue. But in such a mystery the reason is helpless.

The Nominalist theologians thus drove a wedge between truth known by revelation and the doubts of the rational faculty. No longer were they seeking a concord between faith and reason, for faith and reason seemed to be lodged upon different planes, and to harmonize them was like mingling oil and water. Religious philosophy was falling into disrepute. The rope of Nominalism was throttling the windpipe through which the philosophers had breathed. Soon after the beginning of the English Reformation, Oxford men were tearing the heavy folios of Duns Scotus and using them as wastepaper. This symptom of an attitude to Duns Scotus was not a consequence of the Reformation, but a cause. His majestic constructions looked like intellectual wastepaper.

The critics of the fifteenth and sixteenth century fastened with zest upon the minutiae which the schoolmen thought it possible to resolve. A confidence in rational theology ended in over-confidence about the possibility of inference. It is a later scandal, and untrue, that the schoolmen discussed the number of angels who could dance upon the point of a pin. But St Thomas Aquinas, for example, argued whether if angels have local motion they pass through intermediate space, or whether an angel can be in more than one place at one and the same time. On the axioms available to Aquinas it seemed rational to pursue the answers to these questions. On the axioms of the Nominalists it seemed irrational. These answers not being given in Scripture or the definitions of the Church, reason was incapable of finding them. Instead of seeking real solutions to real problems, the Thomists appeared to the Nominalist critics to be merely presumptuous.

To Erasmus and to the early Reformers, educated in a society sceptical of the metaphysical reason, the word *syllogism* stank of absurdity and complacency. These divines, wrote Erasmus contemptuously, think that, like Atlas bearing the heaven upon his shoulders, they are under-propping the Catholic Church with their syllogistical buttresses.

Philosophy was not dead. The Franciscans were still Scotist, the Dominicans still Thomist, and the study of the old ways of thought continued at the universities. But it was no longer the main effort of philosophers. The Nomi-nalists, shrinking from insoluble problems, turned their studies towards logic and the problems of meaning. And thus they carried philosophy away from the realm of theo-logy.

The study of logic, though healthy for the mind, offers meagre food for the soul. Sir Thomas More once said that he 'might as soon obtain bodily nourishment by milking a he-goat into a sieve as spiritual nourishment by reading the schoolmen'.

On top of this internal decay of the school theologians came the humanist criticism, with its lack of interest in the philosophical inquiry, its unprofessional ideas of a less narrow form of education, and its affection for critical and historical inquiry.

The clash between the schoolman and the humanist may not have been inevitable. It is easy to exaggerate the discord between the old learning and the new. Some of the ensuing controversy was not because the schoolmen closed their eyes to new knowledge but because the new scholars were arrogant, contemptuous, and aggressive. Nevertheless, the tradition of the schools often suffered from the worst defects of traditionalism. In 1505 Wimpfeling is said to have distressed the University of Freiburg by trying to prove that Christ, St Paul, and St Augustine had not been monks. Lefèvre of Étaples fell into a long battle when he suggested that Mary Magdalene and Mary the sister of Martha were not the same person. Erasmus believed that the Epistle to the Hebrews was not written by St Paul, doubted whether

the book of Revelation was from the hand of St John the
Apostle, knew that the Trinitarian verse of the first Epistle
of John was found in none of the Greek manuscripts, discerned that the works of Dionysius the Areopagite were
spurious. If the standards of criticism were still vague and
uncertain, they were creating conflict between the new
studies and the outworks of the orthodoxy which the school
theologians were guarding.

In 1514–16 a quarrel over the German scholar Reuchlin
rent the scholars into two camps. A convert Jew named
Pfefferkorn ran a campaign to confiscate Jewish books that
were anti-Christian. Reuchlin was a strange, theosophical,
ranging philologist who was founding the modern study of
the Hebrew language. His reputation for scholarship enabled
Erasmus to compare him to St Jerome. He was already
unpopular with conservatives because he dabbled mysteriously in Hebrew cabbalism. His study of Hebrew disclosed
to him certain weaknesses in the text of the Latin Vulgate
Bible. He defended the Jewish books and attacked Pfefferkorn. In 1511, he wrote a book entitled *Augenspiegel* to
defend the utility for Christian scholars of the Jewish Talmud,
which Dominicans of Cologne were proposing to burn. His
book was condemned by the inquisitors at Mainz and
solemnly burnt at Cologne. Both sides appealed to the Pope,
who finally upheld the condemnation in 1520. The efforts
of the inquisitors to secure Reuchlin's fall appeared to be so
bigoted and ignorant as to drive most of the German humanists into sympathy with Reuchlin and contempt for his
opponents. Two enemies of the Cologne inquisitors, Ulrich
von Hutten and Crotus Rubianus, wrote *Letters of Obscure
Men* (1515) as a skit upon their methods, a skit which
mocks all the 'theologians' in a common ridicule. The idea
of an *obscurantist* was forming.

The line which divides dogma from theological opinion
was not, and is not, easy to draw. Intending no critique
of dogma, the humanists could not trample cynically upon
the conventional theologians without approaching the

foundations of the Catholic tradition. Erasmus had a programme for the recovery of true theology.

In 1503 he published the *Enchiridion militis Christiani* (Handbook for the Christian Warrior), an attempt to expound the lines of this true theology. It was a simpler theology, more primitive, more Biblical, less tangled in logical subtlety and more direct to the human soul, stripped of the layers of glosses and authorities and commentaries. In 1516 he published an edition of the Greek New Testament, and appended a largely fresh Latin translation. For the Gospels he used a poor Greek manuscript of the fourteenth century, for the Acts and Epistles two Greek manuscripts of a similar date, and for the Apocalypse a manuscript of the eighth century which he erroneously believed to be apostolic. But though his version was mostly no better than the Vulgate, which he sometimes altered without sufficient reason, it was much to have begun the use of Greek manuscripts. He wanted everyone to be able to read the Bible in the vernacular, he wanted it circulated to the humblest. He discarded the commentaries of the schoolmen, and sent the student with a caution to the Fathers. He published editions of Jerome and others among the Latin Fathers, made translations from Athanasius and Chrysostom and others among the Greeks. He wanted the Bible to come fresh to the human breast, and wrote a Latin paraphrase of all the books in the New Testament except the Apocalypse.

Compared with this new study of the Bible and judged by this quest for simplicity, the complexities and irrationalities of popular devotion seemed ridiculous. Erasmus and his fellows were impatient, contemptuous, angry with the superstitions of the people. Those superstitions, cults of statues, visits to Madonnas that rolled their eyes or to bleeding Hosts, seemed to be not mere harmless vehicles of a rude devotion, not merely vulgar and credulous, but the bane of true religion. The people cultivated a religion of external acts and substituted a pilgrimage, an indulgence, a relic, for a genuine change in heart and life. It is the better side of Erasmus, the concern for true religion, which turned his satire into the severest form of condemnation. 'Perhaps thou believest that all thy sins are washed away with a little paper, a sealed parchment, with the gift of a little money or some wax images, with a little pilgrimage. Thou art utterly deceived.' 'Without ceremonies perhaps thou shalt not be a Christian; but they make thee not a Christian.' The agelong medieval sense of contrast between ideal and reality was beginning to merge into an educated sense of contrast between the Bible and the religion popularly practised in the Church.

Europe wanted reform, and was not expecting revolution. Like Erasmus, many educated men would have preferred the Church to be ridiculed into good sense and efficiency and purity of life. But a man who is holding property will not be mocked out of it. There were forces more potent at work, both to maintain the existing state of the Church, which would not be altered without violence and illegality, and to ask whether the existing state of the Church was not the symptom of a deep-seated and moral disease. There was a celebrated saying of the sixteenth century: 'Erasmus laid the egg and Luther hatched it.' It is certain, at least, that Erasmus alone would not, and could not, have hatched it. He afterwards said that he would have written his books otherwise if he had foreseen what was coming.

2

Luther

ONE main difficulty for the Pope in the expensive Renaissance world was bankruptcy.

For years the Roman administration had been living beyond its income; and to meet the rising costs, fees for dispensations, exemptions, bulls of indulgence and the like were steadily raised. The fees paid by some eminent churchmen were enormous. Miles of Illiers, Bishop of Chartres, disbursed 30,000 livres in taxes, legal fees, and bribes. Not all this money reached Rome.

In the inefficient state of the administration all kinds of intermediaries took their reward, from the officials of kings downwards. The Pope suffered all the blame while he gained a fragment of the reward. Faced with heavy deficits, he created new offices and sold them; and since each new office possessed a claim upon income, this unwise procedure was equivalent to living on capital and at the expense of posterity. Under Innocent VIII a group of criminals made a large sum of money by forging bulls for sale, and nothing illuminates the financial atmosphere better than that this enterprise was possible and lucrative.

The income of the Republic of Venice was about a million ducats. Even at the best, the Pope's income failed to attain half a million, yet he must bear political, spiritual, and sometimes military responsibilities far beyond those of Venice.

In 1484 Pope Innocent VIII was forced to pawn his tiara for 100,000 ducats. Pope Alexander VI, whose financial acumen was one of his main virtues, balanced the budget. His successor Julius II spent lavishly in all directions in his endeavour to raise the Papacy to its European status in politics and in his magnificent patronage of the great artists and architects. Leo X continued the expenditure. In 1513 he owed at least 125,000 ducats.

He who overspends puts himself for the time into the power of the bank. The financial houses of Europe, like the Medici in Florence or the Giustiniani at Genoa or the Fugger at Augsburg, provided the necessary credits. Efficient in their conduct of business, they often ensured for their own security that the means of ecclesiastical finance were efficiently collected. The bankers began to be familiar with the sources of papal revenue, with exemptions and provisions and dispensations and indulgences, and to expect that they should receive their just share as interest upon their loan and repayment of its capital.

In that expanding world others besides popes needed credit. Kings often needed to send agents, cap-in-hand, to the banks. The Fugger once saved Charles V from political calamity. Archbishops also needed credit, and it was an archbishop whose need for credit fatally linked the cry for administrative reform with doctrine.

THE INDULGENCE

Archbishop Albert of Mainz was a prince aged twenty-seven, brother of the Elector of Brandenburg. He was also Archbishop of Magdeburg (in which diocese lay Wittenberg) and administrator of the see of Halberstadt. To combine these high offices he needed dispensations from Rome. The fees for dispensation on this gargantuan scale being vast, Albert borrowed money from the great banking house of Germany, the Fugger of Augsburg. As security for the debt, he undertook to arrange the proclamation through Germany of the Indulgence which the Pope had recently declared for the purpose of building St Peter's at Rome. The money from the sale of this Indulgence (or phrased less crudely, from the gifts of the faithful seeking the remission of pains in purgatory) went in part to the Pope's building and in part to the bankers in payment of Albert's debt.

These circumstances were bad. But they were not publicly scandalous. They were not known beyond a secret and powerful handful of diplomats and financiers.

The 'pardoner' had long walked familiarly and sometimes laughably across the medieval scene. Tetzel, the Dominican employed to preach this Indulgence, was exceptional in the special and solemn nature of his warrant, not in the unedifying doctrine of his utterances. Subtle theologians could make distinctions which drew the theoretical evil from the 'sale' of an indulgence. In practice the ignorant could not help thinking that they were 'buying' forgiveness for themselves or their beloved in the hereafter, or at least that by their generosity they were doing a good work which the Pope declared to be effective towards forgiveness in the hereafter. 'The moment the money tinkles in the collecting box, a soul flies out of purgatory' – there is no doubt that this proverb was preached.

The Elector Frederick the Wise, ruler of Saxony, forbade the sale of Tetzel's Indulgence in his territory. He disliked the power exercised by the house of Brandenburg, which Archbishop Albert represented, and was proud of his own treasure of relics and indulgences with their revenue-producing privileges. Like other princes he resented the loss of money from his territory. In his castle church at Wittenberg were cases enshrining 17,433 fragments of holy bones and other objects, including the corpse of one of the Holy Innocents.

But his people went across the border a few miles away to hear Tetzel preach in the neighbouring towns. Martin Luther, professor of Holy Scripture at the University of Wittenberg, had for some years been troubled over the doctrine and practice of indulgences. He was pained beyond measure to hear that ignorant people were supposing themselves to have no further need of penitence because they had bought the indulgence. Luther was shown a copy of the

Archbishop's instructions to Tetzel, and was shocked. On All Saints' Eve, 31 October 1517, he fastened* to the door of the castle church at Wittenberg a placard inscribed with 'Ninety-five Theses upon Indulgences'. He announced that he was ready to defend these theses at a public disputation.

Some of the Ninety-five Theses are propositions designed by a theologian to be weighed by theologians. And yet they have not the detached atmosphere of the purely academic disputation. It is evident that the writer's heart is engaged as well as his head. Though the theses are often conservative and contain none of the central doctrines of the Lutheran Reformation, the atmosphere of academic disputation is on occasion banished by a cry of pain. 'The Pope has wealth far beyond all other men – why does he not build St Peter's Church with his own money instead of the money of poor Christians?' That is not a thesis upon the theology of indulgences. But while they echoed the cry of the German people against Italian exactions, the theses were not on the surface antipapal. Luther claimed to suppose that the Pope would disapprove the iniquitous trade if he knew of it. Christians must be told, he wrote, that if the Pope knew what was happening, he would rather see St Peter's in ruin than built with the bones and flesh of his flock.

THE YOUNG LUTHER

At the time of the Ninety-five Theses Luther was nearly thirty-four years old. He was a tough, four-square man of peasant stock, with deep-set disturbing eyes and a character as open as the daylight. His mind was active and vigorous, but he was no gymnast of the intellect, a man earnest and persevering rather than subtle and delicate in discrimination. His friends always respected him with an affectionate and sometimes rueful regard, knowing that he held nothing back from them, erected no screen, allowed them to touch

* The first evidence of nailing the theses comes from Melanchthon 29 years later. It has been doubted whether nailing, as distinct from issuing, occurred. Melanchthon was likely to know.

his real inwardness. He never ceased to be a peasant, and was proud of his peasant blood. He could be rough in language, vulgar, crude, coarse. He had humour and loud laughter, but not wit.

Born in 1483, the son of a prosperous and godly copper miner at Eisleben in Saxony, he studied at the University of Erfurt, where the school of philosophy was Nominalist, and there decided, perhaps after a sudden experience in a thunderstorm, to enter the convent of the Austin Friars. It was in no sense a decadent house, but one where the rule was faithfully kept. There he studied St Augustine and fell in love with his writings. As a pupil of the Nominalists, and as a student of Augustine and the Fathers, he shared in that contemptuous attitude to Aristotelian schoolmen so characteristic of the age. Luther was no humanist. There was a time, in the early days of reform, when it seemed so appropriate for a reformer to be a humanist that he produced a Greek nàme, like Melanchthon and Erasmus and other humanists, and called himself Eleutherius. It was manifestly unsuitable and was rarely used. Some of his later friends lamented that he cared so little for the literature of the ancient world, and thought that it might have helped to soften his roughness. Humanism was European, international, an intellectual aristocracy; Luther was a German, national, a man of the people. It is startling to find that he could play the lute and sang with a tenor voice.

He cared neither for style nor elegance, cared little for the correct texts of ancient documents, remained throughout his life something of a schoolman in his methods and attitudes. But by 1516, and in part for several years before 1516, he had adopted the ideal of a simpler theology, of a return to the springs of Christian truth in Scripture and the Fathers. In 1512, living in the house of the Austin Friars at Wittenberg, he became a doctor and the professor of Holy Scripture at the young university.

He was an earnest friar, practising the prayers and fasts with zeal. After a few years of peace, his conscience ran into storms of scruple. 'I tried as hard as I could to keep the Rule. I used to be contrite, and make a list of my sins. I confessed them again and again. I scrupulously carried out the penances which were allotted to me. And yet my conscience kept nagging. It kept telling me: "You fell short there." "You were not sorry enough." "You left that sin off your list." I was trying to cure the doubts and scruples of the conscience with human remedies, the traditions of men. The more I tried these remedies, the more troubled and uneasy my conscience grew.' He had an overwhelming sense of the majesty and the wrath of God. He felt himself tempted to believe that he was a castaway and a child of destruction, that he could never be redeemed. God loved everyone but him. He was sickened by the idea that God is just.

Led towards St Paul by the vicar-general of his order, Staupitz, and by his own studies in the Bible and Augustine, he found in the Epistle to the Romans the new understanding and peace for which his soul was agonizing. He reached this understanding in no sudden insight, no blinding revelation. In the twentieth century modern scholarship has discovered and examined the courses of lectures which Luther delivered upon the Bible between 1513 and 1518. Through these years his Pauline understanding was growing in precision and clarity and maturity. Though the lectures which he delivered upon the Psalms in 1513–15 were couched in more scholastic and traditional language than he would have used four years later, the beginnings of his Pauline understanding may be found there. Later in life he looked back upon his earlier life and singled out moments of particular apprehension. He remembered how he had been reading the Epistle to the Romans in the tower* and suddenly felt the force of the text 'The just shall live by faith'. His writing shows that the perception came little by little.

* The experience of the tower cannot be dated precisely. It has been argued that it happened after the Indulgence, perhaps in spring 1518. Probably it happened in 1512.

The promise seemed to him to meet the deepest experience of his moral being. The persevering monk must not
trust in his perseverance, his penances, his carefulness. The
righteousness of Christ was promised to all that put their
trust in him. Faith was the channel through which the grace
of the Saviour could flow down upon the troubled soul and
bring peace and new endeavour. This peace of mind and
new endeavour hung not upon the poor little efforts of the
weary Christian but upon a share in an eternal peace and
righteousness beyond his own. The human heart is too
vicious to save itself; forgiveness is a gift, it cannot be won.

Before he heard of Tetzel and the Indulgence he was
proclaiming justification by faith as his Pauline Gospel. It
seemed to him that Wittenberg was accepting the lesson. In
May 1517 he wrote to a friend: 'My theology – which is
St Augustine's – is getting on, and is dominant in the
university. God has done it. Aristotle is going downhill
and perhaps he will go all the way down to hell. It amazes
me that so few people want lectures on the *Sentences* of Peter
Lombard. Nobody will go to hear a lecture unless the
lecturer is teaching my theology – which is the theology of
the Bible, of St Augustine, and of all true theologians of the
Church.'

'I am quite sure that the Church will never be reformed
unless we get rid of canon law, scholastic theology, philosophy and logic as they are studied today, and put something else in their place.'

The Ninety-five Theses contained no mention of the doctrine of justification by faith. But in spite of the silence of
the theses, his attack upon indulgences sprang out of 'my
theology', out of a Pauline conviction of God's grace. The
Indulgence he believed to be pernicious because it was misleading simple souls. He saw it as an external and damnable
symptom of so much that was inwardly wrong with the
Christian teaching of his generation, a teaching which
asserted or suggested that God could be placated by

external acts, by forms, by payments, by 'good works'. Luther did not attack indulgences and thereby reach a doctrine of justification by faith alone. He applied an already appropriated doctrine of justification to judge a particular indulgence.

THE ATTACK UPON THE POPE

Archbishop Albert of Mainz was not a man likely to be interested in the subtleties of indulgence theology. But he was interested in the revenue from the Indulgence and found that the protest by a hitherto unknown divine at Wittenberg was diminishing the sales. He reported the Wittenberg Theses to the Pope. The Pope thought that the quarrel was trivial, and told the head of the Austin Friars to keep his men quiet.

Was the attack upon indulgences heretical? The Dominican theologians, constituted guardians of orthodoxy and natural antagonists to the Austin Friars, believed that Luther was a heretic and tried to prove their case. Since the doctrine of indulgences was doubtful this must be done by proving that Luther was assailing papal power. He had questioned the absolute authority of the pope: to question the absolute authority of the Pope is heretical. The argument rapidly turned itself into a controversy over papal authority and its limits, and the debate upon indulgences was soon left behind in a wider argument.

At first Luther was not pleased to find himself hailed as the leader of an assault upon Rome. People were saying that he meant things which he had not intended. 'The song,' he said, 'was pitched in too high a key for my voice.'

He would have been silenced successfully, perhaps, but for the growing body of support behind him. His earthly sovereign, the Elector Frederick of Saxony, protected him. Frederick doubtless understood nothing of the theoretical argument. But he was proud of his university of Wittenberg, had a Saxon dislike of Italians meddling in Germany, was not displeased at the discomfort caused in the treasury of the Archbishop of Mainz, and trusted his chaplain Spalatin, who was Luther's friend and support. The Pope was not anxious to offend a powerful prince in Germany, a prince who might be of political use in a forthcoming contest over the imperial crown, for the sake of a tiresome quarrel between the friars. And elsewhere through Germany the Theses and the subsequent pamphlets were circulating and gathering public opinion behind them. The ecclesiastical authorities were being resisted, and resisted successfully. German feeling against the distant and vexatious control of Rome began to rise behind Luther like a sudden tide. Tetzel, created a doctor by Rome, could not walk into the streets for fear of violence from the people.

A Diet at Augsburg in 1518 listened to a series of demands against Roman exactions and interference in Germany. To it came Cardinal Cajetan, the great Dominican theologian and restorer of scholastic studies, the legate to whom the Pope had committed the case. Luther appeared before Cajetan on 12–14 October 1518, and despite the promises of his Elector was probably in greater danger than at any time thereafter.

Cajetan was not willing to argue about indulgences. It was a question, simply, of the Pope's authority or rebellion. He ordered Luther to retract or suffer the consequences. Luther was respectful, modest, not truculent; but he would give away nothing. He knew now that he would rather die than retract.

His friends hurried him out of Augsburg by night. If loyalty to the truth meant an attack upon the Pope, an attack upon the Pope there must be. He printed an account of the interviews with Cajetan, appending a commentary which assailed the doctrinal foundations of the claims of the Roman See to divine primacy and infallibility. On 28 November 1518 he solemnly appealed from the Pope to a General Council of the Christian Church.

The advisers of Pope Leo X were not ready for decisive

repression. They sent the German nobleman Charles von Miltitz to bestow the papal honour of the Golden Rose upon the Elector Frederick and to enlist his help against the Turks and Luther. Miltitz lodged the Golden Rose for safe keeping in the Fugger bank at Augsburg, and interviewed Luther on 6 January 1519 at Altenburg. An intelligent diplomat, he observed the state of German feeling and knew that even if he had an army of 25,000 he could not remove Luther by force to Rome. 'Martin,' he said, 'I imagined you were some aged theologian mumbling arguments to himself in a cosy corner behind the stove. I find you are young, and strong, and original.' He persuaded Luther to write a letter to Pope Leo (3 March 1519), submissive in tone, anxious for reverence to the Roman see, but retracting nothing.

Sixteen months after the Indulgence Theses, an unrepressed Luther was still faithful to his Augustinians, and recognized the Pope as in some sense the head of the Church. Whatever contemporary censors might think, Luther would not have been thought heretical by some medieval theologians, even in March 1519.

Through the early months of 1519 Luther was studying the history of the Papacy. He found what he was looking for, grounds to justify doubt about the supreme authority of the Pope. The study of the Bible convinced him that the Indulgence was wrong. The Indulgence, as his antagonists kept reminding him in loud voices, reposed only upon the authority of the Pope. Beginning therefore to contrast the authority of the Bible with the authority of the Pope, he found plenty of writers to persuade him that the Pope was not by divine right the head of all the churches. Supreme authority in the Church belonged to the General Council, and the Pope was the chief servant of the General Council. He was driven a stage further in the argument by the most brilliant and tenacious controversialist of the day, John Eck of Ingolstadt. If quickness and repartee could have won the victory, Eck would have laid Luther low with ease.

In July 1519 Eck met Luther's friend (so far his friend) Carlstadt in a public disputation at Leipzig. Luther was stung by Eck and joined the fray. The disputation was held in the hall of the castle of Pleissenberg, and partly in the presence of Duke George of Saxony. The disputants faced each other in pulpits, Eck with his raucous, rasping voice and agility of answer which belied his stolid-looking face, Luther with his clear, tuneful voice, ascetic appearance, and fumbling modes of argument. In most of the debate Eck was triumphant against both Carlstadt and Luther. His greatest and fatal triumph forced Luther to change his mind and drove him across the highest single fence that divided reform from revolution.

Leipzig lay near the border of Bohemia. To its ruler and citizens the Bohemian John Huss, who had been burnt at the Council of Constance in 1415, was the most notorious of heretics. It was natural for Luther's opponents to spatter him generously but vaguely with the abusive words 'Bohemian' or 'Hussite'. Luther had been educated to believe that Huss was a heretic and indignantly repudiated the names. Eck was determined to show that some of Luther's opinions agreed with the opinions of Huss and therefore that Luther shared in a famous heresy. If Luther had been a nimble controversialist like Eck, he would have evaded the issue with skill. He had the kind of solid, determined mind intent more upon truth than upon victory. And he possessed moral courage, mixed with obstinacy or doggedness. Faced by Eck's nimble manoeuvres and stung by his vituperation, Luther did what Eck had been hoping to make him do – he admitted that Huss had sometimes been right, and that the General Council of Constance which condemned him had been wrong. 'Among the condemned beliefs of John Huss and his disciples, there are many which are truly Christian and evangelical and which the Catholic Church cannot condemn.' There was turmoil, in which Duke George of Saxony could be heard ejaculating: 'A plague upon it!'

Eck's glee was patent. Luther had begun by denying an infallible Pope. He had now denied the only alternative, an infallible Council. Where then shall infallibility be found?

The admission was momentous for Luther's cast of mind. He was a conservative, not by intellect but by temperament. Throughout his life he resented unnecessary change. He intended no revolution, he aimed at purifying the Catholic Church and preserving its truth. But the Leipzig debate cast down the last barrier which restrained his antagonism to Rome. He had publicly and irrevocably identified himself, in part, with a man condemned by the authorities of the Universal Church. Henceforth he expected antipathy and incompatibility between the Bible and the ecclesiastical authorities as now constituted, between the truth taught in the Word of God and the errors taught in the human traditions of papal churchmen. By February 1520 he had advanced far beyond the reluctant, extorted admission of Leipzig. 'We are all Hussites without knowing it,' he wrote, 'St Paul and St Augustine are Hussites.'

He was now a famous or notorious man. The market was eager to buy what he published. Luther discovered to the world that, though he had no bent for subtle argument, he was a polemical writer of genius. The style was appropriate to the man, direct, hard-hitting, Biblical, untwisted. He sent out to his ever-growing public a series of German and Latin pamphlets, easy to read, often attaining beauty of expression, often justifying a charge of extremism. His language quickly ran away with him. 'I am hot-blooded by temperament,' he wrote in 1520, 'and my pen gets irritated easily.' Luther's pamphlets could be repellent. They are often redeemed from being mere broadsides by the disinterested motive and the religious concern which the severity of the polemic cannot conceal. He set his assault upon the Pope in a context of Biblical doctrine and devotion. He turned as easily to writing a commentary on Galatians, an exposition of the Magnificat, a sermon, a message of consolation for the suffering. Luther found no distinction between the two

sorts of writing. He felt himself to have a single aim, the
spiritual and moral reformation of Christendom.

It was natural for a man who was a heretic in the eyes of
many churchmen, and therefore in mortal danger, to
imagine his work as a contest with the principalities and
powers of darkness. His religious ideas of grace and justification made him think of the Christian soul as in God's
fortress, besieged and assaulted by the armies of demons.
He fought his way, psychologically, through the storms of
temptation. He once compared the soul to a decoy goose,
tied in a pit and surrounded with spikes; the wolves leap
at the goose from all sides but fall into the pit and are killed
upon the spikes. His most celebrated hymn, *A safe stronghold
our God is still*, sprang from the deepest instincts of his heart:

> And were this world all devils o'er
>   And watching to devour us,
> We lay it not to heart so sore:
> Not they can overpower us.
>   And let the prince of ill
> Look grim as e'er he will,
> He harms us not a whit;
>   For why? – his doom is writ;
> A word shall quickly slay him.

This hymn was written several years later (1527). But it
helps to explain Luther's unique combination of religious
devotion with embattled pamphleteering.

Among the writings of 1520 three were celebrated:
the so-called Reformation Treatises, *To the Christian
Nobility of the German Nation* (in German), *The Babylonish
Captivity of the Church*, and *Of the Liberty of a Christian Man*.
The second of these was an assault upon the current
doctrine of the seven sacraments. The third was a renewed
statement for the Pope of the doctrine of justification by
faith and its consequences for the moral life of the Christian.
The first of the three was the most effective and revolutionary of all his polemical papers. He thought it the blast

as of a trumpet that blew down the walls of Jericho. He called upon the princes and magistrates of Germany to reform the Church in virtue of their office. The clergy are unable or unwilling to reform their estate. Kings and princes must step in and reform them willy nilly. In a crisis anyone who can act must act quickly. Should we wait for the mayor's authority before we run to put out a fire, even if the fire happens to have broken out in the mayor's house? If an invading army is attacking a city, every citizen has the duty of raising the alarm. Reform is impossible unless the Pope's power in Germany is destroyed. Kings and princes must rise and destroy it. They must abolish pardons, dispensations, annates, exactions, the worldliness of popes and the wealth of cardinals, palls, commendams, the secular rule of the Pope and bishops, whose duty is preaching and praying, not temporal rule. 'It would not be surprising if God were to rain fire and brimstone from heaven and cast Rome into the pit, as once he cast Sodom and Gomorrah.' Princes must end the abuse of excommunications, the excess of idle officials in the Roman Curia, the rule of clerical celibacy, they must diminish the numbers of processions, pilgrimages, vows, jubilees, masses for the dead, mendicants, and beggars. They must reform the curricula of the universities, bring back the studies from the schoolmen to the Bible and a small number of truly good books upon the Bible. The German nation and empire must be freed to live their own lives. The princes must make laws for the moral reform of the people, restraining extravagance in dress or feasts or spices, destroying the public brothels, controlling the bankers and credit.

Is it right for laymen to set their hands upon the Church? Would this be sacrilege? Is it not the duty of the clergy to reform the Church? Luther denounced the notion that the Church consists of the clergy. The Church, according to the New Testament, is a priestly body. The layman also has his priestly vocation in the Church. He is as necessary a part of the spiritual estate as the clerk. The prince is called of God to care for the welfare of his people. If he sees his people robbed or corrupted, it is his duty to protect them. If he may not do what he can do for the Pope, then the tailor ought to be restrained from making his vestments, the cobbler ought to stop making shoes for the bishops, the carpenters should not build houses for the clergy, the cook should cease to cook. The prince is failing in his duty if he does not seek reformation.

THE BURNING OF THE BULL

In the summer of 1520 Germany gathered behind Luther. The dumb or articulate resentment against the ecclesiastical administration and its exactions rose to support him, took him as its mouthpiece. On 15 June 1520 Rome issued the Bull *Exsurge Domine*, condemning forty-one propositions of Luther as heretical, ordering the faithful to burn Luther's books wherever they could be found, and giving Luther two months grace to recant or be excommunicated. Eck, who had written much of it, was given the task of publishing it in Germany. In the flowing tide of feeling he found the task difficult enough. Princes, universities, and even bishops were reluctant to allow the Bull to be published in their domains. Luther met the Bull with a public act of defiance. At 9 a.m. on 10 December 1520, before a crowd of citizens and members of the university, he ceremonially burnt the books of canon law and the papal decretals and a copy of the Bull on a bonfire in the meadow between the wall of Wittenberg and the river Elbe. He watched the paper burn into ashes and then with his colleagues went back into the town. A great crowd of students stayed round the fire. At first they were moved and solemn, and sang the *Te Deum*. Then they started to shout jests, and sang a dirge for the funeral of the decretals. A few of them dressed up grotesquely, pinned a vast mock-Bull to a pole, and drove through the city, preceded by a brass band, collecting the books of Eck and the schoolmen. Then they drove again to the bonfire and burnt books and mock-Bull with another *Te Deum*.

On 3 January 1521 Luther's excommunication was made absolute. The breach was complete, henceforth there could be warfare or submission. 'I said' (at the Leipzig disputation of 1519) 'that the Council of Constance condemned some propositions of Huss that were truly Christian. I retract. All his propositions were Christian, and in condemning him the Pope has condemned the Gospel.' The quarrel was no longer a monkish quarrel, no longer a petty storm between the theologians of different orders, no longer a question of pertinacious heresy. It had moved out upon the stage of European politics. 'All Germany is in revolution,' wrote the papal legate. 'Nine tenths shout "*Luther!*" as their war-cry; and the other tenth cares nothing about Luther, and cries: "*Death to the court of Rome!*" '

It was no longer an affair of professors, courts, ecclesiastics. The peasants near Wittenberg, when they met a traveller on the road, would ask him 'Are you for Martin?' and beat him if he said he was not.

THE DIET OF WORMS, 1521

When Luther burnt the Bull, Charles V had been king in Spain for three years and the elected emperor in Germany for two. It looked as though all Germany might do what England would later do, repudiate the Roman allegiance and declare a national German church. If the German emperor had thrown himself into the national movement and headed it, this might have been possible. But though Charles V was of German stock, and though he knew Pope Leo X to be his political enemy, he was hardly a German sovereign. The basis of his power was in Spain and Naples. He believed in reform as the Spaniards practised it, in orthodoxy less militant but as firm as Spanish orthodoxy. He could not sever Germany from Rome without splitting his realm into fragments.

Twenty-four days after Luther's excommunication Charles opened his first Diet at the city of Worms. He was twenty-one years old, cool-headed, determined, and devout. He gave a safe-conduct for Luther to come to be heard at Worms, and Luther resolved to go. It was an act of courage, for Huss had gone to Constance under a safe-conduct and had been burnt. Luther told Spalatin that he would go to Worms in spite of all the demons and the gates of hell.

At Worms on 18 April 1521, in the presence of the emperor, Luther was asked whether he would recant. He said that he was ready to apologize for the faults in his polemical writings; but he could not condemn his assault upon the Pope. 'Unless I am proved wrong by Scriptures or by evident reason, then I am a prisoner in conscience to the Word of God. I cannot retract and I will not retract. To go against the conscience is neither safe nor right. God help me. Amen.'*

By reason of his safe-conduct he was allowed to depart homeward from Worms, and not until a month later did the Diet declare the Ban of Empire and so outlaw him. Luther thought the Diet had been an anti-climax, almost a waste of time. 'I expected,' he wrote to the artist Cranach, 'that his Majesty the Emperor would have collected fifty doctors of divinity to confute the monk in argument. But all they said was: "Are these books yours?" "Yes." "Will you recant?" "No." "Then get out!"'

THE WARTBURG

By the outlawing of Luther, the Elector Frederick of Saxony was placed in a quandary. Attached by sentiment and by political instinct to the person of Luther, he had no intention of surrendering him to be burnt or hanged. But he thought it imprudent to give the appearance of protecting a man whom the Church declared to be a heretic and a

---

* Luther probably did not say the celebrated words: 'Here stand I: I can do no other.'

majority in the State outlawed. He therefore arranged that Luther should be 'kidnapped' on his way homeward from Worms, and gave Luther warning of the plan. As Luther's cart was passing through the woods near Möhra, five horsemen surrounded it and swept Luther, still clutching his books, away to the castle of the Wartburg and safety. 'Some say I captured him,' wrote the papal legate, 'some say the Archbishop of Mainz. I wish it were true!' At Worms rumour declared that Luther's corpse had been found stabbed and thrown down a mine.

In the Wartburg, known and dressed as Squire George, his whereabouts unknown to the world, he suffered a reaction after the peril through which he had passed. There is an untrue legend that he threw an inkpot at the devil who was struggling with him, and that the ink-stain can be seen upon the wall. It was a time of physical depression and mental temptation. He felt the demons to be about him. He imagined that he heard a devil taking walnuts from the table and cracking them on the ceiling all night. Ravens and magpies, cawing round the towers outside his window, sounded like dismal echoes of the groans in his soul. He doubted for a moment whether he had been right to fight and resist. He rested quietly, strolling to pick wild strawberries, or joining a hunt for hare and partridge. The hunt revolted him, seeing in it a parable of the trapping by popes and priests of the defenceless souls of the poor. Soon he had recovered and was writing again – one of his polemical pamphlets, a sermon to show that private confession was not compulsory, homilies (called Postils) upon the epistles and gospels, a book to prove that monastic vows were wrong. Above all he began to translate the New Testament into German. He had determined that the Bible should be brought to the homes of the common people. He echoed the cry of Erasmus that the ploughman ought to be able to recite the Scripture while he was ploughing, or the weaver as he hummed to the music of his shuttle. He took a little more than a year to translate the New Testament and have it revised by his young friend and colleague Philip Melanchthon. There had been German versions before this, and Luther was neither an accurate scholar at Greek nor a literary genius. But the simplicity, the directness, the freshness, the perseverance of Luther's character appeared in the translation, as in everything else that he wrote. The German Bible (finished in 1534) became, with Luther's hymns, one of the pillars of the Lutheran Reformation.

THE TUMULTS AT WITTENBERG

The rebel, though in hiding, had not been suppressed; and friends thought that the time had come to act against the abuses which he and others had been criticizing. The doctrines of Luther were beginning to be proclaimed in many pulpits of Germany. Not a few friars or monks left or were leaving their convents to preach the new reformation. Young humanists like Philip Melanchthon, Reuchlin's great-nephew, had joined him at Wittenberg. In Basle the crowd cheered the priest when he carried a Bible instead of the Host in the procession at the feast of Corpus Christi. Watched by the students at the university of Wittenberg, Luther had burnt a Bull and the papal decretals. It was not to be expected that students would be content with watching.

They had been told that vows and clerical celibacy and communion in one kind (that is, offering the bread only, not the wine, to the communicant) were wrong. On 29 September 1521 Melanchthon and some of his young men received the communion in both kinds (that is, both the bread and the wine). On 4 December a rioting mob of students destroyed an altar in the church of the Franciscans. On Christmas Eve a crowd rioted in the parish church and sang songs to mock the service. On Christmas Day one of the professors (Luther's colleague Carlstadt) dressed as a layman to celebrate the mass, simplified the liturgy, gave the laity communion in both kinds. In January an ordinance took the ecclesiastical revenues from the brotherhoods and their endowed masses and placed them under the control of a committee of laymen, decreed stipends for priests, relief for the poor, and dowries for poor girls; prohibited begging and brothels; and ordered that the elements at the sacrament should be placed in the hands of the communicants, that communion should be given in both kinds, and that pictures and side altars in the church should be removed. There was some rioting, some smashing of statues and pictures.

With the exception of the rioting, the threats uttered against conservative priests or monks, and the language of three 'prophets' (the so-called prophets of Zwickau) who rose amidst the turmoil, these alterations were moderate enough. They did not appear moderate to that devout Catholic the Elector Frederick. Luther disliked the news. In March 1522 he rode out of the Wartburg, discarded his lay disguise, and appeared in the streets of Wittenberg dressed in his Augustinian habit. He was ready to repudiate private masses, to discountenance vows, and to allow the marriage of priests; but he would have no violence, no riot. He quelled the tumult by his personal force. In March 1523 he approved a liturgy somewhat simplified; and in 1524 Carlstadt was forced to leave Saxony.

THE PEASANTS' WAR, 1524-5

In Germany the central government was weak. Germany was governed by a miscellany of local powers, princes, bishops, city-magistrates, nobles or robber barons, knights. These local powers depended more upon their own strength than upon the weak imperial law. Fights against the private armies of barons or knights and suppression of peasant riots or 'revolts' were epidemic in Germany. Though Luther hated disorder, he successfully resisted the central government and called upon all true men to rise and reform the ecclesiastical potentates, who were the most conservative force in Germany. The fire which was passing through the undergrowth ran into inflammable matter. The peasants were bitter and discontented. Their tumults, under the emblem of a shoe, had long been anti-clerical, they were led by starving disbanded soldiers or bankrupt knights. They joined the simple cries for a Christian land where all property should be common, and believed apocalyptic prophecies by wandering radical preachers like Thomas Münzer.

In 1524–5 a series of peasant risings swept south Germany. The leaders demanded justice, relief, freedom from oppression by landlords, the right to choose their pastor, the restoration to the village community of land once common. They swept through central and south Germany, burning convents and castles. In May 1525 the Saxon peasant army was smashed at Frankenhausen, Münzer was executed, and all over Germany the revolt was suppressed, in some places with barbarity. The suppression strengthened the hands of the princes in governing Germany, and entailed drastic consequences for Luther and his movement.

Luther had been born a peasant and knew the wretchedness of the peasants. He had hit hard at the oppression of the landlords and agreed with many of the peasants' demands. But he hated armed strife. The way of peaceable and insistent demand he believed to be the only Christian way. When the revolt began he travelled round the country districts, risking his life to preach against violence. Shocked by the news of a massacre at Weinsberg, where to the sound of pipes the peasants speared the Count of Helfenstein in the presence of his wife and child, he wrote the most calamitous of his tracts, *Against the Murdering Thieving Hordes of Peasants*. In four burning pages he summoned the princes to 'brandish their swords, to free, save, help, and pity the poor people forced to join the peasants – but the wicked, stab, smite, and slay all you can'. 'These times are so extraordinary that a prince can win heaven more easily by bloodshed than by prayer.' The extremists upon the side of the peasants said that he was a 'toady' for the oppressors. The nobles said that his vehement language incited the peasants to slaughter. Luther refused to retract. 'You cannot meet a rebel with reason. Your best answer is punch him in the face until he has a bloody nose.' His enemies made easy capital from his language. He wrote another pamphlet to defend it; and things were no better.

It was the nemesis of his polemical streak. As early as 1520 a friend warned him not to be so contentious. Though he was well aware that his pen ran away with him, and sometimes regretted it, his simple and enclosed upbringing prevented him from realizing the effect of violent language upon simple minds. Luther, not an extremist, often sounded like an extremist. He imagined a brave citizen meeting a ravening peasant with sword in hand, and had no idea that his language could encourage men to perpetrate outrages on defenceless peasants.

Everyone who hated Roman or clerical power had gathered round him, and not every German who hated Rome was moved by the principles and the motives of Luther. Warriors like Ulrich von Hutten or Franz von Sickingen could cheerfully plot to kidnap the papal legates. Though a small piece of Luther's character was attracted towards such methods of direct action, this was not his way. 'I do not want,' he had written to Spalatin, 'to struggle for the Gospel by violence and murder.' But for a few years he was the voice of a German self-consciousness. Round Luther's cry for religious reformation gathered men who wanted other things besides religious reformation. A wave of German sentiment had rolled behind Luther to carry him onward. But not all this sentiment was pure. The more controversial Luther became, the more he divided Germany. Men who admired when Luther denounced indulgences, hesitated and then withdrew from a frontal assault upon the Pope.

It was natural that they should draw back. This was now a revolution, and heads were likely to be broken. Soon after Luther passed through Erfurt on his way to Worms, the students and townspeople ran amok among the ecclesiastical property of the city, damaging libraries and destroying books. Though Luther denounced this and other illegalities, sane and peaceable men held that if this loosening of society was reformation, they would have none of it. Humanists like Pirckheimer, who once assailed Eck as stoutly as Luther, submitted to Rome. Erasmus had welcomed Luther in the quest for reform, had written a vigorous letter urging Elector Frederick not to listen to the clamour for Luther's arrest, told Pope Leo X that the mode of attacking Luther was hasty. By 1522, Erasmus thought Luther's manner to be objectionable where his matter was true. By 1524, Erasmus was actively hostile, and they engaged in controversy *On Free Will* and *The Enslaved Will.* Saddest of all to Luther, his friend and confessor Staupitz – still suspect to Rome for encouraging Luther, still a friend, and always grateful to Luther for leading him from the husks to living pastures – believed that no reformation could be justifiable if at the same time it endangered the unity of the Church.

Luther had begun as the prophet of Germany. By 1524 he was the prophet of a great party.

THE FORMING OF A LUTHERAN CHURCH

Political Protection

Germany was divided, and after 1524 Luther could have been crushed only by force, that is by civil war. At the Diet of Speyer in 1529 the minority of princes favourable to the Reformation delivered a 'Protest' against the proceedings of the emperor and the Catholic princes. This was the Protest to which the word *Protestant* owes its origin. In 1531 the Protestant princes and cities were linked in a political confederacy, the Schmalkaldic League, determined and able to resist the emperor and the Catholic imperialists. The league was a new power in Europe. By 1539 it included Electoral Brandenburg, Prussia (where the ruler Albert in

1525 secularized the principality hitherto ruled by the Teutonic Order), Electoral Saxony, Hesse, Mansfeld, Brunswick, Anhalt, and other territories with twenty cities of the Empire.

As a new political force, the Protestant league was caught up into a region where religious considerations were not primary. It was not always clear whether the league was defending Protestants against Catholics or the rights of princes against the emperor; nor whether the emperor was defending Catholicism or imperial supremacy. Charles V was afflicted by other tasks and perils besides the Protestants. He was the ruler of Spain, and spent many years managing his Spanish affairs. He was at war with France, and with the ally of the French, Pope Clement VII. In 1527 an imperial army, unpaid and ill-disciplined, sacked the city of Rome and put the Pope into the emperor's power. The Emperor was too busy to turn effective forces against a powerful Protestant league. Nor were all the supporters of the Pope anxious that the Protestants should be suppressed. Just as the French king had not hesitated to attempt alliance with the Turks when it suited his political need, and once allowed a Turkish admiral to celebrate the fast of Ramadan in the streets of Toulon, so French kings preferred a divided Germany. They might execute Protestants in their own domain, but they were not happy to see the Protestants of Germany destroyed. The Counter-Reformation, if considered solely as a political and not as a religious force, failed in part because some Catholics would have found the end of the Protestants a calamity. Even occasional Popes, when in conflict with Spaniard or Catholic German, looked wistfully after the support of Protestant princes.

In Germany the Catholic princes were prevented from effective action by the threat upon their eastern borders. The Turk was in Hungary, and it has been shown how the largest concessions of liberty to the Protestants coincided with Turkish threats of invasion, and how the attempts at severest treatment coincided with Turkish peace.

The Lutheran churches, though they might not easily expand southward, had time to organize their life in peace.

The Confession of Faith

Knocking down idols is easier than replacing the faith which bemused itself with those idols. As soon as men began to reform, without the conservatism of the old law, they must decide how far to go in reforming, what to preserve and what to change. It was agreed that the power of the Pope must be destroyed; monks and nuns freed from burdensome vows, perhaps forced upon them when they were too young to understand what they were doing; the financial system of selling church offices or sacraments must be stopped and the endowments diverted to the support of pastoral needs or of the poor; the people educated and taught the Bible; the priests turned into teachers and preachers; the mass simplified and rendered intelligible; 'recent' doctrines, not found in Scripture, removed. The guiding principle was the doctrine of justification by faith, in other words a shift of emphasis from the external act in religion – cult and ritual and ceremonial – to the mind and heart, to the faith which needs external acts for the sacramental expression of an inward worship.

In the reformed states and cities the first steps were comparatively easy. A German Bible was placed in the pulpit; priests were allowed to marry; monks who wished to be free were permitted to leave their convents; unintelligible rites were suppressed; the people were taught to worship with German hymns; church endowments were diverted from supplying priests who celebrated private masses or from maintaining decaying houses of nuns. Luther himself believed in gradualness. He made suggestions for reform, he encouraged experiment, he left much to local reforming initiative. His liturgical forms removed the sacrificial language from the mass, turned the services from Latin into German, much increased the occasions of preaching, and confined the celebrations to Sundays and holy days (thus

causing the side altars in churches to lose their purpose),
but were otherwise conservative. The communion was
delivered in both kinds, but the elevation of the Host was
retained in many churches. The traditional vestments often
continued to be worn. The conservative nature of the
reformation may be illustrated by the single fact that the
most complete and ornate examples of the medieval reredos
may be found in Lutheran churches of Germany.

In the *Babylonish Captivity* of 1520 Luther reduced the
number of sacraments, on Scriptural grounds, from the
number seven, which had prevailed for 350 years, to three –
baptism, the Eucharist, and private confession. Though
Luther was anxious that self-examination before penance
should not become a burden upon the scrupulous conscience,
sacramental confession continued to be normal in the
Lutheran churches. The elements at the eucharist were
received with the deepest outward reverence, Lutheran
pastors still taught that the bread and wine were the Body
and Blood of the Lord. Luther's historical inquiries convinced him that transubstantiation was a late and irrational
doctrine, not to be warranted by Scripture. He believed
that Scripture plainly demanded a belief in the Real
Presence but refrained from further seeking to define or
describe the mystery of the elements. Though he wished
the mass to be in German when the congregation was
ignorant, he was content with Latin where it was educated. Neither Luther nor Melanchthon thought that they
were founding a new church. They believed themselves
members of the Catholic Church of all the centuries, engaged
upon purifying it from certain abuses recently intruded.

This outlook was canonized in the confession of faith which
Melanchthon presented to the Diet of Augsburg in 1530 and
which as the Augsburg Confession became the broad doctrinal standard of the Lutheran churches. 'This,' wrote
Melanchthon after surveying the Protestant faith, 'is almost
the sum of our teaching. It can be seen that nothing in it is
discordant with the Scripture, or the teaching of the Catho-

lic Church, or the Roman Church as it is known from ancient writers. We are therefore judged unfairly if we are held to be heretics. Our disagreement is over some abuses which have crept into churches without due authority. . . .' Luther at the time was uneasy, and some Lutherans have been more than uneasy since, whether Melanchthon was so anxious for peace in the Church that he was speaking less forthrightly than the truth and the occasion warranted.

Melanchthon

The Augsburg Confession was supported by an Apology, which also won a place among the Lutheran standards of faith and which was also drafted by Philip Melanchthon. The alliance between the two minds of Luther and Melanchthon, who between them moulded the Lutheran reform, is a fascinating study, for they were unequal yoke-fellows. The vehemence of the one versus the pacific nature of the other; the pastoral soul versus the scholar and intellectual; the apostle of the poor and simple versus the apostle of higher education: the pilgrim marching to his God through clouds of demons and temptations versus the moderate student of truth; rough peasant manners versus gentle courtesy; courage versus timidity; stand to the truth though the Church fall versus the reasonable thinker ready to meet opponents half-way if he could; the enemy of Erasmus versus his friend – both of them found the alliance embarrassing and painful. After Luther's death (1546) the discrepancy between master and disciple became a difficulty, arousing argument and dividing loyalties. As long as he lived, they complemented each other. Melanchthon, seeing Luther's faults and regretting them, admired him with a rueful affection and reverenced him as the restorer of truth in the Church. His respect for tradition and authority suited Luther's underlying conservatism, and he supplied learning, a systematic theology (the *Commonplaces*, 1521, much altered in later editions), a mode of education, an ideal for the universities, and an even and tranquil spirit.

In the frescoes in the church of the Virgin at Pirna, St Luke was painted with the face of Luther, St Mark with the face of Melanchthon.

The Organizing of the Lutheran Churches

It was not to be expected that blots which good men had been trying to eradicate for centuries could be eradicated in a moment. An ignorant people could not be educated in a day; dumb or immoral pastors could not be ejected or reformed without inquiry; there was no organization to inquire or to educate. The bishops had exerted an inadequate supervision over the morals of the clergy and the services in their churches, but still a supervision. In the Lutheran states and cities this supervision had collapsed or was collapsing. In some areas bishops still attempted to perform their functions, in others they ceased to make any effort to do so. A few, like the Bishop of Sammland, actively helped to introduce reformed doctrines and pastors. But parochial discipline was confused or non-existent. Few people now knew the law of the church. Many reforming acts cut with a knife into the knot of legal rights and privileges. Every monk who left his monastery, every magistrate who suppressed a private mass and transferred the endowment, every reformer who ejected an incompetent priest from a parish, was driving another nail into the coffin of the existing legal system. When Luther went to visit the parishes, he took with him one theologian and three lawyers. The church could not be reformed without the consent and aid of the law – that is, in a city the magistrates, in a state the prince.

The prince found it the more natural and easy to fill the vacuum left by the repudiation of Rome, because in the later Middle Ages the lay lord had already achieved extensive powers as patron in appointing to bishoprics or to parishes, even in appropriating a share of the ecclesiastical revenues. The magistrates of a free city in the German Empire had already achieved a measure of control over the parochial administration within the city. Throughout the Empire, from Hamburg in the north to Zurich or Geneva in the south, the cities easily accepted the new doctrines and their councils easily undertook the reform and supervision of the parishes. The Reformation did not take ecclesiastical power from the hand of a Church which grasped it. It afforded the opportunity for the cities or the princes finally to wrest power out of a hand from which it was already slipping.

The naturalness of the change may be seen at Nuremberg. In 1524 the provosts, attracted to Luther, revised the liturgy, abolished masses for the dead, and made other changes. The Bishop of Bamberg excommunicated the provosts, declared them deposed from their office, and ordered a new election. The provosts refused to submit; the city council supported them and by menace or persuasion exacted obedience from the clergy. The bishop no longer exercised jurisdiction in the city, and the city council exercised his old jurisdiction, dissolving the monasteries or ordering a parochial visitation. There was no one else to do it.

To contemporaries the removal of episcopal authority appeared less revolutionary than it would appear to posterity. Several schools of the later Middle Ages attributed a theological importance to priest and to pope, but regarded a bishop more as an administrative officer than as an order of ministry integral to the Catholic Church. To throw off the authority of the Bishop of Bamberg felt like an act in no way comparable to teaching a different doctrine of the mass, but comparable to ridding oneself of the incubus of an oppressive and reactionary archdeacon. Many theologians in the sixteenth century, whether reformed or conservative, assumed like many theologians of the fifteenth century that the priest or presbyter was the 'essential' order of ministry. It might be inexpedient that a priest should ordain other priests, but there was no theological objection.

Luther saw no reason why the prince should not reform

the church. On the contrary, it was his duty, his vocation, one of the purposes for which he was called of God. Since reform demanded drastic changes in law, reform was impossible without his cooperation. Though Luther based his belief in the prince's duty upon the doctrine of the priesthood of the laity, his mind was in many ways practical. He saw the immediate need and how it could be met effectively. He asked John, the new Elector of Saxony, who was a convinced Lutheran, to order visitations of the Saxon churches. Out of the visitations arose a new organization, established at Wittenberg in 1542. The prince exercised the old jurisdiction of the bishop by appointing a consistory.

The consistory, the characteristic agent of church government in Lutheran (as later in Reformed) churches, was not created at once in every Lutheran state. The full consistorial system was slow in coming. A consistory was not created in Pomerania till 1563, in Hesse not until 1610, in Waldeck not until 1676–80.

The consistory was normally composed of lawyers and divines, and appointed by the prince. It was regarded rather as a Church court than a civil court, though the distinction had less meaning than it would have a century later. Sometimes the prince presided in person at its deliberation; otherwise he acted by deputy. The visitors went out in the name of the prince, reported to him, referred their insoluble problems to him. The consistory exercised all discipline.

It might have been expected that the doctrine of the priesthood of the laity would have led towards some mode of church government in which the lay congregation possessed a measure of authority. By this doctrine Luther called upon the right of the princes to reform the church. He taught the duty of the ordinary man towards the clergy, to care for true faith and proper sacraments and due order. But confronted by a practical plan for congregational church order, Luther rejected it. In Hesse a wandering ex-Franciscan, Francis Lambert, proposed (1526) a democratic scheme of church government which gave each congregation the right to choose, and in effect to control, its pastor. Luther, to whom it was referred, would have none of it. In a few cities (Ulm, Strasbourg, Reutlingen) a group of elders assisted with the financial administration, to represent the laity in the care of the church, and a measure of such representation had Luther's sympathy. But it never became a reality. Melanchthon seems to have disapproved of it, preferring the tidiness of the consistory. In the cities it was commoner for the municipal government to act as though it was a kind of consistory.

Luther had no desire to give the prince control over doctrine. The episcopal right which he attributed to the Elector was the old administrative function of the bishop, a function mainly secular and legal. He supposed that doctrine was controlled by the Scripture, and by the tradition of the Catholic Church where that was consonant with Scripture. But in a world of religious disunity the personal faith of the ruler was inevitably important in the religious history of his state. In England the changes of ruler conditioned the progress of Reformation, and so it was with several German states.

The power of the princes over the clergy and their property made the governments more efficient in their states. It likewise made the ecclesiastical administration less corrupt and more efficient. The Reformation was remedying part at least of the administrative muddle and incompetence found in the old Church. But it was altering laws; and the process was often untidy. Ideas like the new Protestant relief of the poor were excellent in theory. Practice lagged far behind. The effectiveness of reform varied from state to state.

In the princely anarchy of Germany strong men had always taken the available opportunities to control or to redirect the ecclesiastical revenues. The available opportunities were now multiplied in the necessary transfer of endowments. Monks living in a well-endowed convent left their retirement and dispersed; the convent stood empty, its income unused. Lawyers were changing the destination of endowments from nunneries or from private masses; that part of the endowment should end in a secular treasury was to be expected. Luther did not always grudge this transference, but thought that part of an excessive endowment might reasonably be transferred to the necessary purposes of the state, for these purposes were also religious. He resented genuine misappropriation. 'I hate to see our princes so greedy for bishoprics. . . . The nobles eat monasteries, a diet which will make them vomit, like dogs eating grass.' He once pushed into the room of the Elector to seek his protection for church property. In Saxony itself the whole endowment from confiscated monasteries was given to charitable ends, stipends for pastors or for schoolmasters, a dole for the destitute. In Hesse some monastic houses were turned into hospitals or contributed to the founding (1527) of the university of Marburg, the first university to be founded by Protestants. Some endowments were devoted to the first state attempts to care for the poor, and replace the relief once given by religious orders.

THE BIGAMY OF PHILIP OF HESSE

The power of the prince was illustrated by the bigamy of the Landgrave Philip of Hesse. Philip married at the age of nineteen but contented himself with various mistresses after his wedding. His conversion to Protestantism failed to alter this mode of living. In 1539 he became attached to a young aristocrat of seventeen. Her mother demanded that the marriage, if it could not be public, should be permitted by the chief divines in the Church. Philip requested from Luther, Melanchthon, and Bucer their sanction for a second marriage. He argued that if he were not allowed to marry lawfully, he must continue to live in sin. He threatened that if Luther would not sanction the marriage, he would apply to the Pope and the Emperor.

The threat was not idle. In the past the dispensing power of the Pope had sanctioned the equivalent of divorce for a first wife. The Protestant states repudiated the power of the Pope, and with it the dispensing power. Under a pledge of secrecy Luther and Melanchthon sanctioned the second marriage as the lesser of two evils. Luther was unaware of Philip's sequence of mistresses and said afterwards that if he had known he would never have sanctioned the marriage. He had believed Philip to be in good faith and genuinely suffering from 'weakness'. The effort to justify the marriage by the precedent of Abraham was unconvincing to contemporaries. The marriage was solemnized in the presence of Melanchthon and Bucer. The pledge of secrecy was rapidly broken, and – although some opinion, Catholic as well as Protestant, shared Luther's view that bigamy was preferable to divorce – Europe was scandalized at the Protestant divines.

CATECHISM AND HYMNS

Moved by the gross ignorance which he found upon the first Saxon visitation of 1528, Luther wrote his *Greater and Little Catechisms* (1529), one for clergy and one for laity and children, with short forms for private prayers and grace at meals. Like the German Bible, these became the foundation of parochial instruction and of religion in the home. To the same end he wrote his hymns. He used old religious songs and melodies and adapted them. The first booklet of eight German hymns, including four by Luther, appeared at Wittenberg in 1524, to be followed soon afterwards by an edition of a further thirty-two hymns of which Luther wrote twenty-four. The entire collection was the basis of Lutheran hymnody. They are not designed to teach, nor are they couched in the language of the theologians, but are simple expressions of heartfelt trust and praise.

There was much diversity between the states about their use. Some permitted them in church, others allowed only versions of the psalter; they were always more for private than public use, and were taken into the school and home. Choirmasters sometimes supplemented them with others but as late as 1624 the Saxon synod forbade the use of any book but the original. The congregation was taught them at school, knew them at home, and so sang them in church from memory and without hymn-books. Even in 1697 a Merseburg peasant who took a hymn-book to church and sang out of it was forbidden by his pastor to introduce such novelties.

Luther was a man of the people and fought to bring true religion to the hearts and homes of the people; to show them that religion was not the clerical, ecclesiastical, ritual act performed in church, but the appropriation of a Gospel into the life. It would be naïve to suppose that he achieved in a moment what the medieval church had failed to achieve over centuries. Even in the seventeenth century the reading of the Bible in the country (as opposed to towns) was not common except among the upper classes. Even in the seventeenth century there were complaints that the congregation could not be persuaded to join in singing the hymns. But what success he achieved was chiefly in his four undertakings upon behalf of the simple – the German Bible, German mass, German hymns, German catechisms. It is believed that the Wittenberg press of Lufft alone published 100,000 Bibles between 1534 and 1584. One of Luther's opponents, Cochlaeus, grumbled that the common people loved it and that cobblers and old women studied it and argued about its texts. It was the first German book to be a book of the people. It influenced the development of the language.

LUTHER'S CHARACTER

Luther died in 1546, after some years of ill-health. He began the Reformation, and his experience and outlook were inseparable from the course of its history. The kind of piety – simple, austere, and downright – which became characteristic of north Germany is the best measure of Luther's personality and influence. Despite his learning and his public stature, he never ceased to be a countryman. He always retained his early consciousness of God's grace sustaining his soul amidst temptations and enormities. He always felt himself battling with wickedness, yet without fear. Both his hates and his laughter, it has been said, were titanic. But his hates were not personal, his contentions were not for himself, there was nothing about him that was mean. His hates were directed against the oppressors or misleaders, as he believed, of his beloved German people; and when he thought of his Germans, he thought of the poor and the ignorant. Devoid of façade, with a childlike quality which enabled him to speak to the peasant, he possessed a genius for popular preaching, for clear unpretentious instruction. His mind was graphic and pictorial, fertile in apposite or comic illustrations, perceptive of the parable ready to hand in daily life. His hymns, his German Bible, his catechisms, his eucharistic teaching: these, with the doctrine of justification by faith alone, created the Lutheran tradition of piety, of family and public worship.

The Luther that survived in the memory of Germany was not Luther the friar but Luther the father of a family. During the Peasants' War he married an ex-nun, Catherine von Bora, and lived with her in the empty house of the Austin Friars. The marriage was unromantic. Catherine, plain in features and unadorned in dress, was an excellent and busy housewife. But, said Luther: 'I would not change my Katie for France and Venice, because God has given her to me, and other women have much worse faults, and she is true to me and a good mother to my children.' The characteristic memory of Luther is of a man presiding at his own table, with his colleagues and friends around, arguing with him, or listening to his divinity, his politics, and his humour. One of the friends shamefacedly took out a notebook and began to jot down Luther's remarks. The habit spread, and twelve different reporters made collections. Luther sometimes mocked but neither resented nor forbade these deferential scribes. Twenty years after his death, one of them, Aurifaber, published a collection from a variety of collections. Thenceforth *Luther's Table Talk* became a classic of the Reformation. Rude and outspoken he might often be; 'Dear husband,' said Catherine, 'you are too rude.' 'They teach me to be rude,' replied Luther. He was so outspoken that his enemies leaped to make capital out of the *Table Talk*. It is unreliable as a source for details of history, particularly when the events occurred many years before the date of the reported conversation; and Aurifaber's text was not untouched by improvement or interpolation. But it is a unique and authentic picture of a man and a divine; he who would understand Luther's person and mind cannot neglect it. It is impossible to apply any epithet to him less than the old classical epithet magnanimous, in its original sense of great-hearted.

Meanwhile, through the Swiss valleys into Italy, over the Rhine to France and thence to Spain, over the mountains southward into Bohemia and Hungary and Austria, across the seas to England and Scotland and Scandinavia, rolled the reverberations of the Lutheran thunder. Successful revolt breeds revolt.

3
Calvin

ZWINGLI (1484-1531)

IN Zurich the Reformation came in the way normal among the free cities of the Holy Roman Empire. The leading citizens were influenced by the reforming doctrines; they resisted and repudiated the authority of the Bishop of Constance when he tried to interfere; the city council legislated to reform the churches and parishes, with the advice of its chief pastors, to allow clerical marriage, to remove superstitious images and relics, to suppress the monasteries and use their endowments for education, and to order a vernacular and simplified liturgy instead of the mass. The process began in 1522 and was complete by 1525. As in other cities, the council followed with reforming regulations to control public morals.

Zwingli claimed that his reform was independent of Luther's, that he had been teaching reforming doctrines before he had heard of Luther. An examination of the evidence does not wholly support his claim. Zurich received an impetus from the Lutheran revolt like every other free city in the Empire, and at the time Zwingli was eagerly interested in Luther's teaching and Luther's methods. But the same fuel was everywhere present; so was the same appeal from the Church authorities to the Scripture. The Reformation did not all spring from Luther, it sprang from those conditions of the Church and those states of mind which made Luther possible. Zwingli was not deluding himself in claiming that he held reforming ideas before he heard of Luther. But the news from Wittenberg drastically affected events in Zurich.

Like Luther, but more sympathetically than Luther, Zwingli learnt from Erasmus. He sympathized with the quest for reform by cool ridicule. He had more wit, more philosophy, more learning, less profundity, less religious sense than Luther. His desire to reform the Church was a little more like the desire of the humanist who hated inefficiency and obscurantism than like the desire of the ex-friar who had fought through a storm of temptation to defend the souls of his people. He was less pessimistic about human nature, more hopeful about the destiny of good heathen. But he was not only a humanist. As he studied the Greek fathers to whom Erasmus led him, and as he came under the influence of St Augustine, he found the same religious needs and insights that were central in Luther's heart. Neither Zwingli nor Calvin allowed friends, admiring their intellects and following their reasoning like disciples, to see their inwardness; they captured men's allegiance by the cool force of their minds. Luther always remained a man of the heart, he opened his inward thoughts and feelings to the sight and affection, he captured allegiance more by moral stature than by subtlety of mind. The contrast must not be exaggerated. The more we know of the two Swiss reformers, the less possible we find it to treat them merely as intellectuals. But a measure of this strikes everyone who seeks to penetrate the sources to the character and minds of the three men.

Zwingli felt less reverence for the past than Luther, less respect for traditional ways of worship. The churches of Zurich were transformed in appearance. Relics and organs were removed, pictures and images were sold or smashed, surviving altars were stripped bare of ornament, and the new German order for the Lord's Supper (1525) bore small resemblance to the medieval liturgy. After a sermon and prayers, unleavened bread and wine were placed not upon an altar but upon a table in the middle of the nave, surrounded by the congregation. The ministers faced the congregation, wore lay clothes, and carried the bread in large wooden trenchers round to the silent people sitting in their seats. Zwingli instituted other services almost without liturgical form and composed only of a sermon and prayers.

Luther believed that nothing in the service should be contrary to the Word of God. But as his conservative temperament assumed to be permissible whatever Scripture did not explicitly forbid, he had not sought to abolish the elevation of the Host or the eucharistic vestments. Zwingli, likewise believing that nothing in the service should be contrary to the Word of God, surrounded this belief with a different atmosphere. To his mind the Scripture ought explicitly to sanction what was done in the service; and although he recognized an area of 'things indifferent', such as the wording of the prayers, where the minister or the Church was free to make any edifying rule, he assumed that simplicity ought everywhere to prevail. The change of appearance and worship in the Swiss churches was therefore more revolutionary than in the churches of northern Germany. In some of the Lutheran churches hymnody flowered under Luther's impetus. The Swiss churches thought hymns unscriptural and provided metrical versions of the Psalms. The Lutheran churches continued to use private confession as a sacrament; the Swiss churches did not prohibit private penitence with a pastor but believed the sacrament unwarranted by Scripture, a cause of priestly power, and therefore a corruption.

THE REAL PRESENCE

This difference, as much of attitude as of principle, began to turn upon the doctrine of the eucharist.

It could not be denied that the mass had been the focus of much popular superstition. Zwingli, like Luther, believed that the mass was not a sacrifice, and wished to eliminate the sacrificial language. Unlike Luther, he also believed that the Christian doctrine of the eucharist had been corrupted by the notion that Christ's Body was 'substantially' or 'corporeally' present in or under the elements of bread and wine. His mind sharply distinguished the material from the spiritual, and shrank from the idea that physical objects might be vehicles of spiritual gifts. He always preferred to treat the sacraments rather as symbols and signs of a covenant between God and man than as means of grace. The Lord's Supper was a memorial of the Lord's death and a thanksgiving for it. In his early years as a Reformer he and his friend Oecolampadius of Basle were so engaged upon saying what the Lord's Supper was not, that they rarely and reluctantly attempted to describe what it was. His reading of the Bible suggested to him that the doctrine of the Real Presence (in those days the word *real* was used to mean *substantial* or *corporeal*) was a misunderstanding. The gift is the spiritual gift of Christ's redemption, and a spiritual gift cannot be received physically but only by faith. And when it was put to him that in the text of the Bible Jesus said 'This is my Body', he and Oecolampadius replied that this was the normal mode of metaphor used by Jesus. He said 'I am the door', 'I am the vine'; but no one insisted that these statements be understood literally. 'This is my Body' must be understood to mean 'this is a sign of my Body'. The bread and wine were not vehicles of a present Christ, but signs of a Christ present by faith.

During the last four years of his life, under pressure from his enemies and perhaps some of his colleagues, he made more positive assertions. These signs, though signs of the absent, are efficacious or grace-bearing signs, they are special modes of the universal presence of the divine Spirit, they focus that gift which we also receive when we pray. He never allowed the traditional doctrine that in the Lord's Supper there is a true communication of the Lord's humanity to the faithful soul.

THE COLLOQUY OF MARBURG, 1529

Luther thought that Zwingli was depriving the faithful Christian of that comfortable assurance promised in the

Gospel, and that he was applying rational argument to a mystery beyond all argument. He could not regard the Swiss as faithful men. The Landgrave Philip of Hesse, painfully aware of a political need for unity among the Protestants, arranged in 1529 a conference at Marburg where, he hoped, peaceable discussion would reunite the two sides. At Marburg he gathered Luther, Zwingli, Melanchthon, Bucer, Oecolampadius, and other leading divines. They agreed upon much, but on the eucharist they failed altogether. Luther began the discussion by writing on the table the words 'This is my Body' and announced that he would never depart from them. 'I am not going to argue whether *Is* can mean *is a sign of*. I am content with what Christ said. . . . The devil cannot get out of that.' Thereafter he would never extend the hand of friendship to the disciples of Zwingli. Melanchthon suffered qualms that the difference was not as simple as either side supposed, and hankered after a reconciliation. Luther moved not a step, and the cleavage among the Protestants grew deeper. And as the divines of some Rhineland cities and the Low Countries followed Zwingli and Oecolampadius rather than Luther, those churches began to look for guidance and leadership rather to Zurich than to Wittenberg.

Sword and battle-axe in hand, Zwingli was killed in 1531 at the fight of Kappel between Zurich and the Catholic cantons. He was succeeded as chief pastor by Henry Bullinger (died 1575), of a wise and moderate temper, who directed a European correspondence as Zurich became a guide and a model for other Protestant cities.

BUCER (1491-1551)

Martin Bucer, the reformer of Strasbourg, devoted a main part of his career to reconciling the Zwinglians with the Lutherans. Like other negotiators he sometimes supposed that finding the right formula was the same as reconciling the contending parties, and he never suffered from the fault of being too laconic in his explanations. Luther once called him 'that chatterbox'. But Bucer was more than a mere diplomat or negotiator; he was a man of principle and among the most learned and level-headed of the Protestants. After being an adherent of Luther, he had been convinced by Zwingli's argument that a physical reception of a spiritual gift was impossible and that the channel of reception was faith. But he also perceived the force in the Lutheran contention that the Scripture revealed a true communication of the Lord's humanity in the sacrament. He therefore proposed that the true statement of the matter should use the preposition *with*. The divine gift was not given *in* or *under* the forms of bread and wine – thus far Zwingli was right. But it was given in an indissoluble conjunction *with* them – as the bread is given to the body, so the divine gift passes into the faithful soul. This divine gift was the humanity of the Lord, as the Catholic Church believed it to be. Therefore Luther was right in contending that an objective gift was offered to the communicant, and Zwingli was right in contending that the faithless man could receive nothing but bread.

This is in outline the doctrine which came later to be known as 'receptionism', and was destined in time to become the classical doctrine of non-Lutheran Protestantism. One of its forms is the Calvinist doctrine. For Bucer's long sentences were compressed into a clear and coherent explanation, impossible to misunderstand, by one of his lieutenants. From 1538 to 1541 John Calvin, banished from Geneva, was working under Bucer at Strasbourg.

FAREL AT GENEVA

The city of Geneva, like so many other cities of the Empire, had been growing towards independence, though more slowly than Nuremberg or Strasbourg or Zurich. The arms of the city of Berne, since 1528 the most powerful city of

Protestant Switzerland, supported the desire of the Genevans to be independent of their bishop. The Bernese used the Frenchman William Farel to reform the French-speaking areas of Switzerland under their control, and it was a natural extension of Bernese influence when Farel helped the people of Lausanne to drive out their prince-bishop and become a free Protestant city. Farel tried to work in Geneva but was expelled. In 1533 Berne sent him back into Geneva under diplomatic protection. Sermons, disputations, riots, a siege marked the divided state of the citizens. Before the end of 1535 Geneva was Protestant. It was an independent city but its independence was under the protection of Berne.

CALVIN (1509–64)

In the summer of 1536 Calvin passed through Geneva on his way from Paris to Strasbourg, the haven of Protestant refugees fleeing from France. Born at Noyon in 1509, he studied Latin and theology at the University of Paris and law at Orleans. He published in 1532 a reputable edition of Seneca's *De clementia*. Unsafe in Paris, he retreated to Basle, and in 1536 issued a lucid handbook of Protestant theology, *The Institutes of the Christian Religion*. Passing by chance through the city of Geneva, he was persuaded by Farel to stay. The city council offered him employment as a teacher of Scripture.

Farel was no organizer. The Reformation in Geneva consisted of little but broken statues and more sermons. Calvin, who was trained as a lawyer, had been employed at Geneva for some four months when he confronted the city council with a programme of desirable reforms. He had a tidy mind in practical affairs as well as on paper, and one of the consuming passions of his life was a hatred of public mess. He began to seek an organization of the Church and ministry which should ensure decency and order. Like all other Reformers he assumed that this could be achieved by a systematic reproduction of the practices of the primitive Church as history and the New Testament disclosed them.

His first efforts to organize the Church were stopped by exile, from 1538 to 1541, for Geneva never wished to be organized altogether as Calvin preferred. But the moment he was recalled, triumphantly, he persuaded the city council to establish a series of regulations known as the *Ecclesiastical Ordinances*. Even when these regulations were revised twenty years later by a Calvin firmly in the saddle, they still failed to represent his precise ideal of an ecclesiastical polity. But from 1541 the outline of his programme was being put into practice.

He was a generation later than Luther. Luther married an ex-nun, Calvin the widow of an Anabaptist; and the difference is symbolic. The problem now was not the over-throw of a papacy, but the construction of new modes of power. Luther rested much upon the doctrine of the priest-hood of the laity and derived part of his practical pro-gramme from the doctrine. Calvin recognized that the doctrine was in Scripture and emphasized the theoretical consequences. But what was needed was the authority of a rightly called and purified ministry. In breaking down papal authority, the Reformation seemed to have left the authority of the Christian ministry vague and uncertain. Where authority existed among the Protestant Churches, apart from the personal authority of individual men of stature, it rested with the prince or the city magistrate. Calvin believed that in organizing the Church at Geneva he must organize it in imitation of the primitive Church, and thereby reassert the independence of the Church and the divine authority of its ministers.

There was little that was democratic in Calvin's ideal constitution. The pastors chose the pastors, though the city council could reject the choice. They were to meet once a week for the common study of the Scriptures, and this meet-ing was not voluntary. They chose the teachers, who were responsible for the teaching of Scripture and for education generally, though again the council insisted that the choice should be ratified by themselves. The elders – the most characteristic of Calvin's institutions – were disciplinary officials, It was their duty to survey the morals of their congregations, to ensure that notorious sinners were not permitted to receive holy communion, and to make reports to the 'Venerable Company' of the pastors. These elders were appointed by the councils of the city government, after consultation with the pastors. Every Thursday they were to meet with the pastors in consistory and consider whether there was any disorder in the church requiring a remedy. They were to summon before themselves heretics, parishioners who failed to attend their churches or who treated the ministers with contempt. They were to admonish; and if the sinner was still impenitent they might excommunicate him and inform the magistrate.

This control over the morals of the population was not new. For centuries bishops' courts and city councils had decreed rules which a later generation would think an intolerable tyranny over the liberty of the citizen. Calvin wanted to give this right and duty to the authorities of the Church, not of the State; and where the Church authorities delivered a sinner to the civil power, the civil power would punish him.

Like the councils of Basle, Berne, Zurich, and other Swiss cities, the council of Geneva had no desire to give the power of excommunication to their clergy. At every turn they sought to add provisos in the Ordinances ensuring that the pastors might act only after reference to the council. They added a note to the final text of the *Ecclesiastical Ordinances* which stated: 'These arrangements do not mean that the pastors have any civil jurisdiction, nor that the authority of the consistory interferes in any way with the authority of the magistrates and the civil courts.'

The addition betrayed an uneasiness. In a measure the magistrates had already been forced to allow the right to excommunicate, as a condition of Calvin's return from exile.

They sought to restrict it not only by these ambiguous additions but by insisting that a civil magistrate preside at the consistory, baton in hand, as a sign that he was acting as a civil magistrate and not simply as a lay elder. Calvin at last succeeded in removing the baton in 1561.

The council always retained more control of the elections to the consistory than he wholly approved, and they often interpreted the above clause on jurisdiction in a way which he vehemently disapproved.

The minutes of the consistory after 16 February 1542 are extant. The offences are manifold, and not all are as interesting as the following. A woman knelt upon the grave of her husband and cried *Requiescat in pace*; others saw her and started to copy her. A goldsmith made a chalice. Someone said that the arrival of the French refugees had put up the cost of living. A woman tried to cure her husband by tying round his neck a walnut containing a spider. Another danced. Another possessed a copy of the lives of the saints, the *Golden Legend*. A woman of sixty-two married a man of twenty-five. A barber gave the tonsure to a priest. Another blamed Geneva for executing people for their religious opinions.

Calvin saw danger lurking behind the trivial in moral behaviour. An ordinance of 1547 renewed an older decree of 1535 against the wearing of slashed breeches. But 'we see that, by the loopholes of the breeches, they wish to bring in all manner of disorders'. He was inclined to take a grim view of offences. When several distinguished citizens were imprisoned for holding a dance in a private house, he became (for him) emotional, and declared his intention of uncovering the truth 'even at the cost of my life'.

In 1550 the magistrates authorized the clergy to make an annual visit to the home of each parishioner, with a view to examining whether the household was keeping the rules of the Church.

The Reformation had set out to remedy the corruption, superstition, and immorality of the Church and of society.

The pendulum had swung. The remedy was beginning to work with an effectiveness beyond expectation.

The consistory was indefatigable in its maintenance of the moral order. Its members tried to suppress fortune-telling and sorcery, were pitiless towards merchants who defrauded their clients, denounced short measures, excessive rates of interest, a doctor who exacted high fees, a tailor who over-charged a travelling Englishman. They once compared themselves to dogs which bark when their master is at-tacked. They thought of themselves as charged with the protection of old people, orphans, widows, children, the sick. They attempted to educate the public conscience and somewhat resembled Hebrew prophets, with their courage, their power, and their unpopularity.

The boundaries between the jurisdiction of Church and State had never been easy to define, and they were not easy to define in Geneva. Calvin, the practised lawyer, drafted a revision of the city code for the council, a plan for a watch, a cleaner mode of dispersing refuse. It was not easy to dis-tinguish whether he was offering these suggestions as an interested layman or as the chief pastor of the city. There is a story that when the first dentist arrived in Geneva, Calvin personally satisfied himself that the man was reputable before he was allowed to practise; and though the story is probably apocryphal, it represents a truth about the entanglement of Church and State. The consistory gave its opinions on the bank rate, on the level of interest for war loan, on exports and imports, on speeding the law courts, on the cost of living and the shortage of candles. On the other hand the council, even during Calvin's last years, may be found supervising the clergy and performing other functions which logic would have allotted to the consistory. The council was not backward in protesting against overlong sermons, or against pastors who neglected to visit the homes of the people; they examined the proclamations by the pastors even if the proclamation called the city to a general fast, sanctioned the dates for days of public penitence, agreed or refused to lend pastors to other churches, provided for the housing and stipend of the pastors, licensed the printing of theological books.

It is correct to speak neither of magistrates dominated by pastors nor of pastors dominated by magistrates. Some people served on both council and consistory, and were perhaps not always clear in their own minds whether they were acting as Church or as State. A pastor who dominated the consistory could not help being one of the rulers of State as well as of Church. That was one reason why Calvin worked successfully with a constitution which was not quite faithful to his own ideas.

For Calvin was not the absolute ruler of Geneva pictured by legend and his enemies. There were many matters on which he could not achieve all that he wanted. He wanted the pastors to take the first steps in choosing the pastors, and the council insisted on being associated with the work of selection from the beginning. He wanted the pastors to be present when the council elected the elders, and succeeded in achieving this during his last few years, though the old practice was restored eight years after his death. He wanted the punishment of harlots to be severe, and it was never so severe as he thought proper. In October 1558 the council at last decreed that anyone guilty of a second offence should be marched through the city with a cap on her head, heralded by a trumpeter; but even then the council refused to apply the penalty with rigour. In 1546 Calvin persuaded the council to abolish taverns and establish cafés instead. Stringent regulations determined conduct in these cafés, banning indecorous conversation or bawdy songs, decreeing that no meals should be served unless grace were said before and after the meal, and that a French Bible should be available for consultation on the premises. The cafés proved unsuccessful, for the people preferred taverns, and the taverns perforce were reopened. In 1546 there was an act against the use of non-Biblical Christian names, and again the people were too strong. He wanted the pastors to be ordained with the laying-on of hands, and the council would permit only prayers and a sermon. Nor was he able to persuade the council to return all the ecclesiastical revenues which they had appropriated, like so many cities or princes, at the first rush of reform. This was no matter of principle for him, and he made no strenuous efforts. The question how often the Lord's Supper should be celebrated was nearer to his heart. He believed that frequent, weekly, communion was practised by the primitive Church and ought to be practised by the Church in Geneva. Laymen in the Middle Ages had been accustomed to such infrequent communion that all the Reformers found this change one of the most difficult for the laity to accept. In the Ordinances of 1541 he restrained his request to a monthly communion, and was refused even that. It was to be administered 'for the present' four times in the year.

He was not popular. He was the kind of man who has only disciples or opponents; it was impossible to be neutral about him. He was known and beloved by a few intimates. As a dying man he said of the citizens of Berne: 'They have always feared me more than they loved me.' And the same would be a true verdict upon many of the citizens of Geneva. Some of them are said to have called him Cain, one to have named his dog after him. We hear of rude papers left in the pulpit, of ballads written against him, of men who abused him as a hypocrite and a tyrant, of thirty tennis players suspected of choosing for their game the square outside the church where he was teaching, of a rumour that someone had offered 500 crowns to anyone who would assassinate him. He knew what he wanted and could be ruthless in getting it. Although he could often be gentle, he found it more difficult than most men to be gentle with opponents. Aware that he was faithful to the teaching of the Bible, he identified opposition to himself with contempt for God's Word, and knew that it must be beaten down. He was naturally austere, with no pleasure in food or drink; one almost suspects him of marrying to set an example. He lived quietly in his house on the Rue des Chanoines, with a modest little stipend and simple household and short hours of sleep; he was always grave, he had none of Luther's exuberance and joy in life. There was no abandon, he held himself upon a rein. When he had decided, he was inflexible. 'If he once gets his knife into you,' said a fellow pastor, 'you do not stand a chance.' A manufacturer of toys and playing cards named Ameaux, whose business was affected by the discipline which prohibited card-playing, said at a dinner party that Calvin was a bad man and a foreigner who taught untrue doctrine. The council decided that he should kneel and apologize to Calvin in their presence. Calvin insisted that such an apology was not public enough, and he would not preach again till proper satisfaction was performed. The council condemned Ameaux to walk through the city in a shirt, carrying a taper and asking God's mercy. If Calvin was restrained where Luther overflowed, if he eschewed the coarsenesses which sometimes defiled Luther's conversation, he lacked Luther's warmth and generosity.

He had little room for expediency, but his mind was neither narrow nor blinkered. Whereas Zwingli could be contemptuous of opponents and Luther could rarely see that they were other than wicked, Calvin could see that they had argument and yet that this argument must be beaten down. The air of inflexibility which he succeeded in imparting to much of his work is primarily the air of a man who is convinced by his own logic and who will follow the reasoning to the utmost consequences, whatsoever they may be and whether they are theoretical or practical. The logic may not always be convincing to the abstract logician. The *Institutes*, even in their final form, had a less inevitable coherence than their popular reputation supposed. The sense of coherence is conveyed to the reader as much by the tidiness of the arrangement and clarity of the style as by any relentless development of the argument from its axioms.

He was a man of the intellect, a man of doctrine. Not even his intimates could penetrate to his soul, as any reader of the

Table Talk can penetrate Luther. There was something aloof, secret, reserved. He was a man of books, texts, authorities; he lacked a feeling for natural beauty. If he had other feelings they were usually concealed. It is a surprise to see his tenderness of spirit when his wife died.

It is at first sight extraordinary that he should have dominated a city of which he was not even a citizen until 1559 and where he made no effort to cultivate popular favour. Until 1555 the opposition within the city was powerful. In 1548 he was summoned before the magistrate to explain an intercepted letter, and was so rebuked for his failure in duty that he believed himself about to go again into exile. His disciples tried to discredit the opposition with the name of *libertines*, but they were libertines only in the unusual sense of holding opinions upon Church and State different from those of Calvin. In 1553 Geneva burnt the Spaniard Servetus for his Trinitarian heresies, and thereby shocked the Protestant radicals. Calvin had wished the death to be more merciful than burning, but he had worked to secure the execution, and some good men believed that the severity should be blamed upon him. In the same year a citizen of the libertine group named Berthelier, who was excommunicate, asked the council and not the consistory, the State authorities and not the Church authorities, for permission to receive the sacrament two days later. The council consented. Under the appendage to the Ordinances, it was probably within its rights. Calvin announced from the pulpit that he would refuse the sacrament to any excommunicate person. He expected to fall and be banished, he even preached a farewell sermon. The council said that he must obey their order, but, discretion being the better part of valour, advised Berthelier not to attend the service. The quarrel dragged on until 1555, when Calvin's interpretation of the Ordinance was accepted and the 'libertine' leaders fled to Berne. Calvin was henceforth secure.

One external circumstance helped him. Geneva was the natural refuge for French Protestants fleeing from persecution. The French Protestants looked to Geneva for leadership; and many refugees who came into Geneva were new supports for Calvin. In 1546 not a single pastor out of thirteen was of Genevan origin. 'Good-bye Geneva,' said one of the men who hated Calvin: 'In the end the King of France will be a citizen here.' The refugees were godly folk who had left their homes for conscience sake; every newcomer from France or Scotland or Italy or the Netherlands or England strengthened Calvin's hand. It was the Scottish refugee John Knox who called Geneva 'the most perfect school of Christ that ever was on earth since the days of the Apostles'.

But it would be wrong to suppose that his authority was based upon external support. Not even all the refugees were content with what they found. Clément Marot, almost a poet laureate in Paris, a gay romantic epigrammatic Frenchman, once imprisoned for eating erroneously in Lent, once compelled to abjure Protestant heresy, published in 1541 metrical translations of thirty psalms. A metrical psalter was the chief vehicle of congregational worship in all the Reformed churches. Marot fled to Geneva, and there translated twenty more psalms, to which Calvin wrote a preface; and soon the congregations were singing them. Though it was mediocre as poetry, it met a worshipping need, and ran to twenty-eight editions by 1550 and to condemnations by the university of Paris. But Marot's lively person was not well suited to Geneva. In December 1543 the consistory accused a man of playing tric-trac with him, and he left the city.

The true source of Calvin's authority was in himself. Uncompromising though he might be, he pursued with a single mind what he believed to be the truth; he extorted that reluctant admiration and discipleship which is given to consistency, to courage, and to decisiveness. He always spoke and wrote with a magisterial force, knew what he wanted and where he was going, was as devoid of pomp or cant as of sentimentality. He impressed Geneva with the stamp of his mind; and therefore the Calvinists, wherever they went, shared a coherence and clarity of outlook not shared by Lutherans, Anabaptists, or Anglicans.

In 1559 he founded a college for the higher education of Geneva and of western Protestantism. He staffed it with professors resigned from a similar college at Lausanne, who could not get their city council to agree to the right of excommunication, and placed one of them at its head, the scholar Theodore Beza, later his own successor. It rapidly became one of the great schools of Protestant thought, educating many of the Calvinist leaders of the second generation. The rector, professors, and all the teachers were appointed by the consistory, though with the approval of the council. At first all students were made to subscribe a rigid confession of orthodoxy; but this was abolished in 1576, partly because it excluded those who most needed instruction and partly because it seemed to excuse Lutheran colleges when they forced Calvinist students to sign the Confession of Augsburg.

Calvin's wider influence rested upon the clarity of his theological system and of his Biblical exposition. The first edition of the *Institutes*, published in 1536, was a little book distinguished among theological performances mainly by the lucidity of the arrangement and the Latin style. The book grew year by year – he had leisure to extend it in exile at Strasbourg and allowed the first French translation of this longer edition to be published in 1541. The final and further extended edition was published in 1559; Calvin from a bed of sickness dictating the French translation to his secretaries and even then suggesting additions which might be incorporated into the text. He wrote simply and briefly. There are none of the reverberations of Bucer's prose, none of the vehemence of Luther's. Men might not like what Calvin said; they could not misunderstand what he meant. And as the structure was built from edition to edition, it became clear that the handbook, as extended at Strasbourg, already contained the skeleton of the building and that the additions were illustrating and amplifying and applying to practical circumstances a theology clear to his own mind from the first edition. But in the provision for ministry and organization – the section of the book most momentous in practice – the additions are substantial.

Like all minds of power, he depended upon the influence of others and upon his past experience. The more we know of Bucer, the more evidently derivative are certain characteristic views of Calvin upon theology and church government. But though his stay at Strasbourg under Bucer had been formative, he was no imitator. A man of the Bible and a hard student of the ancient Fathers, he thought and digested and absorbed until the resulting and decisive convictions were his own.

The doctrine of Calvin rested upon a faith in God's special providence guiding the particular events of the world. We are not to think of a general guidance. We are taught by the Bible of his particular guidance in the particular events of individual lives. We read that not a sparrow falls to the ground without the will of the Father. We read that he sent forth a whirlwind in the wilderness, and thus we know that 'no wind ever blows unless he has specially commanded'. We read that he has given babies to some mothers and withheld them from others. This is not fatalism, no mechanical system of a relentless nature, but the personal decrees of an Almighty God. He moves the wills and inclinations of men to walk in the way which he directs. Chance is an appearance to us because his eternal counsel is hidden within his breast.

Luther's ultimate religious act was an utter trust in a redeeming Saviour, his ultimate text 'the just shall live by faith'. Calvin's ultimate religious act was the assent of the will to an everlasting Lord; his ultimate text, 'thy will be done'.

If the circumstances are friendly, the Christian will give all the glory to God and none to himself. If the circumstances are unfriendly and ruin afflicts him, he will recognize the chastening of God and cry with Job 'The Lord gave and the Lord hath taken away; blessed be the name of the Lord'. The Biblical texts of resignation and of confidence were frequently upon Calvin's lips; and no one in Christian history has had better right than the Calvinist to use them.

With this religious interest in the providence of God, Calvin surrounded the old doctrine of predestination with a new atmosphere.

The Protestants had been taught by Luther, by St Augustine, and by the Epistle to the Romans that they could not deserve heaven, that the Christian moral life and its consequences hereafter were to be accepted through faith as a gift of God's mercy and love. God chose some and not others – Scripture taught it, and observation confirmed it.

If all is a gift of God, even the faith by which we appropriate the gift, then from all eternity God must have chosen some to life and bestowed mercy upon them, and left others unredeemed from their sins to die an eternal death. Everyone confessed that this was probing the mystery of an eternal Being hidden from human eyes. Everyone agreed that what the congregations needed to hear was not speculation about the mystery of predestination but 'whosoever repents will be saved'. That predestination was a reality was admitted by all the Christian thinkers of the Pauline and Augustinian tradition. The *theoretical* differences between Calvin or Augustine or St Thomas Aquinas or Luther are small.

But Calvin saw it in the context of his faith in providence. Therefore it possessed for him an importance for religious devotion and practice which it had not possessed for Aquinas nor even for Luther. John Eck had written about predestination as an intellectual exercise to train his youthful mind. Calvin abhorred the notion that this was a detached problem for the mind. The Christian's assurance of his election to eternal life was the deepest source of his confidence, his fearlessness, his humility, and his moral power. 'If God be for us, who shall be against us?' The doctrine, though a mystery, was not a mere mystery for the critics of the lecture room. There were texts about it in the Epistles to the Romans and the Ephesians and elsewhere in the Bible. These texts must have been given that they might convey knowledge, they must be preached from the pulpit and taught to simple people. Every soul should be led in faith to be conscious of his calling, assure himself that God's merciful hand was upon him, until with St Paul he could profess himself persuaded that nothing could separate him from the love of God.

In proclaiming this majestic doctrine Calvin stripped from it the whispering hesitations of his predecessors. He could write nothing obscurely – and therefore he wrote plainly the aweful (*horribile*) consequences: that Christ died on the cross not for all mankind, but only for the elect; that God does not will all men to be saved; that men were created by God whom he decreed from all eternity to be consigned to an eternal destruction. And if anyone cavilled that God was thereby unjust, he replied that *all* men are justly condemned for their sins, and beyond that we cannot see the almighty purpose. We know that God always acts in justice. How that justice works is beyond our sight in this life.

For the next hundred years this was the key question for theologians, for the Catholics almost as much as for the Protestants – the question whether the Augustinian doctrines in this uncompromising expression were the true interpretation of the New Testament. 'I am *not* predestinated,' declared the younger Berthelier violently, 'whatever you and your Calvin say!'

The case of the ex-Carmelite Jerome Bolsec at Geneva is the prototype of a series of controversies which were to disturb Christendom. In October 1551 one of Calvin's colleagues explained the text of John 8.47 upon Calvinist lines. Bolsec, a refugee from France, rose to challenge the contention that Christ died not for all and that faith was a gift settled from eternity upon the elect; he said that these doctrines turned God into a tyrant. While he was speaking Calvin entered the meeting unseen and listened. When Bolsec ended Calvin rose and spoke for an hour. Bolsec was sent to prison. The city council, puzzled by the argument of both sides, and not readily attracted by Calvin's exposition, appealed to the other churches of Switzerland. Calvin found the answers of the other churches unsatisfactory: Berne replied that the matter was a mystery over which men should not fight; Basle and Zurich gave a general and yet qualified support to Calvin; and Zurich blamed Calvin for his method of dealing with Bolsec. Only Farel's Neuchâtel, unsolicited, sent a letter denouncing Bolsec as an Iscariot. The city council banished Bolsec, more for the sake of peace than for the sake of truth. Bolsec had his revenge by publishing (1577) a life of Calvin which is the source of several scandalous legends.

In the long run this was to be the stumbling-block of Calvinism. At first the organizing power and the doctrine of the Church was the attractive force. Men were not drawn by Calvinist teaching and thereby led to organize themselves as Calvinist churches. They were drawn by the Calvinist discipline and thereby led to Calvinist orthodoxy. But the moral and devotional power in the doctrine of election was mighty. The Calvinists were austere, fearless, hardworking, devout men of the Bible. They knew what they believed, they knew what they must do, and they knew by what authority they must do it. For a hundred years they were the most potent religious force in Protestantism.

4

The Reformation in England to 1559

IN Saxony the impetus to the Reformation was first religious and then political. In France and Holland and Scotland the Reformation began as a religious movement which was inevitably caught up into national politics. But this process was not universal. Some reformations began because the nation was developing, and religious change affected the development. In Denmark and in Sweden the Reformation was more a political revolution with religious consequences than a religious revolution with political consequences.

England was unique in its Reformation, unique in the Church established in consequence of the Reformation. The English Reformation was emphatically a political revolution, and its author King Henry VIII resisted, for a time ferociously, many of the religious consequences which accompanied the legal changes everywhere else in Europe.

In England the crown was not by tradition anti-papal. With a fifth to a third of the land in the hands of churchmen, and with the churchmen possessing special and independent rights in justice and in paying taxes, it was not possible for the king to rule effectively unless he used the theoretically supreme power of the Pope as a means of controlling his clergy.

Cardinal Wolsey is an interesting example of this royal power. Henry's chief minister from 1514, cardinal in 1515, and chancellor from 1515 until his fall in 1529, he seemed to wield all authority in the state. But he needed more than royal authority. To rule the state in 1520 he needed papal authority to dominate the bishops and religious orders. He became papal legate with powers which were renewed from time to time and enlarged. These powers were granted on the plea that he needed them for the reformation of the Church. He talked publicly of the need for reform, but was too busy in high matters of state. He closed monasteries to found two colleges, and began to end the abuse of sanctuaries; and so far as he brought the feudal lords under control, he helped the discipline of the church. But he was not himself reformed. He drew the revenues, not only of his archbishopric of York, but of never less than one other see, and of the wealthy abbey of St Albans, though he never visited any of his dioceses until after his fall from power. He took large fees or bribes for private services of every kind, and flaunted his wealth to the world. He kept a concubine by whom he got at least one daughter and a son who was made Dean of Wells Cathedral while still at school.

From 1518 to 1529 Wolsey ruled England as the representative both of king and pope. His unpopular authority in the state, especially his exactions of money, enlarged the bitterness of educated laymen against clerical power and therefore against the Pope. Control by the Pope in this new form was resented because it was making present and effective what had rarely been effective from a remote distance. To be free from papal interference became a goal desired by more laymen and clergy than ever before in England. The Duke of Suffolk struck the table with a great oath, and cried that the old saw was true, that never legate nor cardinal did good in England.

But Wolsey was the king's servant, not the Pope's. Without the king's favour he could not stand for a moment. During the eleven years before 1529 the king already controlled Church as well as State in England, and that with the Pope's complaisance. If there were sufficient hostility to the Pope among his people he would be able to control Church as well as State without the Pope's complaisance. Wolsey fell because the king's desire to be rid of his wife Catherine of Aragon found the Pope in a predicament where complaisance was impossible.

THE 'HEADSHIP' OF THE CHURCH

Henry wished to marry Anne Boleyn. Catherine was ageing before her time, was too bleak to content the bounding energy of the king, and gave birth to a row of offspring of whom all but Mary were stillborn or died in infancy. He could have satisfied his physical desires with a mistress. But higher motives entered Henry's formidable mind and sublimated the issue for him. Catherine had been contracted to Henry's elder brother Arthur. She had therefore been ineligible as Henry's bride and had been permitted to marry him only after papal dispensation. It was possible that the sickly children and the absence of a male heir proved that God's blessing did not rest upon a marriage which was forbidden by God's law. And with the memory of the Wars of the Roses and the Tudor dynasty apparently so insecure, it was necessary for the unity and prosperity of England that a male and legitimate heir should be begotten by the king. Catherine, he now began to believe, had never been his wife. He turned to the Church to declare the fact and to sanctify his marriage with Anne Boleyn.

Pope Clement VII, a diligent and unsuccessful politician, was too weak or prudent to refuse outright. He kept postponing the decision. In favourable circumstances he might have been quick enough to declare what the king wanted. But Henry and Wolsey were asking of him a doctrinal and a practical impossibility. They were asking him to declare that the papal dispensation permitting Henry to marry Catherine had been invalid. A Pope could not declare that the act of a predecessor was invalid without thereby enfeebling his own authority. And among the vicissitudes of Italian politics, the armies of the Emperor Charles V, who was nephew to Catherine of Aragon, sacked Rome in 1527 and captured the Pope. Clement could not gratify Henry VIII by mortally offending Charles V.

In the summer of 1529 the king, in despair of persuading

the Pope to yield, dismissed Wolsey and the policy of persuasion and turned to a policy of menace. The princes of north Germany had successfully excluded the power of the Pope from their dominions. He talked of following this example. He summoned the Parliament of 1529, and allowed the lay and anti-clerical lawyers, released from Wolsey's domination, to draft a series of bills for reforming the ecclesiastical administration.

Since 1393 the chief restriction in law upon papal intervention in the English Church was the statute of Praemunire. In origin this had been intended to exclude from the realm papal decrees which interfered with rights of the English bishops. The courts slowly widened its application. Wolsey was accused under Praemunire, after his fall, on the absurdly unjust ground that he had acted as papal legate in England.

In January 1531 this vague and menacing weapon was turned by the lawyers against all the clergy of England. They were charged with an offence against Praemunire because they had administered Roman canon law in their courts. 'No one,' wrote the imperial ambassador, 'can fathom the mysteries of this law. Its interpretation lies solely in the king's head, who amplifies and declares it at his pleasure, and applies it to anyone he pleases.' The Convocations of the Church, after stiff protest and without verbally admitting guilt, bought their forgiveness for £118,000 (£100,000 for the Convocation of Canterbury, £18,000 for the Convocation of York) and were then forced by the king into recognizing the king as the head of the church – 'especial Protector, only and supreme Lord, and, as far as the law of Christ allows, even supreme Head'.

The formula meant little enough. This was not a repudiation of papal power. The phrase *as far as the law of Christ allows* could cover all manner of limitations. But the lords and lawyers of Parliament were agreed with the king in pressing forward against the Pope. Among the advisers one of Wolsey's lieutenants, Thomas Cromwell, now rose to the top. Experienced in Wolsey's method of controlling Church and State as a unity, he aimed at a similarly unified control achieved by king and Parliament with the Pope excluded from the realm.

In 1532 Henry, petitioned by Parliament, exacted from the Convocations a 'Submission'; that is, an undertaking that, since the canon-making power of the Convocations might conflict with the law-making power of the crown and Parliament, they would enact no new ordinances without licence from the king, and would submit the existing canons to a committee, appointed by the king, for revision. In the same year an Act restrained the payment to Rome of the annates or first-fruits, which in 1534 were transferred to the crown, in 1533 an Act abolished appeals from England to Rome, and in 1534 all the other legal rights and duties of the Pope were transferred to the crown. In the same year the Act of Supremacy declared that the king was supreme head of the Church of England and omitted the saving clause inserted by the clergy in Convocation. The new Archbishop of Canterbury, Thomas Cranmer, declared that Henry's marriage with Catherine was no marriage, and on Whitsunday 1533 Anne Boleyn was crowned Queen. In June and July 1535 Bishop Fisher of Rochester and the ex-Chancellor, Sir Thomas More, were beheaded because they refused to swear to the royal supremacy in derogation of the Pope's authority. In January 1535 Cromwell received a commission to visit churches and clergy throughout the realm.

What were the feelings in the breasts of churchmen when required to repudiate the Pope and accept the royal supremacy during those few years after 1534?

In the south of England, the open objectors were few. It was afterwards claimed by Catholic historians of the next generation that many kept silence with troubled consciences and out of fear; and whether or not the claim is true of many, it is certainly true of some. We have evidence of men speaking against the supremacy to private friends, and since the evidence is only of those who were afterwards

betrayed by those friends, muttering must have been far
more common than we know. All changes in religion are
disquieting. A priest at a church in St Albans said that he
could not forsake the old fashions because he had been
brought up in them. The changes unsettled minds, men
knew not what to expect. Friar Brenchley preached a sermon railing at change, and said: 'Masters, take heed, we
have nowadays many new laws. I trow we shall have a new
God shortly.' At Gisburn in Yorkshire, when the priest
was reading aloud the articles of supremacy, a man stepped
forward from the congregation, snatched the book out of his
hands, and ran from the church. There was fear of the way
the government was moving, a fear of Lutheranism, a fear
that the king would confiscate the lands of the church.
John Smethson, saying mattins with another priest, said:
'I will not pray for the king, for he is about to beggar us.'

Most of the mutterers were simple men. At the top were
a few like Fisher and More, who held on doctrinal grounds
that no Parliament could abolish the Pope's power. Dr
Reynolds, examined on 29 April 1535, said that 'all good
men of the kingdom' held with him, and that 'I have in my
favour all the General Councils, all the writers, the holy
doctors of the Church for the last 1,500 years, especially St
Ambrose, St Jerome, St Augustine, and St Gregory.'
Catholic tradition, he believed, declared the power of the
Pope to be part of Christian truth, and no Act of Parliament
could abolish its hold upon the conscience. This stand must
be taken by everyone in the circle of Queen Catherine of
Aragon, for without the Pope's lawful power Catherine
was not married to Henry. Everyone who thought the
divorce an injustice to be denied in conscience must assert
that the Pope had rightly allowed the marriage and must
therefore assert that the Pope possessed a religious authority
from God as well as an administrative authority from man.

But at the top, such men were few. The higher clergy
made little difficulty about repudiating the Pope. They
regarded the Papacy as a human institution which might

lawfully be removed for the sake of better arrangements. They were ready, surprisingly ready, to sign papers that the Bishop of Rome has no greater jurisdiction in England than any other foreign bishop. They believed with the bishops who declared in February 1535 that the papal power was of man and not of God. The bishops were not time-servers. Tunstall of Durham, humane and honest, had been preaching vigorously in favour of the royal supremacy before he was ordered so to preach. Roland Lee, Bishop of Coventry and Lichfield, was perturbed, not that he was ordered to preach against the Pope, but that he was ordered to preach at all, for he had never yet entered a pulpit. Northern Europe largely accepted the opinions of the Councils of Constance and Basle, a century before, that the Pope was the administrative servant of the Church.

The higher clergy often associated conservatism with 'mumpsimus' and obscurantism; and sometimes they were right. Friar Arthur of Canterbury preached at Herne before a great audience, and blamed the new books and preachers for misleading the people and discouraging fasts and prayers and pilgrimages; he called them Judases, and said that whoever offered one penny to the shrine of St Thomas gained more merit than if he gave a noble to the poor, for the one is spiritual and the other corporal. The simple were conservative, and the simple were ignorant. Cranmer was astonished to discover that a learned man like Dr Reynolds could pertinaciously maintain these opinions about the Pope. The Archbishop of York, Edward Lee, ordered all his curates to read the declaration against the Pope, but pointed out that the order would not be fully obeyed, since many of the curates could hardly read and he knew less than twelve secular priests in the diocese who were capable of preaching.

Though some consciences were troubled, the Marian writers of the next generation exaggerated the amount of inward distress. To abolish the Pope's power was not the most risky of Henry's laws. The country hardly noticed the

Pope's excommunication, and Henry declared that he would not care a straw if the Pope issued 10,000 excommunications.

The ease with which the Pope's power was abolished and the clergy subjected to the law of the land encouraged the king and Cromwell to further revolution. Every other country or city, to repudiate the Pope, suppressed the monasteries. The king and Cromwell turned their eyes upon the monastic lands of England, now helpless before the power of the Crown. Wolsey had already suppressed twenty-eight houses to found his new college at Oxford (later Christ Church) and a school at Ipswich.

THE SUPPRESSION OF THE MONASTERIES

The Protestant states varied in their attitudes to the monasteries. They were agreed that the monastic life was a mistaken form of Christian life, but whether or not it should therefore be suppressed was a matter of disagreement. All Protestant states repealed laws which exacted penalties from runaway monks and nuns. They encouraged monks and nuns to return to secular life. They tried to make it easy for monks to undertake secular work by providing them with pensions from the monastic endowment and by finding them pastoral care, and therefore a parochial stipend, if they were priests. They provided similar pensions, or dowries upon marriage, to nuns who were ceasing to be nuns. They sometimes subjected them to teaching designed to divert them from their erroneous conduct. The more revolutionary states, like the Swiss cities, simply suppressed the monasteries and confiscated their endowments, though providing the necessary pensions from them. Some Lutheran states followed this example. But other Lutheran states – Saxony for a time, Sweden and Denmark especially – permitted some houses to continue until they naturally expired. The lot of a nun thrown upon the world after her enclosure was likely to be harder than the lot of the monk, and in Sweden several convents of nuns drifted quietly in decline for some years. A convent at Maribö in Denmark was not closed till 1621.

England was exceptional in this as in so much else. In the conservative England of Henry VIII there was a pretence of not compelling the monasteries to close.

In the summer of 1535, under the powers conferred as visitor, Cromwell arranged a visitation of the monasteries. Two commissioners, Richard Layton and Thomas Legh, visited the southern monasteries between July 1535 and February 1536. The visitors reported much foulness in monasteries. Not all their evidence has fully satisfied the impartial observer. The smaller monasteries (those with an annual value of less than £200) were suppressed by an Act of 1536. Even after that Act the King had no evident intention of dissolving all monasteries, and himself re-founded two houses during 1537. Even in May 1538 the nunnery at Kirklees received a patent of re-foundation.

But from November 1537 the bigger and wealthier houses began to 'surrender', that is, to dissolve themselves by agreement. Visitors again toured the country to persuade monks to be dissolved. Persuasion was seldom difficult, partly because everywhere it was rumoured that soon they would all be suppressed, partly because some houses already found difficulty in continuing. A not negligible number of monks and nuns were pleased to be thus given their freedom. In May 1539 Parliament passed an act vesting in the crown all monastic possessions surrendered after the Act of 1536. None of the abbots present in the House of Lords protested against it. The dissolution was a peaceable process, with the bloodshed only of the few who refused the royal supremacy. (It is not however certain that the charges would have been pressed against difficult abbots if they had been less difficult about surrender.) The last house, Waltham Abbey in Essex, surrendered to the King on 23 March 1540.

An Act of 1536 set up a Court of Augmentations to receive

and administer the surrendered property. At first it seems to have been intended to hold the property and keep the annual income. Soon the court granted leases, often to servants of the crown; and some lands it became sensible to sell, and thus parts of the property were offered to the public.

The dissolution of the monasteries was by far the most important social event in the revolution. The monasteries were not, and had not been for three hundred years, the moral and spiritual and intellectual power of the earlier Middle Ages. But they were a social fact reaching throughout the European countryside, their lands and their employment dominating so many villages. It is possible to find many houses which would have done credit to the religious orders in any century, but these are still a small group in the total number. Luther's own house at Erfurt, under the guidance of Staupitz, was evidently a place where men of religion tried truly and earnestly to live a religious life. The Benedictine house of Metten in southern Germany was respected by Protestants for its piety. The Carthusians in England were of a spirit which took them bravely to death under the Supremacy Act of King Henry VIII. It is also possible to find houses, more than the fervent, which could rightly be called disgraces. Among the German monasteries there were plenty of scandals over drinking and mistresses. King Henry VIII's commissioners looked for moral iniquity from reasons of state, and though they exaggerated a repellent collection of it, enough is confirmed by other and less partial evidence. But for the most part the monasteries were neither fervent nor disgraceful. They were pleasant, half-secularized clubs for common and comfortable living. Some of the smaller were little more than farms.

Though reliable evidence is difficult to find on such a point, zealous Catholics believed that many monks were indifferent to the dissolution of their houses, provided that they could divide the money among themselves or at least receive an adequate pension. Except upon this assumption, we can hardly account for the ease whereby the greater monastic houses in England 'voluntarily' dissolved themselves between 1536 and 1540. Very few English monks or nuns fled beyond seas in 1539 or 1540 to practise in Catholic countries the familiar life denied to them in England. There are several examples known of an individual retiring to live with his superior; five of the nuns from Kirklees in Yorkshire lived with the prioress at Mirfield for many years; three or four monks of Monk Bretton continued to live with the prior nearby, taking with them some of their library and muniments; Elizabeth Throckmorton, the abbess of Denney in Cambridgeshire, retired to her home with two of the nuns and continued to keep the convent rule, and such unofficial continuity may have been more common than the evidence of it. But it was exceptional; and it is altogether an error to imagine the monasteries as a private army of the Pope. The abbots of Glastonbury, Reading, and Colchester were hanged in 1539, but in England the vast majority accepted without a murmur the royal supremacy and the abolition of papal authority, and examples of an equal complaisance may be found in Germany. The dissolution of the monasteries was not necessary to the destruction of papal authority. But by transferring land upon a vast scale, and creating manifold new rights and interests, it encouraged men who agreed with the Lutherans.

What happened to the money and the land of the dissolved monasteries?

First, it was used to provide pensions for the ex-monks and pensions or dowries for the ex-nuns. These were not large pensions for the ordinary religious, but over most of Protestant Europe they were regularly paid. Some of these pensioners lived a long time, for Fuller said that the last in England died only in 1607–8, and we know that a Cistercian from the house at Bittlesden died as rector of Dauntsey in 1601. Many ex-monks became parochial clergy and for a time enabled the church authorities to avoid large ordinations of new ministers. At Dunstable, out of twelve canons known, at least ten are known to be incumbents in 1556. Other monks, whether laymen or priests, took lay work. The English abbots and priors received large pensions from the monastic revenues. From some of the wealthiest abbeys six new bishoprics were founded by Henry VIII (Westminster,* Bristol, Chester, Gloucester, Oxford, and Peterborough); all the new cathedrals had an ex-monk as their dean, and nearly all had an ex-monk as their bishop. At Peterborough the abbot's palace became the bishop's palace. Between twenty and thirty superiors became bishops within a few years of the dissolution, and some others became heads of colleges or hospitals. Where the old cathedrals had been monastic foundations (Canterbury, Durham, Winchester, Ely, Norwich, etc.), the monasteries were converted into chapters of canons, and many of the old monks continued as new canons – we know, for example, that more than twenty monks remained as prebendaries of Norwich Cathedral, that at Winchester all the monks except four remained, and at Durham twenty-six out of fifty-four.

These endowments of new sees were but a fragment of the monastic lands. In England a small proportion went to education. A few colleges at Oxford and Cambridge were founded or refounded; a small amount of money went into founding schools, especially when the local municipality acquired the site and determined to devote it to providing education, but these foundations could barely have compensated for the loss of monastic schools. In those of the German states where the dissolution was as orderly as in England, larger sums in proportion were diverted from suppressed monasteries into universities or schools. But all governments were in sore need of money, and a proportion of the lands went to help purposes of state, to reward servants of the state. The Crown of England gained an increased annual revenue of well over £100,000.

* Its diocese was the county of Middlesex. The see was suppressed in 1550.

Where the dissolution was disorderly, the fate of the religious might be less happy. In Scotland, where the central government was weaker than in England, the dissolution was piecemeal and sometimes crude. Where the central government was weak, the monasteries were treasure lying defenceless in the transfer of power.

Let us not exaggerate the loss. Everyone is agreed that in all countries of Europe the Church, as a collection of corporations, possessed too much wealth for the health of the state, that some diversion was necessary, and that material transfers of property are always painful and usually accompanied by injustice to individuals. To suppress many of the monasteries was not to harm Church life, but either to cleanse it, or to nationalize, with bare compensation to individuals, farms or country clubs. To anyone who respects the monastic ideal at its best, the loss lay in the groups of devoted communities which were consumed in the general holocaust; in schools, hospitals, and almshouses; in many of the song schools, throwing musicians out of work and making their lot the hardest of all except that of the ex-nuns who would not or could not marry. The gravamen is not that the Church suffered a crippling loss of endowment, but that Protestant sovereigns of Europe, in their need for money, missed a unique opportunity of converting these charitable resources to truly charitable ends like education, hospitals, or the relief of the poor. It would not be so severe a charge if it could be shown that the endowments were diverted to truly national ends. Some of the endowments were so diverted. In other cases, the effect of the dissolutions was to put money and land into the hands of lay lords. Such diversions enabled governments to survive, or to do more, at least for a time.

If the abbey building was in a town, it might be valuable property. If it was in the country, it had probably become useless, impossible either to sell or to use. The English government ordered them to be demolished, but this was often too costly to obey, and the stripped shells of the

houses decayed into ruins that were not yet romantic. At
Lewes a team of workmen, under an Italian expert, used
gunpowder to overturn the bigger columns; and the work
was done rapidly because a relative of Thomas Cromwell
wished to reside there. In Lincolnshire the local officer
reckoned that to obey the order and demolish would cost
more than £1,000, and therefore suggested that he should
render the houses uninhabitable by destroying their roofs
and stairs, and then allowing anyone who wanted stone
to use the walls as a quarry. A few owners were careless in
their use of the ruins. Sir Richard Grenville later turned the
church of Buckland Abbey into a house, and the same fate
befell the nave and transept of Denney in Cambridgeshire.
The great gate of Lord Wriothesley's new house at Titch-
field was sited in the middle of the abbey church. King
Henry VIII used the chapel of the London Charterhouse
to store his tents and 'garden gear'. At Malmesbury a
wealthy clothier bought the monastery as a factory, filled
every room with looms, and planned to build tenements for
his weavers in the grounds. But others became parish
churches, and towns sometimes bought the abbey church
for this purpose. Tewkesbury Abbey, one of the glories of
English medieval architecture, was at first recommended for
demolition as useless and was saved in this way by the
town.

The contents of the houses were not disposed of without
waste. Except for monasteries in Germany and Scotland
where the house had been looted by a mob, the plate and
the jewels, and perhaps some books from the library, were
usually surrendered to the treasury or state library. In
England the contents were then auctioned, often at a sale
held in the cloister or chapter-house, and in this way
speculators or dealers or collectors or conservatives might
pick up glass, vestments, missals, candlesticks, censers,
ladders, organs, pulpits, bricks, and tiles. The woodwork
was often valuable, and so were the lead roofs. There is a
famous later (1591) description of the sale at Roche Abbey

where a monk was trying to sell the properties in his cell and the peasants were wrenching iron hooks out of the walls. A sympathetic conservative bought part of the timber from the church and the steeple. A generation later he was asked by his nephew how he could do it, and he replied: 'What should I do? Might I not as well as others have some profit of the spoil of the abbey? For I did see all would away; and therefore I did as others did.' Some of the contents passed into parish churches, especially in England and northern Germany. One hundred and forty-six tons of stone from Thorney Abbey were granted to build the new chapel of Corpus Christi College, Cambridge. In the tower of Christ Church gateway at Oxford hangs the great bell that once belonged to Oseney Abbey, recast in 1678–9. At the parish church in Richmond, Yorkshire, may be seen the misericord seats acquired from the house at Easby at the dissolution. Such relics are now rare in English churches, for the waste in this auctioneering was great. At local auctions, often in the country, few people could know the real value of the goods. At the sale in Stafford of the Austin Friary, Mr Stamford bid seven shillings and secured an alabaster retable, a door, and a high altar.

Some libraries were poor and small. In the disposal of the better libraries there was loss, not so much by the destruction of texts of the medieval schools as by dispersal. These contents were dispersed into the public book trade, and might find their way into the possession of individuals who would understand little or nothing of their value. In Protestant countries antiquarians, or men of conservative sympathies, or ecclesiastics interested in history, went round the bookshops gathering what they could save and presenting their precious harvest to some institution which would ensure its preservation, as Archbishop Matthew Parker later offered most of his unique collection of manuscripts to his college, Corpus Christi in Cambridge, or Robert Hare gave the manuscripts which he had collected to Trinity Hall and to Caius College, evidently because he thought these societies sufficiently conservative in ethos to value the gift. But the forced dispersal of thousands of manuscripts could not be accomplished without loss, the more because in a new age of printing few men were conscious how irreparable such losses might be. But the losses were casual, haphazard, unsystematic; if the manuscripts were burnt upon a fire, it was like a modern bookseller pulping a useless pile of Victorian novels – dusty old papers dropping into oblivion in attics and rubbish heaps because no one wanted them, not because they were consumed in a holocaust of fanatic zeal.

In parts of England the suppression of the monasteries roused anger and a resort to arms. When the commissioners were suppressing the priory of St Nicholas of Exeter, they left a labourer to dismantle the rood while they went to dinner. A crowd of women assembled, broke into the church, and chased and stoned the labourer until he took refuge in the tower and escaped by jumping out of a window at the cost of a broken rib and at the risk of a broken neck. In Lincolnshire, Yorkshire, and Cumberland popular feeling, gathering to itself more resentments than the dislike of the king's religious policy, issued in a rebellion sufficient to shake the throne – the Pilgrimage of Grace. The defeat of the rebellion hastened the piecemeal suppression or 'voluntary surrender' of the larger houses.

It was not possible to dissolve the monasteries without destroying other objects traditional in devotion but despised even by educated conservatives as superstitious or childish. In 1538 the king's agents pillaged or destroyed the leading shrines of the kingdom, above all the shrine of St Thomas Becket at Canterbury, the loot from which is said to have filled twenty-six waggons and to have included some of the clay from which God fashioned Adam, stones of the prison from which St Peter escaped, and a thorn from the crown of thorns. They brought to London an old statue called the Boxley Rood, of which the eyes and lips could be moved by a mechanism of wires within. The preacher at St Paul's

Cross demonstrated its working to his congregation and then flung the broken pieces among them. An image from north Wales called Darvell Gadarn was burnt at Smithfield, in company with a Franciscan who had been Queen Catherine's confessor and denied the royal supremacy. The statue of Our Lady at Walsingham was removed before the suppression of the priory. In 1545, two years before the king died, an Act of Parliament empowered the dissolution of the chantries – chapels endowed to provide private masses for the soul of their founder or for other objects. But it was not widely executed before the reign of Edward VI, when the Act was renewed and extended.

Though these revolutionary acts commanded the assent of many conservatives, they gave decisive encouragement to those who were not conservative.

ENGLISH PROTESTANTS UNDER HENRY VIII

Upon the site of the present Cavendish Laboratory in Cambridge stood the house of the Austin Friars. Its head in 1520 was Robert Barnes, Miles Coverdale was among its members. It was natural for the friars of Cambridge to be eager to follow the controversy roused by Luther, the distinguished theologian of their order at Wittenberg. With like-minded spirits among the colleges – Thomas Bilney from Trinity Hall, Hugh Latimer from Clare College – they met at the White Horse Inn nearby to discuss German theology, and the group became known to the university as 'Germany'.

The Cambridge group was broken up after 1525, but radicals quietly moved to Germany or Switzerland to study or pursue their plans for reform. Of the many English on the Continent during the reign of Henry VIII, there was Robert Barnes, formerly of the Austin Friars at Cambridge, who studied at Wittenberg, was received back into favour when Thomas Cromwell was friendly to the Protestants, was even used as a royal agent abroad, and was burnt as a heretic at Smithfield in 1540; William Tyndale who succeeded in printing the first English version of the New Testament at Worms in 1525–6, and was strangled and burnt near Brussels in October 1536; Miles Coverdale, also of the Austin Friars at Cambridge, who printed a complete English translation of the Bible at Zurich in 1535, and whose delicate sense of rhythm is still familiar to everyone who uses the psalms in the *Book of Common Prayer*.

In the years 1535–9, while the monasteries were being dissolved, Thomas Cromwell gave a modest patronage to reformers, if they were not radical. Hugh Latimer was elevated to the see of Worcester, Philip Melanchthon was vainly invited to England. Cromwell engaged in diplomatic exchanges with the Lutheran princes of north Germany, and ordered an English Bible to be placed in every parish church. This Bible, printed at Paris and London in 1538–9, was based upon the versions of Tyndale and Coverdale. A reissue of 1540 was given a preface by Archbishop Cranmer of Canterbury.

THOMAS CRANMER (1489–1556)

Cranmer, a Fellow of Jesus College, Cambridge, was employed upon the affair of the king's divorce and made English ambassador to the Emperor Charles V. While in Nuremberg he married the niece of the Lutheran theologian Osiander, and soon afterwards (1532) was summoned to England to become Archbishop of Canterbury. Probably King Henry was not aware that his archbishop-designate was already reforming enough to have a wife, and it was sufficient for Henry that he was warmly recommended by Anne Boleyn. Cranmer was a reluctant prelate, moving slowly across Europe in the hope that the nomination would be withdrawn. Thenceforth he obeyed the king; protesting before his consecration that the oath of fidelity to the Pope should not bind him if it was against the laws of God or the realm; holding the court at Dunstable to determine the nullity of the marriage with Catherine of Aragon;

granting church lands to the king at favourable terms. He approved of the dissolution of the monasteries, though he wanted the lands for education and the relief of the poor. He was not a force in politics. As Archbishop, he continued to devote to study the same amount of time as at Cambridge, three quarters of the day; and part of the remainder was allotted to shooting, walking, chess, or riding, for he was a fine rider. Not even in the heyday of episcopal leisure in the eighteenth century could an archbishop govern the Church effectively in less than a quarter of the day. Cranmer was first and last a quiet scholar, and the Church was ruled more with his assent than at his direction.

He survived the vicissitudes of Henry's reign, partly because he was quiet, partly because he was a useful instrument, and partly because he believed in the royal supremacy and the king's policy, though he made private representation in favour of men condemned, whether for heresy or popery. The time of friendship for reform ended in 1539. The king's vicar-general Thomas Cromwell, advocate of moderate reform and friend of Cranmer, engaged in the ill-fated plan for the marriage between the king and Anne of Cleves, and lost his head in July 1540. In 1539 the repressive Act of Six Articles attempted to vindicate the Catholic faith of the king by decreeing savage penalties for denial of transubstantiation, private masses, private confession, or the need for clerical celibacy, and shocked Protestants hopeful about English progress. Bishops of reforming sympathies – Hugh Latimer of Worcester, Nicholas Shaxton of Salisbury – were forced out of their sees, and before the end of the reign Shaxton was condemned to death as a heretic and driven to recant. Cranmer's wife is said to have disappeared across the seas for four years, and Cranmer said that he wanted to escape abroad. In the streets of London people laid bets that Cranmer would follow Cromwell to the Tower, and on the Continent it was rumoured that he had been executed. But Cranmer survived. Yet in 1539 he had opposed the Act of Six Articles in the House of Lords, and thenceforth his 'heresy' was notorious among the orthodox. In 1543 the king received charges lodged against the archbishop by some prebendaries of Canterbury Cathedral. 'I know now', said Henry jestingly to Cranmer, on a barge by Lambeth Bridge, 'who is the greatest heretic in Kent.' The king frustrated every effort by the conservatives to ruin Cranmer, and left his name among the executors of his will. From servants to dukes, everyone liked Cranmer, and the king among them.

The survival was important in the growth of reforming ideas. The importance of Cranmer's survival to the future of the Church in England consists first in this, that he was an honest man. No rumour of political intrigue or sordid plunder clung to him. If he served the King, he served him on principle and neither from self-interest nor from cowardice. He believed in the doctrine of the godly prince, and believed it in an extreme form. Though he cannot have believed that 'the king', especially that king, 'can do no wrong', he believed acceptance of the king's commands to be a duty to God and man.

He appears to have attained decision in his Protestant convictions only during the last two years of Henry's reign. As late as 1543 he accepted the doctrine of transubstantiation at the royal behest. Almost his sole public contribution to the Protestant cause, before the king died, was to write a liberal preface to the official English Bible which Cromwell ordered to be placed in all parish churches, a Bible intended to educate the people in the Scriptures but also to prevent them from resorting to false and heretical translations, and which after 1543 was permitted to be read only by clerics, noblemen, gentry, and merchants. And yet Cranmer was suspected by conservatives, even conservatives who knew nothing of his wife. They were not misjudging him. By 1546 he believed the doctrine of justification by faith alone, and disbelieved the doctrine of transubstantiation; and Cranmer had an academic, hesitant, slow-moving mind, reluctant to affirm and not liable to sudden conversions. The convictions of 1546 had not been attained without a long and troubled history of scruple and study. Unsatisfactory to Protestants though he might be, his uneasy occupation of the see of Canterbury afforded the moderates among them a quiet encouragement.

THE REIGN OF EDWARD VI (1547–53)

On 28 January 1547 the king died, and at last the gates were open to the reforming party.

The new king, Edward VI, was nine years old, and power was soon in the hands of Protector Somerset, a friend of Cranmer and a supporter of reform. The Act of Six Articles and the heresy laws, though nominally in force until their repeal in November, ceased at once to be effective. Protestant incumbents could freely teach Protestant doctrine, Protestant churchwardens could remove images or alter the appearance of their churches, Protestant printers could publish tracts against the mass. In July 1547 injunctions were issued requiring the destruction of abused images or pictures and the reading of the Gospels and Epistles in English. The difficulty of determining when an image had been 'abused' led to disputes, and the disputes to a further order that all images should be removed. Latimer was summoned to preach, an Act of Parliament decreed that the communion should henceforth be administered in both kinds; a further Act of February 1549 permitted the clergy to marry, and Cranmer's wife began to appear publicly at her husband's table.

THE PRAYER BOOK OF 1549

The reformers wanted first to abolish the Latin mass and to substitute a liturgy in the vernacular. In March 1548 an *Order of Communion* was issued, providing English prayers of preparation to be inserted within the Latin mass. In January

1549 an Act of Uniformity abolished the Latin mass and
made a new Liturgy (the Prayer Book of 1549) the legal
form of worship.

In name it was the work of a group of thirteen divines,
who met at Chertsey and at Windsor and are therefore
known as the Windsor Commission. In fact there is a single
style running through the book, the style of Cranmer's
liturgical genius. That three quarters of the day in his study
was bearing its rich fruit. For a number of years he had been
quietly engaged in liturgical projects; the only one which
reached the public during the reign of Henry VIII was the
English Litany, first used in 1544, and almost in its present
form.

The 1549 Prayer Book was in part modelled upon the
German Protestant church orders. Its principles for reform
were the principles of Luther. The services must be understood by the people and made congregational, the people
must be turned from spectators intent upon their private
devotions into active participants. The laity must be well
instructed, and teaching exhortations were inserted. In
doctrine the idea of a repeated sacrifice in the eucharist
was denied. The most important of the Protestant books
which underlies the 1549 Prayer Book was a liturgy written
by Martin Bucer for Cologne and known by the title of its
1547 and 1548 English translations as *A Simple and Religious
Consultation*. Several German phrases (e.g. 'Whom God
hath joined together let no man put asunder') were taken
from Lutheran books. The ritual was much simplified, but
many old customs of ceremonial and the traditional vestments were nevertheless retained. The 1549 book followed
the Lutheran notion that custom should only be altered
where Scripture demanded, not the revolutionary Swiss
doctrine that Scripture must give a warrant for every
action. A travelling English merchant rightly described its
communion service as being 'after the manner of the
Nuremberg churches and some of those in Saxony'.

Lutheran services adapted the liturgies of the Middle

Ages. Cranmer likewise used the medieval liturgies of England, especially the use of Sarum. He made an office of Mattins, like certain Lutheran orders, which had already fused the old services of Mattins and Lauds in the medieval Breviary. He made an office of Evensong by working directly upon the old Breviary offices of Vespers and Compline. At the solemn moments of sacramental rites he often retained the words and outward signs of the medieval rite, above all in the consecration prayer of the eucharist, which was strongly reminiscent of the canon of the Roman mass. But the diverse elements upon which he worked, traditional or Protestant, were taken up by his careful scholarship and transmuted into a beauty, at once delicate and austere, of liturgical prose and poetry. Liturgies are not made, they grow in the devotion of centuries; but as far as a liturgy could ever be the work of a single mind, the Prayer Book flowed from a scholar with a sure instinct for a people's worship.

The future question of the English Reformation hung in great part upon Cranmer's Prayer Book, whether English Protestantism would follow this attempt to mould the best of the old with the best of the new, or whether the event would prove the mixture to be no essential unity, but a patchwork, so skilfully created by a master craftsman that only time and stress would show it to be a patchwork of incompatibles.

Even before the book was published, it was hardly able to content Cranmer himself. In the latter part of 1548 his mind moved towards the eucharistic doctrine taught by the Swiss Reformers, and the traditional formulas of the mass no longer pleased him. He was influenced by his friend Nicholas Ridley, now Bishop of London; and by eminent refugees from the Continent whom he invited to England – Martin Bucer from Strasbourg, who became Regius Professor of Divinity at Cambridge; the Italian Peter Martyr Vermigli, who became Regius Professor at Oxford; John à Lasco from Poland. While Bucer taught the moderating doctrine later to be called after his pupil Calvin, Peter Martyr and à Lasco were both Zwinglians after the manner of Zurich. 'Praise God,' wrote a young English Zwinglian to Bullinger at Zurich, in September 1548. 'Latimer has come over to our doctrine of the eucharist, and so has the Archbishop of Canterbury and other bishops, who until now seemed to be Lutheran.' From the moment of publication, the 1549 book was disliked by both sides; by the conservative because it was too radical, by the reformer because it was too conservative.

Under the Duke of Northumberland as Protector, the English reforming party succeeded between 1550 and 1553 in doing all that a German or Swiss city had done. They produced a new and simplified liturgy in the vernacular, with a Swiss doctrine of the eucharist, published a new statement of doctrine conforming at least in outline to the pattern of Swiss theology (the Forty-Two Articles of 1553), stripped the churches of images and side altars, replaced the high altar with a holy table, forbade the use of ceremonies other than those expressly provided in the Prayer Book, and appropriated to secular use a proportion of church property. They weakened the authority of the bishops, by extending the policy of Henry VIII to replace it by a direct exercise of the royal supremacy. Where the bishops refused to accompany reform, they were removed from their sees – Bonner of London, Gardiner of Winchester, Tunstall of Durham, Day of Chichester, Heath of Worcester – and replaced. In appearance, the ancient system of church government was continued; in fact, the rulers of the Church were the council of State, as in Wittenberg or Nuremberg or Zurich. Two of the new bishops, Hooper of Gloucester and Coverdale of Exeter, had long been exiles on the Continent, were warm adherents of Zurich, and disapproved of ancient episcopacy while they were being consecrated bishops. Hooper was even lodged in the Fleet prison for a time, to force him to withdraw his objections to some of the external accompaniments of episcopal consecration.

THE PRAYER BOOK OF 1552

This book was still a liturgy, a modified version of the 1549 book, and not yet the simplified sermon and prayers and psalms of Zurich or Geneva. If Cranmer now believed that the Swiss were right in their idea of the eucharist, his mind was congenitally cautious, and was perhaps made the less revolutionary by a human reluctance to jettison most of his life's work in liturgical study. Martin Bucer wrote a scholarly book known as the *Censura* (1551) to prove what was wrong with the 1549 book, and his moderate critique influenced Cranmer. Bucer objected to kneeling, vestments, prayers for the dead, the clothing with a white garment or chrisom at baptism, the anointing with oil, the exorcism. Thus the ritual of the 1552 book was much simplified.

It had been claimed by conservatives like Bishop Stephen Gardiner that the 1549 book taught the Lutheran or Roman Catholic doctrine of the Real Presence in the elements, the doctrine which Cranmer had ceased to believe. The various passages which had been claimed by Gardiner were altered in the new book. The most important of these was the sentence at the receiving of holy communion.

The 1549 book: 'The Body of our Lord Jesus Christ which was given for thee, preserve thy body and soul unto everlasting life.'

The 1552 book: 'Take and eat this in remembrance that Christ died for thee, and feed on him in thy heart by faith, with thanksgiving.'

The 1552 sentence was thus a perfect vehicle for those Swiss doctrines which taught that the eucharist was primarily a memorial of a sacrifice and that the gift was a spiritual gift received by the heart and not the hand.

Cranmer consented to the removal of old ceremonial practices, and called the altar a table, but still called the minister a priest and retained kneeling to receive the sacrament. In October 1552 a Scottish chaplain, whose

name is not given by the source but who is commonly
believed to have been John Knox, preached a bitter sermon
against this kneeling. The council suspended the publication of the Prayer Book, and asked Cranmer to reconsider
the question. Cranmer refused to give way, and a compromise was reached by inserting into the book the so-called
Black Rubric, which declared that in requiring communicants to kneel 'it is not meant thereby that any adoration
is done, or ought to be done . . . unto any real and essential
presence there being of Christ's natural flesh and blood'.

This explanation never contented the reformers who
accepted the Swiss principle of Scriptural warrant for
everything in church. The traditional atmosphere which
still hung unmistakably about the Prayer Book, the obvious
inheritance from the medieval liturgies, the use of the sign
of the cross in baptism or the ring in marriage, the formal
and liturgical nature of the prayers, the requirement of
kneeling – all were objectionable to the Calvinist and
Zwinglian. In the reign of Queen Mary, it was rumoured
among the English exiles on the Continent that Cranmer
secretly agreed with them, and that he had composed a
Prayer Book a hundred times more perfect than that of
1552, but had been prevented from publishing it by
'wicked clergy'.

In 1553 the English Reformation was still external to
most of the people, still an affair of legislation. The parishes
had been affected by the dissolution of the monasteries;
they were more affected by the abolition of the Latin mass,
the introduction of two vernacular liturgies in quick succession, the transformation in the appearance of the churches
and of the clergy who officiated in them. Congregations are
naturally conservative and resent change. There must have
been many parishioners in the country who sympathized
with the Cornish rebels of 1549 when they described the
English liturgy as a 'Christmas game' and wanted the
Latin mass and communion in one kind to be restored. The
Reformation in England had captured the genuine allegi-

ance only of a few instructed theologians and some educated merchants and other members of the middle class, particularly in London, and was supported for less unmixed motives by noble potentates. In 1553 England was by no means a Protestant country. It was made more nearly Protestant by the reign of Queen Mary.

THE REIGN OF MARY (1553–8)

Half Spanish, the daughter and confidante of Catherine of Aragon, sometimes treated by her father as a bastard, Mary grew up with an attachment to Rome so fervent as to be fanatical. During the few years of Protestant change under Edward VI, she was subjected to indignities and persecutions over her desire to keep her mass. She came to the throne at the age of thirty-seven, already an embittered spinster. The marriage, arranged in 1554 with the son of the Emperor Charles V, Philip of Spain, was the most disastrous act of the reign. He was eleven years younger than she, and charming. In 1555 she convinced herself that a baby was coming, and on 30 April the bells of London were rung and a *Te Deum* was sung in thanksgiving for the birth of an illusory child. Her personal happiness, as well as her hope for a Catholic England, was dependent upon a child and heir, and from the frustration of these hopes she never recovered her balance.

Her object was to restore the Catholic faith; and from the nature of her own parenthood, this must mean the restoration, not of the non-Roman Catholicism of her father, but of the authority of the See of Rome. The five deprived bishops were restored to their sees, and Gardiner became Lord Chancellor and her chief adviser. Ridley, Latimer, Coverdale, and Hooper were imprisoned; and so was Cranmer, for a protest against the Latin mass, though an Act of Parliament restored its legality only after he had been imprisoned. Some 2,000 clergy were ejected because they had married, though some crept back into livings where they were less well-known. Peter Martyr and other refugees were freely allowed to leave England, and Englishmen who felt it prudent to depart found easy ways to leave the country. At her coronation on 1 October 1553, Mary promised to maintain the rights of the Holy See as well as the liberties of the realm. An Act of Parliament repealed all the legislation of the reign of Edward VI concerning the prayer books, uniformity, and the marriage of the clergy. The Convocation of Canterbury declared the doctrine of transubstantiation to be true.

This was not equal to reinstating papal authority. The queen found it easier to restore the Catholic Church of 1546 than the Catholic Church of 1528. The English Parliament had no desire that papal authority in England should be restored. It preferred her to marry an Englishman and not a Spaniard, and gave offence by a petition in that sense.

Nor was it easy to restore the churches to their appearance before 1547. Bishop Bonner demanded that the pyx should be hung again over the altar, that there be a stone altar, a crucifix, a rood loft, censers, vestments, and a sanctus bell; and since many incumbents or churchwardens or mobs had destroyed or sold these articles, compliance with the bishop's orders was at first impossible. The Londoners showed such fierce hostility that the imperial ambassador Simon Renard was momentarily afraid of revolution. The churchwardens' accounts of the age show that the renewed roods were more makeshift than the old demolished roods.

The laity suspected that if they received Reginald Pole, the papal legate, as their new Archbishop of Canterbury, they would be putting into jeopardy their possession of the old monastic lands. By canon law, church property was inalienable. The Commons feared that legally the restoration of the Pope must mean the expropriation of many of the leading landowners in the country. Their fears were increased when Pole refused to commit himself to an absolute assurance about former church lands. On 7 November 1554 Pope Julius III at last gave a sufficient assurance.

Later in the month Pole was allowed to land at Dover, and was received in London amid loud popular enthusiasm. On 30 November, 500 members of Parliament knelt to receive his absolution for the disobedient and schismatic acts of the kingdom of England, and descended to the chapel to sing a *Te Deum*. Six days later Convocation submitted to the legate, and likewise received absolution. But the Act of Parliament which repealed the Acts of Henry VIII against the Pope also established the laity in continued possession of the former church lands. Mary started to give back her own lands, but the process soon languished.

The queen re-established a few monastic houses, Westminster Abbey being the most important. Since the old monastic lands were not available by law, every monastery must be newly endowed, and lack of money limited the number of houses which could be founded. An attempt to re-found the monastery of Glastonbury failed because the endowment was not sufficient. The monasteries were peopled, for the most part, with monks and nuns from the dissolved houses.

The Burnings

In December 1554 three old statutes against heresy were re-established. On 4 February 1555, the first of the Protestants, John Rogers, was burnt at Smithfield.

In the course of the next three years and a half, nearly three hundred people, high and low, rich and poor, were burnt as Protestant heretics. They included five former bishops: Ferrar of St David's, Hooper, Ridley, Latimer, and Cranmer. Ridley and Latimer were burnt together at Oxford on 16 October 1555. Two Spanish friars were sent to Oxford to argue with Cranmer and persuaded that moderate and hesitant mind to admit more evidence in the Fathers for the papal supremacy than he expected. At the end of February 1556 he submitted to the Catholic Church and to the Pope as its supreme head, declared that he believed all the articles of the Catholic faith, and denounced the heresies of Luther and Zwingli. On 18 March he signed a document of penitence that he had abused his archbishopric and had declared the divorce of King Henry VIII. On the day appointed for his burning, it was raining, and he was placed upon a platform in St Mary's Church while Dr Cole preached at him. At the end of the sermon Cranmer prayed, in deep penitence; and then, to the astonishment of the congregation and dismay of the authorities, he revoked all his recantations. He said that he had not believed them, but had signed them in the hope of saving his life. At the stake he held his right hand in the rising flame.

Thus the government, acting on what it thought to be principle, forced into the depths of humiliation the man who had been Archbishop of Canterbury for more than twenty years. Cranmer was not an unscrupulous time-server. He had been no worldly ecclesiastic sharing the spoils of a rich Church with an absolute sovereign. He was a scholar and a man of conscience, a genuine believer in the royal supremacy, who had been brought at the last to an intolerable dilemma when the crown ordered him to repudiate the royal supremacy. His humble mind saw that the questions were not at all simple. But he was a man of religion; and a man who was so ready to see both sides of an argument that he might have been persuaded to some genuine half-recantation, if the government had been less fanatical. No one believed in toleration. Protestants like Cranmer or John Philpot approved of the burning of the extreme heretics as strongly as did Queen Mary. But these men, who had held leading offices in the church under Henry VIII or Edward VI, were not of the same sort as the old-fashioned heretics. What they had taught, they had taught under the favour and authority of the government of England. It was impossible to expect men of learning and integrity to alter their opinions because England had now a different government.

Against some of the accused the authorities could claim their heresy to be so grave that not even Protestants would deny the penalty. Others they could charge with blasphemy in church. The English government burnt fewer Protestants than the French kings or the Spanish governors in the Netherlands. But those included not only the radicals of a tiny minority, but eminent representatives of opinions widely held among influential clergy and laymen. Mary was not executing a few unpopular fanatics, but some of the chief leaders of a party in opposition. No one in the country, under the age of thirty-five, knew what a papal England was like, and the Pope was wanted only by conservative ecclesiastics, who now believed that Catholic orthodoxy could not be preserved without a recognition of papal authority. England received back the Pope at Mary's behest, not because the English wanted him.

Most of the people wanted Protestantism as little. But in parts of the country hostility to the old order ran surprisingly deep. The bitter anticlericalism of Wolsey's day made even simple laymen hate papal restoration. At the end of August 1554 Suffolk villagers tried to burn a church with an entire congregation at mass inside. In the same month indignant peasants cut off the nose of a Kentish priest. In February 1555 Renard reported his fear of a rebellion if the burnings were not stopped. On 29 August 1556, 1,000 people cheered through the streets a roped chain of twenty-two men and women from Colchester on their way towards burning. Two of the revived Franciscans at Greenwich reported that the people threw stones at them when they went abroad.

Who was responsible for the persecution?

Not the Spaniards of King Philip's entourage in London. No one saw the peril more clearly than the clever ambassador, Simon Renard. He sent report after report to Philip, urging that the bishops should be restrained, recommending that there were other ways than these perilous public burnings, that secret executions would be better, or banishment, or imprisonment. He anxiously observed the sympathy of crowds with the victims: how they gathered round the ashes and wrapped them reverently; how they uttered menaces against the bishops, or wept in compassion.

The burnings began after Pole arrived; and the bishops who sat in the courts to condemn heretics were sitting under his jurisdiction as papal legate. Pole wanted mildness to be tried before execution; but he believed that execution was right if mildness failed. Renard thought the coarse and quaint-humoured Bonner to be the most deplorably active among the bishops; and the records of the Protestant victims sustain this reputation. Stephen Gardiner, Chancellor till his death in 1555, carried a large responsibility. Other bishops took a share. The queen and her close advisers killed men and women neither from policy nor from vindictiveness, but from conscience, to purge the realm before Almighty God.

The courage of the martyrs was not expected by the authorities. Believing that English Protestants were few and shallow, they expected recantations. They achieved recantations, of which the most important was that of Sir John Cheke, formerly tutor to King Edward VI, who was kidnapped near Brussels and would not face the fire. But they overestimated the ability of human beings to adopt opinions because they are commanded. The steadfastness of the victims, from Ridley and Latimer downwards, baptized the English Reformation in blood, and drove into English minds the fatal association of ecclesiastical tyranny with the See of Rome. The old anticlericalism, the old hatred of Wolsey and his power, the resentment against the Pope's authority, received a new and terrible justification. Five years before, the Protestant cause was identified with church robbery, destruction, irreverence, religious anarchy. It was now beginning to be identified with virtue, honesty, and loyal English resistance to a half-foreign government.

Everything hung upon the baby that never came. All over Europe men knew that the Princess Elizabeth must succeed and that with her would come another, and Protestant, revolution. Rumours of Mary's illness, reports of her death, spread through the Continent, dismaying the adherents of Rome and strengthening the morale of Protestants. The English exiles in Germany found it easy to borrow money on the credit of their English estates, so convinced were the European bankers that they would soon be home and in health and power. Every calamity which afflicted one of the persecutors was recorded and remembered as a judgement of God – the chancellor of Salisbury diocese who died on the day before he was sending ninety persons to be examined; the gaoler of Newgate who died with flesh rotting; the agent destroyed by lightning at the arrest of a Protestant; the sheriff of London stricken with paralysis. If there had been a baby, the political complexion of England would have changed overnight. But the queen sat wretched in her rooms, or walked the corridors like a ghost, or yearned after her absent and indifferent husband, or sat on the floor with her knees drawn up, while men whispered, in fear or hope, that she was dying.

She died in the early morning of 17 November 1558; and Cardinal Pole died a few hours later.

THE ACCESSION OF ELIZABETH

The religion of Elizabeth is an enigma but not because she was silent upon the subject. She spoke freely to foreign ambassadors, less freely to her councillors; but the resulting information is so confused that we do not wonder at the Spanish ambassador, who wrote in despair: 'After all she is a woman and inconstant.' Religion being at the core of English diplomacy, it is unquestionable that sometimes her descriptions of her faith were intended to please King Philip II of Spain, or the King of France, or the Huguenot or Dutch or German or Scottish lords. She was inclined to tell people what they wanted to hear. Seeing her affirmations through the eyes of others, we hesitate to trust them. She was once charged by a hostile critic with 'atheism', but absurdly. She has been charged by historians with being 'secular', but the charge is an anachronism. She has been charged less absurdly, but still improbably, with thinking all religions much the same. She kept the inmost creed of her soul as secret as her real intentions about marriage; she talked volubly about marriage, she was in perpetual dalliance with suitors, but no one can penetrate the inner mind; and perhaps, like a woman, she could not always fathom her own heart. Its mechanism was not simple. She had been living so dangerously during the reign of Mary that to conceal its complexities had become natural.

In consequence, historians still argue whether, in making England Protestant during 1559, the queen and her advisers were pushing a reluctant Parliament or whether the House of Commons was pushing a reluctant queen.

As the daughter of Anne Boleyn, she must be Protestant. Under Mary she had suffered for the Protestant cause; she was hailed by the growing Protestant party as their champion; the exiles hurried back from the Continent. For all her diplomatic talent she had no dealings with the Pope and withdrew the English envoy in Rome without ceremony. At Christmas 1558 she ordered the Bishop of Carlisle not to elevate the host, and on his refusal left the church after the Gospel. At the opening of Parliament on 25 January 1559, when she went in state to Westminster Abbey, she was received by the abbot and monks with candles, incense, and holy water, and dismissed the monks, saying: 'Away with those torches, for we see very well.' She summoned Protestant preachers, and surrounded herself with Protestant lords, especially the former secretary of Somerset, William Cecil. With a treasury impoverished and a land undefended, with the French claiming the English crown through Mary Queen of Scots, with a Spanish army in the Netherlands, with two thirds of England Catholic, it was imprudent to be a Protestant. But by birth, education, and conviction a Protestant she must be. She told the Spanish ambassador openly that she could not marry Philip II because she was a heretic.

She was the daughter of Henry VIII; and it is certain that she was personally attracted to a religious settlement like that of her father, though considered in generalities, not adopted in all its detail. Her ideas of that settlement included a Catholicism without the Pope; the royal supremacy; a preferably celibate clergy; the Real Presence in the eucharist. In March 1559 she told the Spanish ambassador that she was resolved to restore religion as her father had left it. This was not a practicable programme, because no one in the country wanted it. The reigns of Edward VI and Mary had made the Catholics more Roman and the Protestants more Reformed. She was ruling a divided people, among whom some wanted the Pope and others the Prayer Book for which Cranmer and Ridley and Latimer had died.

Seven years later she told a Spaniard that the Protestants had driven her farther than she intended to go, and she was speaking truth as well as diplomacy. But she had no choice. If a Protestant, then despite her talk about the Lutheran Confession of Augsburg, despite her affirmation that she disagreed only with three or four things in the mass, she had no alternative to the Prayer Book hallowed by fire.

It was the fortune of Queen Elizabeth and of England that policy agreed with her preference. A violent change, a down-with-idolatry campaign, might not only have provoked revolution in the north of England, but might have invited the armies of France or Spain. She must retain the Spanish alliance and the good will of King Philip II as the best protection against the French. She was advised to go warily: 'Glasses with small necks, if liquor was poured into them suddenly and violently, would not be so filled, but would refuse to receive it.' So far as possible she aimed to reconcile the moderate conservatives like Bishop Tunstall of

Durham, and therefore to establish a religion which a conservative might accept.

Not without strong opposition in Parliament, a Supremacy Bill offered her the Supreme Headship. She accepted the power but refused the title, and became Supreme Governor. Both conservative and radical disliked the title of Head and were better pleased with the new word. Since the Prayer Book of 1552 was the only possible liturgy, it was reissued under an Act of Uniformity, but with important amendments in a conservative sense. A rubric declared that the ornaments of the church and the ministers should be those of the second year of King Edward VI, a year when the traditional vestments were still worn and the churches still retained much of their medieval appearance and furniture. The Black Rubric of 1552, which declared that no adoration of any Real Presence was intended by kneeling at the communion, was omitted. Above all, the Zwinglian formula which the 1552 book had ordered at the administration of the holy communion was kept, but was to be preceded by the more traditional formula of 1549 – 'The Body of our Lord Jesus Christ which was given for thee, preserve thy body and soul unto everlasting life.'

MATTHEW PARKER

The vacant See of Canterbury was conferred upon Matthew Parker, a man known to have been friendly to reform under Edward VI. During the reign of Mary, Parker had been deprived of his preferments as a married man and lived quietly in England. He was like Cranmer in being retired and scholarly; more persevering than able, in the eyes of the government he possessed the supreme merit of being a moderate man who would conciliate.

The Marian bishops were not ready to cooperate with the government. They opposed the bills steadily in the House of Lords. Archbishop Heath of York refused to crown the queen. In the event only two of the seventeen

Marian bishops (those of Llandaff and of Sodor and Man) retained their sees under Elizabeth. 14 bishops, 12 deans, 15 heads of colleges, and between 200 and 300 clergy resigned their offices or were deprived.

This refusal of the conservative leaders made Parker's task far more difficult. He must rely upon the divines in sympathy with Protestantism.

But many of the divines of the Protestant party were not as moderate as they had been under Edward VI. Those who had been exiled upon the continent had learnt the doctrines and the practices of the Swiss and Rhineland churches. They had themselves been divided on whether the 1552 Prayer Book was a truly reformed book. At Frankfurt the exiles quarrelled bitterly. The less extreme wing, led by Richard Cox, contended that the 1552 Prayer Book was the book for which the martyrs of England died; the more extreme wing, led by John Knox, contended that it still contained the dregs of papistry. These were the men now flooding back into England, and upon some of them the government must rely for its moderate policy.

On 17 December 1559, Parker, after election by his Dean and Chapter, was consecrated Archbishop of Canterbury. The government wanted all to be done in the ancient ways, and hoped that four Marian bishops would agree to consecrate. The hope was vain; Parker was consecrated by Barlow the Henrician Bishop of Bath and Wells, Scory the Edwardine Bishop of Chichester, Hodgkin the suffragan Bishop of Bedford, and Coverdale the translator of the Bible and Edwardine Bishop of Exeter. Parker's difficulties may be judged by the vestments of the ministers. Barlow wore a cope, the legal vestment. Scory and Hodgkin evidently had scruples about a cope, and wore surplices. Coverdale evidently had scruples about a surplice and wore a black gown. It was soon plain that whatever the Ornaments Rubric intended, the traditional dress of ministers was not enforceable. Old exiles, now new bishops, like Grindal and Jewel, threatened to resign their sees upon the issue. So far from securing that the cope should be preserved, Parker was struggling to preserve the surplice.

Most of the parochial clergy remained at their posts through these vicissitudes. A few in each diocese followed the Marian bishops into retirement or exile, but the great majority of the clergy continued to minister in their parishes through all the changes. An Augustinian canon of Dunstable named John Stalworth was forced to leave his religious order with a pension when the house was dissolved in 1539. He subsequently held livings under Henry VIII, Edward VI, Mary, and Elizabeth, and he died the rector of Greatworth in Northamptonshire in 1590. Though he lived longer than most, this career was not untypical. Hugh Curwen, who had been Marian as well as Protestant Archbishop of Dublin, saw nothing odd, when pleading to Elizabeth for an English see, in recalling that he had served her and her sister Mary for eight years and a half. Nicholas Wotton, who refused bishoprics with passion, was Dean of Canterbury and Dean of York jointly from the reign of Henry VIII to the reign of Elizabeth; but he was less a dean than a diplomat salaried by deaneries. Some were open to the imputation of being Vicars of Bray. Dr Andrew Perne was Master of Peterhouse from 1554 to 1589. When in 1557 the corpses of Bucer and Fagius were exhumed and burnt as heretical in the market square at Cambridge, in company with a pile of Protestant books, Perne was Vice-Chancellor and lent his countenance to the proceedings. Three and a half years later the Senate passed a unanimous grace restoring to Bucer and Fagius their degrees and a public service was held to do them honour; Dr Perne was again Vice-Chancellor. Pamphleteers of Elizabeth's reign coined the Latin verb *pernare*, meaning 'to be a turncoat'. But Perne was exceptional, for a majority of the Marian heads of Cambridge and Oxford colleges were removed after the accession of Elizabeth.

Some clergy were content with lower motives, knowing

that the alternative was possible starvation and certain discomfort. We have the report of a conversation between two clergymen summoned to St Paul's Cathedral in London to make the new subscription before the commissioners. They met outside the door.

Dr Kennall said: 'What do you mean to do today?'

Dr Darbyshire replied: 'What in conscience I am bound to do, to wit, not to subscribe.'

'What!' said Kennall. 'I think you are not so very a fool as to refuse to subscribe, and thereby lose so good livings as you have!'

Darbyshire said: 'I must do that which is secure for my soul, whatsoever becometh of my livings.'

'Before God,' said Kennall with great vehemence, 'if ever you get so good, and so many, and so near together again, I will give you my head!'

Many clergy were ignorant, simple, poverty-stricken, and generally 'unreformed'. Others, more capable of decision, were convinced that the Church needed reform. They were not all happy with what they saw around them in the shape of reform, but they preferred the vernacular to Latin and a wife to a concubine and knew that their parishioners had souls which must be baptized and fed and married and buried. Whatever the status of the Pope, the canon law, or the scholastic philosophy, the people still needed sacraments.

But in 1559 the religious and ecclesiastical model of an English Reformation was still to be determined. So far it was only certain that, in some manner or other, the Church of England would be Protestant.

The Reformation everywhere had political consequences; but in England beyond all other states the political motive was entangled with the reforming ideas. By 1558 Protestantism had struck roots into the country – that was evident from the martyrs under Mary and the attitude of London towards them. But the Reformation as a *reforming* force had hardly begun. The appearance of the churches had been altered, the monasteries dissolved, the clergy permitted to marry, the images and the chasubles destroyed or sold, the independent power of the church curtailed, the secular authority of the bishops weakened. But the clergy were as ignorant as ever. And Protestant doctrine penetrated little farther than the homilies which they were compelled to read and the liturgy which they were compelled to use. A substantial body of lay opinion (the more substantial the further away from London) preferred the old ways. The leading reformers, with the exception of Matthew Parker, disliked the relics of the old ways still remaining and wanted to alter the new establishment further, to conform with the patterns of Zurich or Geneva. The end of the revolution had not been reached in 1559. Some say that the accession of Elizabeth was the beginning of the English Reformation, not its end.

5

The Growth of Reformed Protestantism

THE Swiss pattern of a reformed church became the norm for Protestant churches outside the Lutheran churches of north Germany and Scandinavia. They were not agreed about the relations of Church and State, being divided into Calvinist or non-Calvinist. They were agreed upon a doctrine of the eucharist denying that the grace of the sacrament was given 'in' the bread; upon an austere simplicity of ceremonial in worship; upon a recognition of the high importance of moral discipline; and upon a driving attempt to bring the Bible into every home.

They made their conquests mainly in the countries where the government was Catholic and hostile. The most conservative reformations were in those countries where the government sooner or later took charge of the Reformation and blessed it – the north German principalities, Denmark, Sweden, England. The least conservative reformations were in those countries where the government resisted by force, and where the religious revolution required a political revolution also – France, the Netherlands, Scotland. The more hostile the State, the more likely that the Protestants would be Calvinist, for Calvinism established an authority of the ministry free from spiritual subjection to the State authorities.

But the Reformed began to expand at the expense, not only of the Catholics, but of the Lutherans in north Germany. The name *Reformed*, indeed, first came into common use when opposed, not to the Catholics, but to the Lutherans.

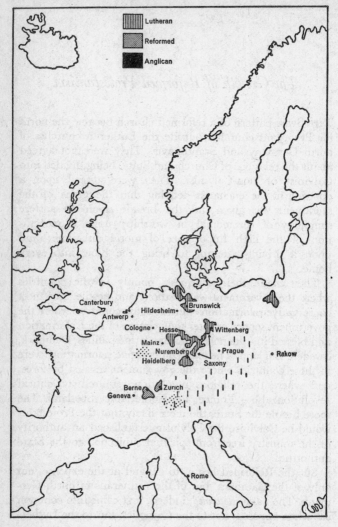

Protestantism in 1529.

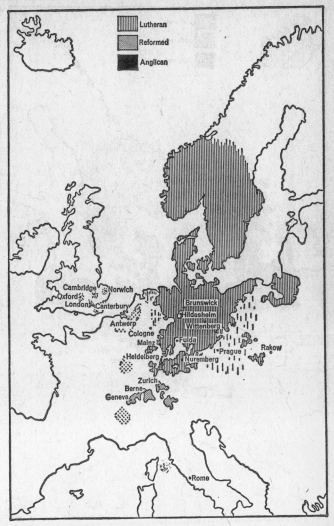

Protestantism in 1555.

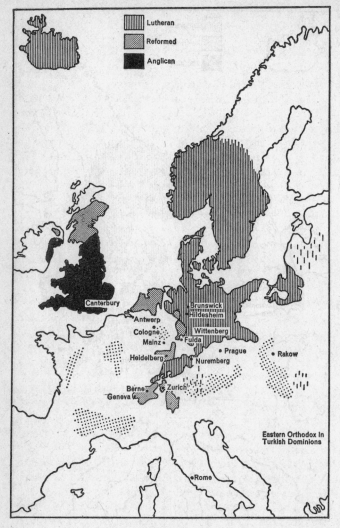

Protestantism in 1600.

GERMANY

The Divisions of Lutheranism

Within a year of Luther's death in 1546, German Protestantism faced destruction.

The Emperor Charles V at last achieved a peace with France at the Treaty of Crépy in 1544. The Turks were busy in Persia and the eastern frontiers were quiet. He won to his side the Protestant Duke Maurice of Saxony, who coveted the title and domains of the Elector of Saxony. His armies advanced northward and at the battle of Mühlberg in 1547 crushed the Saxons and captured the city of Wittenberg and the person of the Elector John Frederick. The Landgrave Philip of Hesse was enticed to the court by a subterfuge and also imprisoned. The Electoral title and all the Electoral domains of Saxony except Thuringia were given to Duke Maurice as his reward. It looked as though the Emperor could end the Protestant revolt by force.

The Interim, 1548

At the Diet of Augsburg in 1548 the Emperor ordered the religious settlement known as the Augsburg Interim. This permitted the Protestants, until the final decision of a General Council, to retain the legal marriage of clergy and the use of the cup in the sacrament. It permitted them almost nothing else, and the question followed whether it was enforceable. Bucer fled from Strasbourg to England; other divines fled northward; the imprisoned John Frederick tried to move his university from Wittenberg – which was in the lands wrested from his domain – to Jena in Thuringia. At Jena gathered the bitterest opponents of the Interim, the fiercest and most uncompromising among Luther's disciples. They summoned Melanchthon to join them.

Melanchthon refused to go. He had fled from Wittenberg just before its capture by Spanish troops, but soon returned there and received an assurance from Duke Maurice that the Protestant Church of Saxony would be preserved. He was a man congenitally ready to meet opponents half-way whenever he could, and reluctant to desert Wittenberg, which he saw as the morning star of the Reformation. With Maurice's help he succeeded in modifying the Interim – to make it more tolerable – into the Leipzig Interim of December 1548, containing credal formulas patient of a Lutheran interpretation but agreeing to government by bishops (so long as it was not exercised against God's Word) and to a Latin liturgy, seven sacraments, vestments, and fast days. Provided that the essential doctrines of the Gospel were free, Melanchthon was content to accept the enforcement of Catholic ritual and ceremonial even when he disliked them. In a letter to Karlowitz he said that he was a man of peace and imprudently criticized Luther's vehemence and irascibility.

Charles V reckoned without the affections of the people. It was found that Protestant faith and practice had taken roots in popular devotion. In south and central Germany a superficial acceptance of the Interim was enforced by Spanish troops, in Saxony and Brandenburg evangelical-sounding formulas made it workable. But north Germany was in open revolt. The emperor likewise reckoned without the traditional independence of German cities and princes. Even in southern Germany he found the people obstinate against the restored mass, and a difficulty in finding pastors, for many Protestants refused to conform and many Catholics were doubtful of a settlement imposed without the approval of the Pope.

If Charles V had not destroyed the Lutherans, he had divided them. Philip Melanchthon was the one disciple of Luther with a European stature, the one person who could have guided the Lutheran churches. With half or more than half the Lutherans his reputation was now ruined. Their confidence in his leadership was gone, they believed him to be corrupting the evangelical faith and to be treating with ungodliness. In a few months he lost the headship of a

Church and became the head of a group of theologians. The Lutherans were divided into a moderate party based upon Wittenberg and led by Melanchthon, and a strict or extreme party based upon Jena and Magdeburg, and led by Matthias Flacius Illyricus.

The Lutheran churches never recovered the unity which they lost after the Augsburg Interim of 1548.

The Peace of Augsburg, 1555

Politically they were soon restored to safety, for the emperor could not maintain his power. Assisted by a new Turkish invasion, by alliance with the French, and by Duke Maurice of Saxony, the Protestant league extorted from the emperor the Peace of Augsburg (1555). Every land that was Lutheran before 1552 might remain so legally, and for the future every ruler of a state was given the choice between the old religion and the Lutheran, and his subjects were to abide by his decision or peaceably leave the state – the famous principle of *cujus regio ejus religio*, though the actual phrase is later. The treaty established the basis of religious peace in Germany for sixty years. Protestantism was no longer in peril.

But the disagreement over the Interim inaugurated long years of argument among the Lutheran churches. Flacius Illyricus was the most learned, militant, and quarrelsome churchman of the sixteenth century. A native of Istria near Venice (hence the surname), he spoke Italian as his mother tongue and never spoke German fluently. Melanchthon thought him only an ungrateful pupil, a viper whom Wittenberg had nourished unawares. Flacius was driven by a determination to defend 'faith alone' to the death. He possessed something of Luther's annihilating quality as a pamphleteer, and poured out broadsides against Philip Melanchthon and his party, known henceforth as the Philippists. Not only against Melanchthon. There was hardly a school of thought in Christendom which Flacius failed to controvert. With a passionate affection for orthodoxy upon high religious grounds, he combined more than a touch of the crank and the fanatic. Melanchthon, dying in 1560, wrote a little paper of reasons why he was not afraid of death. On the left side are the words: 'Thou wilt be redeemed from sin. Thou wilt be freed from care, and from the fury of theologians.'

As the Reformed faith began to spread northwards into Germany, the touchstone of Lutheran faith became the doctrine of the eucharist. Melanchthon always held that the distinction between '*in* the bread' and '*with* the bread' was not simple, and had produced a revised text of the Augsburg Confession in 1540 which made room for the Reformed.* The Philippists were soon being accused of crypto-Calvinism, of favouring a Reformed doctrine of the sacrament. The stricter Lutherans sometimes confessed that Catholicism was nearer than Calvinism to orthodoxy. Melanchthon wished to meet the Swiss where he could, to work with them peaceably. There were other sources of strife. The Philippists could not allow that Luther was above criticism. The strongest plea of the strict Lutherans was that of faithfulness to Luther.

The Formula of Concord

In 1577 a partial settlement of the debates in Lutheranism was achieved by the publication of the *Formula of Concord*.

The *Formula* was not the posthumous triumph of Flacius Illyricus, some of whose views it condemned. But it contained an uncompromising exclusion of the Reformed doctrine of the Eucharist and of the Calvinist doctrine of predestination. No Philippist could subscribe to it. The *Formula* was made obligatory upon ministers in the Lutheran states which accepted it, and established more religious peace than had existed since the days of the Augsburg Interim of 1548.

* Known as the *Confessio Variata*.

Most of the Lutheran states (86 states or cities and some 8,000 pastors) accepted the *Formula of Concord*, and for a moment it looked as though the Lutherans were united. But not all states accepted it. The King of Denmark threw his copy of the *Formula of Concord* into the fire. Bremen, Anhalt, Nuremberg were important among the few who refused to accept it and remained Philippist. The continued existence of these Philippist churches encouraged the growth of Reformed Protestantism in Germany. In sympathy they were as near to Calvin as they were to the strict Lutherans, and little by little some of the Philippist churches could hardly be distinguished from Reformed churches. The Reformed made rapid strides in Germany, because a large party among the Lutherans came to believe that in important respects they were right.

It is nevertheless an illusion of popular history that the Lutherans lost their vigour and expansiveness after the Peace of Augsburg in 1555. Most of the Lutheran lands were nominally Lutheran before 1555, but several of the greatest, like Prussia and Sweden, were adequately organized during the second half of the sixteenth century, and in Germany the Lutherans were strongly consolidating their territories up to the Thirty Years War. They made a momentous acquisition as late as 1598, when the city of Strasbourg, once the city of Martin Bucer and of John Calvin, received the *Formula of Concord* and became Lutheran. Even the Palatinate, where Calvinist presbyteries were introduced from 1570, and which was to become the keystone of the German Reformed Churches, became stiffly Lutheran for seven years after 1576. Because the Lutherans sometimes criticized each other, it must not be inferred that they had lost dynamic. Vehemence is rather a sign of energy than of weakness. The old picture of a Lutheran Church static and declining before the inroads of the Reformed and of the Jesuits is a legend of Church history which modern studies have rewritten.

Between 1556 and 1559 the Elector Palatine Otto Henry

made the Palatinate Protestant. At the same time Duke Christopher of Württemberg, a state which had been Protestant since 1534, fully organized the church with the aid of the theologian Johann Brenz. In 1568 the duchy of Brunswick came over to the Protestant side. Oldenburg was organized by a strong Lutheran church order of 1573. A series of church orders reorganized other states.

One important mode of spreading Protestant territory after 1555 was by absorbing the lands of the bishoprics. Those of Germany were also secular lordships. To make the see of Magdeburg Lutheran was to protestantize not only a diocese and an ecclesiastical administration but a principality and a secular administration.

The Catholics claimed that to protestantize a diocese was illegal. To the Peace of Augsburg in 1555 they added a clause known as the Ecclesiastical Reservation, ordering that if a bishop or abbot became a Protestant he lost his office and the chapter or convent or patron must proceed to a new election. The Protestants refused to accept this clause and repeatedly protested against it.

This mode of securing these territories was simple: to get a Protestant bishop elected. Then the bishop allowed liberty for the Augsburg Confession within his territory, and appointed Protestant canons to ensure the succession. It was easiest where a bishop was not elected by a chapter but nominated by a Protestant prince. In this way Brandenburg united to itself the territories of the three sees where the Elector possessed the right of nomination – Brandenburg, Havelberg, and Lebus. It was less easy, but still inevitable, in sees where the lands were surrounded by Protestant territory or located in a great Protestant city. However Catholic the canons of the chapter, however reluctant to elect a Protestant, it was politically impossible to elect a person who would not be acceptable to the neighbouring power. In this way Saxony absorbed the sees of Meissen, Merseburg, and Naumburg. The chapter of Merseburg, where the Protestant canons were in the majority, demanded the younger son of the Elector of Saxony as their bishop (December 1561); he was eight years old, and henceforth the Elector ruled the diocese in the name of his son. Three years later, when the bishop of Naumburg died, the Elector surrounded the place of election with troops, promised money and prebends, and was satisfied when that same younger son (now aged twelve) was elected to the see. In 1585 the Protestant chapter of Bremen elected an aristocratic boy aged ten to the archbishopric. From similar motives the staunch Catholic Duke of Bavaria put his son Ernest into the see of Freising at the age of thirteen. The Catholic Chapter of Halberstadt elected (1567) the grandson of the Duke of Brunswick, aged two, in the desperate and vain hope of receiving Brunswick protection for the see. The child was elected on condition that he be brought up in the Catholic religion. But the old duke was buried by a Protestant abbot with Protestant prayers, the child was educated as a Protestant, and though he was at last consecrated bishop with Catholic rites, he refused to attend mass and declared himself an adherent of the Augsburg Confession.

Thus several of the old episcopal principalities were taken into the new system.*

The Emperor declared this way of circumventing the Ecclesiastical Reservation to be illegal; but after negotiation, he began to wink at it, and watched complaisantly while the great sees of Magdeburg, Lübeck, Verden, Minden, Halberstadt passed into Protestant hands.

The greatest ecclesiastical principalities were the three Archbishoprics of Mainz, Trèves, and Cologne. Despite many Protestants among their citizens and a few among their canons, none of them succeeded in electing a Protestant archbishop; and after 1555 the one conversion of a

---

* The worst of the troubles over election by a chapter occurred at Strasbourg between 1592 and 1604, where the Protestant canons elected a Protestant bishop (aged fifteen), the Catholic canons a Catholic bishop, and the friends of each side brought the contest to open war.

German archbishop to the Protestant faith, at Cologne in 1582, proved the gravest setback to the Protestant cause before the Thirty Years War.* Not far from the Rhineland and north-west Germany lay the most formidable army in Europe, the Spanish army of the Netherlands, and it was the political and religious interest of Spain to protect the Catholicism of the Rhine bishoprics.

But the Protestant faith was not spread merely by political measures with prince-bishoprics. Its true expanding power was evident when both sides regarded liberty for the Augsburg Confession as a likely prelude to the protestantizing of that territory. In a state like the Archbishopric of Mainz, where the ruler was unfriendly but not zealous, Protestants continued to make rapid inroads. In the south German lands, which a modern age would regard as solidly Catholic, in Austria and Bavaria and Tyrol and Bohemia, they were growing in numbers and power through the sixties of the sixteenth century, usually among the nobility and in the cities among the middle class. In 1568 the Emperor Maximilian II was pressed into allowing a measure of legal liberty† to the Lutherans of Austria, and four years later he permitted a similar freedom in Bohemia. As late as 1575 it still looked as though the Protestants might end by converting all Germany.

Of the German states which accepted Reformed doctrine and polity, the most important were: the Palatinate, permanently though moderately Reformed after 1583; Bremen, a Philippist Lutheran Church which became Reformed in 1580, while it continued steadily to repudiate the name of Calvinist; Anhalt, counted among the Reformed states by 1595; the main part of Hesse, counted as Reformed by 1605; and the ruler, but uniquely not the people, of Brandenburg.

* For the Cologne election and its consequences, see pp. 311–13.

† The nobles, and their households and tenants, were permitted freedom of Protestant worship on their property, but not in royal cities or market towns. They had to testify in writing their adherence to the Augsburg Confession and undertake not to injure the Catholics in their religious practice, their stipends, or other rights.

In 1613 the Elector John Sigismund of Brandenburg, who had been allowed by his father to study at Heidelberg in the Palatinate, became a Calvinist. That two out of the three Protestant Electors of Germany (Saxony, Palatinate, Brandenburg) should be Reformed worried Lutherans everywhere, and especially when Brandenburg was rising in power and importance. But unlike the Palatinate, where the neighbourhood of the upper Rhine and Switzerland made the Reformed influence inevitable, in Brandenburg the people were deeply Lutheran. Unable to force them into a Reformed polity, the Elector John Sigismund secured a legal place for Reformed teaching within the state of Brandenburg, and the two continued together, with Lutherans in the majority.

If they were called Reformed, or even if they were called Calvinist, the German churches did not usually follow the Swiss pattern of church government. If, like Bremen, they were Philippist in origin, they usually preserved the Lutheran form of consistory. If, like the Palatinate, they were governed by a prince, the prince kept a hold upon the consistory even where he permitted the introduction of Genevan elders. The Elector Palatine Frederick III presided normally at the consistory; his grandson Frederick IV presided once a month. Nowhere in Germany was the pure Calvinist form of government established successfully. The German Reformed looked rather to Zwingli and his successors at Zurich, who disapproved the free right of excommunication without reference to the magistrate. Only on the Lower Rhine, by association with the Calvinist Netherlands, were true presbyterian synods created, at Wesel in 1568 and Emden in 1571. For a long time the Philippist churches refused any confession of faith but the Augsburg Confession.

Erastus (c. 1524–83)

In the Palatinate, the clash between Church and State, between the Zurich and Genevan ideals of ecclesiastical polity, came into the open. Thomas Lüber, known better to the world by his humanist name of Erastus, was a pupil of Bullinger at Zurich and came to Heidelberg in 1558 as physician to the Elector Palatine. From 1560 the Calvinist Caspar Olevianus attempted to introduce the Calvinist consistories and discipline into the Palatinate. Erastus became his chief opponent; and when the Elector Frederick III was persuaded at last to introduce a presbyterian discipline, in 1570, it was under stringent limitations, though not stringent enough to prevent Erastus being troubled for several years by a process in the Church courts.

During his life Erastus printed no work against the presbyterian claim of excommunication. But he wrote and circulated theses against the right of excommunication, upon the general basis that if excommunication carries civil penalties its exercise must be given to the magistrate alone. These theses were produced after his death and published at London in 1589. In Britain (but only in Britain) the name Erastianism was soon being applied, unjustly to Erastus, as a term to describe any theory which advocated excessive control of the Church by the State.

Lutheran and Calvinist

The Lutheran churches slowly grew in order and learning. The older universities of Tübingen, Rostock, Greifswald and Leipzig were reformed, and after the foundation of Marburg (1527), other new universities were founded at Königsberg (1544), Jena (1558), Helmstedt (1576) and Giessen (1607).

Martin Chemnitz of Brunswick (1522–86), a pupil of Melanchthon, turned himself into the most learned Protestant theologian of the century. He helped to systematize Lutheran doctrine further. His famous book was *An Examination of the Council of Trent* (four parts 1565–1573), which contained the most complete of all contemporary justifications of the Protestant movement. As the various states were organized by church orders, the administration of education and of the relief of the poor became far better organized.

In divided Germany Lutherans would not allow either the mass or the Calvinist worship in Lutheran states; the Calvinist consistories would discipline anyone found holding Catholic or Lutheran doctrines of the Real Presence. Because there were more separated Protestant states in Germany than elsewhere, the religious disunity of Germany was more manifest.

Protestant Germany was not an underlying unity with differences of opinion. The Calvinists were more friendly to the Lutherans than the Lutherans to the Calvinists, but they gave exceeding provocation by their open claim that the Lutherans were still stained with the inheritance of papistry, and by their conscious superiority. 'Hoeschel, *though a Lutheran*,' said Scaliger, 'is a learned man.' Until 1648 the Lutherans never forgot that they and the Roman Catholics were the only legal religions of Germany, and that the status of the Reformed was as illicit as that of the Anabaptists. They believed the Calvinist denial of Real Presence to be an intolerable breach of Catholic faith. They were seldom conscious of a common unity among Protestants. The Lutheran professor Polycarp Leyser defended the thesis that if the errors of the Calvinists are compared with those of the Papists, the errors of the Calvinists are worse. Devotion was made a sinew of war when there was published *A Prayer Book against the Calvinists*. Though Leyser's view was not held by a majority, the stricter Lutherans believed it loyalty to truth that they should not fraternize with the Reformed. When Theodore Beza met the Lutheran Andreae at a discussion about reunion in Montbéliard, they could not shake hands at the end. The death of thousands of Huguenot martyrs in France appeared to the Lutheran Hutter a just judgement of God upon a sect which had broken the religious peace. There was an outcry against the Philippist Calixtus when he took luncheon with a Reformed court chaplain in Berlin. 'Is it possible,' asked Calixtus, when under fire for befriending Reformed theologians, 'that hatred has risen to such a pitch among us that the Reformed are not fit for a man to walk across the street with? I will not avoid the company of good men, be they Calvinists or Papists.'

The quarrel spread across Germany, weakened the political power of the Protestants in Germany and Poland and France and Hungary and Transylvania, opened doors to the Counter-Reformation, and dissipated pastoral energies into controversial divinity. But even controversial divinity was still divinity, and knowledge acquired for warlike purposes was more useful than a dumb and vegetable ignorance.

Some Lutherans were not afraid to use Calvinist writings. They were ready to translate books of English Reformed piety. Lutheran students included in their tours Marburg, or Heidelberg, or Leyden; and the Lutheran university of Tübingen gave a friendly welcome even to vehement Calvinist students. The Philippist Lutherans were far friendlier to the Reformed, and there is an isolated case of a union: Pelargus, the superintendent at Frankfurt, went over from Philippism to open Calvinism; some Lutheran clergy continued to support him, he ordained both Lutheran and Reformed pastors, and the university allowed the degree of doctor to members of both confessions.

John Durie was a Scottish minister who in 1628 was made chaplain to the English merchants at Elbing in Prussia. Agonized at the religious strife of Germany, he devoted the rest of a long life to devising a union of Lutheran and Reformed, if not of all Protestants, in a common and simple confession of faith based upon the Apostles' Creed. He travelled the length and breadth of Europe, from London to Transylvania, from Geneva to Stockholm. The Swiss Churches took his cause into their prayers; the Swedish State expelled him. A man of wide sympathy, vague divinity, and small knowledge of affairs, he proved that in the cause of Christian unity sentiment and affection are not enough.

The Reformed found it absurd to say that the Lutherans, for their errors, were no part of the true Church. 'I dare not deny,' Richard Hooker wrote of the Lutherans, 'the possibility of their salvation, which have been the chiefest instrument of ours, albeit they carried to their grave a persuasion so greatly repugnant to the truth.' As the sixteenth century turned into the seventeenth, they began to look upon the Lutherans with a still critical but ever more favourable eye, by reducing the number of essentials of faith upon which they insisted. In 1631 the French Synod of Charenton at last recognized the Lutherans as brothers and resolved that they might communicate in their churches and even be sponsors for their children. The Swiss churches were freely hospitable to Lutheran refugees during the Thirty Years War.

FRANCE

The conversion of France lay nearest to Calvin's heart. French was his native tongue, he was a French theologian, he communicated by letter with his friends, and his Genevan academy trained evangelists for France, carrying the French Bible published by Olivetan in 1535 and the Psalms translated by Marot.

The French government, though it executed for heresy from the first, was provoked into a more stringent persecution. On 18 October 1534, the citizens of Paris, Orleans, Blois, and elsewhere awoke to find violent and grossly irreverent placards pinned to the walls of the main streets, and one placard upon the king's bedroom door at the castle of Amboise. They had been smuggled into France, and their distribution had been well organized, not without opposition from wiser heads among the Protestants. Queen Margaret of Navarre, the friend of reformers, believed that the placards must have been written and distributed by an enemy to discredit them. She was wrong. King Francis I undertook a solemn procession to the cathedral of Notre-Dame, with relics and burning lights, to purify the city of Paris, and at a banquet in the bishop's palace declared his purpose of eradicating the poison from the state. More than thirty-five Lutherans were burnt, and many more fled the country.

The government thereafter persecuted, and often ferociously. The worst sufferers in the early years were the Waldensians of Provence, who lost several hundred simple people in a murderous raid (1545) which was dignified or excused by the romantic name of 'crusade'. But though 'Lutherans' (as they were called until after 1560, when the name Huguenots became common) were persecuted, it was not always easy for the government to persecute them consistently. Nor can a people for ever tolerate cruelty if it is public, partly inefficient, and exercised against a large number of apparently good men and women.

For France, despite appearances, was not a political unity. The crown was powerful, was steadily Catholic, and since the Concordat of Bologna (1516) exercised great and calamitous authority over the endowments of the Church. But the country was broad, the nobles troublesome and independent, the corruptions of ecclesiastical life glaring, and over the border, and after 1558 across the Channel, were Protestant states. Merchants and landowners received the new doctrines, opened their Bibles, and found hope for reform of the Church; and though often in peril and losing many to the fire and the scaffold, they could not easily be suppressed everywhere or at once. It needed only a weakness in the crown – a minority, a regency – for political factions to form round the leading nobility in the contest for power. By 1560 the Huguenots were numerous enough throughout France to be an important element in the political struggle.

The universities, and other humanist circles, were often drawn towards reform. Bands of undergraduates from provincial colleges were sometimes strong on the side of the Protestants, sometimes armed for the defence of Catholics. In 1560, 400 students at Toulouse demanded a church, sang the Psalms of Marot publicly, and were suppressed. The great medieval university of Montpellier drew many students from Germany and other Protestant lands.

Reform appealed especially to the noblemen of the countryside and the merchants of the towns, while the peasant remained staunchly conservative unless he followed his feudal lord. Much depended upon the sympathies of the local lord. In Normandy, Admiral Coligny sympathized with reform, and under his guidance or inaction the churches were able to organize. In Navarre and the surrounding lands congregations were formed, for the Bourbon king and his queen of Navarre were friendly. In Orleans and the Orléanais, for similar reasons, the Calvinists made progress, as they did in Dauphiné and Provence in the far south, where some inheritance from the Waldensians and medieval heresy may have combined with a political tradition of independence. The majority of the people of Paris, Bordeaux, and Toulouse always remained Catholic. Lorraine and the north were controlled by Catholic noblemen, Guise and Montmorency.

At first the Huguenot services were held in secret; in a private house, in a barn, in a wood or field. Some congregations exacted an oath on admission that the member would never reveal the names of other Protestants. The ministers, of whom there were too few, were partially protected by disguise or assumed name, and were moved if their identity became known in the town. Though they held their first national synod at Paris in 1559, the centre of organization and advice was Geneva. They used Genevan psalms and Bible and forms of services, and in the desperate shortage of ministers drew many from Switzerland. In some parishes, the priest quietly adopted Protestant opinions and continued to instruct his flock. A number of other priests and friars were ejected, and adopted the role of pastor. In Lent 1560 a monk named Tempeste preached the Reformed Gospel at Montélimar without even removing his habit. In 1561 an Augustinian at Montauban preached a notable course of Lenten addresses and at Easter unfrocked himself publicly, before joining with the Huguenots in the eucharist.

But French experience with unfrocked priests and monks was not always happy. Their motives were doubtful, and they were hated beyond measure by the ecclesiastical authorities. Huguenot consistories established rules under which ex-priests or ex-monks might be admitted. They looked to Switzerland for help, and sent students to be instructed for the pastorate at Geneva. Between 1555 and 1562 Geneva supplied at least eighty-eight pastors to the Huguenots, and Berne and Neuchâtel supplied others. The Swiss cities denuded their pulpits for the sake of the French. During 1561, as the Huguenots began to come into the open, a French town might drive out its priest, break the statues in the church, and appeal for a pastor – and sometimes none could be sent. Geneva was helped in 1558, when Berne expelled a number of pastors from Lausanne and elsewhere because they were insistent upon Genevan consistorial discipline in Berne territory; many of these expelled pastors were sent into France.

Early in 1561 the French government formally protested to the Republic of Geneva against the sending of preachers who caused sedition or dissent in the kingdom. Thereafter Geneva was careful to wink at the unofficial aid which their pastors and citizens were supplying.

In 1561 Admiral Coligny reckoned that there were 2,150 Protestant congregations in France.

There exists a contemporary account of the growth of the Protestants in the little town of Castres in Languedoc. In 1559 some citizens of Castres travelled to Geneva to buy Bibles and other books, and asked for a pastor. At the end of 1559 the Venerable Company chose Geoffrey Brun, whom Berne had recently expelled from the territory of Lausanne. In April 1560, members of the congregation guided Brun safely to Castres, took him into the town under cover of darkness, and lodged him with a leading citizen named Gaches. In the Gaches house the services were held, always by night and under conditions of secrecy. But after a month the meetings in the Gaches house were known outside, and they moved the services to the house of another Protestant. Meanwhile the congregation was growing. After only six months Brun decided that he must have a second pastor and returned to Geneva to find one. While he was away, a pastor travelled from Toulouse to preach and baptize, but was observed and expelled.

Now it was 1561, and the Huguenots were coming into the open. In February 1561 Brun's new assistant renewed the services in private houses. On 18 April another new pastor began preaching publicly in the old schoolhouse, and though he was ordered by the magistrates to desist, he refused to obey the order. Brun himself came back from Geneva, and soon the magistrates themselves joined the congregation. The flock was now too big to meet in private houses, and so they took over public buildings and released Protestant prisoners by force. Henceforth the town was a Huguenot town.

The synod of Paris (1559) organized a national system of presbyteries. Each church was governed by a consistory, the minister with lay elders. Above this was a district assembly, the colloquy, and above that a provincial synod, and finally at the apex the national synod. For many years the state of the country prevented much of this from being more than a paper organization, but there is plenty of evidence that in many districts the consistory and colloquy worked with effectiveness.

In 1559 France, through inflation and a European crisis of credit, was bankrupt; and at the worst moment for public order, the king died. On 30 June 1559 King Henry II was struck in the right eye by the point of a splintered lance in a tournament, and though several eminent physicians made hasty experiments on the eyes of four criminals beheaded for the purpose, he died ten days later. The new king, Francis II, already married to Mary Queen of Scots, was not yet sixteen, and sickly. He in his turn died on 5 December 1560, and the crown passed to a younger brother,

Charles IX, aged ten. His mother, Catherine de' Medici, spent the remainder of her years balanced uneasily between the two great factions of nobles. On the one side were the Guises, headed by the Duke of Guise and the Cardinal of Lorraine: Catholic, allied when possible with the Spanish. On the other side were the Bourbons, headed by the Prince of Condé (for the natural head of the party, Antoine de Bourbon, King of Navarre, though married to a devout Protestant, was weak and vacillating), backed by the three Châtillon brothers (the Cardinal of Châtillon, Admiral Coligny, and d'Andelot): friendly to the Huguenots, and allied when possible with German Protestant princes or with Queen Elizabeth of England.

The power of the French crown could not stand the test of a minority and the regency of a foreign Queen Mother. In the struggle for power the central government was weakened and the provinces asserted themselves. There would probably have been civil war, not unlike the English Wars of the Roses, if the religious question had not also divided France. Even in 1560–1 contemporaries distinguished between 'political' Huguenots and 'religious' Huguenots, the political being the lords who resented the power of the Catholic Guises over the crown and were prepared to use the religious contest as an instrument. Their leaders varied in their outlook. Condé was disreputable in his private life, Coligny was a devout and noble Protestant.

In the weakness of government, the Huguenots could not help illegality. It was not possible to stand aside and watch friends burnt when they had the power to stop it. They began to protect their assemblies for worship with a watch of armed men. At Caen they took possession of deserted churches; elsewhere they sometimes expelled the occupants before they took possession. In Montpellier they besieged the canons in their cathedral close. In the spring of 1560 the Huguenot church of Rouen numbered 10,000, with four pastors and twenty-seven elders. At Dieppe the congregation was bold or rash enough to build a 'temple' in the heart of the town, in a classical style like the Coliseum, but the government destroyed it. In towns where the majority was Protestant, concealment became impossible and absurd.

They could not meet without protection, and the public authorities would not protect them. At Valence in 1560 the younger Huguenots seized the Franciscan church and armed gentlemen protected their services. At Nîmes the congregation met in the suburbs and celebrated the Genevan liturgy under an armed guard of pike and arquebus. On 26 August 1560 a congregation of 7,000 met in the market square at Rouen, sang psalms, and listened to a preacher standing on a chair and surrounded by 500 men with arquebuses.

The occupation of churches by Huguenots was repugnant to the Catholics, who regarded it as sacrilege. The Huguenots had no sense of sacrilege; they were the Church of God, purifying their buildings and restoring true religion. If nearly all the citizens of a town were Huguenot, they thought it mere justice that they should meet for worship in one or more of the empty churches.

A conspiracy – in which the religious motive was a small part, or a pretext – to capture the king and win tolerance for the Huguenots (the Tumult of Amboise, 1560) was betrayed to the Guises and smashed. The country was upon the brink of civil war.

Was it right for religious men to join in a rebellion against the legitimate sovereign? Many communications upon this theme passed between Geneva and the Huguenot leaders. At one end Calvin believed that the powers that be are ordained of God, that no one had the right to rebel against a legitimate sovereign. As late as 1562 Beza made a famous retort to the King of Navarre, suggesting passive resistance: 'Sire, it is truly the lot of the Church of God, for which I speak, to endure blows and not to strike them. But may it please you to remember that it is an anvil which has worn out many hammers.' At the other end the great lawyer Anne du Bourg, awaiting execution for heresy in his Paris prison (1559), wrote a pamphlet contending that any monarch was illegitimate who forced his subjects to live contrary to the will of God. Between these extremes, there was much room for argument. The Guises captured the king and ruled him – was not a rebellion against the tyrants of the king in truth a defence of the king? Ought not a Christian to fight to save his king from an illegitimate despotism? Even Calvin agreed that such a fight was permissible – but on one condition, that it be led by the chief magistrates or by princes of the blood. And so when Condé mobilized his forces it was possible for Geneva to approve those who rallied to his standard. Beza was a decided advocate of this opinion. The Huguenot consistories allowed themselves to be used as a civil and military organization as well as a religious government.

The Colloquy of Poissy

Surrounded by clanking swords and mutual recrimination, Catherine de' Medici beat about like a fluttering bird in a cage. Turning for help to Coligny, she issued a decree ordering that all prosecutions for religion should cease and all prisoners be released. The refugees in Switzerland and England poured back into France. Congregations of Huguenots met openly in towns where they were a minority; and popular riots and disorders ensued. For September 1561 Catherine summoned the Colloquy of Poissy, a meeting of the theologians of both sides, in the effort to make them live together.

They assembled in the refectory of the Poissy convent near Paris. On the Catholic side sat the Cardinal of Lorraine and forty or fifty bishops with attendant theologians. At the bar stood Beza, supported by the leading pastors of France and joined later by Peter Martyr from Zurich. Before the king and his mother and the princes of the blood the theologians stated their case. It seemed like one of those staged disputations which had helped to establish Protestantism in Zurich and other Swiss cities. But its atmosphere was very different. The ranks of prelates sat hostile, conscious of their power; and Beza's private letters show that he was inwardly less confident than appeared in the bold front which he presented to the assembly. It was symbolic that no seats were provided for the Calvinists, who appeared more like defendants in a court. If Catherine aimed at an agreement or toleration, she must have been quickly disillusioned. As Beza and his colleagues entered, a cardinal said audibly: 'Here come the Genevan dogs.' Beza heard it, and turned, saying: 'The Lord's sheepfold needs faithful sheepdogs to drive off wolves.'

He began to conciliate them, declaring the Reformed faith in all the main articles of the traditional creed. The bishops heard him at first with a silent respect. It has been shown that the Cardinal of Lorraine, at least, genuinely intended to find peace if peace should be possible. Even when Beza began to declare the disagreements upon the Bible, justification by faith, the traditions of the Church, the bishops kept silence. He declared that the Reformed do not believe the bread of the eucharist to be mere bread, nor make Christ absent from the Lord's supper; but in respect of his local presence 'we say that his body is as far removed from the bread and wine as the highest heaven is from the earth'.

He was interrupted by a cry of 'Blasphemy!' And only Queen Catherine's command enabled the conference to continue. It dragged onward fruitlessly, and petered out in October 1561. Catherine, imagining that the Huguenots were stronger than they were and fearing the power of the Guises, issued the Edict of January 1562, ordering the Huguenots to return the churches of which they had taken possession and banning Huguenot public worship within the walls of a town except in private houses, but allowing public worship anywhere outside the walls.

The Protestants had thereby won legal recognition, however tenuous. They were aware how much they had won. Some believed that, if the liberty given by the edict lasted,

they were sure of making France Protestant. They hardly
expected it to last.

The Outbreak of Civil War

On 1 March 1562 the Duke of Guise, with 200 armed men,
halted at Vassy in Champagne on his journey towards Paris.
It was Sunday; and near the monastery chapel, where the
Guises intended to hear mass, 600 to 1,000 Protestants were
holding service in a barn. They were meeting illegally,
unless a barn be a private house, for they were within the
walls. No one knows who began the fight, whether the
congregation first threw stones at intruding Guise retainers
or whether the retainers first fired. At least forty-eight members of the congregation were killed or mortally wounded
and many others injured.

The example was infectious through the provinces. At
Toulouse nearly 3,000 Huguenots, including women and
children, were murdered. Catholic mobs attacked Huguenot
congregations everywhere. Huguenot mobs sacked Catholic
churches. The Duke of Guise took possession of the king and
of Catherine de' Medici. The 'Wars of Religion' had begun.

It is the tragedy of the Reformation. Everyone, Catholic
or no, confessed that the Church of France was corrupt and
must be reformed. The Calvinists proposed that it be reformed according to the Word of God; and their ideals
were taken up into the political whirligig, mingled with the
greed and fear and passion of mankind, poured out in
blood, and trampled in the dust. Religion divided an already
cracking France, and thirty years of civil war or suspicious
truce were the consequence – a civil war of murder, killing
innocent priests on one side and innocent pastors on the
other, and of loot, burnings, exhaustion, and massacre. It
was not continuous (1562–3, 1567–70, 1572–6); and after
1576 the wars were more political than religious. The Duke
of Guise was assassinated in 1563, Condé was captured and
shot in cold blood in 1569, Coligny was murdered with

thousands of others in the massacre of St Bartholomew's Day 1572. And in the intervals of 'peace' there were many killings.

'But for the war,' wrote the Venetian ambassador Correro in 1569, '. . . France would now be Huguenot, because the people were rapidly changing their faith and the ministers were much respected and exercised authority among them. But when they passed from words to weapons and began to rob, destroy, and kill, the people began to say: "What kind of religion is this?"'

One of the Ten Commandments, when literally interpreted by Swiss divinity, caused havoc and resentment among the moderates whose sympathies might have been won for the reforming cause: no graven image; an Old Testament precedent for destruction. If non-religious mobs on both sides sometimes looted churches, religious fanatics destroyed statues and roods and pictures and stained glass because they believed themselves ordered by the Word of God, to be obeyed above the laws of men. Nothing more easily alienated the law-abiding. In Caen cathedral even the tombs of William the Conqueror and Matilda were wrecked. Pastors exhorted to moderation, Huguenot generals threatened the death penalty for loot, to no purpose against zealotry. On 21 April 1562 Condé heard that the churches of Orleans were being invaded and hurried with Coligny to the great church of the Holy Rood. Seeing a man high on the wall in the act of toppling a saint from his niche, Condé snatched an arquebus from one of his men and took aim. The climber shouted down: 'Sir, wait till I have smashed this idol and then I will die if you like.' In the market square at Montauban in August 1561 the offending idols were solemnly burnt on a pyre while choirs of children chanted the metrical version of the Ten Commandments.

But it would be wrong to imagine that most of the destruction was religious zeal. On the contrary; not only are civil wars occasions of popular loot, since they destroy local government, but this civil war was fought, in good part, between bands of hired mercenaries whose religion was plunder. When the news of the massacre of St Bartholomew's day at Paris reached Orleans, and it was obvious to the meanest intelligence that further massacre was imminent in Orleans, 400 ruffians arrived from the countryside intending to compensate themselves for their losses in the past war; and individuals often took the occasion, when government had collapsed, to avenge their scores or fill their pockets. The military task was calamitous for the religion of both sides. The orders of colonels were more decisive than the sermons of pastors or the warnings of distant Geneva.

Henry IV

At each peace or armistice the Huguenots preserved a legal recognition, tenuous if the tide of war had flowed against them, generous if the war ended favourably. On 1 August 1589, the last son of Catherine de' Medici, Henry III, was stabbed by a half-witted Dominican friar, and left the Bourbon Henry of Navarre, a Huguenot, son of the weak Antoine and the Huguenot Jeanne d'Albret, as the legitimate sovereign of France; and France at last had a man of force and decision as king. It took him five years to conquer his own kingdom against the Catholic league and its Spanish allies, who would not recognize a Protestant king. He confessed at last that he could give peace to the country only by becoming a Catholic.

Some writers have contended that Henry IV was always a political and not a religious Huguenot, and have pointed to the scandals of his private life, his contemptuous procession of mistresses. There was a popular story of the time that he said 'Paris is worth a mass'. But there is now some doubt that the change of allegiance was as troublesome to his soul as it was to his mind. Not for nothing was he the son of Jeanne d'Albret, and had imbibed the Protestant faith, as he often said, in his mother's milk.

Troublesome to his political mind, for it was certain that a change to Catholicism would lose him the support of some Huguenots, his faithful followers, and not certain that it would win the intransigent among the Catholic league. But the moderate Catholics, and the '*politiques*' who had ceased to care much for religion and cared mightily for peace, pressed him with the argument that the kingdom was 'more like a brigand camp than a kingdom' and could have peace only if he became a Roman Catholic. The great majority of Frenchmen were still Catholic, and 'can tolerate a Turk better than they can a heretic'. The king of France must consult the welfare of his realm, and the alternative might be the Spanish domination of France. Even two or three Huguenot ministers in his entourage were brought to consent to the argument, believing that here lay the best hope for French Protestantism. This was not common with the Huguenots. 'Can it be,' he was asked by his personal pastor Gabriel d'Amours, 'that the greatest captain in the world has become so cowardly as to go to mass for fear of men?'

'Come into our church and cleanse it,' cried the moderate Catholics. 'I am entering the house,' Henry told an anxious Huguenot deputation, 'not to live in it but to cleanse it.' He seems to have been persuaded that the differences between the faiths were trivial, of order and ceremonial. The wisest and ablest of his advisers, Sully, a Huguenot, recommended him to change with the plea that a man might be saved in either religion provided that he held the essentials of creed and charity.

Henry refused to make too detailed a profession of his faith in all the articles of the Church of Rome, and made a general assent. On 25 July 1593 he was received in the old abbey church of St Denis, and took an oath upon the Gospels to renounce heresy and to live and die in the Roman Catholic and Apostolic religion. On 17 September 1595 Pope Clement VIII solemnly absolved Henry's ambassadors and proxies in the square before St Peter's, exacting as conditions that the king would go four times a year to confession and communion, would hear mass daily, observe the fasts, and recite litanies on Wednesdays and the rosary on Saturdays. He must bring up his heir as a Roman Catholic, and establish the religion in his ancestral state of Béarn.

France, there was no doubt, was not going to be a Protestant country.

The Edict of Nantes, 13 April 1598

There was no doubt also that the Huguenots were remaining, and legally. They were perhaps a fifteenth of the population, though in some areas a majority. The accession of Henry IV weakened the idea of one religion in one state (*un roi, une loi, une foi*) held everywhere in Europe until this moment. During his first months or years as a Catholic sovereign, he could not afford to tolerate them fully, since there were many voices ready to accuse him of deceit, and the forces of the Catholic league in Brittany were not reduced till 1598.

In 1598 he at last felt free to act, and the resulting Edict of Nantes is a landmark in the history of toleration and freedom. The Germans had settled the question of religious disunity (for the time) by dividing Germany into Protestant and Catholic states. Elsewhere in Europe, with only Poland and Ireland as special exceptions, a state was either Catholic or Protestant. Now France was trying the momentous experiment of a state where Catholics and Protestants lived side by side.

The Edict of Nantes provided that the Protestants might have liberty of conscience anywhere in France, and children of both religions were to be admitted to all hospitals and universities and schools. The Protestant might worship on estates of the chief Protestant noblemen, and in all cities where worship had been held from January 1596 to August 1597, including two cities in every bailiwick of the kingdom, but not within five leagues of Paris. They might establish their own schools wherever they worshipped. They were assigned public cemeteries for their use, and became eligible for all offices of state.

As they needed cemeteries, so they needed their own law courts. Courts were created to try cases in which Protestants were concerned, at Paris with six Protestants (soon reduced to one) out of sixteen judges, in the south with equal numbers of Protestants and Catholics. The Protestants were given an annual grant from the treasury of 225,000 crowns, and the temporary possession of certain important fortresses as a guarantee of their safety.

And meanwhile the Catholics were given not only the recognition of Catholicism as the established religion of France, but one practical boon – freedom for the mass in Protestant towns.

It cannot be asserted that the edict worked perfectly. Killings leave behind them ineradicable bitterness, and the existence of the legal safeguards in the Edict was evidence of insecurity. The university refused to admit Protestant students, still less to allow Protestant professors. The Archbishop of Tours and several bishops asked for prayers in the churches that the edict in favour of heresy might not become law. 'I,' said Pope Clement VIII, 'am the most grieved and disconsolate person in the world. . . . I see the most cursed edict that I could imagine, . . . whereby liberty of conscience is granted to everyone, which is the worst thing in the world. . . . I absolved him and recognized him as king . . . and in return for all this I shall become the laughing stock of the world.' In some parts of France the Edict of Nantes was evaded for several years. At Huguenot doors rude persons sang a ditty about a Catholic girl's cow wandering into a Huguenot service. There was at first a little bloodshed, and much bad feeling. To Henry's wrath, the Huguenot synod of Gap (1603) solemnly reaffirmed its belief that the Pope was Antichrist. But not all was bad feeling. At Castelmoron a compact has survived whereby the inhabitants of both religions solemnly agreed to use together the parish cemetery and the belfry. From 1601 the Huguenots were allowed two deputies-general at court to report breaches of the Edict. The king transgressed his own Edict by allowing the Parisian Huguenots to build a great church at Charenton, nearer to the city than the statutory five leagues.*

It is an epoch of history. France, because France could do no other, was going to test whether a man might be a good citizen though his religion be not that of the crown.

HOLLAND

Spain ruled the Netherlands; and Spain was the most devout and powerful of the Catholic states. Yet the Netherlands were open to Protestant influence of every kind. To the east, the north German states were Lutheran or Reformed; to the west, after 1558, England was both Protestant and fearful of Spanish power; to the south, after 1562, Huguenots were fighting the Guises and the Catholic league, and epidemically achieved the legal right to exist. The citizens of the Netherlands were prosperous, their cities mercantile, their ports wealthy, their education advanced, their people the kind among whom reforming ideas spread rapidly. The Spanish crown, determined by reason of devotion and by reason of state to suppress heresy with fire and sword, met the only part of the Spanish Empire where the Protestants were numerous enough to be a political force.

By 1564, therefore, a political controversy existed in the Netherlands comparable with that in France on the eve of civil war: two parties in the state, one Catholic and eager

* After the murder of Henry IV (1610) the political independence of the Huguenots offended the growing autocracy of the crown under Marie de' Medici and then Richelieu, and the political privileges which made the Huguenots an independent corporation in the state were finally taken from them in 1628. But the Edict of Nîmes in 1629 re-affirmed the religious concessions of the Edict of Nantes. (For Louis XIV and the history of the subsequent Revocation of the Edict of Nantes, see *Pelican History of the Church*, vol. 4, pp. 17 ff.)

to retain and extend the power of the crown over local liberties; the other not precisely Protestant, for it included Catholic noblemen, but resenting extensions of royal power, anxious to preserve local and traditional liberties, and wanting toleration for the Protestants, now too numerous to suppress despite all that stake and scaffold had done.

The Catholic ruler of the Netherlands was a foreign and absent ruler, Philip II of Spain. The party which wanted toleration (or, on its extreme wing, the suppression of Roman Catholicism) easily appeared as the party of patriots, the defenders against foreign armies. On the other side the party of the crown possessed an advantage more weighty than anything possessed by the Guises in France. The king could call upon the wealth and troops of the strongest military power of the day.

Philip wished to unite the Netherlands, with their varying traditions and two languages, as a Spanish state. Rulers of the later Middle Ages or of the Reformation who aimed at increasing royal authority found the easiest means in extending their control over the Church. To this end he created (1559) three new archbishoprics and fourteen bishoprics, to which he retained the nomination, he encouraged the Spanish form of inquisition, and in 1565 he savagely reinforced the already ferocious decrees against heretics. By 1565 the Netherlands opposition was beginning to identify itself with resistance to the religious policy of the Spanish king, and therefore with the Protestants.

In 1566 the congregations began to worship in the open fields, sometimes under armed guard and with barricaded approaches. A congregation of seven or eight thousand met in a field near Ghent; fifteen thousand outside Antwerp; twenty thousand at a bridge near Tournai, where a third of the congregation was armed and the preacher escorted to his pulpit by a hundred mounted troops. Like the Huguenots they were desperately short of ministers. Francis Junius arrived from Geneva to be pastor to the congregation of Antwerp, though he was just twenty years old.

In such circumstances of popular feeling, any public event could start a tumult. (Half a century later a Catholic procession through the streets of a town in south Germany led fatally towards the Thirty Years War.) That August of 1566, at a procession to conduct a colossal statue of the Virgin round the streets of Antwerp, a rough mob broke into the cathedral; the old woman who sold candles and trinkets near the door was mocked and began to throw things – and thereafter popular passions ran across the cities of the Netherlands, the statues in the churches were smashed, pictures torn from the walls, stained glass shattered, the chests of vestments broken, the missals torn, monasteries sacked, prisoners freed. As in France, Protestant pastors struggled to restrain and suppress the lawlessness.

The riots divided the people into warring parties, and the country was already at civil war. Philip of Spain resolved thereafter to rule the Netherlands by martial law; and on 1 December 1566 a Calvinist synod at Antwerp declared armed resistance to be permissible. William of Orange, the Silent, tried to hold together a moderate party; but in 1568 he threw himself into the leadership of the anti-Spanish and Protestant movement, and formally became a Calvinist in 1573.

As late as 1587 the Protestants were still calculated to be only one tenth of the population. But the Calvinist organization was the organization of resistance to Spanish taxation and to the bloody rule of the Duke of Alva. William the Silent, among the Calvinist leaders, struggled for compromise with the Catholic majority, and thus for the union of the Netherlands, until his assassination in 1584.

In France the religious war ended in a state within a state. In the Netherlands, it ended in the division of the country into a Catholic south and a Calvinist north (1579) – the distant origins of modern Belgium and modern Holland. The north achieved an uneasy recognition by Spain in 1609 and a free recognition of independence only in 1648.

SCOTLAND

While Spain was the most centralized monarchy in Europe, Scotland possessed a weak crown, weak constitutionally and weak because from 1542 the sovereign was a minor and a woman, Mary Queen of Scots. More obviously than in France, almost as evidently as in aristocratic Poland, the Protestants could spread their ideals provided that they secured the support of the lords. The practices of the Scottish Church were as unreformed as those of France, its humanist critics despised its corruption, and its lands lay temptingly. England was a refuge for any Scotsman of reforming ideals who felt himself not safe in his own country.

As in France and the Netherlands, the Reform was entangled in the political strife of Scottish factions. One party looked to French support, accepted French money, tried to rule Scotland with the assistance of French troops, wanted to increase the power of the crown in the person of the French Regent Mary of Guise, and was identified with the maintenance of the Catholic religion. The other party looked to English support, accepted English money, wanted the assistance of English troops and ships, and was identified with reforming ideals and antipathy to the Catholic bishops. In December 1557 a band of lords calling themselves the 'Lords of the Congregation' formed themselves into a league or 'covenant' with the avowed purpose of defending the Word of God. In 1560, Queen Elizabeth of England, who could not risk a Catholic and pro-French Scotland in her rear, sent money and ships and an army to Leith; the French Regent and troops were expelled, and the Scottish Parliament repudiated the authority of the Pope and abolished the mass. It accepted a Confession of Faith drafted by John Knox. But a Book of Discipline, intended to introduce the Reformed polity of church government where moral supervision would be exercised by a consistory and elders, was not given legal force. A Scottish General

Assembly was formed, the equivalent of the Huguenot national synod, and confirmed a service book after the Genevan model known as the Book of Common Order. The edition of 1564 was bound up with the metrical psalms; and since the psalms were the popular and congregational element in the book, the whole book of prayers came to be known at last as 'the Psalm-Book'.

The presbyterian polity, despite this refusal of legal sanction, was slowly introduced into the parishes. The disciplinary register of St Andrews already begins in 1559. But it was slow to be accepted, even by the people. For 130 years the ecclesiastical history of Scotland is a history of the attempt to create or to reject a system of presbyteries with a legal status and independence. When the crown and government were weak, the presbyteries were given legal force. When the government was strong, the rights which they claimed were withdrawn or diminished.

In Huguenot France, in Holland, and in Scotland, the Protestant movement took a Calvinist form between 1559 and 1567. In each country the Reformers had to persuade the people, and organize a Church, in the teeth of the power of the crown. In each country their pastors had been trained at Geneva or had received the deep influence of Genevan teaching. In each country the appeal to the people, and the ruthless suppression of 'idolatry' in the churches by popular violence, caused the moderates to shrink back. But in Scotland the civil war was brief and blundering, and with English help the Protestant cause triumphed easily.

A powerful France would not have allowed Scotland to be so quickly made Protestant. The outbreak of the French wars of religion destroyed the European power of France and left Mary Queen of Scots helpless upon her uncushioned throne. If the Huguenots failed in France, they indirectly helped to make Calvinism victorious in Scotland.

As Henry IV of France proved that a Protestant king could not rule a Catholic people, the tragedy of Mary

Queen of Scots proved that a Catholic queen could not rule a Protestant people. The sixteenth century knew no instance of a ruler different in religion from the majority of his people. *Cujus regio ejus religio* could mean that a ruler had the right to compel his people to conform to his religion. It could also be inverted, and mean that a people had the power to compel their ruler either to conform to their religion or to abdicate. Mary wanted her mass in her private chapel at Holyrood; Knox declared that one mass was more fearful to him than if 10,000 men were landed to suppress true religion. Like Henry IV of France, she toyed with the idea of changing her religion. It looked in 1566 as though she might establish her power and remain Catholic. The murders of Rizzio and Darnley ended all hope. In April 1567 she married Bothwell and thereby lost even Catholic support. She was forced to abdicate that year.

But the short reign of Mary, and the victory of Knox, were important for the strong Calvinism and the characteristic ethos of Scottish Protestantism. The more agonizing the war for liberty or survival, the more revolutionary and decisive the change in religion. The war had been won with comparative ease; and yet the reformation had been established *against* the crown and under the guidance of Knox, most rugged of the disciples of Calvin.

The English established their reformation with the help of the crown, with such important help that for a few years the existence of their Church seemed to depend upon the life of Queen Elizabeth. A majority of English Protestants were never afraid of 'interference' by the crown in the Church, for they owed their welfare and freedom to that interference. The Scottish established their Reformation against a Catholic queen, and early associated their Protestant faith with a sense that they must safeguard the rights of the Church from the meddling of a hostile or unworthy ruler. A presbyterian doctrine and polity reached the affections of many Scotsmen in the Lowlands before the union of the crown with that of England in 1603.

THE MARTYROLOGIES

The Protestant movement had been accompanied, at times, by mob rule, land grabbing, and political and military faction. The armies of William of Orange helped to make Holland Protestant, the fleet and army of Queen Elizabeth of England helped to make Scotland Protestant, the troops of Alva or of Parma kept the southern Netherlands Catholic. It is naïve to think that force did not contribute substantially to the successes both of Reformation and Counter-Reformation.

But the Protestants held their people, and built their congregations, against bloody and systematic persecution. It was not quite inevitable that the disciples of Luther or of Calvin should have been treated as heretics for the pyre. The policy of burning Lutheran and Calvinist was soon modified of necessity in the Catholic German states. Unfortunately they could be burnt successfully in Italy and in Spain, and Italy and Spain determined the Catholic attitudes to the Reformation. In Marian England, in France, and in the Netherlands – and to a lesser extent in Scotland – the Protestant communities were created by courage and conviction of a high degree. Francis Junius preached a sermon to a meeting in Antwerp while several men were burning in the market-place outside and the light from the flames was flickering upon the windows of the room. Several of the leading Reformed pastors upon the Continent, like the five English bishops, ended their lives at the stake. They were supported by a host of simple people.

Reformed theologians distrusted the old custom of celebrating a calendar of saints, for they believed the reverence paid to saints to derogate from faith in the one Saviour. But at a very early date Protestant writers began to collect historical materials and stories about the deaths at the stake and upon the scaffold. The earlier part of the *History of the Reformation in Scotland* by John Knox has some of the characteristics of a martyrology. Dutch writers published a series of such martyrologies. The most famous and influential were the *Book of Martyrs* by Jean Crespin, a French lawyer who fled to Strasbourg and then to Geneva, and who collected the moving and painful agonies of the Huguenot victims; and the book originally of the same title by the Englishman John Foxe, who fled abroad during the reign of Queen Mary and wrote his *Book of Martyrs* at Basle between 1556 and 1559. His work, in its later editions known as *Acts and Monuments*, was influenced by that of Crespin, but Foxe's own genius and the different matter made it a great book in its own right. Both Crespin and Foxe were willing to include the death of persons who might doubtfully be claimed for the Reforming cause, and Foxe included at least two persons who had not died at all; but when every allowance is made to modern criticism, they contain much material still indispensable to the historian of the age, and they were sources of power and faith in the Protestant communities to which they were addressed. In England the Convocation of 1571 ordered a copy of Foxe's book to be placed in all cathedrals; many parish churches followed the example, and a few are still to be found in English churches. Among the Huguenots and the English Puritans, these martyrologies deepened the attachment to the Reformation and encouraged a strong anti-Roman understanding of church history.

PURITANISM

Puritan was an adjective first used in the fifteen-sixties as a term of abuse. It soon came to mean precise, over-strict, over-severe, failing to make allowances. As such it was used to ridicule those who were guilty of absurd severity or rigidity.

But there is more than one view on what is too severe. The courtiers of Charles II, in their hatred of Roundheads, required little severity or strictness to justify the charge of puritan. The Reformation age was not of this mind. It set out to remedy the immoralities of the Church and society. As a whole the age was earnestly moral. Among the Spaniards of the Counter-Reformation, the city councils of Switzerland, Pope Paul IV or Cardinal Borromeo, the Lutheran burghers, the Scottish pastors, the leaders of English reform, Catholic and Protestant, predestinarian or Arminian, Calvin or Ignatius Loyola, Philip Neri or William Laud, Johann Arndt or Jeremy Taylor – the tone of western Europe was reforming and often therefore strict. If the epithet *puritan* is removed from its special use to condemn the hypocrite, the canting, and the bizarre, it may be merely one way of describing the moral ideals of the Reformation and Counter-Reformation; and its distaste for posterity arose because some practical expressions of these moral ideals proved to be less tolerable than others.

Moral rigorism was not confined to Calvinists. Whatever the Reformation was failing to do, it was altering public practice about the pomps and vanities of this world. Puritanism will not be understood unless it is seen as part of a climate of European opinion.

Sometimes the word has been used loosely to include Protestants of the left wing who likewise lived austerely and were men of the Bible, even if they controverted the doctrines of Calvinism. There is some justification for this wider use. Not all puritans believed in a presbyterian polity for the Church, not all presbyterians could rightly be described as puritan. But the puritan idea may be found at its most distinctive and coherent and authentic among the Calvinists. The doctrines of Calvin clothed the moral idea, embodied it within an atmosphere of Scripture and particular forms of devotion and religious customs. Though puritanism and Calvinism were not identical, the puritan ideal is best understood when seen among the Calvinists.

To possess a stern standard of public and private morality, and at the same time to have power to use the force of the state to compel those standards, is to ask at once for unpopularity and at last for rebellion. On three successive Sundays in 1561, five or six hundred people went through Montpellier with flags and tambourines, leaping about the streets and chanting: 'In spite of the Huguenots we shall dance.'

The moral discipline was exerted through the consistory, which acted as a kind of permanent commission of inquiry into the well-being of the community. Even in Geneva the action of the consistory was never perfectly free, and in other Calvinist countries like Holland and Scotland its freedom was either limited drastically or attained only for short periods. Among the Huguenots of France and the puritans within the Church of England its acts carried no secular penalty whatever, and its authority thereby depended solely upon its moral prestige. Nevertheless the existence of the consistory, however restricted or however voluntary, went far to maintain the high ideals of discipline which the reformers set forward. There the leaders of the congregation maintained the moral law, encouraged each other, established a corporate judgement upon sin, stabilized orthodoxy, and repressed misconduct.

The hinge of Calvinist morality was the doctrine of predestination. The sense of contrast between the good men and the bad, the children of darkness and the children of light, is evident throughout puritanism. The doctrine of election was in part the cause, in part the expression of this contrast. The man of faith believed that he had been called by no virtue or quality in himself, but by a free and loving act of God's grace; by walking in good works he was to establish to his own heart a conviction of that call, for its evidence was a good life; he was to seek for the heartfelt assurance of his own salvation in God's love. He knew that if God once bestowed his grace, God would not suffer him at last to fall away.

The Calvinist might not have this assurance and yet might often be in a state of grace. It was not an evidence of damnation if he failed to possess this assurance. But assurance was believed to accompany the rock-like faith which issued in goodness. And as he looked about him, he knew that the human race was divided into sheep and goats. He knew that he was ignorant who were sheep and who were goats, that this was a secret hidden within God's everlasting counsel. But knowing that the human race was thus divided into light and darkness, he could not help thinking, and sometimes acting, as though he shared the eternal fore-knowledge and knew who was in the night, perpetual night. The better puritan worked out his own salvation and left in mystery the salvation of his neighbours.

In 1570 Thomas Cartwright, Lady Margaret's professor of divinity at Cambridge, recommended in his lectures a presbyterian system of church government for England. He was removed from his professorship. In the following years a number of ministers built up a voluntary system of presbyteries, especially in London, Northamptonshire and Essex. Their plans won support in the House of Commons. In 1588–9 the anonymous 'Martin Marprelate' published libellous tracts against the bishops, and in the ensuing hunt the presbyteries were largely suppressed.

Though not condemning drama for edifying and instructive ends, the puritans were unfriendly to the theatre in its main forms. Despite the glories of the Elizabethan stage, they often condemned it justly. The theatre seemed to them to encourage immorality by representing drunken men or whoremongers and by making the audience laugh instead of hate. Calvin would never permit the wearing of the clothes of the other sex, on the ground of Deuteronomy 22.5; and on stage boys habitually took the part of women. After Calvin's death the moralists exhibited an ever-growing sternness against the theatre. In 1572 the Huguenot synod of Nîmes, on behalf of the French Reformed churches, forbade all plays except those which aimed to educate.

In 1584 Dr Reynolds at Oxford denounced plays for interrupting the studies of the university. In 1599 he published *The Overthrow of Stage Plays*, in which he criticized all the educational arguments in favour of theatre for the young, held that to counterfeit wantonness led morally downwards, and said that though he was no enemy of poetry and reasonable recreation, he doubted whether some of the hours spent at the theatre ought not to be spent at sermons. If the more rigorous moralists were thus ready to attack the use of the theatre in education, nearly all moralists attacked the scurrility of the professional theatre in London. All the Scriptural and moral arguments were adduced, the harlotry on the stage, the use of the audience as a rendezvous for prostitutes, the use of Sunday as the customary day for plays, the trumpets blowing to summon the audience just as the bells were tolling for afternoon prayer. The City of London excluded them, and they moved southward into Southwark.

But with the rise of the anti-puritan party in England the dramatists were encouraged. In the fight against puritans, the theatre was a sharp weapon, and took vengeance by its parody. The puritan's moral criticism was inflated into censoriousness, his assurance into pharisaism, his contempt for fashion into ostentatious singularity, his readiness to be unpopular into a mania for persecution. 'I am glad,' said Zeal-of-the-land Busy, the scathing caricature of a puritan in Ben Jonson's play *Bartholomew Fair* (1614), 'I am glad to be thus separated from the heathen of the land, and put apart in the stocks for the holy cause.' All parodies, where truly humorous, possess a touch of truth, and the theatre seized upon the odious qualities of the puritan underworld. 'Thou art the seat of the Beast, O Smithfield,' Rabbi Busy apostrophized the fair-ground, 'and I will leave thee! Idolatry peepeth out on every side of thee.'

By such abuse the name of puritan became honourable among some good men; as this of 1641: 'In abusing this word (puritan) . . . they can so stretch and extend the same that scarce any civil honest Protestant which is hearty and true to his religion can avoid the aspersion of it.' Among others the name stood for hypocrisy, or severity, or even political faction. Puritan strength lay with merchants of towns, members of corporations. Such men kept puritan ministry in existence, despite the disfavour of authority, by subscribing to provide a 'lecturer' in their parish church. They chose a lecturer who would preach a Calvinist faith and secured for him the right to occupy the pulpit.

The puritans encouraged the keeping of journals as a religious exercise. They were interested in moral histories, in times and modes of conversion, in special leadings or providences, and in their own offences. It was part confession, part self-discipline, part a spreading of their lives before the Lord. For the same reason they delighted in pious little biographies. Izaak Walton was no puritan, he was a high churchman of the Restoration, and he published the first of his charming *Lives* in 1640. But behind this model of the genre lay a mass of puritan writing, the sober hagiography of the new age. Samuel Clarke collected a newer and more puritan Foxe, in the years 1650–2, with the lives of men who are not even names except to the historian.

A Puritan Squire

Squire Bruen lived near Tarvin in Cheshire during the first quarter of the seventeenth century. He rose at five a.m. in winter, between three and four a.m. in summer, and spent an hour or two in meditating upon the Bible, interceding for his family, or writing out a sermon which he had lately heard, to such purpose that when he died he left many orderly volumes of manuscript devotions in his study. He observed the text 'seven times a day will I praise thee' at fixed points during the day. He woke his household by ringing a bell for family prayers, and though most of his prayers were extempore, he always began with a collect to convince the ignorant who thought a set form to be unlawful. He chose godly men from the neighbourhood to be his servants, catechized them, and held meetings with them to discuss cases of conscience; and after evening prayers the servants used to continue their devotions in the kitchen. He bought two large Bibles and put them on lecterns in his hall and parlour that the servants and visitors might consult them. When he discovered playing cards in the room of a visitor, he said nothing but carefully removed the four knaves from the pack. Once at a dinner given by the sheriff, a toast to the prince was proposed. As the cup passed along the line they looked to see what he would do. He said, 'You may drink to his health and I will pray for his health . . .', and so passed the cup. On Sunday when he went to church, a mile away, he called the neighbours and tenants, and they went together, singing Psalm 84 on the way. After morning service he usually stayed with a few others, and repeated the sermon or sang psalms till the evening service began, and afterwards he returned home with his company, discussing the sermon and again singing psalms.

In Tarvin church he removed the stained glass and put in white glass at his own expense. He paid the stipends of several preachers or lecturers, especially a godly preacher at Tarvin, where the incumbent was decrepit. On one Sunday in the year the people of Tarvin held a wake where there was much drinking and dancing. Bruen summoned three of the best ministers in the country, who kept the parish together by such constant preaching and praying that the pipers, pedlars, bear-wards, players, and gamesters went away fretting; and when this was repeated for three years the wake was abandoned.

His motto, which he used to write on the title page of his books, was Hallelujah. He keenly observed particular providences, and kept a journal of them, from which these extracts have survived:

1601. My servant going with his cart laden, fell down, and the wheels being iron bound, went over his leg, yet hurt him not at all: *Laus Deo*, praised be God.

1602. My son John going into the field, took up a scythe to see how he could mow, the scythe entered into his stocking to the shin-bone, shaving the hair, and came out at the back side of his leg, and touched no flesh nor skin: *Laus Deo*, praised be God.

1603. One that dwelt in my farm in Wimble-Stafford, seeing two godly persons going in the way, said to one with him, I will dance, swagger, and swear, to anger yonder two puritans, and so he did, to their great grief; but presently the revenging hand of God was upon him, so that immediately he fell sick, was carried home in a cart, and within three days died most fearfully: All glory to God.

To his tenants he was always charitable, not exacting high rents, encouraging their labour, making an annual allowance to buy winter clothes for the poor, visiting them when sick, sometimes giving them his good suits. In times of scarcity he fed many at his table. His hospitality was bountiful, and far from the conventional portrait of a puritan. Twenty-one people were sharing his dinner when his second wife died; young gentlemen 'of the best rank' came to study in his house; his table was well supplied, for he bred pigeons and conies to help his kitchen. He was three times married, with at least twelve children, and in his engraved portrait is wearing a sizeable and fashionable ruff. His generosity so overflowed that he fell into debt and in his old age needed to close the house for three years and live quietly in Chester while his fortunes recuperated.

Such men were impregnated with Biblical texts; conscious of the imminent hand of God upon every act and moment; denying the possibility of chance; so teaching the utter depravity of man since the fall of Adam, and the glory of redeeming power, that it was appropriate that the great puritan epic should be Milton's *Paradise Lost* (1667); watering the soil of prayer with devotional and spiritual writing; certain of God's victory at last.

Though frugal and thrifty, they did not share the medieval ideal of poverty. They condemned and sometimes mocked the hair-shirt and the scourge, they believed not at all in a fugitive and cloistered virtue. Though representative of the ascetic world-denying strand of Christianity which in another age issued in monks and friars, they were not ascetic in the old sense of the word. A good man worked, and if he worked he might receive prosperity, and he was right to enjoy his prosperity, as he enjoyed other natural gifts like a wife and children. There was no suspicion of marriage or of the begetting of children. But he practised early rising, days of fasting, temperance at all times, austerity in dress, and he kept few personal comforts in his house. Even a wealthy puritan might use platters like his poorer tenants. His ideal was to keep his station in society, simply and modestly, and cut away the trivialities and decorations that diverted. The Christian was to live in the world and use its gifts as God's steward. As it was a religion for the fighting man, so it was a religion for the merchant, the magistrate, the labourer. The talents were to be used, not buried in a napkin. Luther's doctrine of the blessedness of all right earthly vocations received an austere and decisive expression among the Calvinists.

Upon the text of Deuteronomy 23.19 the medieval Church condemned usury and included all interest under the ban. To prohibit credit would have shattered the prosperity of Europe. The later schoolmen devised formulas to allow interest on public loans. The views of the Reformers were not radical. The negative judgement of the Church through the centuries was not lightly or quickly set aside. Luther was hostile to usury; he was even more hostile to peasants who used the ban upon usury to refuse payment of their rent or their debts. The Swiss were more ready to be radical. Calvin ended the prohibition by arguing that this Deuteronomic law applied only to the polity of the Hebrews and was not intended to be universal. The sole guide is the law of charity. Extortion is always wrong, excessive rates are wrong, lending to the poor is wrong, but normal loans may be to the reasonable advantage of all the contracting parties. Interest is not to be condemned unless it transgresses the law of love.

The arguments of Calvin were accepted slowly among the European divines. In 1564–5 Bartholomew Gernhard, pastor of the church of St Andrew in Rudolstadt, refused communion to two gentlemen who had loaned money at four to six per cent, and after public disputes was forced out of office. In 1587 five preachers at Ratisbon fiercely attacked all rates of interest, comparing the lender to a thief and a murderer, and like Gernhard claimed the authority of Luther; and were expelled the city when they refused to obey an order to be silent upon the subject. Some Lutheran and Catholic writers continued into the seventeenth century to declare all usury immoral. In England Parliament allowed interest up to ten per cent in 1545. The Act was repealed under Edward VI in 1552, but in 1571 interest was again permitted and never thereafter attacked by government. The Church authorities were but slowly reconciled to the legality. In 1638 a Protestant divine, the Dutchman Claude Saumaise, at last argued in his book *On Usury* that interest was now necessary to civilization and that free competition would benefit society by lowering costs.

The truths behind an alleged connexion of puritanism and capitalism are these: first, that Reformed divinity, being less chained to precedent, adjusted itself a little more rapidly to the new economy; and secondly that (other things being equal) those who practised thrift, temperance, honesty, and consideration for others, and who believed an active life as a layman in society to be a vocation from God, were more likely to be successful merchants than those without these qualities.

Calvinist Worship

The Swiss principle demanded Scriptural authority for all things in ecclesiastical polity and the worship of the Church. Simplicity was godly, all else was distraction. The medieval church seemed to the Reformed like an over-furnished clutter, a shop of antique junk, where the worshipper could not apprehend true holiness because his vision was screened by trinkets, side altars, statues, coloured windows, pomp, vestments, saints, and ceremonies, as though the listening ears of prayer were deafened by the clangour of ritual noise. Some simple folk, especially women, regretted the loss of colour, the departure of the statues and banners. Not so the true Calvinist. He felt as though he had been present at a cleansing of the Temple, elevated and purged in spirit, conscious of a wind of Hebraic purity rushing through the church, sweeping away squalor and superstition and the ornaments which anchored his soul to the earth. A homilist of 1563 has preserved an imaginary conversation between a woman and her minister.

'Alas, gossip, what shall we do now at church, since all the saints are taken away, since all the goodly sights we were wont to have are gone, since we cannot hear the like piping, singing, chanting, and playing upon the organs that we could before?'
'But dearly beloved, we ought greatly to rejoice, and give God thanks, that our churches are delivered of all those things which displeased God so sore, and filthily defiled his holy house.'

Therefore they removed ritual acts, preferred extempore to formal prayer, used ordinary instead of unleavened bread in the sacrament, would not have their ministers distinguished by a special garb either in church or out of it, discarded the ring in marriage and the sign of the cross in baptism, and believed that all services ought to contain a sermon expounding the Word of God. Reacting always against unintelligent or unintelligible ritual, they were vehement advocates of religious instruction, catechizing, schools, Biblical knowledge. The chief weakness of Calvinist worship was the inclination to exhort out of season as well as in season, to make the homily overlong, to turn extempore prayer manward instead of Godward.

Luther wrote great hymns and most Lutheran churches accepted hymnody. To the Reformed, hymns were not Scriptural and therefore not allowed. In France and Geneva the metrical psalms of Marot and others were the sole hymnody. In the England of Edward VI Thomas Sternhold, a layman, wrote metrical translations of thirty-seven psalms. John Hopkins added seven more, and then English Calvinists like William Whittingham added still more, until all the Psalms received metrical versions. The 1582 edition also contains metrical versions of the canticles in Mattins and Evensong, of the Veni Creator and the Athanasian creed. Sometimes the metrical psalter was bound up with the Prayer Book. It was formally sanctioned for use at the beginning and end of morning and evening prayer and before and after the sermon. One of its versions – that still known by words and tune as Old Hundredth – has survived into every modern collection of hymns. More than 600 editions are known, the last in the catalogue of Cambridge University Library being dated 1845. Much abuse has been poured upon the metrical psalter, as rhyming doggerel, unworthy as a vehicle for the thoughts which it enshrined. But a part of the abuse was poured by those who hated congregational singing as untuneful and wanted choir music only, or by persons advocating non-Scriptural hymns instead of metrical psalms, or by those who resented its tunes as 'Genevan jigs' and associated the words with a puritan spirit. These are not metaphysical poetry; they were designed as popular religious songs, and are to be in part judged by that standard; as the 1582 edition stated on its title page, they were meant to be used not only in church but in private houses, so that the people might lay apart 'all ungodly songs and ballads, which tend unduly to the nourishing of vice and corrupting of youth'. Here is the first verse of the twenty-third Psalm, a translation by William Whittingham:

> The Lord is only my support
>   and he that doth me feed,
> How can I then lack anything
>   whereof I stand in need.
> He doth me fold in coates most safe
>   the tender grass fast by,
> And after drives me to the streams
>   Which run most pleasantly.

It may be bald, and a harsh critic of the Calvinists might

raise his eyebrows at the word *drives*. But it would hardly be just to call this simple sincerity by the name of doggerel. These psalms were sung to hornpipes at country feasts (*Winter's Tale* Act 4 scene 3) or by soldiers on the march. It was natural that a verse from the psalter should spring to the lips of Oliver Cromwell at the battle of Dunbar (1650). The version called Sternhold and Hopkins taught the people of England, and of early reformed Scotland, more about the Christian religion than any other single book outside the New Testament.

6

The Radicals of the Reformation

A REVOLUTIONARY movement always produces a wing
which will reform the revolution. Whatever else the Reformation succeeded in doing, it created a kind of piety called
by the contemptuous 'the religion of the mechanicks'. It
brought religion into the family, urged every man and
woman to seek for the confirmation of his faith in the Bible,
set forth the concern of God for his individual children with
a force and emphasis never previously tried in the history of
Christendom. The cobbler took his Bible home, and pored
over it, and found truth for himself. He found there the word
of life, and saw no need of education, of academic study, for
understanding it. If the inspiration of the spirit alone could
enforce it in his heart, the inspiration of the spirit alone
could expound its truth. The rising tide of literacy, which
printing made possible, was beginning to burst the bonds of
ecclesiastical tradition at the moment when the old modes
of ecclesiastical discipline were in question. These simple
folk believed that every man had an equal right to search
doctrine for himself from his Bible. They found apocalyptic
visions, and the dragon cast into the bottomless pit, and
they dreamed of the kingdom of heaven and of the saints,
and sought to gather a little remnant of the faithful and of
Babylon, and were contemptuous of the rich and the
learned. 'God useth the common people and the multitude
to proclaim that the Lord God omnipotent reigneth; as
when Christ came at first, the poor receive the Gospel,
not many wise, not many noble, not many rich, but the
poor.'

THE ANABAPTISTS

The members of these little groups came to be known generally as Anabaptists, because several articulate leaders agreed in denouncing the baptism of infants. But the name Anabaptist was applied loosely and widely as a term of abuse. It covered a multitude of different opinions.

For the most part the little groups were barely organized, quiet meetings to read and study the Bible, with much diversity among doctrines and practices. They found their most fertile soil in the cities of Switzerland, the Rhineland, and Holland. But because their enemies condemned them all as Anabaptists, we must not infer that they agreed among themselves or formed a coherent body of teaching. For the most part they rejected the baptism of infants. They believed that the true Church was called out of the world and therefore most of them repudiated the idea that the magistrate should uphold the true Church. The so-called Anabaptist Confession of Schleitheim (1527), the document nearest to a confession agreed by the early Anabaptists, proclaimed adult baptism and separation from the world, including everything popish, and from attendance at parish churches and taverns. It condemned the use of force, or going to law, or becoming a magistrate, or the taking of oaths.

The outside world eyed Anabaptists with horror. In the hands of religious eccentrics or ignorant fanatics, freed from the restraints of a common and historical tradition, the little groups could end in blasphemy and crime. At the extreme left was the apocalyptic spur with which Thomas Münzer helped to goad the German peasants into their calamitous jacquerie of 1524. There were wild prophecies of the approaching end of the world, plans for a new kingdom of God to be established by force. The doctrines propagated by bizarre prophets readily set aflame the tinder lying ready.

John of Batenburg, formerly the mayor of Steenwijk in the Netherlands, appears to have held that anyone unconverted ought to be killed, that churches may be plundered, that divorce is obligatory if one party to a marriage is unconverted, that property is common and polygamy right, and that he was Elijah to prepare the second Coming. Though he considered baptism unimportant he was known as an Anabaptist. With such associates were the peaceful Anabaptists ruined in public opinion.

Münster

At the end of 1533 the Anabaptist group at Münster in Westphalia, under the leadership of a former Lutheran minister Bernard Rothmann, gained control of the city council. Early in 1534 a Dutch prophet and ex-innkeeper named John of Leyden appeared in Münster, believing that he was called to make the city the new Jerusalem. On 9 February 1534 his party seized the city hall. By 2 March all who refused to be baptized were banished, and it was proclaimed a city of refuge for the oppressed. Though the Bishop of Münster collected an army and began the siege of his city, an attempted coup within the walls was brutally suppressed, and John of Leyden was proclaimed King of New Zion, wore vestments as his royal robes, and held his court and throne in the market-place. Laws were decreed to establish community of goods, and the Old Testament was adduced to permit polygamy. Bernard Rothmann, once a man of sense, once the friend of Melanchthon, took nine wives.

They now believed that they had been given the duty and the power of exterminating the ungodly. The world would perish, and only Münster would be saved. Rothmann issued a public incitement to world rebellion: 'Dear brethren, arm yourselves for the battle, not only with the humble weapons of the apostles for suffering, but also with the glorious armour of David for vengeance . . . in God's strength, and help to annihilate the ungodly.' An ex-soldier named John of Geelen slipped out of the city, carrying copies of this proclamation into the Netherlands, and planned sudden coups in the Dutch cities. On a night in February 1535 a group of men and women ran naked and unarmed through the streets of Amsterdam shouting: 'Woe! Woe! The wrath of God falls on this city.' On 30 March 1535 John of Geelen with 300 Anabaptists, men and women, stormed an old monastery in Friesland, fortified it, made sallies to conquer the province, and were only winkled out after bombardment by heavy cannon. On the night of 10 May 1535 John of Geelen with a band of some thirty men attacked the city hall of Amsterdam during a municipal banquet, and the burgomaster and several citizens were killed. At last, on 25 June 1535, the gates of Münster were opened by sane men within the walls, and the bishop's army entered the city. The cages where corpses of Anabaptist leaders were hung are still hanging on the tower of St Lambert's Church.

For a hundred years and more the ill-omened name of Münster was enough to destroy the arguments in favour of religious toleration, enough to prove that Anabaptists, however law-abiding, were better suppressed. 'At the moment,' wrote one of their early assailants, 'they are peaceful, law-abiding lambs, but soon they may be wolves, as rebellious as before.' 'God,' wrote Zwingli's successor at Zurich, Henry Bullinger, 'opened the eyes of governments by the revolution at Münster, and no one thereafter would trust Anabaptists who claimed to be innocent.'

If we leave aside the catastrophic fringe of lunacy, the groups, as they developed, began to cohere in four areas: (1) the Swiss, founded by Conrad Grebel and Felix Manz at Zurich in the time of Zwingli, (2) the south German, led at first by Balthasar Hübmaier and Hans Denck, but after their deaths by the Tyrolese engineer Pilgrim Marbeck; (3) the Hutterite brethren in Moravia; (4) the Mennonites of the Netherlands and north Germany.

At Zurich about fifteen people, members of a little group for Bible study, refused to have their children baptized. Early in 1525 an ex-priest in the group named George Blaurock made a profession of faith and was baptized by Conrad Grebel; and thereafter baptized the remainder of the group. A few days later there were further baptisms of adults at the village of Zollikon down the lake, and soon Blaurock and Grebel were travelling round the country, baptizing men and women in streams, and holding simple services in houses or in fields. In 1526 the city council of Zurich ordered that all Anabaptists should be drowned. One of the Anabaptists, Felix Manz, was tied to a hurdle and thrown into the river. Blaurock was whipped through the streets and expelled from the country. He moved into the Tyrol but was captured and burnt in 1529.

The Hutterites

From 1526 a little group, partly under Swiss influence, established itself in Moravia. After schisms and painful vicissitudes, one of the divisions maintained itself peacefully, as the Hutterite Brothers, from 1556 to 1620. Jacob Hutter was executed in 1536, but stamped his particular group with the conviction, based upon the early chapters of the Acts of the Apostles, that community of goods was the practice of true Christians.

They gathered the community into a 'brother-house' – the *Bruderhof* at Nikolsburg still stands. The *Bruderhof* consisted of several large and several small buildings. The ground floor was used for the common life, dining hall, school, nursery, kitchen, laundry, weaving sheds, smithy, workshops. The roofs were high and steep, and in the attics lived the families. Each *Bruderhof* was managed by an elected steward, and the sacrament was celebrated in the dining hall. The ordinances were in some ways reminiscent of the rule of a medieval monastery, and altogether these Hutterite communities were a fascinating manifestation, in a family context, of the old ascetic ideal.

The profit motive was excluded for the individual, but not for the community. 'Private property,' affirms an early Hutterite document (1545), 'is the greatest enemy of love, and the true Christian must render up his will and become free from property if he would be a disciple.' It was a principle that all materials should be used, as far as possible, on the premises, so that hides were tanned and shoes cobbled within the *Bruderhof*. Where this was impossible, they freely bought materials like metal from the world outside, but they would never 'trade', would never buy with the intention of selling, they would only buy that they might be enabled to sell the fruits of their labour. 'We think it wrong to buy something and sell it and take the profit, so making the thing more expensive to the poor and taking the bread from their mouths, and thus the poor man cannot but become the mere servant of the rich.' Everyone who joined must learn a craft. Like most of the peaceful Anabaptists they were pacifist on principle and would not allow the manufacture of swords, spears, or guns. They paid the normal taxes, but refused levies openly directed to a military end, and allowed their goods to be sequestered in payment. All work was to be careful, solid, reliable, without haste. No one could bequeath property. All that a man used reverted on his death to the community.

Hard work, careful manufacture, an austere life, and restrained consumption meant wealth. In the time of peace between 1564 and 1619 the Hutterites of Moravia became celebrated, for they could manufacture the best objects at a lower price than was possible elsewhere. They were famous as doctors, clock-makers, copyists, cutlers, designers of furniture, above all of maiolica. Their bath-houses were frequented by Catholic noblemen, their services demanded to manage farms or breweries or saw-mills. In 1609 they sold iron bedsteads to an Austrian nobleman, in 1611 a richly gilded carriage to the Margrave of Brandenburg, in 1613 an ornamental clock to the Cardinal von Dietrichstein. Old Moravian inventories of furniture contain entries such as 'a blue Anabaptist jug mounted in silver and gilded', and fair examples of the maiolica ware may now be seen in museums. Their great physician, Zobel, was called to minister to the Emperor Rudolf II. Probably at the height of their prosperity there may have been 100 communities, with 20,000 people or more.

The outbreak of the Thirty Years War ended their age of peace and plenty. In 1620 imperial troops sacked Nikolsburg, and in 1621 the government persuaded the bishop, or head, to disclose one store of their 'treasure' (which they buried in the ground), the capital of their working community, much magnified by popular legend and slander. In 1622 they were expelled from Moravia, and a remnant fled eastward. Through Slovakia, the Turkish lands, and the Ukraine, they came during the years 1874–9 to South Dakota in the United States, and there and in the Canadian provinces to the north communities of Hutterite brothers may be found, 120 brother-houses (1954) with about 10,000 souls, practising community of goods, learning English at school and speaking German at home, reading at their services the old sermons of the seventeenth century and allowing no new sermons, but allowing farm machinery, cars, telephones, and electric light.

The Mennonites

Community of goods, despite Münster and the Hutterites, was found only among scattered groups of Anabaptists, and elsewhere came rapidly to be interpreted, in the orthodox manner, as 'bearing one another's burdens'.

For a time, however, there were other unique customs, of which traces may also be found among the Hutterites. The ultimate conviction of the movement was its belief in the pure congregation, the society of saints, the congregation of the truly converted, drawn from the world, and drawn not merely as individuals but as a society. This was the root of the attack upon infant baptism and upon churches established by law. This was the root of the desire to withdraw the members, socially as well as spiritually, from the general life of the world.

The need to refuse military service, or to pay certain taxes, were manifest difficulties in peaceable living. But the desire for absolute purity suffered more agony even than these. What was to happen if a true Christian married an unbeliever? A Swiss tract of 1527 asserts that the believer must divorce the unbelieving partner, or rather must behave as though the marriage had never been. In 1536 Melanchthon heard the examination of an Anabaptist in Thuringia, and believed that the defendant maintained an erroneous faith to be an immediate ground for divorce. Other traces of this agony are occasionally found in the movement. But sensible leaders came to see that the rigid view was here untenable.

A second source of agony was the excommunication. In the traditional churches excommunication carried secular penalties, sometimes a social ostracism by law. The Anabaptists would have nothing to do with the law. But they believed that exclusion from the pure community must carry a social exclusion. Menno Simons (died 1561), the chief of the Anabaptist leaders in Holland, adopted it during the fifteen-thirties.

In 1556 a member of the Emden congregation named Rutgers was excommunicated. His wife believed that she ought not to shun her husband, and was herself excommunicated. The ensuing controversy, whether or no she was rightly excommunicated, split the Mennonite movement for a time. The severe decision was condemned by a conference of south-German Anabaptists at Strasbourg in 1557, and Menno Simons, who at first objected to the ban, appears to have been won, till near his end, for rigidity. In north Germany and Holland the movement split into a liberal and a rigid wing.*

* The Old Order Amish Mennonites in U.S.A. still practise a form of the ban – refusal to eat at the same table even within the same family, refusal to work together on the farm.

Under these circumstances all Anabaptist groups, even to the eighteenth century, strongly preferred marriage within the community, and hence it became common for first or second cousins to marry. The engagement was announced from the pulpit, and among the Swiss Mennonites the deacon would make the man's proposal of marriage to the girl's family.

A number of other interesting customs appeared among the Mennonites. At first the sacrament was often celebrated in silence, without liturgy or formulas. After communion there was often a rite of foot-washing, the sexes sitting apart, which ended with a kiss of peace and a 'God bless you'. In Thuringia Anabaptists retained their own version of the Lord's Prayer, with the clause 'Give us the eternal heavenly bread'. The more severe groups retained an extreme simplicity in dress, furniture, food. The Sunday before the communion the congregation met for self-examination and might on occasion determine not thereafter to proceed with the communion. Baptism was usually by affusion, as in the traditional churches, and not by immersion. Peculiar habits of extreme American Amish Mennonites at the present day, like the refusal to wear buttons and insistence upon hooks and eyes (because buttons entered dress as ornaments), came in little by little as fashions changed and every acceptance of a new fashion was a compromise with the world.

The Waterlanders

By contrast the liberal wing of the Dutch Mennonites, known as Waterlanders, were able to adapt themselves more freely to the society in which they lived. Founded upon tolerance, they rapidly began to modify the early rigidity in several directions. Despite the pacifist principle, never abandoned, they raised and presented a large sum of money to William of Orange in his camp at Roermond (1572), and in the next century they were accused of allowing their merchant ships to sail with guns as a protection

against pirates. By 1581 they were permitting their members
to hold office, at least minor office, under the government,
provided that the office did not include shedding of blood.
They denounced, but tolerated, marriage with non-
Mennonites. By 1620 they are said to have allowed Calvinists, baptized in infancy, to join them without being
baptized. They slowly replaced silent prayer with prayer
by a minister, and they began to sing psalms. The Dutch
states, on the whole, treated them well, exempting their
almshouses and orphanages from taxation, allowing them
to affirm instead of taking oaths, and to commute their
military service for money payments. In consequence
members of these little God-fearing sober groups established
themselves in Dutch life, as bankers, merchants, scholars,
painters (including Ruysdael). They had outlived the
memory of Münster.

THE SOCINIANS

Upon the fringe of the Anabaptist movement there sprang
up a group whose bond of union was more directly theological – those known variously as Socinians, Arians, or
Unitarians.

The cauldron of ideas among the early Anabaptists
threw up speculations which called in question the decisions of the early Church – especially upon the nature and
person and birth of Christ. It was inevitable that the
doctrine of the Trinity should be re-examined and criticized
in the light of the Biblical texts. Luther himself declared
that words like *Trinity* and *of one substance* were not necessary
to Christian language, though he held absolutely to the
ideas which they sought to express. At Lausanne in 1534
Viret drafted an orthodox confession without using the
words Trinity, person, substance. Calvin was content not
to use the Athanasian creed. The movement was reacting against scholastic subtlety, against theological
speculation; and some of the language used by traditional

thinkers about the Trinity could justly be, called technical.

It must not be supposed that the Unitarian of the sixteenth century was a rationalist critic of the eighteenth, or even a humanist of the Renaissance. He was a student of the Scripture who eschewed all appeal to reason or to authority and found for himself a certain conclusion. Beside the Biblical text, all the Christian centuries were for him as nothing. *Against the whole world since the Apostles* was the title of a book by an Anabaptist leader named Campanus.

Most Anabaptists, in this matter, stood upon the side of ancient orthodoxy. Most Anabaptist churches were hardly concerned with the question. They used no creed, were content with a mode of worship which hung closely upon the Biblical text. When an anti-Trinitarian named Adam Pastor arose among the German Mennonites, Menno Simons and the strict leaders excommunicated him. But a less stringent discipline elsewhere was of another mind.

Of the early radicals who adopted anti-Trinitarian thought, the most famous and influential was the Spaniard Michael Servetus. A surprisingly high proportion of the anti-Trinitarian leaders were refugees from Italy or Spain. By 1530, as a young man of nineteen or twenty, Servetus was famous for his Trinitarian oddities to the Protestant pastors of the Rhineland. He believed in a doctrine of the Trinity to the tragic end of his life. He thought it his mission to destroy the erroneous forms and technical terms framed by subtle schoolmen and philosophers.

He was a remarkable and versatile young man. He learnt medicine and made brilliant speculations in anatomy, guessing at the circulation of the blood. He edited the geographer Ptolemy with skill. In 1537 he was lecturing in Paris on astrology and casting horoscopes for money. In 1546–8 he published three revised editions of his book on syrups. Amid this versatility he earned his living as a scholar, editor, and corrector for the press, until the expected end of the world should shortly come. Practising as a physician near Lyons, and outwardly a Catholic while internally he condemned the Pope, the Trinity, and the practice of infant baptism, he was discovered (not without assistance from Calvin at Geneva) and condemned by the Inquisition as a heretic. He escaped from the prisons of the Inquisition at Vienne, by the expedient of asking to go for a walk in the garden still wearing his nightgown and nightcap. The rumour spread, even to distant Wittenberg, that he had fled to Paris and died insane. Passing through Geneva during a week-end, he attended afternoon church and was recognized in the congregation.

He was burnt in an open space outside the wall of Geneva on 27 October 1553.

Servetus was no wise or humble seeker after truth. He was odd, cantankerous, unbalanced, abusive, and arrogant. But by (almost) inviting Geneva to burn him, and burn him on grounds of pure intellectual error, he served the cause of Christian charity more than many better men. He was not the first man to be executed by Protestants for heresy, nor was he near being the last. His death, as we shall see, brought Christendom closer to ending the ghastly procession of conscientious killings.

Rakow

The Reformation made headway in Poland because each lord of the manor won a practical freedom to choose his own religion. In the private chapel of a great estate, any doctrine was secure provided that the proprietor supported it. Anabaptists fleeing eastwards found a haven in several of the great Polish estates, and thence exercised magnetic attraction upon the scattered Reformed congregations. For a time they found similar refuge in Hungary and Transylvania.

A church called the Minor Reformed Church of Poland

came into existence, professing Anabaptist principles and holding anti-Trinitarian doctrine. It was based upon a few of the great estates, the most important being those at Vilna in Lithuania, where it was backed by the Lithuanian Chancellor Prince Radziwill (died 1565), and at Rakow, the property of an Anabaptist magnate named Jan Sieninski. Sieninski, whose wife was a convinced anti-Trinitarian, founded for her sake a new town upon his estates, called it Rakow after the crab (*rak*) upon his wife's coat of arms, and granted it a charter of incorporation (1569) which provided for a wide toleration. 'I, Jan Sieninski . . . make known to all . . . that I will not rule over the religion of the aforesaid Rakovians in which they differ from one another . . . nor will I permit agents to rule over the same, but each of them, as the Lord gives him grace, and as his knowledge of the truth leads him, shall cherish his religion in peace with himself and his descendants.' Rakow collected the radicals from other Polish estates, refugees from Moravia and Germany, one or two Polish nobles who sold their estates and distributed them to the poor, and simple enthusiasts believing that Rakow would be the new Jerusalem. After a few years of religious anarchy, the citizens of Rakow wanted to turn the town into something like a Hutterite *Bruderhof*. They tried to organize the town upon a strict application of New Testament texts. Like everyone else, high or low, the ministers were urged to earn their bread with their own hands. They encouraged the freedom of serfs and community of goods, discouraged appeals to law courts, sports, and public dancing, established factories for paper, cloth, and pottery, and set up (1600) a press to print Unitarian literature. In 1602 a college in which every student must also work at a trade was founded and endowed by Jacob Sieninski, the son of the founder.

Sozzini

In 1580 a leader of power sought admission to the church of Rakow – Fausto Sozzini, after whose latinized name of Socinus the Unitarians would later be generally known. Sozzini, like so many of the early radicals, was Italian by race, a scion of an eminent Sienese family one member of which, his uncle Lelio Sozzini, had already distinguished himself in the cause of radical Protestantism (three other uncles had been suspected of or charged with heresy). As a secretary in Florence, he won theological repute with a lucid and orthodox treatment of Scriptural authority. Retiring about 1575 from Florence to Basle, he wrote but did not print his most celebrated work, *On the Saving Work of Christ*, setting forth a view of Calvary as atonement by example. Henceforth a convinced and critical radical, he journeyed into Poland, and remained there from 1580 till his death in 1604.

He was refused admission to the Church in Poland. They said that he must be (re-) baptized, and he could not believe that baptism was a necessary ordinance in the Church. Despite much subsequent pressure he never submitted and never received communion in Rakow. Yet he worshipped with them, shared their synods without being a formal member, and came inevitably to be a leader.

Since they agreed only in negations, Sozzini stepped into the space for constructive thinking. Among his hardest tasks was to persuade a synod at Chmielnik in 1589 to jettison the belief in an imminent millennium. He defended the pacifist doctrine with an unfanatical moderation, persuaded the churches nevertheless to pay taxes and allow their members to seek redress in the law courts, to hold private property, to invest money at interest, or to serve as magistrates provided it was not thereby their duty to inflict capital punishment. He gave the Unitarian movement a body of doctrine and the traditional Christian method of coherent thinking. It was a hinge of his teaching that, despite the anti-Trinitarian conviction, the members of the movement would be faithful to the New Testament only if they worshipped Christ as divine.

In 1605 the year after Sozzini's death, three of his

disciples published at Rakow the so-called Rakovian Catechism (Latin edition 1609). This catechism became for the Socinians what the Augsburg Confession was to the Lutherans. It was dedicated (without permission) to King James I of England, and was burnt by order of Parliament in April 1652. A succession of Lutheran and Calvinist professors exercised their pens and their students in refuting it. It somehow succeeds in being constructive while denying not only the doctrine of the Trinity but those of original sin, baptismal regeneration, predestination to death, vicarious satisfaction, and justification by faith alone. It came from a world of radicals some of whom denied yet more.

The End of Rakow

The Socinians did not live unmolested. Sozzini himself was smeared with filth by a young Catholic in the streets of Cracow, beaten and almost lynched by a crowd; his papers were burnt upon a fire in the market square. The safety of the Socinians depended upon the weakness of the Catholic crown of Poland, their peril that in an age of war pacifism rendered them open to the charge of treachery. The third generation of the Sieninski family, the grandson of the founder, became an ardent Catholic during his studies at the University of Vienna. In 1638 two students of the Rakow academy threw stones at a crucifix provokingly erected on the Rakow border. The Catholic Bishop of Cracow exhibited the broken fragments of crucifix at the Diet in Warsaw, and thereafter the press was suppressed, the college closed, and the Socinian inhabitants expelled. On the site of the Socinian church, the bishop in 1640 laid the foundations of a new Catholic church, and a century and a half later travellers could still see the ruin of the baptismal pit where adults had been immersed.

Thus the centre of Unitarian thought passed from Poland to the more radical among the Dutch Mennonites. But in England, Holland, and Germany of the seventeenth century the name and work of Sozzini were by no means to be forgotten. For he, and those like-minded, had raised a fundamental question for the left wing of the Reformation; whether by the authority of Scripture alone, and without any reference whatsoever to the early Church and its teaching, the Trinitarian language could be defended.

THE ENGLISH INDEPENDENTS

'Your Anabaptists,' wrote John Jewel, the Bishop of Salisbury, apostrophizing the Catholic countries of the Continent in 1567, '. . . we know not.' It was not quite true. King Henry the Catholic burnt thirteen Dutch Anabaptists in one year. Queen Elizabeth the Protestant burnt two Dutch Anabaptists in 1575. The Thirty-Nine Articles (1571), with their defence of arms and oaths and their denunciation of community of property, show that vague reports from Europe, and immigrants, entered England. A few foreign Anabaptists reached London during the reigns of Edward VI and Elizabeth. But the Articles were fighting a shadow.

The little groups flourished wherever religion was unsettled. And the religion of Elizabethan England was still, in a manner, unsettled. Neighbour to the Protestant countries where Calvinism reigned, England chose a middle road. The Calvinist antagonists of doctrinal caution or liturgical conservatism had no wish to separate from the Church of England, they wished to reform it from inside by lawful means. The fiercer their assault, the stiffer grew the defence of the Church of England as by law established. And on their own left wing, at least from 1567, were a few groups or congregations who could not bear to worship in churches where surplices were used or men knelt to receive the sacrament, and who withdrew to illicit, secret, hunted meetings. Most of these congregations were led, and some of them formed, by Anglican ministers who had been suspended or removed for failure to comply with the church order in England. They found it impossible to worship with the Prayer Book, the formal liturgy, the surplice, the sign of the cross in baptism, or to tolerate the discipline exercised by lawyers through public courts. Though most of them were simple men, one or two of the leaders were instructed, even learned. Some of them rejected infant baptism; and as they were driven out of the country and found a refuge in Holland, the example and influence of the Dutch Mennonites began to be important. In most congregations the idea of a *covenant* was fundamental – each member bound himself by a solemn covenant with God to a holy life, and upon the existence of this covenant was based a moral discipline exercised by the other members of the congregation.

The Reformation appealed to the open Bible. The Reformers had desired and planned that the simplest labourer in the fields might be able to read it for himself. In the seventeenth century the labourer was beginning to read for himself, and with potent consequences. By their vernacular Bibles the main Protestant churches thrust into the popular consciousness a religious dynamic, a flood which could not for ever be channelled within the banks of an artificial canal, not even by a censorship more efficient or more rigorous than anything possible to the authorities of that day. The England of the middle seventeenth century was to test what happened when the 'mechanick', the brazier and the feltmaker and the coachman, went into the Bible to fetch their divinity for themselves. Some Reformers, like the early Luther, preached the priesthood of the laity. Was it meant that a layman, or even a woman, might at any time speak in the congregation – as Colonel Henson, of Cromwell's army, pushed his way into the pulpit at Aston and preached – whether the minister willed or no?

The Reformation had embarked upon reforming the Church. If you begin to reform, how far shall you reform, and when will you consider your reform to have succeeded? It had been agreed that one purpose was the removal of scandalous and unworthy men from ministering in the parish churches; yet some unworthy men could still be found ministering in parish churches. The Reformation must be carried yet further, the work was but half done. And if the Protestant authorities of the land refused to allow the work to advance, perhaps it was better to abandon the parish church with its unworthy incumbent, and to meet apart, with godly men dedicated to an earnest faith.

The authorities in Church and State said that parsons must wear a surplice, and that communicants must kneel at the sacrament. Believing it forbidden by Scripture to kneel at the sacrament, some parishioners came and sat. The parsons must turn them away. Ungodly to kneel, but ejected from communion if sitting, they turned away to make their own assembly with arrangements, as they believed, more Biblical. Schism was a sin – 'but surely,' wrote Francis Cheynell, 'the Archbishop was rather schismatical in imposing such burdens upon tender communicants, than the people in separating from external communion.' So at least it was argued; and to the contrary, it was alleged that the principle would justify disobedience to all laws. 'I think I may safely say', said one outraged critic in 1657, 'this is an Anabaptistical Münster principle, at the bottom.'

In 1581 Robert Browne, formerly upon the left wing of the numerous puritans at the University of Cambridge, gathered a separated congregation in Norwich.

Browne adopted certain ideas found among Anabaptists – that the Church shall consist only of true Christians, that the congregation binds itself in a 'covenant', elects or deposes its own ministers (and therefore each congregation is sovereign over its own life and order), that magistrates shall have no part in religion, that established and 'national' churches are wrong, that a spouse may separate from an unbelieving partner. After imprisonments for fierce denunciations of the authorities in Church and State, he fled (1582) with many of his congregation and his chief colleague, the teacher Harrison, to Middelburg in Holland.

At Middelburg the congregation split into quarrelling groups, and a few months later Browne left for Scotland and another imprisonment. Back in Norwich he re-created a congregation. In 1585 he submitted to the Archbishop of Canterbury and returned uncomfortably to the Church of England, dying as an Anglican vicar of Achurch in Northamptonshire forty-eight years later.

In 1593 a stringent Act against puritans and separatists passed Parliament, and in the same year three of the leaders – Barrow, Greenwood, and Penry – were executed for writing hot pamphlets against the establishment in Church and State. Until the outbreak of the civil war in 1642, the main home of English separatists was Holland. The most celebrated group came from Nottinghamshire and the surrounding district, Scrooby, Gainsborough, Bawtry, Babworth, Workshop, Austerfield. Several of the leaders held all set forms in worship to be un-Christian, Smyth held that the use of a book when singing psalms was unlawful. Though the Scriptures were publicly read, they were often accompanied by a prophesying or running commentary of devotional exposition.

The little congregations, each supreme over its worship, were earnest in their endeavour after Scriptural worship. Some English congregations revived the agape or love-feast, a common meal of the congregation held before the Lord's Supper. Others adopted a rite of foot-washing. They practised mutual examination and corporate moral discipline at weekly meetings. John Robinson, in his famous speech to the church before the *Mayflower* voyage in 1620, expressed the sense of all these groups that light was yet to be found in faithfulness to the Bible. 'He was very confident the Lord had more truth and light yet to break forth out of his holy word . . . The Lutherans . . . could not be drawn to go beyond what Luther saw, for whatever part of God's will he had further . . . revealed to Calvin, they will rather die than embrace . . . You see the Calvinists: they stick where he left them . . For though they were precious shining lights in their times, yet God had not revealed his whole will to them . . .'

Like the Mennonites, the English separatists were not always an edifying spectacle. There was a Babel of dissenting schisms and mutual excommunications. The nature of a moral discipline exercised by the congregation was still half formed and required much experience before it ceased to waste away in criticizing the whalebones in the petticoats of a pastor's wife. One of the oddest aberrations was the act of at least two English Anabaptists (especially John Smyth in 1608) in baptizing themselves, on the ground that there was no pure church to receive them. In 1610, thirty-two of Smyth's little congregation applied to be admitted to the Waterlander Mennonites, and after five years of doubt were received.

The English Baptists, like their counterparts in Europe, baptized by the traditional method of affusion. But both on the Continent and in England isolated ministers taught and practised baptism by immersion. Some of the Mennonites in the Netherlands adopted immersion in the early seventeenth century, and in 1641 the English Particular Baptists (as those of a Calvinist theology came to be known) formally adopted the rite of immersion. It was thenceforward to become characteristic of the Baptist movement. In 1640 there were seven Baptist congregations in London, and forty-seven elsewhere in England, but many other Baptists were overseas, in Holland or New England.

NEW ENGLAND

In New England the radical movement took a new form. The country was planted by a mixture of trading settlements encouraged by London investors and of refugees from the religious policy of the English government, whether Presbyterian, Independent, Baptist, or Roman Catholic.

The charter of the Virginia Company (1606) provided that the true Word of God was to be preached both to colonists and savages, and from 1609 papists were excluded. The settlement intended to reproduce the Church of England across the Atlantic. The clergy were to use the Book of Common Prayer, every plantation must provide a church, there were penalties for failing to attend worship, the clergy were supported by a form of 'tithe', each clergyman to receive from his parishioners 1,500 lb. of tobacco and sixteen barrels of corn.

But even in Virginia the establishment was modified towards a little more control of the clergyman by his congregation. There was no history of private patronage, no bishop west of the Atlantic, no rite of confirmation. The local vestry rapidly assumed an importance which it did not possess in England.

In 1620 the *Mayflower* sailed, and so began the settlement at Plymouth. This is the earliest of the plantations directly intended to be a refuge from religious persecution. Of the 149 on board the *Mayflower*, a minority of thirty-five were separatists from the Leyden congregation. Forty-one adults signed the *Compact* in the cabin of the ship – the covenant to establish the government of the colony. They later bought out the London merchants who had financed the voyage, and in 1629 secured a minister to suit their polity and ideals. But they remained for many years a little group.

In 1628 there was a settlement at Massachusetts Bay. In 1630 this was taken over by the Massachusetts Bay Company, a much stronger and much less extreme group of English puritans headed by John Winthrop, a Suffolk squire. Many of these were friends of the Church of England, at least in that they never discouraged their members from attending parish churches when in England. Yet the church polity which they reached at Salem and Boston in Massachusetts Bay was a unique kind of established Congregationalism. They tried to practise the ideals of contemporary

English Puritans. They refused to use the Prayer Book and established the moral discipline, though not exercised through a consistory as in the presbyterian pattern, but through the governing court. In 1631 they determined that no one should be a citizen with suffrage unless he was a member of the church in the colony. In 1643 there were 15,000 inhabitants and only 1,708 citizens. This gave a measure of power to the clergy, who determined admission to membership of the church; and as in the Spanish colonies, overseas service attracted a high proportion of decisive men. But the final word lay with the governing court. Thus the mode of Church government resembled that of Zurich more than that of Geneva. It was codified and declared in the *Cambridge Platform* of 1648.

Connecticut, New Hampshire, and Rhode Island were all founded, in their different ways, by groups who resented the limiting nature of the Church establishment in Massachusetts. Connecticut was founded in 1635 by like-minded persons who resented the autocratic and quasi-theocratic constitution, and wanted any man of good character, whether church member or not, to have a vote. Rhode Island was founded by the extreme Independent Roger Williams, when he was convicted of separatism and banished from Massachusetts in the deep winter of 1636. Here grew a little community consecrated to tolerance and freedom of worship, welcoming the dissidents whom Massachusetts banished.

Maryland was another community which aimed at toleration. Charles I gave a charter in 1632 to George Calvert, Lord Baltimore, who was a Roman Catholic and attracted Roman Catholic refugees as well as Protestant colonists.

Meanwhile the king of England and his Parliament fell to blows, and the anarchy of war afforded new occasions to the left wing of the Reformation. Modern Congregationalism descends from a harmony of ordinary English puritanism, moulded in the unique conditions of Massachusetts with a few of the more radical ideals of the early Independents, and then carried back across the Atlantic to the open opportunity of England in the age of Oliver Cromwell.

7

The Assault upon Calvinism

LIKE Catherine de' Medici under the threat of civil war in 1562, like William the Silent when the Netherlands were being torn apart, like the Swedish kings, the English government sought for a moderate constitution, sufficiently reformed to satisfy reasonable Protestants, sufficiently conservative to satisfy the Catholics who were not determined to be Papists. The question remained whether English Protestants could be satisfied by anything short of the Swiss pattern, which in all the surrounding lands – France, the Netherlands, Scotland – was winning the assent of reformers.

No German Protestant state of that age dared to attempt a unity between Lutheran and Reformed. Either the German state was formally Lutheran and the Reformed pastors were excluded, or it was formally Reformed and the Lutheran pastors were excluded. Yet from motives of policy and personal inclination, and with the opinions of the country divided by the religious see-saw from Henry VIII to Mary, Queen Elizabeth of England intended to hold together, in an external conformity of moderation, persons whose opinions might differ as widely as Lutheran differed from Calvinist.

The result was neither expected nor desired by either party: the growth within the bounds of one establishment of two great schools of religious thought, two schools partly incompatible in outlook, at first antagonists, each trying to dominate or expel the other, in the course of the conflict losing the extremes upon either wing into formal dissent, but at last coming to live side by side, if not with comfort at least with a measure of respect – the two schools of Calvinist and Episcopalian. And their mutual hostility and mutual relation, entangled with the political strife of king and Parliament, generated that unique offshoot of the Reformation which after 1836 would come to be known as Anglicanism.

Queen Elizabeth and her advisers aimed at securing a compromise; a middle road between the jangling parties which divided the kingdom; a 'golden mediocrity', if like Archbishop Matthew Parker one believed moderation to be right; a 'leaden mediocrity', a 'mingle-mangle', as some of the disciples of the Swiss preferred to call it.

But moderation and compromise are ideals which often fail to command loyalty. The Roman Catholic upon his side, the Calvinist upon his side, pursued a programme of restoration or of reformation. The strength of the opposition to middle roads lay with the Calvinists, because most sensible people admitted that further reformation was needed. In contemporary Germany the Lutherans were not finding it easy to defend their conservative Reformation against the inroads of the Reformed churches. The Calvinists commanded the allegiance of many among the thoughtful divines of England. They represented European Protestantism, the idea of a reformed and reunited Christendom, the faith of Scotland and Switzerland and the Netherlands and the Palatinate and the suffering Huguenots of France. And behind them, some lay lords wanted bishops abolished for material reasons. Other Protestant states secularized the lands of bishops as well as of monasteries; England had so far only secularized the monasteries and diminished the income of bishops by unscrupulous bargains. There was treasure to come. The doctrinal desire among godly and reforming Calvinists that Matthew Parker should be the last Archbishop of Canterbury received a measure of hidden support from men who were neither Calvinist nor godly.

An apologia was needed to defend moderation upon ground of Christian principle.

In the earlier years of the reign of Queen Elizabeth, it was not clear what the non-Calvinist school was teaching. They were not Lutheran, for few of them accepted the Lutheran doctrine of the eucharist, and many of them accepted as true the Calvinist doctrine of predestination. The Thirty-Nine Articles, which reached their final form in 1571 and to which assent was demanded from the clergy, taught the classical doctrines of the Reformed Protestants, that men are justified by faith alone, that the grace of sacraments is received only by men of faith, that the Church can teach nothing which Scripture does not contain.

If Elizabethan bishops had a guide to doctrinal authority, they looked to Bullinger of Zurich, with whom several of them had been friendly during their exile under Queen Mary. They were united by loyalty to the queen and to the national settlement of religion, and by resistance to the Calvinist who refused to accept that settlement. They did not argue, at first, that bishops were apostolic, or even that they were the best mode of Church government. They argued that the English government of Church and State might lawfully organize the Church with bishops, and if they so organized it they were not repudiating the authority of Scripture. Thus far they were like the Lutherans; concerned, because they were the defenders of the moderation of Elizabeth and Parker, to show that abuse does not necessarily forbid use; that it was a false principle and 'rotten pillar' to assert that nothing abused under the Pope may be retained in the Church.

Richard Hooker

In 1584 Richard Hooker was appointed Master of the Temple in London. His 'lecturer' – that is curate, over whom he had no control – was Walter Travers, who had been ordained by a foreign presbytery and was the author or part-author of the *Book of Discipline*, the standard of English Calvinist polity. Travers proposed that Hooker should not preach until the congregation issued its 'call'. Hooker refused the proposal, and master and lecturer preached against each other's doctrines, Canterbury versus Geneva – with Travers the more lively and popular, for Hooker was short-sighted and read his long manuscript dully, with eye close to the paper. Hooker then went to two country parishes in succession, Boscombe in Wiltshire and Bishopsbourne near Canterbury. To preach for Canterbury against Geneva demanded that Canterbury should say something as positive as the systematic Calvinism which it was opposing; and the outcome of this controversy was the classical defence of the moderate Elizabethan mode of reformation. Hooker designed *Of the Laws of Ecclesiastical Polity* in eight books. Books 1 to 4 were published in 1593, Book 5 in 1597. Hooker died in 1600. Books 6 and 8 appeared only in 1648, and Book 7 in the first complete edition of 1662. A long argument over the authenticity of these posthumous books has reached the conclusion that the bulk of them all is Hooker's work, though the possibility of deft touchings by interested hands, especially in Book 6, cannot quite be excluded.

The Calvinists contended that all things done in church must have positive warrant in Scripture, and on this ground attacked the English Prayer Book and the polity of the Elizabethan settlement. Hooker's defence was at bottom a justification of the place of reason in religion. Apart from that area where God has issued direct commands in the Scripture, there is a wide area where the government of Church and State must accord with the natural law of God, which may be known by the general reason of mankind and of which ecclesiastical or civil laws must seek to be the practical expression. Human laws do not moderate the details of practice for all time. Human society is changing, and a State or a Church may order whatever practice is edifying and expedient, provided its order obeys the Scripture law or is in harmony with the natural law. State and Church are united; and therefore the godly prince has the right and duty of legislating, in ecclesiastical polity as in civil, always provided that his laws are in harmony with natural law and not contradicted by Scripture. The literary beauty of Hooker's prose, and the measured tranquillity of his reasoning, raised the book far above the controversies of the age to which it was addressed.

It was a new note in Protestant thought. The union of Church and State, the justification of the power of godly princes in religion (a justification which went so far as to defend elements of the English polity which posterity has agreed with the Calvinists in thinking abuses), the general tradition of Swiss theological thought upon justification and the sacraments – there is little new here except the mode of expression. The momentous innovation was the rational method of defence, in which Hooker rested in part upon St Thomas Aquinas. The Reformation was becoming assured, when it could use the schoolmen instead of despising them.

But there is another novelty, besides the theoretical, in Hooker. Intent upon defending the Elizabethan settlement as wise, expedient, and Scripturally permissible, he devoted his fifth and longest book to the Prayer Book, so hotly attacked by its puritan critics. Through his serene apology comes an affection of the heart for this liturgy, seen against the background of a great tradition, not only as wise and expedient, but as a ripe fruit of the Christian centuries, bearing within itself the loveliness of a reformed and Catholic devotion.

Apostolic Succession

Hooker, at least in his earlier years, was not ready to contend for bishops as the only authorized ministry. He defended them, partly because the English settlement preserved them and he was defending the lawfulness of the entire settlement, and partly because he valued the customs of the Catholic centuries which could not be shown to have been wrong. In the books published posthumously, he used stronger language upon the apostolic authority of bishops.

Among his contemporaries, some divines – Hadrian Saravia, Matthew Sutcliffe, Thomas Bilson, Lancelot Andrewes, John Overall – argued that bishops were part of the authentic ministry warranted by Christ. Hooker had pleaded that they were not unscriptural; this new group claimed that they were the ministry founded by Christ, demanded by Scripture and by apostolic practice. They believed in a divine authority, transmitted in the Church through the centuries. The Church was not at liberty to change the order established in the first age. They did not therefore infer that Lutheran or Calvinist churches upon the continent were not churches, for as yet they felt no sense of isolation from the broad reforming traditions of the Continent. The Continental reformations, they argued, had been less fortunate than the English. 'We do not deny,' wrote George Downham, 'that silver is good, though gold be better.' 'If our form be of divine right,' wrote Lancelot Andrewes to the Huguenot Peter Du Moulin, 'it does not follow from thence that there is no salvation without it, or that a church cannot exist without it. He is blind who does not see churches existing without it.'

To claim that bishops were of divine right in the Church was indeed an assault upon Calvinism. Though Lutherans often claimed powers for their superintendents or general-superintendents when controverting the Calvinist polity, this English claim was unique in the Protestant churches. Sweden, which also preserved its consecrated bishops in a conservative reformation, was too Lutheran to whisper such a claim during these years.

By 1590, therefore, it began to matter to some divines whether the English bishops were in line and succession to the bishops of the Middle Ages. In consequence, to deny this continuity began to matter to Roman Catholic fighters. If there was a claim that these Protestant bishops were Catholic bishops, it was suddenly important that the claim be repudiated.

The Nag's Head Story

About 1590, an old clergyman named Thomas Neal, formerly the professor of Hebrew at Oxford, who had been Bonner's chaplain and never truly reconciled to the Elizabethan Church, was said to be telling a remarkable story. It was rumoured that he claimed to have been present at the consecration of Archbishop Matthew Parker; that so far from attending it in due form at the chapel of Lambeth Palace, he had been present at a tavern in Cheapside, the Nag's Head; that there, because no Catholic bishop could be found to consecrate, Parker and others knelt upon the floor of the tavern before Scory, the deprived Edwardine Bishop of Chichester, and Scory had placed a Bible upon the neck of each, saying: 'Receive the power of preaching the Word of God sincerely.' This rumour circulated among the Catholic recusants at the turn of the century, and appeared at last in print. It was widely believed, and the question was the quarrel of the hour. In 1613 Francis Mason, chaplain to the Archbishop of Canterbury, produced the relevant extract from Parker's register in the Lambeth Library, a description of the consecration from the State Papers, and even an eye-witness, the Earl of Nottingham (formerly Lord Howard of Effingham, commander of the English fleet against the Armada), who claimed to have been present at the consecration and the dinner which followed. In 1614, finding that the Roman Catholic writers asserted the register entry to be a forgery, Archbishop Abbot took four other bishops and four Roman Catholic priests, then imprisoned in the Tower of London, and caused them to examine the entry in the register. Though the rumour faded away into disrepute, it was a sign that the authenticity, or the reverse,

of the Protestant bishops had begun to matter to both sides
in a way that it would not have mattered to Calvin or
Luther.

The Study of the Fathers

The case for bishops proved to be more defensible than
could have been supposed half a century before. For
scholarship was not standing still, but was slowly improving
in critical and comparative power. In 1642 the Dutch
historian Gerhard Voss proved that St Athanasius had not
written the Athanasian creed. The Huguenot David
Blondel finally proved that the Isidorian decretals, which
had posed for 700 years as letters of early popes, were a
forgery of the ninth century. This scholarship was not
partial in shattering old tales. Blondel distressed fellow
Protestants by proving that the story of Pope Joan – who
was said to have succeeded to the papacy in male disguise
and given birth to a baby during a procession, a story much
used by Protestant warriors – was a late fabrication. The
two so-called epistles of St Clement were first printed at
Oxford in 1633. A Latin version of Ignatius of Antioch had
been printed by Lefèvre of Étaples in 1498, but nearly all
Protestant scholars believed the letters to be forged in favour
of bishops, until James Ussher showed (1644) that an un-
interpolated version was genuine. The discovery changed
the ground upon which the argument over the ministry
had been conducted since the days of Luther.

The advance of scholarship put St Augustine in a new
perspective. As the colossus among the early expounders
of St Paul, he dominated the Reformation. In 1600 or
1630 he was still the greatest of the Fathers. But it was
now plain that there was more variety and discrepancy
in the early Christian understanding of the Bible than
had hitherto been supposed by either side in the controversy.

The Fathers, it was found, supported the more radical

Protestants a little less, and the moderate conservatives a little more, than had been expected.

In the religious atmosphere of 1600–30 we sense a change of mood. Something fresh in the air of Protestantism is blowing through the palaces of doctrine and morals, coming mysteriously, impossible to seize and entrap. Part of it is the maturity of the Reformation: ripeness arising from security and growth, from the knowledge that the worst dangers are past; a readiness to appropriate the best devotions of the Catholic centuries where they are profitable; a willingness to study the philosophers, to read Plato and Aristotle, to use the schoolmen with discrimination. In the early days of reform they had to cry aloud for truth, and these cries could sound raucous and strident, the trumpet-notes of dogmatism. Though still sounding the trumpet in 1600, they were weaving the notes into a richer harmony of sound – prayer, the life of sanctification, the care of the troubled conscience, the place of the intellect in religion. You may discern the fresh wind across Europe, in many varied forms: in the noblest of Lutheran devotional writers, Johann Arndt; in the new metaphysical and mystical interests of English poets, from Spenser to Donne and Vaughan; in the Platonic philosophy of an Englishman like Thomas Jackson, or the idealism soon to be taught by the Cartesians in France; in the ethical inquiries of puritan and Jesuit divines; in the power which Spanish mysticism was beginning to exert in the Church of the Counter-Reformation.

> Teach me, my God and King,
> In all things thee to see.

In Spenser, Donne, Herbert, Jackson, Arndt, this nature mysticism, or consciousness of a sacramental universe, was eliciting among Protestants the attachment to an ancient and Catholic tradition of devotion, and so causing them to raise their eyes beyond the Reformed churches and take a larger view. A wider horizon must benefit the conservatives of the Reformation. It encouraged Lutheran affection for traditional modes of prayer, or English attachment to liturgical worship.

The fortress of Calvinist teaching was assailable in its two weak bastions: whether the dogma of absolute predestination, however supported by texts of Scripture, was not incompatible with other texts of Scripture and with the total revelation of God's nature; and whether the text of the New Testament vindicated the claim that the polity of pastors, elders, and consistories was the only polity ordered by Scripture.

ARMINIUS

Jacob Arminius studied under Beza at Geneva, travelled in Italy, and was a professor at the University of Leyden in Holland from 1603 until his death in 1609. The other professor of divinity was Francis Gomar, a Calvinist with an inflexible mind and a conscientious talent for setting the eternal decrees in their most repellent guise. Arminius began to contend that the New Testament revealed a loving God and that this was incompatible with the interpretation which consigned many mortals to hell without regard to their conduct. The controversy between Gomarist and Arminian waxed warm; and after the death of Arminius forty-six ministers assented to a document known as the *Remonstrance*. This declared that election to eternal life is conditional upon good works in this life, that grace can be resisted and lost, that Christ died for all men. The Remonstrants introduced into the argument an attack upon a Church independent of the State, and thus the doctrinal conflict became entangled with Dutch politics.

In 1618–19 the Reformed Churches held a synod at Dort, the assembly which came nearest to being a General Council of the Reformed Churches. It was attended by delegates from England, Scotland, Switzerland, Hesse, the Palatinate, and all the main churches of the Swiss tradition – except the French Huguenots, who were discouraged by their government, and the Elector of Brandenburg, because most of his subjects were Lutheran. The synod confronted the Arminians, now led by Simon Episcopius. In so large an assembly of the Reformed, including even an English bishop, it was impossible to canonize the extreme language of Gomar. But the synod determined that the cause of election is the pure grace of God, without regard to good works, that grace once given cannot be lost altogether, that Christ died only for the elect, that grace is irresistible. The States-General banished the Arminians, who refused to conform.

Episcopius and the banished leaders took refuge across the border in the Spanish Netherlands or in France. After 1625 they achieved a toleration in Holland, in 1630 they were permitted to build a church at Amsterdam, and in 1634 to establish a seminary. Protesting partly against Calvinism on grounds of reason, Episcopius led them slowly into a more rationalist and anti-dogmatic attitude towards all creeds and formularies, and they began to have affinities with the Socinians. They always remained a tiny community (twenty-six churches or chapels by 1841) but eminent in scholars like Gerhard Voss, Hugo Grotius, and Jean Leclerc. The Arminians were the first sign in Christendom of that rational anti-dogmatic school which was to take the leadership of Protestantism by the end of the seventeenth century.

THE STUART KINGS AND THE ENGLISH BISHOPS

It was not necessary for a 'godly prince' to be an episcopalian; it was necessary for him to keep control of the consistory and the laws of the Church. In north Germany this was often achieved through 'superintendents' or 'general-superintendents', in Sweden and England through bishops. In the Calvinist churches the consistory amounted to an assembly elected by clergy or people, with a claim to legislate apart from the secular authority. 'No bishop no king,' said James I of England at the Hampton Court Conference of 1604 – with the more feeling, because ever since he could remember anything, he had been trying to strengthen the weak royal authority in Scotland amid the claims of the presbyteries and the sermons of the pastors. His son Charles I might have kept his head upon his shoulders and a semblance of power if he had been willing to compromise upon the equation 'no bishop no king'. Therefore both these kings steadily discouraged the puritans and encouraged the anti-puritan party within the Church of England. Charles I began his reign by asking for a list of clergy to promote; and William Laud marked the list with the letters P (for Puritan) and O (for Orthodox). The antagonists of Calvinism were parading for the assault.

Something about an English king distinguished him from the godly prince of Germany or Sweden. While everyone agreed that a lawful ruler was called of God, and that obedience was a Christian duty, it would not have been so natural for a Lutheran to write that a divinity doth hedge a king. Offspring of an ancient line, crowned with the anointing of medieval ritual, he retained an aura of mystique which neither Renaissance nor Reformation at once dispelled. It is curious to find the Catholic king of France touching the scrofulous to heal them until a few years before the French Revolution. It is much more curious to find the Protestant sovereigns of England, from Elizabeth to James II, continuing to perform the same ritual cures, and to note that the last reigning sovereign to touch was Queen Anne in 1714. (A lady asked George I to touch her – he let her touch him.) King James I had been educated in Scotland, undertook the duty reluctantly, and began his first rite by preaching a sermon against superstition. But this reluctance faded, and Charles I had no qualms. The supernatural aura of the anointed head was long in dying, and must be reckoned with when judging the unusual English forms of the doctrine of divine right.

The English Bible

The first achievement of the Stuarts became one of the greatest legacies of the English Reformation: the Authorized Version of the Bible.

Twice the government of England had authorized a Bible for reading in parish churches, and ordered church-wardens to buy it: the Great Bible issued by Cromwell and Cranmer in 1539; the Bishops' Bible of 1568. To authorize a version was part of moderate reformation. The Great Bible had been planned to drive out the unofficial versions, like that of Tyndale, with their too acrimonious notes and comments. These various versions were not independent translations. Each grew out of its predecessor, using the old when it was good, and many phrases of Tyndale's came right through all the versions.

But in the Elizabethan age neither of the authorized versions rivalled the most popular of the unofficial versions – 'the Geneva Bible'. The English exiles at Geneva during the reign of Queen Mary published in 1557 a revised translation of the New Testament, a complete Bible in 1560. This was a careful revision of the Great Bible, in the light of the scholarship of Calvin and Beza and contemporary French versions. This version is popularly known as the Breeches Bible, because in Genesis 3.7 Adam and Eve 'sewed fig-leaves together and made themselves breeches'.

This was not only a scholarly edition and an improvement of style. It included maps and tables, and was the first English Bible to possess verse numbers, which had been introduced by the printer Robert Étienne in his Geneva edition of 1551. (Étienne is said to have numbered the New Testament while journeying from Paris to Lyons.) Verse numbers were a startling new convenience to readers, preachers, and students; and the Genevans further considered the convenience of the reader by producing an admirable and cheap edition for the pocket. The appearance of the Biblical page was never changed after the Genevan

Bible of 1560, and became sacred: printed in Roman type, following Beza's custom of using italics for words supplied in translation, and with the verse divisions. It was now much easier to find a single text, less easy to follow a continuous story or a sustained Pauline argument.

King James I did not form his view of scholarship by impartial inquiry, for he unjustly believed the Genevan Bible to be 'the worst', finding its notes to be 'very partial, untrue, seditious, and savouring too much of dangerous and traitorous conceits'. But he cared much for the matter, selected some forty-seven scholarly translators, and provided inadequately for their remuneration by church preferments. They were divided into six companies, of which two met at Oxford, two at Cambridge, and two in London, and these distributed the books of the Bible between them. Ordered to follow the Bishops' Bible of 1568 and not to alter without necessity what the people were accustomed to hear, they nevertheless adopted much from the Genevan Bible, and something from the Douai Bible which the Roman Catholic recusants published in 1582–1610. They were required not to add the controversial notes whereby Geneva had given offence. When the revision had been completed at the three centres, it was reviewed by a commission of twelve, and then by Bishop Bilson of Winchester and Dr Miles Smith, who reviewed the whole, put the finishing touches, and added a preface (by Smith) which is a noble statement of the aims of the translators in the context of the Reformation view of the Bible. Their object, they declared, was not to make a new translation, but to make an old one better.

A notice on the title page stated that it is 'appointed to be read in churches'. It does not appear that the use of other versions was thereby rendered illegal, but the king's printer was given the sole right to print and could prevent rival printers from issuing other versions. Even the New Testament of the Bishops' Bible was reprinted as late as 1618 or 1619, and its use is found at the end of the seventeenth century. The Genevan Bible continued to be widely used in popular devotion, and some puritans suspected the King James version as prelatical. It won its way slowly, and then on its merits of scholarship and literary form.

The slow growth of the English versions is evident in the Book of Common Prayer. The Psalms are printed almost as in the revised (1540) edition of the Great Bible, and being hallowed by recitation were not changed. The Magnificat and Nunc Dimittis are in a revised version of an independent translation made probably by Cranmer. The Epistles and Gospels were not changed to the King James version until 1662. The dates were not introduced into the margin of the Bible until 1701. They were based on the calculations of Archbishop Ussher of Armagh in his *Annales Veteris et Novi Testamenti* of 1650–4, which determined the creation of the world at 4004 B.C.

While the King James version was becoming hallowed, Greek scholarship was not standing still. Sixteen years after it appeared, the patriarch of Constantinople, Cyril Lucaris, gave the king of England the great Biblical manuscript of the early fifth century now known as the Codex Alexandrinus (in the British Museum). This was a better Greek manuscript than any known to the translators of King James. The task of scholarly revision was stored for the future.

The Laudians

The English anti-puritan school of religion, often called Laudian after its most eminent bishop,* was attacked by its enemies under the name 'Arminian'. The Arminians in Holland assailed the doctrine of the Calvinists, especially the doctrine of predestination. The episcopalians in England assailed the doctrine of the Calvinists, especially the doctrine of the presbytery. The difference was important; but hostile contemporaries were not wholly

* William Laud, Bishop of St David's 1621, of Bath and Wells 1626, of London 1628; Archbishop of Canterbury 1633; executed 1645.

wrong in using the word Arminian to describe the Laudians. A few of them repudiated the whole doctrine of predestination in its Augustinian form; many of them repudiated the extreme statements of it found among the Calvinists of the third generation.

But the momentous difference between puritan and episcopalian was rather devotional than doctrinal, even though doctrine guided devotion and devotion affected the language in which the doctrine was preached.

The episcopalian school had begun in a defence of the Prayer Book and the episcopal polity against its puritan critics. Thus was generated an association between the high* Anglicans and a care for external reverence, for due ritual and ceremonial, an association which amidst many vicissitudes has never been lost. Consider the phrasing of a poem *The British Church*, by George Herbert:

> A fine aspect in fit array,
> Neither too mean, nor yet too gay,
>   Shows who is best.
> Outlandish looks may not compare:
> For all they either painted are,
>   Or else undrest . . .

Then the poet contrasts her who sits over-painted upon the hills, and her who sits shyly in the valley improperly clad and with hair unruly:

> But, dearest Mother, what those miss
> The mean, thy praise and glory is,
>   And long may be.
> Blessed be God, whose love it was
> To double-moat thee with his grace,
>   And none but thee.

And none but thee – here is the claim to a uniquely favoured reformation. Evidently the poet is not so much concerned with truth as a sign of this favour. It is the 'fine aspect in fit

---

* The word *high* is an anachronism here. It was first used about 1687, to mean 'stiff for the Church of England', especially against dissent.

array', the due externals, the form and the liturgy, the reverence which is sober and not meretricious.

It is characteristic of the English Arminians that the most important works in that age, in the eyes of posterity, are not works of formal divinity, but two books of prayers; the *Manual of Private Devotions* (*Preces Privatae*) of Lancelot Andrewes, fetched mainly out of the Psalms and the ancient Greek liturgies, and given posthumously to the world in 1648; and *A Collection of Private Devotions, in the Practice of the Ancient Church*, published by John Cosin in 1627.* This latter was not formed in accordance with the Calvinist tradition and language of piety. It was first published for the benefit of the Protestant ladies at the court of the queen of Charles I, Henrietta Maria, whose Roman Catholic ladies used their breviaries in the royal antechambers, and was intended to be 'as like to their pocket offices as he could, with regard to the ancient forms before Popery'. Compare it with puritan books of piety, and you will find that the difference lies not in doctrinal content, but in devotional atmosphere. The eccentric puritan Prynne was scandalized because Cosin seized upon the more conservative parts of the Prayer Book and lifted them into prominence. Prynne was jarred by the word 'devotion', disliked the phrase 'ancient Church', the assumption that pictures and images were lawful, the open opportunity for private confession. Cosin claimed authority, especially from the early years of Queen Elizabeth. Prynne declared that in those years the Popish relics had not been so fully cleansed as afterwards, and that Cosin was wrongfully attempting to 'rack and screw them to our aged and noontide seasons of the Gospel'.

The Laudians reintroduced art into churches, stained glass windows, crosses, even crucifixes. They gloried in church music, and put back the organs which had been removed. They raised the holy table again upon steps, called it an altar, and fenced it with rails. (Sanctuary rails of the

* The famous version of the Veni Creator – 'Come Holy Ghost our souls inspire' – was written for this book.

sixteenth century are known; most rails in English parish churches are not earlier than the nineteenth century, but a high proportion of the older rails were installed under Laud or after the Restoration.) Laud used the secular authority vested in Star Chamber and High Commission to enforce reverent ornaments and conduct in church. He aimed at obedience and uniformity. He tried to compel clergymen to wear surplices, to repair their chancels, to bow at the holy name, to use the Prayer Book and no other. He mended decayed buildings. He attacked dirty linen, neglected sanctuaries, ecclesiastical courts subject to long delays and absurd litigation, ignorant or idle or immoral clergy, universities rent asunder, puritan lecturers building a church within a church. At Durham Cathedral, Cosin painted and gilded the statues.

The Catholic ethos of worship and prayer and liturgy, which Andrewes and Laud derived from the Book of Common Prayer, was not compatible with the doctrine or the worship of the English Calvinists. English divines who were controverting Calvinism were in no sense deriving their divinity from Arminius. Richard Montague, the Englishman who came nearest in doctrine to the Arminians of Holland, did not begin to read the writings of Arminius until May 1625, and he had already been attacking Calvinism for several years – 'All the Calvinists in the world, come on, I care not.' But Laud and his followers were abused, in Parliament and out of it, by the loose word Arminian, which their puritan opponents conceived as half-way towards popery. Probably the charge was not unjust. Montague, though with a measure of diplomacy, once gave the papal envoy Panzani to understand that he could accept all the articles of the Roman Catholic Church except transubstantiation, and told a friend that it was his duty to 'stand in the gap against puritanism and popery, the Scylla and Charybdis of ancient piety'.

In 1625 Nicholas Ferrar retired from a London and parliamentary career to Little Gidding in Huntingdonshire, was ordained deacon by Laud, and with the families of his brother and brother-in-law lived a community life. Twice a day they attended the offices in the tiny church, twice a day they had prayers in the house, and at every hour during the day some members of the community joined in a little office of prayer, so that the whole psalter was recited daily; and during the night at least two members of the household were watching, and the psalter was again recited. The community exercised charity towards the neighbouring folk, visited the sick and taught the children, and at home exercised their skills in binding and illustrating books. Though Ferrar died in 1637, the families continued their devotions until they were raided and dispersed by troops in 1646.

From 1621 to his death in 1631, the poet John Donne was dean of St Paul's. His sermons were the best examples of 'Laudian' preaching; perhaps the best examples of Protestant preaching. Their divinity was that of the Reformation, their language that of the age when English literature flowered.

Laud pursued a not contemptible ideal. Believing in the entire unity of Church and State, he wanted Church and State harmoniously to teach the people to do right, to respect authority, to be loyal and reverent.

The age when an archbishop could compel unwilling men to external reverence was passing. Leighton, Prynne, Bastwick, Burton, Lilburne – the names recall conscientious men, troublesome, fanatical, eccentric, being made public martyrs by losing their ears, being whipped through the streets, standing in the pillory. Critics of the English settlement had long ago been driven from office, the largest number between 1604 and 1607; but the effect of Laud's endeavour was to drive some of them towards nonconformity, flight beyond seas to Holland or the Americas, separation from the parish church, and resort to conventicles. At the accession of King James in 1603 the separatist movement of Baptists and Congregationalists was negligible in number. By 1641 it was still small, but no longer negligible. Intelligent men of stature had passed into separatism, and the high-minded imprudence of Laud was in part responsible.

England had tried to hold together a right wing and a left wing upon Cranmer's Reformed liturgy and Elizabeth's settlement; and the attempt seemed to be failing for ever, as the two wings of the Church, puritan and episcopalian, each claiming to be the authentic Church of England, each denouncing the other as faithless or disloyal, moved towards mutual exclusion, while Crown and Parliament turned towards civil war.

CHARLES I AND SCOTLAND

To repress the puritans of England was one thing, to repress the presbyterians of Scotland another. The Scots looked back upon a presbyterian Reformation.

King James I went slowly (which was wisely) about the task. Ridding himself of Andrew Melville, the most presbyterian of all the Scots, to a Continental exile, he restored step by step the diocesan jurisdiction of bishops in Scotland. In 1610 he fetched three of them to London to receive consecration from English bishops. In 1618 he caused five articles to be brought before an assembly at Perth. They required the Scots to receive five points of English practice – kneeling to receive the sacrament; private communion of the sick; baptism in private houses in case of necessity; confirmation of children by a bishop; the celebration of Christmas, Good Friday, Easter, Ascension, and Whitsunday. Though the assembly accepted the five articles by eighty-six votes to forty-one, they remained a dead letter in most parishes. It was hard enough to persuade a congregation suddenly to kneel even if they had not been taught for two generations that kneeling at the sacrament was unscriptural, perhaps idolatrous.

But undoubtedly the English polity was making its way slowly. The operation was less difficult than posterity has believed it. There was much moderate opinion in Scotland of the kind which in England disliked the puritans.

Charles I, succeeding to the throne in 1625, began his reign with an Act of Revocation which was intended to bring order into the church and crown lands of Scotland. It was suspected by the Scottish lords of being the first step towards questioning their right of possession. The surest way to raise ecclesiastical antagonists was to create insecurity in the breasts of those who had profited from the transfers of land at the first rush of reformation. James balanced the power of the nobility against that of the presbyterians, Charles threw the nobility into the arms of the presbyterians.

In 1633 Charles came to be crowned at Edinburgh, with Laud as his adviser and an elaborate liturgy of coronation which seemed popish to Scotsmen. In 1635 he appointed John Spottiswoode, Archbishop of St Andrews, to be Chancellor of the kingdom. In 1636 the bishops drafted canons for the Church of Scotland. Canon I declared excommunicate all those who denied the royal supremacy in causes ecclesiastical. The canons forbade extempore prayer in public worship, caused the holy tables to be replaced by altars, and contained no reference whatsoever to General Assembly, kirk session, presbytery, or elders.

The king and Laud wanted the Scottish bishops to receive the Book of Common Prayer, that there might be a uniform order for the whole kingdom. The bishops thought that the Scots would be readier to accept something not known to be English. The Scottish Book of Common Prayer, drafted by the bishops of Ross and Dunblane with Laud's advice, is of high interest as the liturgical programme of what was for the moment the strongest anti-Calvinist group in Protestantism; even stronger than the Lutherans, though the Lutherans were supported by the people and the Laudians by a minority, in that the liturgical and episcopalian tradition created minds almost as likely to assail Luther as Calvin, and in that they were backed by the sovereign of one of the great European states.

The book agreed in the main with the English book, but reverted to the more traditional atmosphere of the first (1549) English Prayer Book, with hints (at least) of a eucharistic sacrifice and prayers for the dead. It conceded something to Calvinist consciences by substituting the word *presbyter* for *priest* and omitting many lessons from the Apocrypha. In 1637 a royal proclamation at every market cross ordered this to be the only form of worship in Scotland and required every parish to buy two copies before Easter.

In the face of popular turmoil, the Scottish bishops postponed the introduction of the book. The king ordered them to proceed in St Giles's Cathedral in Edinburgh, on the fourth Sunday in July. As the dean began to read the service, an instant clamour interrupted him. The bishop tried to restore order, a stool and missiles were thrown,* and though the rioters were thrown out they continued outside, and roughly treated the bishop after service. The Scottish council promptly and willingly suspended the book.

King Charles, obstinate with the obstinacy which took him to the block, rebuked the council and insisted on the book. And so began the long course of tumult which led to the Scottish National Covenant, a solemn bond to resist the innovations recently introduced into the Kirk; and then to war, which linked the Scots with the Parliamentary malcontents in England, and at last to the Solemn League and Covenant of 1643, whereby English Parliamentarians and the Scots bound themselves to extirpate 'prelacy' and introduce a presbyterian polity in both the kingdoms of England and Scotland.

---

* The famous story that it was a vegetable-seller named Jenny Geddes who threw her stool at the bishop is first mentioned about 1670. A stool purporting to be the stool is preserved in the National Museum of Scotland.

CIVIL WAR AND CROMWELL

The English civil war was not a religious war; it was a battle over the constitution. But with the power of the king to rule and levy taxes and the rights of Parliament, the strife between Laudian and puritan was entangled. It now looked as though all that the puritans wanted would be established in the Church of England. An Act of Parliament abolished the Star Chamber and High Commission in 1641, another ejected bishops from the House of Lords in 1642. With the outbreak of civil war in 1642, the royalist members disappeared from London to the side of the king, and Parliament was left to begin its own reform of the Church in the parts of England where troops could enforce its law. An ordinance declared bishops, deans, and chapters to be abolished and their land to be confiscated.

The Execution of Laud

The fear of Roman Catholicism was a part of English patriotism. Laud and his party, the king and his Roman Catholic queen, roused fears, rational and irrational, that they were encouraging the Church of Rome. The king had pursued a foreign policy of friendship with Spain; the archbishop had restored into English parish churches customs or ornaments which many people associated with the Church of Rome. In 1641 the Irish Roman Catholics rose in revolt and massacred thousands of Protestants; and yet the king talked of using Irish troops to repress the Scottish and English rebels, and his secretary was found to have negotiated with the Pope for money and arms. A fear of 'barbarous' Irish invaders, and a fear of Rome, were in 1641 the same fear. And these fears, rational or irrational, were like a tumbril driving little Archbishop Laud, inflexible idealist, to the block.

The House of Commons resolved to accuse Laud of treason as early as December 1640. But, lodging him in the

Tower, they could not decide what to do with him. In May 1643 there was a rumour that he would be banished to America. That autumn they resolved to put him on trial. The solicitor for the prosecution was William Prynne, who claimed to have lost his ears at Laud's command and who had no belief that emotion should be kept out of law courts. Laud was charged with attempting to overthrow the rights of Parliament, with levying ship money illegally, and with trying to overthrow the reformed religion of England and to reconcile the Church of England to the Church of Rome. The evidence was an incongruous medley of crucifixes, altar rails, letters to Roman Catholic priests, and persecuted puritans. The prosecution failed, as well it might, to prove treason in the courts. Accordingly a Bill of Attainder was brought into Parliament; the cries of the London mob conquered the reluctance of the peers, and the Long Parliament, in executing Laud, took a step in the course whereby Englishmen would for years associate the puritan programme with injustice and illegality.

The Westminster Assembly

The House of Commons, engaged in appropriating executive powers which hitherto had belonged to the king, was inclined to take a parliamentary form of the royal supremacy and govern the Church as it governed the State. It appointed ministers to parishes; created committees to administer the confiscated revenues; controlled pew rents; declared that Scottish pastors might become English incumbents; appointed a committee to eject scandalous ministers and a committee to relieve plundered ministers. It recognized that the ministers must be consulted, and summoned to Westminster an assembly of 121 ministers and thirty lay members of Parliament. This assembly met in the Jerusalem Chamber of the Dean's Lodging, and sat from 1643 to 1649.

Believed by some of its members to be like a national assembly of a Reformed Church, with all the authority of such an assembly, it was believed by the Commons to be the adviser of the Commons. The leading ministers of the assembly were Presbyterians and Calvinists, and wished to establish in the Church of England the disciplinary system of elders and presbyteries. Like the governments of other Calvinist countries, Parliament was unwilling to concede these far-reaching powers of discipline and excommunication.

The Westminster Assembly contained others besides convinced Presbyterians. English lawyers like John Selden, distrustful of clerical domination of every kind and therefore of all forms of Calvinist polity, determined to keep the lay control of the Church as a safeguard of reasonable liberty in opinion and morals. There were ten or eleven Independents in the assembly, who talked a great deal and resisted at every turn the legal establishment of presbyterianism, fearing with reason that the new presbyteries would repress the Independents. It was in this sense that Milton wrote his famous line, so hostile to the presbyterians – 'new presbyter is but old priest writ large'.

The military alliance with the Scots against the king, the Solemn League and Covenant of 1643, of which one condition was the quest for a uniform church polity in England and Scotland, drove the Commons to accept more of the presbyterian claim than its members liked. An ordinance divided London into twelve 'classes'; another abolished the use of the Book of Common Prayer and replaced it with the Directory of Public Worship, a much more flexible order of worship deriving from the Scottish, and so remotely from the Genevan, tradition. In 1645 Parliament ordered the establishment of presbyteries throughout the land, and the election of elders. But it refused to concede to these presbyteries the unrestricted right of excommunication. The elders might excommunicate only if certain clear offences were committed, and for any other offences they might only excommunicate if it were sanctioned by the parliamentary commissioners in that province. The Westminster Assembly petitioned against this system and secured a small modification, but still there was the right of appeal from the elders to a parliamentary committee.

In 1646 the system, in theory, began to work. In practice it worked, not without inefficiency, in London and Lancashire and in other scattered areas. All incumbents must take the Covenant and must use the Directory. The Assembly, which began by trying to revise the Thirty-Nine Articles in a Calvinist sense, preferred to draft a new formulary of faith, the Westminster Confession, and the doctrinal parts of this Confession were ratified by Parliament. It contains a well-phrased and uncompromising statement of Calvinist divinity, and soon became the classic exposition of English and Scottish presbyterian doctrine. It is still the formula to which the candidate for the Scottish ministry must give a (general) assent. The Assembly also prepared a longer and shorter catechism, and the shorter catechism became the customary catechism in Scotland and later among English nonconformists.

Except in Scotland, the work of the Westminster Assembly was ephemeral.

Parliament never ruled the whole country. Even the instructions about taking the Covenant were widely disobeyed. Richard Baxter, later the leader of the English presbyterians, prevented his people at Kidderminster from taking the Covenant, and persuaded the ministers of Worcestershire not to offer it to the people. And when at last the king was beaten at Naseby in 1645 and the whole country made its peace, the armies, and not the Parliament, ruled the country. In name they were the armies of the Parliament; but the troops felt loyalty to their commanders, not to Westminster, and from 1647 the army became a rival of the Parliament in the struggle for power.

Robert Baillie, one of the Scottish envoys to the Westminster Assembly, confessed that the presence of the Scottish army was the mainstay of the presbyterian establishment in England. For the English army was rather independent than presbyterian in its leadership. Oliver Cromwell and many of his colonels believed in liberty of worship. Among their troopers the officers often conducted prayers or preached sermons. They wanted liberty of worship for themselves, and for the numerous little Independent or Baptist congregations which sprang up in the country through the absence of repressive discipline during the war. Some of them adopted republican opinions, while the majority in Parliament still aimed at a constitutional monarchy. A few adopted the opinions of a Leveller democracy. Parliament played into their hands by failing to pay them before they were disbanded. And so the army came to rule the country.

The Execution of Charles I

The king's death was necessary to the republican party. The fanatical party among the soldiery thought that they were the Lord's instruments in beheading the king. The execution was thought wicked by the English and Scottish presbyterians. But the presbyterians gained no reputation in English posterity by their resistance. Ultimately the king's death benefited no ecclesiastical party but the old episcopalians. The destruction of the king and its consequences ensured at last that of the two old schools of religion in Protestant England (puritan or episcopalian), it was the second which would secure the leadership of the Church of England.

The king himself believed in the episcopal tradition; and upon theological as well as political ground. He was as capable as any of his bishops at arguing the Scriptural texts with Scottish divines. His death not only evoked a European sympathy, but in some eyes made him, like Laud, a martyr for the episcopal polity and the Book of Common Prayer. Shortly after his death appeared *Eikon Basiliké*, a portrait of the king's last hours with what were alleged to be his private devotions, and fifty editions, despite attempts at suppression, appeared during 1649. Its frontispiece showed the king kneeling at a table, on which was the Bible, his royal crown lying on the floor, in his right hand a crown of thorns, and his eyes elevated to a crown of glory above.

Written by a moderate churchman, John Gauden, it helped to turn Charles from the king executed by rebels into the martyr persecuted by fanatics.

The Church under Cromwell

The end of civil war in England created a religious condition hitherto unique in Christian history – a great state under a military ruler who himself preferred Independency, looked to the best of the little but now growing groups as the finest religious force of his commonwealth, and used as one of his secretaries the greatest of Independent publicists, John Milton. It was difficult to create a religious establishment out of earnest men who denied that the magistrate could rightly intervene in religion; and the bulk of the country was still inclined to be moderate Anglican or Presbyterian. Even under Cromwell, the Independents were a minority on the fringe of the establishment. But the Independent ideal secured, for the first time in any large state, toleration. This toleration had limits. The papists were excluded as disloyal to England; the high Anglicans were excluded as disloyal to the régime, and were forbidden to use the Book of Common Prayer. Nevertheless it was a régime of genuine toleration. In 1650 the Act compelling attendance at the parish church was repealed. The Englishman was still compelled to go to corporate worship on Sundays; but since such compulsion was not enforceable, this repeal was important to Cromwellian religious liberty. Though Cromwell preferred a godly puritanism, his establishment was liberal enough to allow the spread of ideas, mystical and critical, latitudinarian and rational, enthusiastic and pietistic, which allowed the religious thought of England to push its elbows out of the ropes in which Laud or the Westminster Assembly preferred to confine it.

The control of a new and broader establishment was allotted under Parliament to the Committee of Triers, who had the sole power of examining the fitness of candidates for pastoral office. The committee of 1654 numbered thirty-eight, and was composed of Presbyterians and Independents, with a few Baptists. An Independent, John Owen, greatest of Congregational theologians, became Dean of Christ Church and Vice-Chancellor of Oxford University; others became the heads of Magdalen College, University College, and Jesus College in Oxford, of Pembroke Hall in Cambridge, and of Trinity College Dublin. Their administration was rarely helpful to scholarship. The apartments in Whitehall, once occupied by Archbishop Laud, from 1650 were occupied by the vehement Independent Hugh Peters, chaplain to the Council of State. In 1653 the 'Barebones' Parliament attempted to test whether the country could be governed on purely Biblical principles, and the Independent congregations had their due part in nominating members to that futile assembly. Independent congregations met in some of the great churches of the country – Westminster Abbey, Canterbury, and other cathedrals. A little group of Fifth Monarchy men met for a time in a corner of St Paul's Cathedral. Exeter Cathedral was divided by a brick wall, with a Presbyterian congregation on one side and an Independent congregation on the other. In Chester and Dover and Bristol the Congregational church met in the castle, doubtless because it was strong among the troopers of the garrison. In 1658 the Independent churches came together, above-ground at last, to a national conference at the Savoy, and from 100 to 120 Independent congregations sent representatives to the confernce. By 1660 about 130 Independent ministers were incumbents in Cromwell's 'established' church; some of them had been elected thereto by the congregations, but it is a mark of the breadth in the movement that many others had accepted appointment at the hands of a patron. There were still a few Congregational churches, as at Bury St Edmunds, who preferred to remain outside even an establishment designed to suit Congregationalists. The state and incomes of the 'established' clergy were much helped by government grants from the old lands of bishops and chapters.

The attempt was swept away in the Restoration of King Charles II. But the events of the Civil War, the Commonwealth, and Protectorate ensured that in England, as in New England, Congregationalists and Baptists had come to be a permanent feature of religious life. It was impossible to go back successfully to the repressions of Archbishop Laud.

The Quakers

The religious confusions of the English civil wars afforded a unique opportunity for little groups of every kind, conventional or unconventional. Blasphemous cranks or odd zealots, who in an age accustomed to toleration would have caused little comment, were so shocking to contemporary opinion that Presbyterians chronicled and catalogued the heresiarchs and their 'doxies', made lists such as Christendom had not seen since St Epiphanius catalogued his heresiarchs towards the end of the fourth century. The apocalyptic streak made its appearance again. There were the Fifth Monarchy men, who intended to bring in the monarchy promised in Daniel 2.44, where Christ should reign upon earth for a thousand years. There were the Muggletonians, adherents of an eccentric London tailor who claimed that he and his cousin were the two witnesses of Revelation chapter 11, rejected preaching, and taught that only preachers with short-cut hair should be heard and that reason was made by the devil. And many others are to be found in the catalogues, with little opportunity for the historian to penetrate behind what they are said to have taught to the reality which they taught. The corpulent constable Richard Sale walked through the streets of Derby, barefoot, dressed in sackcloth, ashes on his head, sweet flowers in his right hand and stinking weeds in his left. In November 1652 a Furness tailor named James Milner, after fasting for fourteen days, prophesied that Thursday 2 December would be the first day of the new creation, when a four-cornered sheet carrying a sheep would be let down from heaven. It is important to remember these events when contemplating the next generation and its fear of enthusiasm. Most of these upsurges of piety died with their originators. A few were destined to a long history, even the Muggletonians lasting as a tiny group into the reign of Queen Victoria.

Upon the extreme radical wing of those ideas which were still known as Anabaptist, the piety was usually marked by a fierce reaction against all external forms. The Reformation had been a protest against institutionalism, against substituting external forms for an inward reality, against salvation by the purchase of an indulgence instead of true contrition. Far to the left wing, the simple and earnest 'mechanick' questioned the utility of all forms. Many Independents denounced the use of set patterns of liturgy that all worship might be 'free'. In the Civil War there were groups of Seekers, who waited for the direct inspiration of the Spirit and felt a repugnance from all external forms, even the sacraments, even the reading of the Bible.

Of all these groups, one alone, as odd as many others in its origins, survived and outgrew the bizarre touch of its birth, and at last would command public and national respect – the Society of Friends, to call it by its title of a century and a half later. Fox's first adherents came from existing cells of Seekers.

George Fox (1624–91)

George Fox was the son of a godly weaver of Fenny Drayton in Leicestershire and of a mother who was 'of the stock of the martyrs'. He was apprenticed to a shoemaker, but at the age of nineteen, as the Civil War began, he became a wandering Seeker, not attending churches – 'steeple-houses', as he called them – but walking in the fields or orchards with his Bible. His family prescribed marriage, others said he should join the army, a clergyman advised tobacco and psalm-singing. About 1647 or 1648 he became an evangelist with a Gospel. Part of his message was that of many Anabaptists – a repudiation of oaths and military service, a radical suspicion of external forms of religion, a belief that the simplest might wait upon the Spirit and that

learning and study afforded no advantage in interpreting
the Bible – 'the Lord opened unto me that being bred at
Oxford or Cambridge was not enough to fit and qualify men
to be ministers of Christ, and I stranged at it, because it
was the common belief of people.' The practice of silent
prayer at meetings was common among the Mennonite
Waterlanders. Part of Fox's message is found among the
more mystical of the Anabaptist groups of the sixteenth century, a Denck or Schwenckfeld,* or later a Boehme; a message which in essence was the old immediacy of the medieval
German and English mystics like Tauler and the author of
The Cloud of Unknowing, yet stripped of the Catholic and
traditional environment of monastic practice. We need no
external guide, no minister, no authority, for we have
immediate knowledge of the Christ within, the 'inner light',
the seed of divinity within the soul. It has been argued that
this teaching is so similar, sometimes even in its phrases, to
the earlier mystic indwelling preached by radical Protestants that Fox must have received their direct influence,
especially that of Jakob Boehme. But Fox has not been
proved to have known Boehme, and probably the way of
approach or cast of mind was found among those groups of
Seekers who were the earliest home of his spirit.

Mysticism lodges in the breasts of an élite; and in the
contemporary atmosphere to persuade the tinkers and the
bagmen to dwell upon the light within was to invite the
eccentric. Fox himself learnt in the spirit to refuse to bow
or to take off his hat to anyone,† to use the pronouns *Thee*

---

* Caspar Schwenckfeld (1490–1561), who taught an unsacramental
mysticism of indwelling, sought to create no community, but his disciples
continued. By 1618 the group survived only in Silesia. In 1734 about
200 emigrated to Philadelphia and there is now a Schwenckfelder Church
in Pennsylvania, with a membership of between 2,000 and 3,000.

† At Launceston Assizes in 1656 the judge ordered the hat off, and
asked for Scriptural evidence in favour of keeping it on. Fox replied:
'Thou mayest read in the third of Daniel that the three children were
cast into the fiery furnace by Nebuchadnezzar's command, with their
coats, their hose, and their hats on.'

and *Thou* to all men and women whether they were rich or poor, never to say *Good evening*, never to call the days of the week or the months of the year by their names but only by their numbers. He was driven by his spirit to enter the Church of St Mary at Nottingham and denounce the preacher in the midst of his sermon; in the Midland counties he kept interrupting services, was beaten by an enraged congregation at Mansfield-Woodhouse, was put in the stocks and in several gaols. At Lichfield he went up and down the streets in unshod feet upon market day, crying: 'Woe unto the bloody city of Lichfield!' He approved of one William Simpson, who testified against London by walking naked through the streets; he taught the conviction of moral perfection, present as Christ's perfection, and almost a personal infallibility, of spirit-inspired utterance. His rival for the leadership of the movement, James Nayler, whom Fox converted to the inner light in 1651, began to allow himself to be worshipped as the Son of God; and in October 1656 Nayler entered Bristol in a downpour, riding upon a horse with his followers strewing garments in the way and crying 'Holy, Holy, Holy'. There was in the earliest years little to distinguish Quakers from other fanatics. Indeed the name *Quakers* was originally applied to another group, and transferred to Fox by way of abuse.

They were preserved for posterity, partly by the profound nature of some of their teaching, partly because Fox could inspire an extraordinary devotion (and not only from the easily enraptured), and partly by the growth in the stature of Fox himself. As he matured, he proved to possess a hard head, well capable of distinguishing the practicable from the absurd. In 1652 he interrupted a service at Ulverston Church, and his words struck the squire's lady in the congregation, Margaret Fell of Swarthmore Hall. She gave him refuge, and her husband, an eminent lawyer, was pacified on his return. There is no doubt that the Fells helped Fox to a riper understanding of humanity and of the world. After Fell's death he married the widowed Margaret (1669).

Fox proved to have organizing capacity. He was quick to recognize the disadvantage to Quakers through refusal of baptism and church marriage, and instituted a system of registration of births, marriages, and deaths – a record which was to be invaluable until a national system of registration was created in 1836. By 1670 his Friends of the Truth had found stability, without losing the doctrine of indwelling light and the unsacramental quietism which was their reason for existence.

The Episcopalians

From 26 August 1645 the Book of Common Prayer was forbidden, even in family worship, under penalty of a year's imprisonment. But the ordinance establishing the Directory never received royal assent, and in the eyes of the royalists could not repeal the Act of Parliament establishing the Book of Common Prayer. Loyalty to the liturgy became part of loyalty to the Crown.

The ordinance was not uniformly enforced. When the decapitated body of King Charles I was brought for burial to St George's at Windsor, the mourners asked that Bishop Juxon might read the funeral service in the Book of Common Prayer; and the governor of the castle declared that the Directory was the only permitted form. But in private chapels and drawing-rooms a few clergy and laity continued to use the old liturgy, and even Oliver Cromwell's daughter Mary was married according to its rite. A few retired bishops continued to ordain quietly from their retreat. Parish priests got round the law by reciting the Prayer Book from memory, or by inserting minor alterations, or by framing their own liturgy out of Prayer Book materials. Strict Anglicans believed that this tampering with the liturgy was as illegal as the use of the Directory. But there was no attempt to organize a Church underground. Of the bishops, Juxon retired to his country seat and his fox-hunting; Wren was imprisoned in the Tower; Brownrigg is believed never to have visited his diocese of Exeter during seventeen years;

Duppa said: 'I secure myself . . . as the tortoise doth, by not going out of my shell.' The bishops remembered the days of war and the execution of Laud, and preferred obscurity to valour. Stories in another sense became famous; how the aged Bishop Morton, asked by a traveller for his name, replied: 'I am that old man, the Bishop of Durham, notwithstanding all your votes.' The surviving bishops rarely felt it prudent or possible to act in this spirit.

Something like 3,000 incumbents were ejected by Parliamentary committees. Early in the eighteenth century Dr John Walker compiled a martyrology entitled *The Sufferings of the Clergy*, in which amid infinite labour and much valuable material he reckoned the number of dispossessed incumbents at about 10,000, as though the clergy of the Church of England were almost all episcopalians staunch enough to suffer. The calculation rested upon an assumption that the episcopalians were as dominant in 1645 as they were after 1662; and this is not true. About two thirds of the parishes in the Church of England were not disturbed by the ecclesiastical changes.

But in the retirement of the London streets and of the English countryside, in the exile of Paris and the Hague, the strict episcopal school was identified with the royal cause. The young King Charles caused grief and hesitation by negotiating with the Scottish Presbyterians, and even on one occasion by signing the Covenant. But after 1653 there were no more vacillations. The cause of the king was the cause of 'the Church of England' and the cause of the Church of England was the cause of the king; and by 'the Church of England' was meant the Book of Common Prayer and the polity of bishops, priests, and deacons. The Cavalier squire, who in 1641 hated the bishops like a puritan, now looked hopefully for their revival with the return of the king. The repression was too tolerant to kill the Laudian school, it was persecuting enough to renew the word *puritan* in a yet more odious sound. 'I,' wrote the gentle Sancroft, 'look upon that cursed puritan faction as the ruin of the most glorious Church upon earth!' The presbyterians might resent the execution of the king, might wish for Charles II, might dislike the Independents and the government of Cromwell; but they had opened the floodgates of revolution, and in the eyes of the strict royalists they were cast with Cromwell into a common pit of damnation.

For the first time in the history of the Reformation, English Protestant churchmen were now refusing communion with the Reformed churches of the Continent. The episcopalian exiles were not quite agreed upon the point, for John Cosin argued that communion with the Huguenots was lawful. But he was the exception. The Huguenots had presbyteries, the very name was ill-sounding, and Huguenot pastors were unpalatably sympathetic towards the puritan régime in England, seeming to excuse the 'impiety' which had overthrown the old polity of the Church of England.

The restoration of Charles II in 1660 brought with it the restoration of the Prayer Book and the bishops. But in important respects it was impossible to return to the state of the Church before the civil wars.

First, the Church of 1641 was restored, not the Church of 1640. Star Chamber and High Commission were not revived. The High Commission had been the English form of a Lutheran consistory, the ecclesiastical court through which the royal supremacy was effectively exercised. No adequate substitute was provided. The result was therefore an unwitting comprehensiveness. Cromwell left English religion more varied. It could no longer be narrowly confined by a machinery of discipline. The limits of opinion and practice within the Church of England were thereafter to be widened steadily.

Secondly, the religious cleavages were deeper. In the age of Cromwell the high churchman had grown higher, the puritan more decisive in his resistance to bishops and Prayer Book. English nonconformity was henceforth permanent within the national life.

Thirdly, the rulers of the Church of England had been made more conservative than ever. The Calvinists wanted reform, and had failed. By the mode of their failure it became difficult to reform anything, and various medievalisms long disapproved by reformers were preserved in England until the nineteenth century or beyond. It was a puritan saying that Queen Elizabeth swept the Church of England and left the dust behind the door. The civil war consecrated even the dust. This unusual conservatism applied above all to the Prayer Book. Hallowed first by the burning of its chief author and of the Marian martyrs, and then by the customary growth of holy association, it received a new sacredness from its 'illegal' abolition. It was now part of the constitution, of allegiance to the crown, of legality. Thus it became more difficult to make alterations of substance in the Prayer Book, whether it were desired to relieve puritan consciences or later to adjust the devotions of the people to the needs of new generations.

Lastly, the Protestant Churches were further divided. Since Zwingli disagreed with Luther, the Protestants had been divided into Lutheran or Reformed. But despite the rising political power of Lutheran Scandinavia, the Reformed Churches took the lead, and as late as 1620 it seemed possible that with England in the Reformed camp a harmonious alliance would be achieved.

The collapse of the puritan school in England ended these hopes. Reformed divinity henceforth encountered the criticism, not only of the north Germans, but of a powerful body of English high churchmen; while, amid the little groups of English nonconformists and with growing power across the Atlantic, Congregationalists and Baptists refused to accept the Calvinist polity.

The English civil wars were not only momentous for the history of English and Scottish religion. They affected all the posterity of the Protestant Reformation.

Part Two

THE COUNTER-REFORMATION

8

The Counter-Reformation

CATHOLIC REFORMATION

THE name of Counter-Reformation suggests a fight against Protestantism. There was a political aspect of the Counter-Reformation, a league of Catholic powers ready to crusade against the new Protestant states. There was also a true sense in which the fight against Protestantism encouraged the reforming movement within the Roman Catholic Church. But it did not create it. The conflict with Protestantism gave to reform a new edge, to cut through the vested interests and administrative conservatism which everywhere frustrated reform. It gave to reform a dynamic, a vitality, an affection for ancient ways, and a mistrust of Protestant ways.

The vested interests were so powerful that no reformation, not even a Catholic reformation, was possible without an increase in the power of the secular state. Part of the difficulty was the independent power of the Church within each state. Part of the difficulty was the interest of the Roman court in maintaining all its financial and legal rights throughout the Church. Even a Catholic Reformation, in Spain, France, or Southern Germany, had as one consequence a further restraint upon the power of Rome in those countries, and derived its effective impetus as much from Catholic sovereigns as from the moral and intellectual leadership of popes or divines.

The fight against the Mohammedans in southern Spain welded Spanish State and Church into a unity of crusading fervour. The Spanish crown already exercised a decisive power over the Church through the Inquisition, which was a royal weapon, and through the normal restraints which a national monarchy placed upon papal action. By 1550 the wealth of the newly discovered Americas was flowing into Spain; and new economic power, joined to the political status given by royal marriages, elevated the country to a leading place in the states of Europe. After 1562, France, split in two, was out of the political race, and Spain became the strongest power in Europe, without rival in means or in influence. By its rule of the Duchy of Milan and of Naples and Sicily it was able to dominate Italy, and the old titanic conflict of the Middle Ages between Pope and Emperor turned itself into petty bickerings between Pope and Spanish king; but only bickerings, for after 1562 the Pope depended as politically upon the king of Spain as ever medieval Popes had depended upon Saxon or Hohenstaufen or Angevin. Spain led the rest of Europe in military prowess, navigation, discovery. Spanish Catholicism was like a magnet, attracting towards itself the Catholicism of the Counter-Reformation.

Cardinal Ximenes, primate of Spain from 1495 to 1517, conducted a reformation of the Spanish Church on lines which would have been traditional if the royal power had not been so directly engaged. He enforced poverty among the monks and friars; dissolved religious houses which failed to conform to his standards, or stripped them of their endowments and devoted the revenues to hospitals or to impoverished monasteries; compelled incumbents to reside upon their benefices, to expound the Scriptures, and to educate children; and created the university of Alcalá, designed to train scholastic theologians and the clergy, where the study of the Hebrew and Greek languages was encouraged.

Here the leading scholars, some of them imported from Italy, warmly adopted the reforming and critical ideas of Erasmus. In the Spanish Netherlands, Vives edited St Augustine and devised enlightened schemes of education. Perhaps in no other country in Europe were the principles of Erasmus so zealously adopted, by a few eminent men, as a guide to reform. They were subjected to a battery of criticism in 1520–2 by a heresy-hunter, Zuniga, who tried to persuade the Spanish that Erasmus was responsible for Luther, but without evident success. Alcalá rivalled Salamanca for the intellectual primacy of Spain. Between 1502 and 1517 a group of scholars, under the personal direction of Ximenes, produced the Polyglot Bible in six volumes, a Bible in Hebrew, Greek, and Latin texts, and a critical apparatus. The volumes were to be sold only with papal approval (not obtained until 1520) and therefore the publication was delayed until 1522, and the New Testament of Erasmus was known in western Europe before the Polyglot version. The critical attitude of the cardinal was more conservative than the critical attitude of Erasmus, but his scholarship was by no means inferior. In 1512 appeared a Castilian translation of the Gospels and Epistles, frequently reprinted, so that the Spaniard had little difficulty in buying a copy in his own tongue.

But after 1530 the Erasmians of Spain encountered the disapproval of the Inquisition. They were a small group of educated men, and their ideals took no hold among the people or among most of the Spanish clergy or monks. In 1537 the Inquisition prohibited the reading in Castilian of the works of Erasmus, and ordered his Latin editions to be expurgated. The inquisitors began to expect, and to hunt, Lutherans. They found a little evidence. A group in Seville was discovered to have smuggled Spanish Bibles from Geneva. Solemn burnings in 1558–60 destroyed the few powerless Protestants, and probably some others. Once in the chase, the inquisitors were hard to satisfy. In Italy the destruction of Protestantism was as rapid.

New Orders

Medieval Catholicism sought its highest expressions of devotion in the monastic life. The age-old method of reforming the church was to found new orders, or new forms of old orders. In Italy and Spain new orders were founded during the first half of the sixteenth century. It was easier to found new orders than to reconstruct the old, partly because reformers, even within a religious community, are always likely to divide it, and partly because the monastic endowments across Europe were part of that system of worldly wealth and vested interest which was the most conservative force in the Church. Single monasteries or groups succeeded in reforming themselves, and some houses needed no reform. The most successful attempt at reconstructing an old order was that of Matteo da Bascio (died 1552), an Italian Franciscan of peasant stock who sought to revive the primitive simplicity of St Francis of Assisi and to observe the letter of the testament of St Francis. He insisted upon a beard, and wore a four-pointed hood upon his coarse brown habit. He later left his group and became an itinerant evangelist; but the group was recognized by the Pope in 1528, and the name of Capuchin – from the brown pointed hoods – is first found in a papal document of 1535. The Capuchins directed themselves to pastoral charity, lepers, hospitals, popular evangelism, eschewed those magnificent houses and city churches of older Franciscans, refused to encourage scholarship, and built little communities of mud or wattle far out in the country or mountain. They were fought at every turn by the Observant Franciscans, whom they were silently criticizing by their reform and from whom they were attracting good men. They endured an attempt at forcible suppression during the thirties, and they were almost suppressed when their superior, Bernardino Ochino, most popular of Italian preachers, turned Protestant (1542). Until 1572 they were prohibited from founding houses outside Italy, but thereafter they spread rapidly, and second to the Jesuits were the great religious order of the Counter-Reformation. The fear of towns and of scholarship was modified, and in 1619 the order at last acquired formal independence. The Capuchins, in a manner, were typical of what friars could do to reform the Church.

But most of the new orders were of a new age, and a new spirit – Theatines (founded by Gaetano da Thiene in 1524); Somaschi (1532); Barnabites (1533); Jesuits; and looser groups named 'oratories', like that brotherhood of prayer and pastoral works in Rome called The Oratory of Divine Love (1516), or the group of secular priests founded by St Philip Neri in 1575, which raised the name of Oratory into that of a great religious institute. Though these orders were in a line of descent reaching back through the friars, their ethos and their institutions were novel. They were not withdrawn from the world. Their intention was pastoral endeavour and parochial renewal. They lived severe lives, preached, established orphanages or hospitals or homes for fallen women, educated children, and undertook the relief of the sick or destitute. Even the new order for women, the Ursulines (1535), at first designed its members to live at home and worship in their parish churches while they lived the life of charity and social endeavour. If we seek a single theme running through the reforming endeavours of the Catholic Reformation, it would be the quest for a more adequate clergy – better-trained and better-instructed priests, priests resident in their parishes, bishops resident in their sees, pastors fervent and self-sacrificing and missionary-minded, trained as confessors, celibate, mortified, able to teach in school, wearing canonical dress; a priesthood uncorrupted and incorruptible, educated and other-worldly. From Gaetano da Thiene near the beginning of the century to St Philip Neri near the end, the conservative reformers directed themselves to this end. And in spite of the novelty of their ideas or institutions, they were proving that the traditional ways of the Middle Ages were practicable. There might, for example, be legitimate argument whether the enforced celibacy of the clergy was Scriptural, or desirable, or harmful, or useful; but the Counter-Reformation gave an answer to those radicals who argued that in the light of medieval concubinage it was impossible.

THE JESUITS

Ignatius Loyola appears first in the pages of history during 1515, at Pamplona in Navarre, accused of 'great crimes' in

Guipuzcoa in the company of a clergyman. He claimed before the court that he was an ecclesiastic, but the court found that he was not upon the list of the vicar-general and that he was usually observed to be wearing a leather cuirass and breastplate and to be carrying sword, dagger, musket, and various other weapons. We do not know what he had done, but evidently he was not yet aspiring to sanctity.

On 21 May 1521, while he was defending a breach in the castle wall of Pamplona against French invaders, a cannon ball shattered his right leg and wounded his left. The ensuing surgery almost killed him. The leg, which was set wrongly and had to be broken again, was set wrongly a second time, and the same process was repeated. He was left with a misshapen right leg, and knew that he would not fight again. Reading the *Life of Christ* by Ludolph the Carthusian and the devotional literature which were the only books near his bed, brooding or day-dreaming gloomily over his future, and once seeing a vision in the night of the Madonna with her Child, he determined to become a saint. 'Suppose I did what St Francis or St Dominic did?' He would begin by undertaking a pilgrimage to Jerusalem. At the sanctuary of Montserrat he hung his sword and his dagger by the statue of the Virgin and watched all night before her altar, like a knight dedicating himself anew in chivalrous vigil.

Continuing on his way towards Jerusalem, he was prevented from entering Barcelona by a plague which was devastating the town. He therefore halted at Manresa, intending to stay a few days, and remained for nearly a year. During the weary months he devoted himself to austerity, praying for seven hours a day, flagellating himself three times a day, rising at midnight for prayer, leaving his hair and nails uncut, begging his bread. Luther found that such endeavours failed to bring peace of mind. Ignatius found the same. His conscience began to torture itself, he felt bound in his confession to go over and over the same sins, he harassed his mind to find what he had forgotten to confess, he fell into a condition of scruples. Luther discovered the way of escape by reading the Epistle to the Romans. Ignatius discerned his way of escape through a concentration of his iron will upon obedience to the suffering Christ, an obedience formed by obedience to the precepts of his Church. It was his confessor who ordered him to eat, and so he abandoned the resolution to eat nothing till exhaustion supervened. Luther broke his self-will by subjecting it to the grace of God. Ignatius broke his self-will by forcing himself to obey the representatives of the Church. If faith was the ground of all Luther's work, obedience was the key to Loyola's.

While his body was suffering and his mind fermenting at Manresa, he wrote the first sketch of *The Spiritual Exercises*, a book which reached its final form at Rome in 1541. (The manuscript of 1541 has survived, with his corrections, but it was not printed till after papal approval of the Latin translation in 1548.) It is not a book to be read. If it is not used experimentally, it is nothing. There is no style, nothing to attract. Ignatius was never articulate about religion. The book contains a series of exercises in prayer – described without ornament, but with Spanish realism. By subjecting a person to these exercises he aimed to train him to master his will. The subject is to enter a solitary cell for a retreat of a month in silence, interrupted only by the liturgy and by communications with his director. He is to consider himself and his corruption and foulness, to look upon himself as an ulcer poisoning society, to see with the eye of imagination the length and breadth and depth of hell; and in imagining he is to use every sense, to hear men screaming, to smell them burning, he is to ask to feel in himself the pain which the damned suffer. Then he is to turn to the grace and mercy of God, to Bethlehem and Nazareth and Calvary, with the same near-physical imaginings. ... And so the month of discipline is to pass, driving the subject to feel the terrible consequences of self-will, his helplessness without the mercy of Christ and his Mother – the Christ of beauty and of kindness, who has delivered him from these torments though he has not deserved it, lifting him little by little from the proximity of agonies to contemplate the peace and the glory of Mount Sion, from living upon Calvary to living with the Resurrection. The month was planned to lead to an act of will – the choice of a new way of life. This new way is to be lived by obedience to the teaching and the ordinances of the Church. Obedience to a superior is the condition of a soldierly service of God and of a total self-abnegation in the individual. The soul undertook to obey the Church, as the bride of Christ, and to sacrifice its own judgement; to practise confession, frequent communion, the recitation of the hours of prayer; to maintain such institutions of the Church as monasteries, the celibacy of the clergy, relics, fasting, indulgences, pilgrimages; and to defend the scholastic theology, the Church's tradition and the decrees of the Popes. The book ends with 'Rules for Thinking with the Church'. In these rules comes the celebrated hyperbole that he is to be ready to believe that what seems to him white is black, if the Church declares it to be so. (Contrary to a common opinion, however, it has been shown that for many years there was no regularity about the practice of these exercises by Loyola's disciples.)

In 1523 Loyola went as a pilgrim to Jerusalem. In 1526 he was a student at Alcalá preparing himself for ordination. His rigours and his little groups of prayerful friends made the Spanish Inquisition suspicious of him, and for a time he was imprisoned. He tried again at Salamanca and was imprisoned. In 1528 he tried again at the University of Paris, where he was again denounced to the Inquisition. He had begun at last to learn wisdom and prudence in picking his disciples. At Paris in 1534, his first six men joined him in a brotherhood – Francis Xavier, also from Pamplona, Faber (Pierre Le Fèvre), Lainez, Salmerón, Bobadilla, and Rodríguez.

In a chapel on Montmartre (15 August 1534) the little band vowed to go to Palestine to work for the conversion of the Turks; or if this proved to be impossible, to offer themselves to the Pope to be sent on any work which he chose, even if it were a mission to the Turks or other persecuting powers. By 1538 it was clear that Palestine was impossible; and though the mind of Xavier was already turning towards the Indies, they offered themselves to the Pope. They had become aware of the crying needs of Italian parishes, and became known as educators of children, as conductors of missions or retreats, as popular preachers, as chaplains to hospitals. At Rome in the spring of 1539 they formed a 'Company of Jesus' which was to instruct the children and the illiterate in the commandments of God. Its members were to take a special view of obedience to the Pope, to go wherever the Pope should send them. The priests of the Company, though bound to recite the hours of prayer, were not to do so in choir, that they might not be withdrawn from the works of charity.

It was not a good time for founding new orders. In the Papal court, reform made a stumbling beginning under Pope Adrian VI (1522-3), remained quiescent or worse under Clement VII (1523-34) and by 1539, with Paul III as Pope, began markedly to influence public opinion in Rome. Persons with revolutionary ideas could be found in high places. The canonist Guidiccioni, whom the Pope consulted about the Jesuits, believed that all the existing male orders except four (perhaps except one) should be suppressed. At last, on 27 September 1540, the Society was established by a Bull entitled *Regimini militantis ecclesiae*.

The Society was in no sense designed to be a weapon for fighting the Protestants. Nor at first had it any reputation for intransigence. The Bull of 1540 declared its object to be the propagation of the faith, and the phrase 'propagation *and defence*' of the faith was not added till 1550. Nor was it in origin an autocratic society. Ignatius himself was less autocratic by temperament than John Wesley. But between 1540 and 1555 the Society grew so rapidly in numbers, influence, and range of activities that it could only be directed, perhaps could only have been held together, by a strong hand at the centre. And while Ignatius was not temperamentally an autocrat, and would probably have been content if another had governed the society which he had founded, he stamped it with his own religious ideals and therefore with the virtue of obedience at the centre of its devotional life. The rule of obedience taught in *The Spiritual Exercises* was not new. It may be paralleled in the rules of St Francis of Assisi, and its origins go back to the Rule of St Benedict and beyond. Yet he succeeded in imparting into his Society an atmosphere of religious obedience which easily fitted the autocratic constitution desirable for practical reasons, and which culminated in the special promise of obedience made to the Pope by fully professed members of the Society.

They intended to be a society of priests ministering to the heathen and the poor, and especially educating the children or the illiterate. Ignatius spent much energy in resisting the tendency of his more devotional followers to turn the society into a conventional, even a more contemplative, order. They established orphanages, houses for prostitutes, schools, centres of poor relief, in Sicily even a kind of banking institute for destitute peasants. Others among the new orders modified the obligation of the religious to say the offices in choir, but Ignatius carried this to a revolutionary abolition. There should be no common recitation of the office; thus the oldest obligation of the monastic community disappeared.

It is interesting to observe the balance with which the mature Ignatius, once a zealot and ascetic extremist, ruled his order. Though he maintained a severe and austere life for himself, he would allow no one to practise discipline so strenuously as to harm his health. He would even force some young ascetic, discovered to have been fasting beyond the rule, to eat a meal in his presence. His men were to be fit for hard work in the world. The success of the Jesuits sprang largely from this readiness to adjust the old ideals of the monks to the needs of the new generation.

The hierarchy of the order was complex. The novitiate lasted two years instead of one, and was different from the old enclosed novitiates in containing a period of work in a hospital and a barefoot pilgrimage. Then the novice took the simple vows of poverty, obedience, and chastity, and passed into the 'scholasticate', where he received a severe course of higher education, and might be received at the end into full profession of vows and membership of the Society. If received, he could later be allowed to take a fourth vow, that of personal obedience to the Pope; and those 'professed of the fourth vow' were the governing body of the Society. They were not numerous – in 1556 they were only 43 in number, out of 1,000 members. This governing body was summoned only to elect a General or at the will of the General (except in exceptional circumstances where the General was insane or incapable), and the General held office for life, restricted only by the advice of four elected assistants. The constitution in theory attributed no more power to the General, and exacted no more obedience from the fathers, than some medieval orders. But the old abbot had been limited by custom and enclosure and a body of tradition and a written rule, whereas the Jesuit General was administering a new body which needed strong government to control its rapid expansion and harmonize its various activities.

Their work became diverse as their numbers grew. The mission to the heathen was not allowed to drop – perhaps, indeed, it always remained as primary to the Society as were the struggles against the heretics. On 7 April 1541 Francis Xavier, with three Jesuit companions, embarked at Lisbon for the Indies. He was the first of a long line of missionaries to the Indies and the Americas.

In 1540 the Society was still a little group, primarily for education and pastoral work among the poor. By 1556, when Ignatius died, it had more than 1,000 members and had become one of the powerful forces in the Catholic world, by its ministry not to the poor but to the upper ranks.

This happened chiefly through its hold upon higher education. It began by teaching the urchins of the Roman slums. It ended by teaching princes and princesses.

The Franciscans had begun by a ministry to the poor and had soon produced professors at the university. The parallel extension of the Jesuit work was less of a change than among the Franciscans. Education of children, to be effective, must lead them upwards. The primary school cannot be efficient unless the secondary school is efficient, and the secondary school will not be efficient unless the university is efficient. The first Jesuit secondary school was opened at Messina in 1548. The good sense of Ignatius exacted modern methods, fresh air and exercise, admirable teaching of Latin in the spirit of the Renaissance, care of good manners. Soon they were educating the upper classes of Catholic Europe. And meanwhile, colleges were founded in university after university, the first at Padua in 1542, the chief at Rome in 1551. The Company of Jesus became a teaching order, the leading body engaged in the higher education of Catholics. And since its educational methods were effective, more effective than any other methods in contemporary Europe, it found itself educating aristocrats and kings. The association of the Jesuit with the Catholic court, an association to be perilous to both sides, was founded upon intelligent schoolmastering.

The Jesuits in Germany

Teaching the Catholic faith in the universities, they were brought into direct controversy with the swiftly spreading influence of the Protestant divines. Their own plan of reform encountered notions of Reform, and those notions in absolute conflict with their ideals of obedience to the Holy Roman Church. Their study of theology was first for pastoral uses, then for controversial uses, and finally it became an end in itself, an academic discipline. Ignatius, despite painful diligence, was never a scholar. But two of his original six, Lainez and Salmerón, rapidly gained a place among the leading theologians of Catholic Europe and were among the Pope's more stalwart defenders at the Council of Trent. And from the moment (1542) that Jesuit Fathers were summoned by Catholic bishops to work in Southern Germany, they found that they were at once leading resistance to Protestant thought and seeking to confute Protestant theologians. In 1549 they began to teach at the Bavarian University of Ingolstadt, henceforth their German base. In 1552 the German college was founded in Rome; and from that time Ignatius regarded the battle against heresy as a primary task of his Company. He was succeeded as General by Lainez, the ablest theologian and controversialist among the early members.

For in 1555 sober men thought that the conservative cause in Germany was lost. Protestantism was still spreading in the Catholic lands like Austria, Bavaria, and Bohemia.

It had been difficult for the old theologians to resist the new theologians, except at the most superficial level of controversy. John Eck, by his cleverness, produced little handbooks which scored points against the Protestants. But at a deeper level the learned divines had been on the side of Reform. The universal belief that reform was necessary, the aridity and staleness of the older scholastic tradition, its fruitlessness in a world dominated by the insights of humanism, the second-rate quality of many of the defenders – these rendered the traditionalist apologetic scanty and unconvincing, during the first forty years of reform. There were exceptions; Spanish friars like Alfonso a Castro or Dominic Soto were already in the forties and fifties creating a new apologetic towards Protestantism. But as scholarship improved and confidence returned, as the theologians found much common ground with the Protestants in the study of the Bible and of the ancient Church, the controversy became less unequal. The conservatives discovered how in the new world they could defend the old ways, and were sometimes surprised to find that the old ways were defensible.

In Germany the *Catechism* of the Jesuit Peter Canisius (published in 1555) is a mark of this changing atmosphere.

It was written in a style to be understood, it was lucid and attractive and supported by Biblical texts, it was not (as a catechism by Eck would have been) armed to the teeth against assailants. It was an uncontroversial statement of the Catholic faith, and won praise even among Protestant divines. Canisius toured the Catholic south, stirring the princes to the defence of their religion, disputing and preaching, founding colleges and institutions. For much of the century even informed Germans supposed that the founder of the Jesuits was Canisius.

It should not be forgotten that controversial disputations or pamphlets formed one of the least important parts of the battle against the Protestants. The only way to counter the Protestants was to reform the Church. In the Bavaria of 1550, for example, all the old abuses were continuing, and continuing in spite of a pious prince. The clergy were often illiterate, the monasteries often like country inns, the vicarages commonly contained a concubine and numerous progeny, there were many drunken priests. This was the condition which invited the Reforming ideals from the north to spread southward, and some of the Bavarian middle class were already affected by the teaching of the Lutherans or of the Anabaptists. The only way to stem the tide was to reform the Church. It was pastoral endeavour as well as militant antagonism which was at the base of the Counter-Reformation advance in South Germany. 'The best way to fight the heretics is not to deserve their criticisms,' said the nuncio Bonomi in 1585. But this pastoral endeavour was an action of the state. In Bavaria the pious prince Albert summoned Jesuits to his aid and reformed the parishes of his duchy with a soldierly severity. And to expel heretics or destroy Anabaptists or burn false books was for every Catholic sovereign a part of his endeavours to reform his parishes.

CONTARINI AND CARAFFA

The Protestants – Luther, Henry VIII (if he was a Protestant), Calvin – appealed to a future General Council of the Church. The memory of the fifteenth-century councils was still potent. The most traditional of reformers looked to a General Council to reform the Church in head and members and, after the German revolt, to bring peace. The difficulty lay in the question when a General Council was free, who might attend it, and what might be its agenda. Papal divines held that the Pope alone had the canonical right to summon a General Council. Protestant divines could not expect, or did not expect, fair dealing at a Council summoned and arranged by their principal opponent. A moderate peacemaker, like the Emperor Charles V, was confronted with the formidable and unlikely task of summoning, or causing to be summoned, a Council which sensible men upon either side would recognize to be a true Council, of an authority and prestige comparable with the great Councils of the primitive Church.

Many moderates, especially in Germany, were passive in the growing schism because they looked for remedy to a future Council. They might not want Luther, but they wanted reform, and they suspected the Popes of failing to call a Council because they wished not to be reformed. The Germans wanted 'a free Christian Council in German lands'. By 'free', most Germans meant that it must be independent of the papacy. The Emperor Charles V wished the Council to meet in Germany, partly because he was a good Catholic and partly because he wanted and needed a united Germany.

The Pope and his advisers followed their predecessors of a century before in eyeing with suspicion and fear any Council which a German Emperor, however Catholic, might convoke. Their fear sprang as much from the fact that the vested interests of the papal court were afraid of the 'reform in head and members' on which everyone was theoretically agreed, as from the memory that any General Council raised constitutional hindrances to the freedom of papal action. They remembered how the Council of Basle had lectured the popes like a nagging wife. They remembered how the

Council of Constance had deposed popes and elected a new pope. They feared that a General Council outside their control would conduct a revolution in which Catholicism would be transformed and the See of Rome swept into insignificance. They admitted that sooner or later a Council must be held, but they were determined that this Council should be under the presidency of the Pope or his legates, should be held in the traditional manner with bishops attending, and should be as immediately under the direction of the Pope as the Lateran Council of 1512–17. They thought that the popes were capable of reforming the Church by papal decree, so far as it needed reform. If a Council could not be avoided, it should be held at Rome or in the papal dominions. They sometimes believed that no new decrees were needed, and that the nations needed only to enforce the existing canon law. 'What is the point of a Council,' said Cardinal Campeggio at the Diet of Augsburg (1530), 'when the Lutherans do not obey the canons of earlier Councils?' 'We . . . have no need of a Council,' said Luther to the papal nuncio in 1535, 'but Christendom has need of a Council, whereby it may recognize its inveterate errors.' Between these opposing viewpoints it took long years for the Emperor Charles V and the Pope Paul III to agree upon the place and time and agenda of a Council.

Paul III Farnese (Pope 1534–49) was the Pope who recognized that a General Council must willy nilly be summoned, and abandoned the policy of his predecessors that a Council must at all costs be avoided lest Rome perish in the ensuing constitutional conflict. In his personal habits Paul was no great example of a reformed Pope, for he suffered from a numerous and avaricious family. But reformed or not, he was convinced by the urgent need to reform the Church from within. And his performance was courageous. Though he elevated a nephew aged fourteen to be a Cardinal and sent the red hat to his school, he also elevated several Catholic leaders of reforming zeal or humanist sympathy: Fisher, Contarini, Sadoleto, Caraffa, Pole. The reformers were given an immediate opening. In 1536 he appointed a commission of nine – including Sadoleto, Caraffa, Contarini, and Pole – to produce a memorandum on reform. In 1537 they issued a *Report of a Select Committee ... on Reforming the Church* (*Consilium de Emendanda Ecclesia*). They recommended that residence be made compulsory, that a certain standard should be exacted of persons to be admitted to benefices. Though they were oddly silent upon ignorance and the need of education, they recognized the peril in indulgences and superstitious devotions. They were unpalatably frank in their denunciations of monastic abuses, the misuse of episcopal authority, the avarice and irresponsibility of the cardinals, the prostitutes in the city of Rome, and the claims of extreme canonists that the Pope, even if he sold benefices, could not commit simony. Unpalatably frank, for the text soon leaked out and was published by Protestants in Germany. A picture was circulated of three cardinals sweeping a church with foxes' tails instead of brooms.

The Catholic Church was no monolithic uniform structure. The medieval Church contained a wide range of opinion, and now the Pope found himself pressed by two different schools. Everyone agreed upon reform. But must reform mean an approximation towards the Protestants, conciliation and concession, an allowing of clerical marriage or the cup to the laity, an eschewing of the admitted abuses of the doctrine of merit by encouraging a more Scriptural teaching of justification by faith? Or was reform rather to be obtained by fighting the Protestants, refusing all concession, developing the unprotestant elements of devotion in the medieval tradition, strengthening the authority of the hierarchy?

The history of the Counter-Reformation is in part the history of the triumph of the conservatives and the militant over the conciliatory and the liberal.

Among the cardinals elevated by Paul III and among the

authors of the *Consilium de Emendanda Ecclesia*, two have been seen as symbols of the rival schools: Cardinal Contarini who patronized the early Jesuits, and Cardinal Caraffa who organized the Theatines. Contarini* studied philosophy among the humanists, was then a civil servant in the city of Venice, attending the famous 1521 Diet of Worms as the Venetian ambassador, and was still a layman when Pope Paul III made him a cardinal in 1535. Humane and courteous, he was for seven years the guide and inspirer of the Catholic Reformation. He believed that the Protestants had a measure of truth in their pleas upon merit, and to express the doctrine of justification he was ready to find formulas which would satisfy both Protestant and Catholic. He believed that the traditional abuses, even the highest, even the abuses of the Roman Curia, must be ended.

Colloquy of Ratisbon, 1541

The policy of conciliation reached its climax in the Colloquy of Ratisbon in 1541. There Contarini, accompanied by the most moderate of German Catholic divines, and possessing vague but liberal-sounding instructions from Pope Paul III, sat round a table with the most moderate of German Protestant divines, Melanchthon and Bucer. Contarini exceeded his instructions. The Pope demanded that the supremacy of the Pope must be recognized at the outset. Contarini saw that the demand would wreck the conference, and postponed it to the last item on the agenda. John Eck, who though no moderate was attending the conference, caused trouble to the pacific programme but was at last brought to heel. And under Contarini's leadership the conference attained the astonishing success of agreement upon the doctrine of justification by faith.

Moderate men who engage in ecumenical conferences need to remember that not all the members of their respective churches are moderate men. Luther was suspicious

---

* Despite many histories, he had not been a member of the Oratory of Divine Love at Rome.

when he heard what was happening. He found the agreement incredible. In Rome Cardinal Caraffa protested bitterly against the theological betrayal. The French king, Francis I, suddenly afraid that the Emperor Charles V might succeed in uniting Germany on the basis of a religious peace at Ratisbon, protested with equal vehemence against the concessions. The German Catholics of the right wing thought that concession was illusory, and must go further, to intolerable limits if it was to satisfy the Lutherans. Meanwhile the conference at Ratisbon was itself breaking down upon the article of transubstantiation, which Contarini could not abandon and the Protestants could not accept. Pope Paul III declared that he would not tolerate ambiguous formulas, and the opportunity of peace had gone.

In Italy Cardinal Contarini found himself everywhere rumoured to be a heretic. He died in the next year, 1542.

The failure of Contarini opened the way to the opposing party. Reconciliation was now believed to be a mirage, and the proper policy for the Church was to define its doctrine and condemn error more precisely.

In the same year that Contarini was at Ratisbon, Caraffa recommended the Pope to found a new and powerful Inquisition into heresy. He and his school believed that the way to purify Catholicism was by assaults upon heresy, and that the policy of conciliation was encouraging the growth of heresy. A small but distinguished crop of Italian conversions to the Protestants during 1542, including the famous Bernardino Ochino of the Capuchins and Peter Martyr Vermigli of the Augustinians, lent substance to the belief. The Roman Inquisition was founded by a Bull (*Licet ab initio*) of 21 July 1542, appointing six cardinals (including Caraffa) as inquisitors-general and subjecting all Catholics to their authority. They were given power to imprison on suspicion, to confiscate property, and to execute the guilty, while the power of pardon was reserved to the Pope. Caraffa would not wait for a grant from the papal treasury, but bought a house which he fitted with offices and dungeons and shackles. He issued a set of rigorous rules for inquisition, of which the fourth ran: 'No man is to lower himself by showing toleration towards any sort of heretic, least of all a Calvinist.'

This new Inquisition was a dead letter outside Italy, for the Catholic sovereigns had their own courts and would not countenance a new system of papal courts within their territories. Within the papal territories it was successful and disastrous. A series of crude hunts for heretics suppressed much else in the process, including some humane thinking and intelligent discourse. The Inquisition began to look with suspicion upon the learned societies, to control the book trade and the printers. Italian humanism, colourful and eccentric, suffered its first blow at the sack of Rome in 1527, and now needed to conform in a more disciplined world.

In 1555 Caraffa was elected to be Pope as Paul IV. He was seventy-nine years old, choleric and impulsive, passionately devoted to two objects alone, objects not easily compatible – the Catholic restoration, and the downfall of the Spanish power in Italy.

The incongruity between these objects almost destroyed the reforming value of the pontificate. The Pope was forced to use Lutheran troops to fight the Catholic Spaniards. He heaped reproaches upon Queen Mary of England and upon Cardinal Pole, Archbishop of Canterbury, who restored England to the Church but were nevertheless within the Spanish alliance. He was forced to use worthless nephews for his political plans against the Spaniards, and subsequently to ruin them because he found them to be corrupt and criminal. His short pontificate as Paul IV affords the clearest demonstration of the dilemma of all the Popes until 1870 – the dilemma whether it was possible for a reformed Papacy to be also the centre of Italian politics and a power among the powers of Europe. Throughout his reign he was indefatigable in the search for reform, repressing public scandals, taking care to select good men (such care that by 1558 fifty-eight bishoprics were vacant), exhorting, guiding public opinion. He drove back to their sees all of the 113 bishops living in Rome except the ten or twelve who were needed for the administration. He forced every Jew to wear a yellow hat and live in a ghetto with only one exit. He caused to be published the first Index of prohibited books. The *Decameron* of Boccaccio was upon the list, until it should be bowdlerized. The decree forbade all books, however innocuous, written by certain authors or published by certain printers. Large numbers of Protestants, all the works of Erasmus without exception, even if not about religion, King Henry VIII, Staupitz, Machiavelli, Rabelais, Peter Abelard, and even two editions of the Koran were found upon this eccentric list. It caused a great burning of the books throughout Italy, and was altogether ignored in France and Spain. At Venice more than 10,000 books were burned on the Saturday before Palm Sunday. Sixtus of Siena was sent to Cremona, where there was a great Hebrew school (for the destruction of the Talmud was ordered), and reported that he had burnt a store of 12,000 volumes. The disaster was diminished by the rulers of Italy; Duke Cosimo of Tuscany ordered the friars of San Marco to refrain from burning any of the books which were gifts from his predecessors. It was mercifully modified by the Index of Trent in 1564. But its impact upon the Italian booksellers, in spite of a regulation to protect their interests, was disastrous.

Under an Inquisition with extended powers and a Pope ready to suspect everyone, there was almost a reign of terror in the city. 'Even if my own father were a heretic,' said the Pope, 'I would gather the wood to burn him.' He imprisoned Cardinal Morone, heir to the mantle of Cardinal Contarini. He entrusted Daniel of Volterra (who was therefore nicknamed the Trouserer) with the task of clothing some of the nakedness of the Sistine Chapel.

If the Pope of 1459 is compared with the Pope of 1559, the spectator observes a different air, almost a different world; a difference not dependent upon the contrast of the individual personalities. By 1559 the Catholic Reformation, so hopelessly longed for by godly men throughout the past decades, had at last attained power in Rome. It is true that individuals governed and directed the change. But it is not only a contrast of individuals. It would have been almost unthinkable for the Pope of 1459 to be elected in 1559, or vice versa. On the one side is a world of Italian Renaissance: gay, humane, corrupt, reasonably content with the old ways and the old abuses, still thinking of crusades against the Saracens when it thought of crusades at all, valuing the ascetic life deeply but regarding the ascetics as men to be admired rather than imitated by the world. On the other side is a world in earnest: seeking discipline and order, not only admiring the friars but wanting the Church to conform to the ascetic or puritan pattern, suspicious of nudes and pagan statues, fiercely struggling to diminish or eradicate the venality of church administration.

The atmosphere of religious, moral, and intellectual life was being transformed. Bishops who had once been tranquil in their non-residence now issued circulars denouncing non-residence. Secretaries who once drafted the seamier documents of the indulgence traffic were now loud in denouncing the abuses of the indulgence. Humanists who once hired their pens to immoral literature were not ashamed to publish books of devotion. In the fifteen-fifties some of them still inserted pagan phrases or legends into their writings to the Pope, but the phrases now looked strange. Peter Aretino had lived in a kind of harem at Venice and made money out of writing obscenities and panegyrics. While the Counter-Reformation triumphed, he engaged in writing ascetic books, acquired a reputation for pious fervour and hatred of heretics, and died in 1556 as a Chevalier of St Peter, asserting with brazen effrontery that he had refused the offer of a cardinal's hat.

Learned Italy was returning to the piety of the Church; Italian poets were turning to sacred poetry, Italian artists to devout practice. And not only in Italy was the atmosphere changing. The Portuguese Inácio de Azevedo was the son of a priest, the grandson of a bishop, the son and the grandson of nuns. When he learned of his birth, he held it to be a fourfold sacrilege, believed himself called to a life of sacrificial reparation, joined the Society of Jesus and its Brazilian mission, and was murdered by pirates in mid-Atlantic. The wave of moral severity, which in another part of Europe was creating puritanism, was now strengthening the hand of the Catholic reformers.

THE COUNCIL OF TRENT

The Council of Trent is important, in the first place, because it failed to meet until 1545.

The Cardinals, if they must have a Council, wanted it at Rome. The Emperor Charles V was determined to have a Council in Germany. For long years papal diplomacy was directed to securing that a Council never met. The legate Aleander offered welcome advice to Pope Clement VII: 'Never offer a Council, never refuse it directly. On the contrary, show you are willing to comply with the request, but stress the difficulties in the way. Thus you will be able to ward it off.' 'Commit yourself to nothing,' the legate Cervini warned Pope Paul III at the eleventh hour, 'until it is agreed that the Pope is absolute master of the Council.'

The postponement, perhaps a fatal postponement for Christendom, was made easier because Charles V was usually at war with the King of France. France, fearing a united Germany, feared a General Council. The French king was almost as anxious as the Roman cardinals to put off the Council indefinitely. After repeated false starts under Pope Paul III, who saw that the danger in not summoning was now greater than the danger in summoning, the Council was at last enabled to meet in 1545, because the Emperor and the French king signed the Peace of Crépy in 1544, containing a secret clause whereby King Francis pledged himself to further the Emperor's plans for a Council.

As early as 1524 the name of Trent was mentioned as a possible site: a little town on the south side of the Alps and the Brenner pass, under the rule of a Catholic bishop, in Italy, easy of access to Italian bishops, and yet also within the Holy Roman Empire and therefore complying with the German demand that the Council must meet 'in German lands'.

The Council of Trent opened after an infinity of delays upon 13 December 1545, with only twenty-eight bishops present. The Emperor and the Pope wanted the Council to perform different functions. The Emperor hankered for religious peace in Germany, by reforming the abuses and corruptions of the Church and by giving to the Lutherans certain concessions, like the marriage of the clergy and communion in both kinds. He therefore desired the Council to attend to the questions of discipline and leave the questions of doctrine, which his experience of divines led him to think insoluble. The Pope on the contrary instructed his legates, who presided, that the Council must first treat the questions of doctrine. It was therefore agreed that doctrine and discipline should be treated in parallel. But of the three sessions during which the Council sat (1545–8, 1551–2, 1562–3) the first was chiefly concerned with the doctrinal definitions believed needful upon the questions in controversy with the Protestants, and the last was chiefly concerned with those efforts at disciplinary regulation and correction which the traditionalists meant when they used the word *reform*.

The Fathers of the Council felt no obligation to be tender to the Protestants. In the session of 1545–8 they were mainly from areas unaffected by Protestant ideas, and they wished to condemn what appeared to them to be erroneous doctrines. Confronted by the doctrine of justification by faith alone, they declared that faith alone was not sufficient for justification, but must be accompanied by hope and love. Confronted by the Protestant appeal to the Scripture, they declared that unwritten traditions and Scripture were to be received with equal reverence. Confronted by the Protestant declaration that the sacraments of the Gospel were three or two in number, they affirmed that the sacraments were neither more nor less than seven. Protestant scholars believed that the Hebrew Bible was the source of the authentic text, and therefore put the Greek apocrypha upon one side as instructive for morals but uncanonical (the question had never been settled by the medieval theologians). The Fathers of Trent declared that the Latin Vulgate was the canonical and sacred text. The Protestant divines believed that the doctrine of a repeated sacrifice of Calvary in the mass, a doctrine which they attributed too sweepingly to the Catholic divines, was perilous and unscriptural; and they abolished 'private masses' root and branch. The Fathers of Trent declared that in the mass there was a truly propitiatory sacrifice of Christ, and commended those masses at which the priest alone communicated. The Protestants contended that the liturgy should be in a language understood by the people. The bishops declared that the mass should normally continue to be in Latin.

These definitions or decisions effectively ended the hopes of the Emperor and other moderates that the Council might seek a measure of reconciliation with the Protestants. It is not to be denied that the fear of Protestantism led the bishops towards direct confutation of its doctrines. There were rumours in the Council, from time to time, that Protestant armies were marching upon Trent. The bishops sometimes felt themselves to be legislating under an imminent threat from heretical force. In 1552 a Protestant army under Maurice of Saxony was but a few hours' march from Trent, and the Council hastily adjourned. But it should be observed that the doctrinal decrees of Trent, because they were sometimes given a polemical tone, sounded more hostile to the Protestants than they really were. In the early sessions of the Council, when the most momentous of the doctrinal decrees were passed, the numbers of bishops present (about sixty) was still comparatively small. But even within this number, there was sufficient variety of opinion to illustrate the diversities of medieval theology. One bishop, Nacchianti of Chioggia, even believed that all things necessary to salvation are contained in Scripture, and protested his right to continue to believe this until the Council declared otherwise. The bishops of Trent, in framing their decrees, needed to allow a breadth which men of diverse opinions could accept as the authentic teaching of the Catholic Church. The decrees of Trent were framed with care; their language was designed to allow more liberty of opinion than their Protestant critics believed. The care with which they were framed has only been fully evident during the twentieth century. During the last fifty years the Görres Society has been engaged in publishing the minutes of the debates and discussions which lay behind the formal promulgation of the canons.

One example will suffice: the decree of 8 April 1546 upon the canonical Scriptures. Later critics of the Council contended that this decree elevated tradition into a second source of revelation, outside and independent of Scripture: an unwritten word spoken by Christ to his apostles and guaranteed by its acceptance in the Catholic Church. Many defenders of the Counter-Reformation understood the decree in this way. But the minutes of the discussion show that, if the decree is patient of that interpretation, it was not intended by all the disputants. Some bishops would have liked all the 'traditions' of the Holy Roman Church to be declared sacred. Other bishops felt that this was too generalized; that the only traditions which could claim this sacredness were 'apostolic' traditions, traditions handed down in the Church from apostolic times. It was suggested that a list of apostolic traditions might be framed in the canon; and this was rejected on the ground that a list might unwittingly omit an apostolic tradition and thereby cause Christians to neglect or repudiate it. The clause was therefore framed to sanctify only traditions 'which have always been maintained in the Catholic Church'; and it is clear that some of those who framed it were thinking not of an unwritten heritage of doctrine but of certain practices, like the keeping of Sunday or the baptism of infants. Though the decree was intentionally directed against certain beliefs of Protestants, it was less hostile to the Protestant doctrines than was afterwards believed. And the same measure of diversity may be found among other decrees, even those on the eucharistic sacrifice or justification by faith.

Yet it is certain that the immediate effect was calamitous for the programme of the peace-makers.

In October and November 1551, after a period when Pope and Emperor were in vehement conflict, Lutheran representatives at last arrived at Trent to prepare the way for their theologians. They refused to participate in the Council unless the bishops would begin to discuss the questions of doctrine again from the beginning and regard as null all the decisions which had been taken. Understandably; and it is equally understandable that the papal legates and the bishops should have rejected the suggestion with warmth. By the word *Council*, the two sides meant different assemblies. One assembly at Trent could not serve for both.

The Council was not under the immediate control of the Pope, who never came to it. His legates presided and received frequent communications and instructions from the Curia at Rome, just as the representatives of the Emperor or the kings of France and Spain received frequent instructions from their respective sovereigns. The majority in the Council was Italian; but as the number of bishops rose (in the last session of 1562–3 it was over 200) the successive Popes needed to exercise vigilant diplomacy through agents at Trent. It was important to the Popes that the Council should not be swayed by the political desires of the Catholic monarchs, and that the Council should not reform Rome itself – Rome alone must reform Rome. The Spanish bishops held strenuous opinions about the 'divine law' which insisted that a bishop reside upon his see, and complained of the hundred and more bishops from various countries who resided in Rome. The Papal Curia, though it might admit excess, held strenuous opinions that the central administration of the Church needed bishops who were not residing upon their sees, and that this administration must not be weakened through the doctrinaire fervour of Spanish bishops. The Catholic princes of South Germany, like the Emperor Ferdinand, wanted the Catholics permitted communion in both kinds, and a married clergy; the demand (1562) had to be skilfully turned aside, and celibacy reaffirmed. But for most of the time the diplomatic labours of the papal legates were not arduous. The Council, though not an assembly of papal dependants, had no intention of being a revolutionary assembly; and at its close in 1563 the Fathers officially reaffirmed all the decrees passed in the different sessions and officially requested the Pope to confirm them. They asked the Pope for new editions of the Index (that published in 1564 imported prudence into Caraffa's original Index), the catechism (1566), the missal (1570), and the breviary (1568). Their decrees were formally confirmed by Pope Pius IV in the Bull *Benedictus Deus* of 26 January 1564.

The disciplinary decrees of the Council were henceforth the canonical basis of the Catholic reformation. They were often sweeping in their impact. The office of indulgence seller or 'quaestor' was abolished. Bishops were given effective powers of supervision in their dioceses. The Council removed many of those exemptions from episcopal control which during the Middle Ages made the office and work of a bishop so frustrating and so likely to produce litigation. The patterns of devout shepherds of souls, whether bishop or priest, were described by the canons, but these were liable to be no more effective than the admirable exhortations of earlier Councils. The Council of Trent took one practical step to this end, a measure in the long run the most important of all the measures decreed there. It ordered that the bishop of every diocese where no university existed should establish a seminary to train boys and young men to the priesthood. The Jesuit colleges provided some precedent. The new training educated the clergy in theology and fostered in them disciplined habits of devotion. Probably the institution of seminaries was more efficacious than any other canon in promoting the chief aim of the Catholic reform – an instructed and pure-hearted priesthood.

Nothing in the history of the Church has proved more intractable than the problem of turning an illiterate clergy into an educated clergy. The Protestants were shocked to find priests mumbling in the mass words as meaningless as any magical formula, and in their own way set out to instruct the clergy – by establishing schools and colleges, by instituting clerical meetings for study, by encouraging scholarship in the bestowal of benefices, by turning the pastoral emphasis away from the sacraments in favour of the due and efficacious preaching of the Word. The Roman Catholic Church likewise used all these methods, not excluding a more urgent emphasis upon preaching. In 1538 the city of Rome had forgotten that the surplice was the proper garment in which secular priests should preach; for the secular priests hardly ever did preach, and the congregations were accustomed only to friars and other religious, who preached in the habits of their order. The Jesuits, and later the Oratorians, attempted to remedy the defect as part of their vocation of a reformed priesthood – a Jesuit was listed as a 'reformed priest' at the Council of Trent. As the Protestants thundered against 'dumb dogs' and demanded that pastors should be preaching men, the Council of Trent laid its obligation upon bishops and clergy that they should preach.

It is easier to legislate than to see that the law is executed.

It was not difficult to assert that the clergy must be educated and must preach sermons. It was more difficult, and took far more time, to secure that the sermons which they preached were not offensive to instructed ears. It was easy to legislate that a seminary should be instituted in every diocese. It was long years before there were seminaries in most dioceses and before many of those seminaries were purveying an education worthy of the ideal which inspired their foundation. It is possible that in the Protestant countries the problem of ministerial education was made easier to solve because the revolutionary changes in the ecclesiastical constitution gave the authorities a hand less tied, and also allowed a somewhat larger proportion of endowment to be diverted into education. But in Protestant as in Catholic countries a long age of endeavour was needed.

In the Protestant countries the reform was often carried through by the princes against the Pope. In the Catholic countries the process was not so different – it was carried through by the ecclesiastics with the active or reluctant assistance of the princes. In Catholic France and parts of south Germany the decrees could not even be received, and Spain helped itself to what it preferred. It was not easy to reform the episcopate when so many Catholic kings, including those of France and Spain, exercised an almost absolute control over the choice of men to be bishops. As late as June 1569, the Venetian ambassador in Paris said that at the French court 'they deal in bishoprics and abbeys as merchants trade in pepper and cinnamon'. The Council of Trent was an effective reforming council mainly in Italy; elsewhere it was an encouragement and stimulus to reform. The decrees were accepted by some French provincial councils in 1580–4, and solemnly in 1615 by the representatives of all the French clergy, at a brief moment of independent assertion. Spanish councils of clergy consented to them forthwith (1564) but could not put them into practice without leave from the crown. In south Germany, thanks to the skill of the papal legate Commendone, the bishops and Catholic princes (except the Emperor) received the decrees of Trent in 1566, though with a few reservations.

POPE PIUS V

The reforming party in the Church was helped to overcome the conservative traditions of Rome by the new political predicament of the Pope. Considered as a political sovereign, the Pope was less important to the European powers in 1565 than in 1510. In 1510 Julius II made the Papal State one of the powers of Europe, maintaining the political balance between France and Germany and so preserving papal independence and sovereignty. In 1565 all this was changed. The Pope was much poorer, for Germany and England had defected, France was fighting a civil war, and fees and dues were not paid. The Spanish Cardinal of Compostella wrote with a cool cynicism to the Emperor Charles V in 1555 that the Pope must reform the Church, because he was now too poor to do anything else. The rules of the Council of Trent hampered traditional and lucrative sources of profit, and made the Papal State a less happy ground for adventurers ready to be ordained in exchange for a fortune. Then Pope Paul IV (Caraffa) attacked the Spanish in Naples with his armies, was defeated, and threw the Papacy under the dominance of Spain for forty years.

In 1565 Michele Ghislieri, the Grand Inquisitor of Pope Paul IV (though no disciple or favourite), was elected Pope and became Pius V (1565–72, canonized in 1712). A holier man than Paul, he looked upon reform with a similar contempt for compromise, politics, and diplomacy. He was another ascetic with a decisive mind, a body which made him look nothing but skin and bones, and a way of life which was still that of a strict friar. He once said that the Church had need neither of cannon nor of soldiers, that its weapons were prayers and fasting, tears and the Bible. But he was prepared to use other weapons than the spiritual when they were available. He encouraged the killing of Huguenot prisoners. He sent the consecrated hat and sword to the Duke of Alva to show his gratitude for the reign of terror in the Netherlands.

Edicts imposed savage penalties for simony, blasphemy, sodomy, concubinage. They limited luxury in dress or in banquets, expensive marriages or marriage settlements. They expelled all the prostitutes from Rome within six days, unless they would marry or enter the convent of the Penitents – a decree which was not carried out in its full rigour, but those who preferred not to brave the perils of flight were confined to a special quarter, which was walled in and where special sermons were arranged for their instruction. Another edict forbade all residents with houses to visit taverns. The Pope was narrowly dissuaded from imposing the death penalty for adultery. Parents were subjected to special penalties if they failed to send their children to Sunday schools. Priests, who had commonly dressed like laymen, were compelled to wear clerical dress and to shave off their beards. Physicians and doctors were forbidden to wear the biretta. Doctors were not to visit the sick for more than three days without receiving a certificate that the patient had confessed to a priest. The Pope tried to restrain the luxury of banquets, of weddings, and of dress; his police raided jewellers' shops to confiscate the world's baubles; his taxes discouraged carriages; his decrees limited dowries and forbade shopkeepers to hang out signboards with saints painted upon them. He thought it unfitting that pagan images should decorate his residence, and gave a few of the classical statues to the Roman people. He wanted to give away many more, including some of the great statues housed in the gallery of the Belvedere, and allowed them to remain only on condition that the collection should not be open to the public. He approved of the covering of the statue of Neptune on the fountain at Bologna and hired an artist to clothe more of the frescoes, though in general he did not further drape the nudes. Gossips began to say that Pope Pius wanted to change the whole city of Rome into a monastery.

Sumptuary legislation of this sort was impossible to enforce effectively in the Rome of 1570. Outside the power of the papal government it was altogether ineffective. The Pope published a decree abolishing bull-fights, but the Spanish bishops dared not publish it. These sumptuary laws were more important as a symbol of a programme and an ideal than as a practical venture in moral government. In the realm of administration the Pope ran into those obstacles which had frustrated the reforming efforts of his predecessors. The Pope once professed that the Church needed no wealth. In fact, Rome contained a great civil service, a network of administration, and the papal government could not be carried on without money. Offices had been sold for money; and in moments of imminent bankruptcy, popes had created more offices, with incomes attached, in order to find capital. To clear out the hangers-on, the corrupt and petty officials from the papal court, was not only an act of administrative reform. It meant finding huge sums of money to compensate persons who had bought offices in good faith and would now find their offices and their income abolished. Pope Pius told some officials dismissed from the Penitentiary that 'it is always better to die of hunger than to lose one's soul'. He said that it was preferable for the Curia to be ruined rather than Christianity. But common justice could not sweep away the bureaucrats of Rome without making provision for them. He tried to force every priest and bishop who had a cure of souls outside Rome to go back to his benefice, and even imprisoned in the Castle of Sant'Angelo some bishops who failed to obey the order. It was an attempt to cure the symptom rather than the disease. Yet it was much for the future that a Pope should have attempted so fearless a reformation of the Papal administration. 'Men in Rome,' said the Venetian ambassador Tiepolo, 'have become a great deal better – or at least they have put on the appearance of being so.'

In 1568 the Pope reformed the Breviary. He adopted some of that programme which Cranmer had wanted earlier – making it clearer and simpler, restoring the Psalms and the reading of the Bible to their dominant place, removing passages from the non-Scriptural readings that were spurious or incredible. He restrained the issue of indulgences; and in every way he attempted to carry into practice the decrees and the spirit of the Council of Trent. In St Maria Maggiore in Rome may be seen the copy of the decrees of Trent which Pope Pius V used. The historian Pastor looked upon that little book with deep emotion, and commented: 'It became in his hands the hoe by which he uprooted a whole world of weeds.'

Charles Borromeo

The strength of the movement at its best is seen in the work of Charles Borromeo, Archbishop of Milan from 1560 to 1584. He experienced one of those colourful conversions so exuberantly plentiful in the Counter-Reformation. The nephew of Pope Pius IV, a beneficed clergyman at the age of twelve, a pluralist and an archbishop at the uncanonical age of twenty-one, a cardinal at twenty-two, a devotee of hunting in a manner criticized as unfitting for a cardinal, a lover of splendour and display who clothed his 150 retainers from head to foot in a livery of black velvet, he suddenly received holy orders at the age of twenty-five, undertook the *Spiritual Exercises* of Ignatius, tried to resign most of his lucrative sinecure benefices, dismissed half his retinue and prescribed austere rules for the other half, lived on bread and water one day a week, used a scourge of spikes upon his body, and began to preach sermons – which the people thought striking, for they had never heard of a cardinal preaching. His abilities and his standing at Rome enabled him to play a large part in the last session of the Council of Trent (1562–3). The Council created a commission to ensure that its decrees were observed, and another commission to draw up a revised catechism in Catholic doctrine; Borromeo helped to direct the work of both these commissions and revised the first draft of the catechism. It is characteristic of the Counter-Reformation that this famous catechism should have been designed not for the child or the illiterate, but for the instruction of the parochial clergy. He helped to revise the Breviary, as Trent had decreed. He attempted to carry out in his archdiocese the disciplinary decrees of Trent. Trent had ordered him to reside in his diocese, but he had the greatest difficulty in persuading the Pope to allow him even to visit it. He succeeded in persuading Pope Pius V and lived at Milan, the first archbishop to reside in the diocese for many years. He held provincial and diocesan synods of his clergy as Trent had ordered. He was the new model of a Catholic bishop, constantly engaged in visiting his parishes. He established not one seminary but three in Milan and three more outside it. He put these at first under the control of the Jesuits, but later lost his confidence in the Jesuits and founded a teaching society, the Oblates of St Ambrose, for the purpose. He founded a 'Swiss college' to train priests for Catholic Switzerland. He instituted an educational society which by the time of his death was controlling 740 schools. He was a grimly austere, often unpopular, heroic man, ready to risk life in a plague or his comfort in a fight with the governor. He died in 1584 and was canonized in 1610.

THE ENGLISH RECUSANTS

Every state which became Protestant lost churchmen by flight or banishment. A small number were not reconciled to change and preferred to maintain their traditional worship in other lands. These men were not attracted by the whitewash and the destruction or by seeing vestments, pyxes, images, copes, altars and censers being sold on the open market.

The circumstances of England might have been expected to encourage a larger number of these recusants than in Scotland or in the north German princedoms. For the bishops of Queen Mary, almost to a man, refused to accept the new régime of the Church, and carried some 200 other clergy away at the first rush. The rule of Edward VI and then of Mary convinced some English conservatives that Catholicism needed the Pope. The government in London, though secure enough unless invaded from abroad, had not mastered the wilder and simpler north, and sometimes needed to be tactful in ruling Wales, still more tactful in ruling Ireland. In the north of England and in Ireland great lords acted with an independent spirit. And just as the Protestants under Queen Mary were heartened by the absence of a baby and the knowledge that a Protestant would succeed, so the conservatives were now heartened by the spinster condition of Queen Elizabeth and the knowledge that the heir to the throne, Mary Queen of Scots, was a Roman Catholic. Lancashire and the northern hills, like Ireland, were as yet barely touched by reformation.

The adherents of the Pope did not at once cease to attend their parish churches. It was their habit to attend; and they were liable to fines if they failed. In 1563 a committee at Rome declared that this attendance was not permitted; but they disregarded the opinion, and if they were not readily reconciled to the vernacular liturgy, their children quietly became accustomed to it. Many of them were helped by the moderation, the Catholic atmosphere, of the English liturgy; and some justified their attendance and conformity during the first few years on the plea that the Pope had not pronounced decisively against Elizabeth by excommunicating her.

Pope Pius V was partly responsible for the tragedy of the English Counter-Reformation.

In 1568 Mary Queen of Scots fled from Scotland into England, was imprisoned, and gave the growing opposition a rallying-point. She told the Spanish ambassador that if

Spain would help her, she would be Queen of England within three months and mass would be said again all over the country. At Rome two cardinals discussed anxiously with the Pope how best to aid the coming insurrection. In November 1569 the Catholic north rose in revolt. The Earls of Northumberland and Westmorland, with a banner of the Five Wounds, 12,000 crowns from the Pope, and the promise of Spanish help, raised the standard of revolt. They desecrated the holy table in Durham cathedral, tore the English Bible in shreds, set up the mass again, and were soon suppressed in terrible executions. Not knowing that the rebellion had collapsed, Pius V issued the Bull *Regnans in excelsis* (1570) which excommunicated and deposed the Queen, declared that she and all her adherents were no part of the Body of Christ, and released all her subjects from their allegiance. The Bull was smuggled into England by a chaplain of the Spanish embassy, and a gentleman named Felton pinned it to the gate of the Bishop of London's palace in St Paul's churchyard and paid with his life. The language of the Bull was foolish, and its promulgation was resented by King Philip II of Spain, who was the chief earthly hope of the Roman see but had not been consulted. Thus the Pope stamped English Catholics with the imputation of treachery.

Once the character of traitors was given to them, the numerous innocent were thrown into the same bundle with the few guilty. Most English disciples of the Pope were as English as they were Roman, and had no wish to destroy the Queen for the sake of Mary Queen of Scots and the Spaniards. But since the Pope had proclaimed to the world that it was impossible to be a faithful subject of both Queen and Pope, every Roman Catholic in England, everyone who now refused on grounds of the old religion to attend his parish church, was a possible betrayer within the gates. If a man owed money to a recusant, he might raise popular feeling against him or denounce him to the authorities. If a man stole from a recusant, or took an action against him, the recusant could not be sure of justice, might not even dare to plead. The plot after plot surrounding Mary Queen of Scots, the fruitless efforts to plan for a Catholic succession to Elizabeth, the subsidies from the Pope to Irish rebels, above all the threat from Spain, deepened the fear of Roman Catholicism in the popular mind of Englishmen.

The rise of nationality, and its accompanying sentiment of patriotism, met the older medieval ideals of an international Christendom and generated conflicts of loyalty and troubled consciences. Elsewhere the conflict was made less painful by circumstance or by diplomacy. Pius V, least diplomatic of all the popes, succeeded in creating this conflict of conscience in its naked form. While most English papists were loyal to the Queen of England, some recusants felt obliged to regard their loyalty to the Pope as choosing the commands of God above the commands of Caesar, and so justified the national fears of conspiracy and foreign invasion. It was true that 180 monks and friars sailed with the Spanish Armada; that King Philip II and the then Pope agreed to elevate the exiled Cardinal Allen into the offices of Lord Chancellor and Archbishop of Canterbury if the invasion should succeed; that at the time of the Armada Allen printed a nasty tirade denouncing the Queen as a bastard, a usurper, and a heretic; that a band of 700 English exiles marched with the Spanish army of the Netherlands to prepare the invasion, and that in 1580 a papal secretary wrote an official answer that Elizabeth was the cause of so much injury to the Catholic faith that 'whosoever sends her out of the world, with the pious intention of doing God service, not only does not sin but gains merit'.

So began the penal legislation.

The Parliament of 1571 subjected to the penalty of treason anyone who reconciled another to Rome or was himself reconciled to Rome. The Act made every recusant priest implicitly liable to death on a charge of treason. The first priest to be executed was Cuthbert Mayne in 1577. Subsequent legislation, from 1581, made the treason explicit. In 1585 the priest was guilty of high treason if he remained in England, and it became a felony to shelter or receive a priest. It is impossible to say whether Mayne and his successors were executed for high treason or martyred for religion, since the two had now become identified. Mayne was charged with administering the Lord's Supper after a papistical manner, and with distributing trinkets; but he was also bound to confess that while he was loyal to the Crown now, he would need to assist any invaders who thereafter might endeavour to recover England to the obedience of the Pope.

Here is an exchange during the Durham Assizes of July 1594:

THE PRESIDENT: Thou art condemned for most vile treason against the Queen's Majesty.

INGRAM: My Lord, I die only for religion, and for the same religion by which, and no other, your lordship and this whole bench must all be saved if ever you will be saved.

JUDGE BEAUMONT: Thou art impudent . . . the law tellest thee that thou diest for high treason . . .

INGRAM: There is no Christian law in the world, that can make the saying and sacrifice of the mass treason; as well might the celebrating of the maundy of Christ's disciples be made treason, as the saying and hearing of mass be made treason.

The predicament of English recusants had become intolerable. A dispensation obtained from Rome in 1580, allowing a qualified profession of loyalty, made matters no better, for the qualifications seemed to undermine the value of any profession of loyalty by a recusant.

Meanwhile the exiles upon the Continent organized themselves. It was clear that recusancy in England would die without assistance from Rome and beyond the seas, for without that assistance it had become impossible to supply priests, theology, or sacraments. In 1568 Allen founded an English college at the new university of Douai, and thence a college was founded at Rome in 1576. The Douai College sent 438 priests to the English mission before 1603. Before 1603 there were also colleges at Lisbon, Madrid, Seville, and Valladolid. Allen created an effective mode, however perilous, of stemming conformity and encouraging faithful recusants. To his trained, zealous, courageous men, Roman Catholicism in England owed its continued existence. During the years between 1577 and 1603, 123 priests were executed, and some sixty men or women who had been guilty of harbouring or assisting them. The best of the priests, like the Jesuit Edmund Campion, were men with a pure spirit of pastoral care, refined by the readiness to face martyrdom. The lesser men, like the Jesuit Robert Parsons, were political schemers without scruples.

It was inevitable that these pressures should divide the recusant body. There were men who believed that they could be good Catholics and loyal to Queen Elizabeth, and others who believed that this was impossible. The difference began to divide the recusants into two parties, those who wanted Jesuit control over the secular priests, because Jesuit control insisted upon the more rigorous opinion, and those who resisted it for the same reason. In the English colleges at Rome and Rheims, whither the Dutch wars forced the Douai college to move for fifteen years, in the castle at Wisbech where many recusants were confined, the difference led to accusations of schism and heresy. It led to a demand by the secular priests for a bishop, since the presence of a bishop would overthrow or minimize the authority of the Jesuits.

The endeavours of brave or unscrupulous men could do little more than maintain the allegiance of the few. The returns at the accession of James I in 1603 show that there were 8,570 recusants in the country. The highest numbers were in Cheshire and Lancashire, nearly 2,500 being in the diocese of Chester. Other estimates of the real extent of recusancy were much higher. There may have been as many as 360 priests still working quietly in the country, and perhaps 100,000 or more Catholics who conformed occasionally to avoid fines. In the north, yeomen and farmers and even townsmen might be recusant. Simple people might refuse to go to church because they disliked change. Mrs Porter, the wife of a tailor at York, when summoned for not going to church, replied that 'her conscience will not serve her, for things are not in the church as it hath been aforetime in her forefathers' time'. But, except in the north and in Ireland, the continued allegiance to Rome depended upon the continuity of a Catholic family of squires. The country people could not remain Roman Catholic without the sacraments; the sacraments were not obtainable without the priests; the priests could find shelter and protection only in great houses. The number of 'priest-holes' now to be found in country houses has been exaggerated by legend or piety. These skilfully constructed hides are more often found in the south than the north. The most effective were built into the house in such a way that no hollow spaces, or spaces unaccounted for, could be observed by the most experienced searcher. At Hindlip Hall in 1606 the pursuers had almost certain knowledge that there were priests in the house. They were right; four men were concealed. The house was torn apart in the endeavour to find them, but in vain. They were found after several days, only because they were starving and forced to surrender themselves. These uncomfortable hiding-places show romantically how Elizabethan and Stuart recusancy depended upon faithful squires. This relation between the county family and the priest imparted to Roman Catholicism in England a characteristic stamp which it bore until the emancipation of 1829, and which the vast changes since 1829 have not wholly eradicated.

In the plot of 1605 to blow up the king and the Houses of Parliament while they were sitting, most of the conspirators were Catholic; and it was shown that the superior of the Jesuits, Father Garnet, possessed a knowledge of the plot through the confessional, and outside the confessional a vague information that something of the kind was afoot. The Roman Catholics of England were ignorant of the plot, and nearly all would have disapproved if they had known. But Guy Fawkes became to the English people the third symbol, like the fires of Smithfield and the Spanish Armada, to prove the disloyalty of Roman Catholics. A service for the annual commemoration on 5 November was ordered, when sermons were preached resounding with eloquence rather than charity.*

Despite the Gunpowder Plot, and epidemical though fewer executions of priests, despite yet more stringent penal laws, the recusants were justified in expecting the Stuarts to be more tolerant and favourable. High policy conducted negotiations for a Spanish marriage under James I, and married Charles I to a Roman Catholic queen Henrietta Maria, who was allowed to bring with her a bishop and twenty-seven priests, though a majority of these were later dismissed. In 1623 a bishop was at last consecrated, as Bishop of Chalcedon, for the Roman Catholics of England, though his successor was compelled to leave the country in 1631. One of the Secretaries of State resigned his office on becoming a Roman Catholic, was elevated to be Lord Baltimore, and later became the founder of the state of Maryland. Under Charles I papal agents appeared at court and mass was celebrated before large congregations in the chapels of the queen or the foreign ambassadors. Even Dr Godfrey Goodman, the Anglican Bishop of Gloucester, submitted on his deathbed to the Church of Rome. Recusant peers were not debarred from sitting in the House of Lords until 1678. Charles II, in exile during the Commonwealth, acquired those Roman Catholic sympathies which were

* These annual services continued to 1858. By the middle of the seventeenth century the day was the occasion of excitable behaviour and fireworks among the apprentices of London. From about 1673, when the Duke of York (the future King James II) married Mary of Modena despite the hostility of the Commons, an effigy of the Pope was sometimes burnt. At the end of the eighteenth century the effigy began to be called a guy.

seldom evident in either his public or his moral life, but which appeared on his deathbed.

Suspicion of Rome became almost a part of the national character, a part of patriotism, a part of the Englishness of a man, and a rock upon which Stuart kings were to destroy themselves.

COUNTER-REFORMATION DEVOTION

In devotional life as in doctrine, it has been suggested that the Protestants drove the Catholics into valuing even more highly the practices which they criticized or destroyed. A Spaniard or an Italian heard of sacrilegious feet trampling upon the dust and bones of godly men, heard that vile northern mobs hurled bricks at a statue of the Blessed Virgin, heard of the Virgin outraged and blasphemed though she had consoled the Church through centuries – the Virgin whose delicate queenly portrait in St Maria Maggiore at Rome had been painted from the life, so it was believed, by the hand of St Luke himself; and was moved in the heart to make reparation, to restore the beauty and the poetry which the north was stripping, to cherish the images or the relics more fervently than ever, to listen more readily than before to the stories of relics bleeding or tears pouring from the eyes of statues, which he decorated with still richer jewels.

But the belief that here Rome valued what the Protestants denied because the Protestants denied it is not warranted by evidence. The student of devotional life during the fifteenth century sees many of the forms often associated with the Counter-Reformation. The new piety of the age of Trent, the new warmth, encouraged by the European stature of Spanish religious culture, took these older forms and extended them.

Though the Counter-Reformation pruned its mass and its breviary, its devotional power was more personal than liturgical. The laity were encouraged to make their communions more frequently and therefore to go to confession more frequently, but their devotions at the mass rather accompanied, than were derived from, the liturgical forms. It was observed by hostile critics as an aggressive act when Jesuits walked publicly in the streets with a rosary in hand or at the belt. In the churches it was an age of lavish ornament, costly furnishing of sepulchres and altars, of coloured lamps and precious candlesticks. The retreat slowly became a custom, mainly rising from the administering of the *Spiritual Exercises* of Ignatius and later much encouraged by French writers of the seventeenth century. Educated laity were encouraged to use the Bible for devotional purposes, in authorized translations of the Vulgate. The devotion to the Virgin Mary, though like most devotions extended during the later sixteenth century, hardly acquired important new forms; the Angelus became widespread as a devotion only during the seventeenth century. Some theologians, like the Spanish Jesuit Suarez, developed the idea of Mary as in a manner cooperating in man's redemption; and theologians usually refrain from such speculations unless they are accompanying or justifying or restraining a current in popular piety. In eucharistic devotion there were further extensions. The old haphazard conditions under which the sacrament was reserved in churches, being sometimes kept in cupboards in the sacristy even in Italy, slowly gave place to a more uniform arrangement whereby an elaborately furnished tabernacle was constructed upon the high altar of the church. The modern form of the service of Benediction, where the Host is exposed for veneration and the people blessed with it, took shape at this time. Frequent communion and a strong devotion to the Virgin often accompany a dwelling upon Christ's human nature and human love. Teresa of Avila and Francis de Sales popularized the cult of St Joseph. The early Counter-Reformation was too austere to encourage extravagant language, but as it developed it ceased to be afraid of emotional warmth. Pierre de Bérulle (died 1629), who introduced the Oratory into France, was marked by a fervour of affection for the human nature of Jesus, publishing in 1623 *Les Grandeurs de Jésus*, a title which itself marks the difference from the Catholic devotion of a century before. His successor as superior of the French Oratory, Charles de Condren (died 1641), shows a similar mingling of affectionate language to the human Jesus with strongly evocative language about the eucharist. Another Oratorian, John Eudes (1601–80, canonized 1925) left the Oratory in 1643 to found the 'Congregation of Jesus and Mary', a community of priests dedicated to the Hearts of Jesus and Mary; and although the important development of the cult of the Sacred Heart waited until the visions of Margaret Mary Alacoque in 1673–4, its origins should be sought in the work of Eudes. In 1648 he established in his congregation a feast in honour of the Heart of Mary.

The physical 'miracle' associated with sanctity continued to be valued, as in the Middle Ages. The body which remained incorruptible or gave an odour of fragrance, the relic which cured, the nun who rose in the air and remained suspended there, the face which shone with an unearthly light, the stigmata of the crucified upon the hands and feet (as of Sister Mary of the Visitation, the nun of Lisbon who was consulted by the Spanish naval command before the sailing of the great Armada),* the ring of flesh upon the nun's finger, the heart which the fire of a spiritual love raised to a material temperature of burning, the nun who ate nothing for many years – these physical and psychological accompaniments were valued uncritically by the people, not uncritically by the ecclesiastical authorities. It is one of the most curious contrasts between the Protestants and the Counter-Reformation that among the Protestant churches this popular element in the medieval outlook dropped away so readily. The king of England continued to touch for the King's Evil, the practitioners of Protestant medicine were hardly emancipated from material magics,

---

* It was afterwards alleged that her stigmata were fabricated; the allegation is suspect, for the Spanish government discovered that she favoured Portuguese independence, and wished to discredit her.

their astronomers were still astrologers, their chemists were still alchemists, their witch-hunters were as zealous. But the alleged accompaniments of mystic ecstasies disappeared with the convents which had begotten them, were suspected as popish, and were not missed.

Mysticism may broadly be defined as the direct apprehension of the divine by a faculty of the mind or soul. The Protestants were suspicious of any such claim, which seemed to suggest that the divine might be found in a natural knowledge or experience apart from the knowledge of the Scriptures. Many leading Catholics, especially the Jesuits, were also suspicious of an unrestrained mystical claim, on comparable grounds. The early Spanish mystics were often in trouble with the Inquisition.

Teresa of Avila (1515–82), of noble family, was a nun from the age of sixteen, a Carmelite at twenty. The Carmelites were not 'unreformed'; but Teresa demanded higher standards, and (from 1562) founded seventeen convents in the teeth of opposition. In 1561–2, at the order of her Dominican confessor, she wrote her autobiography, a narrative of nervous illness and ecstasies and religious visions, mingled with a profound apprehension of the growth of the soul through prayer towards union with God; a farrago, unique in Christian history, of the childlike and the mature mind, grandeur without arrangement and with the minimum of punctuation, a feminine and uninhibited version of St Augustine's *Confessions*, which much influenced her. No important Christian author has written with more abandon. The reader knows, even if he were not told by one of her friends, that she wrote rapidly and without erasures. The Inquisition confiscated her manuscript, and she recovered it only with the help of King Philip II. In *The Way of Perfection* (1565) and *The Interior Castle* (1577), she went again over the same ground, *The Interior Castle* being intended to replace the autobiography, which the inquisitors still kept. The castle is the soul, its keeper God indwelling; and the life of prayer is a movement through the rooms of the castle from the outer ring to the light at the centre. In the midst of these devotions of the cloister, she was showing herself a woman of capacity and business, a mistress of practical detail, organizing her order, protecting it from powerful onslaughts. She was sainted in 1622.

In 1567 she met for the first time a young student of Salamanca, Juan de Yepes, known now as St John of the Cross (1542–91). Under her guidance he founded in 1568 the first house of discalced (barefoot) Carmelites at Duruelo, not far from Avila. He spent several months of 1577–8 in prison, died persecuted by his prior, and was not sainted till 1726; his works were first published at Alcalá in 1618, with many mutilations and suppressions. Not until an edition of 1912–14 was the authentic text adequately known, and he was declared 'Doctor of the Church' in 1926. A Spanish poet of lyrical purity, he poured the mystical ideal into a series of odes with commentaries, *The Ascent of Mount Carmel, The Dark Night of the Soul, The Song of the Spirit, The Living Flame of Love.* With John of the Cross, quiet and enclosed, publishing little, designed not so much for the layman as for the religious, writing lyrics for the heart, not pandering to the emotions but carrying the heart upwards into a purer air, the mystical tradition within Christendom touched one of its rare summits.

The part-theological, part-devotional reaction against Augustinianism, which we have already observed in Protestantism among the assailants of the Calvinists, and which was marked in some of the Jesuit divines, received its most attractive statement in another French writer, Francis de Sales (1567–1622), Bishop of Geneva (not resident at Geneva but at Annecy) 1602–22, sainted in 1665. In 1609 he published the *Introduction to the Devout Life*, in 1616 the *Treatise on the Love of God*. The *Introduction* marks a new phase in Catholic piety. As the Jesuits were the medieval religious orders coming out into the world, so the *Introduction* is the piety of the convent coming out of the cloister and taking charge of lay life. Perfection is possible for everyone, and not only for the especially religious. The busiest man is not to leave ascetic sacrifice or the prayer of contemplation to the monk and the nun, but may in his manner practise them in cities and courts and family life. The silent wordless mental prayer of the contemplative is within reach of all. Thus, like the contemporary Jesuits, Francis de Sales portrayed the life of devotion as easy, or at least as much easier than everyone expects. Unlike all Augustinians, whether Lutheran or Jansenist, he held a most optimistic view of the powers of the human will, which seems to rise towards God by its free acts, lured onward and upward by his beauty and sweetness. What Molina and some of the Jesuits are in theology – the opposite of the doctrine of justification by faith alone – Francis de Sales is in piety. Though for an austere taste there is too much sweetness of the spirit, few devotional books have conveyed such a feeling of charm or of psychological skill. He was fully aware that the courtier or the governor cannot say his prayers or mortify himself like the nun. But he was contending that the daily round and common task afford ample opportunity for self-abnegation to him who will seize them. He encouraged a weekly receiving of the holy communion. He was the first of Catholic writers to take spiritual direction out of the cloister and recommend all laymen to the guidance of a director.

The Use of Latin

In 1660 Latin was still the language of European scholarship. It had ceased to be the language of everything else that mattered to the life of man. As the vernaculars had become the tongues of literature, whether prose or poetry, so they had become the vehicles of worship in all the churches outside the Roman Catholic and Eastern Orthodox. Even in scholarship much of the best was now written in the language of the people.

Thus the growth of vernacular tongues to the highest respectability separated Latin as the liturgical language. Until the seventeenth century Latin was in some measure a living language. It continued to live in corners of the adult secular world, among the civilian lawyers and the scholars. But for the most part it was shrinking back within the Church and the classroom, no longer a true medium of life and exchange, but a dead language, to be mastered by the children, essential to the educated man who wished to understand his civilization and its past, but now principally a ritual and a liturgical language. Latin was not a 'dead' language in 1500, for Erasmus used it as the literary expression of the highest contemporary prose. Such a form of living literature was no longer possible in 1660. And therefore the language of Catholic liturgy became more remote, more clerical, more ritualistic at the end of the Reformation than at the beginning, and partly in consequence of the Reformation. As the old Slavonic liturgies were becoming canonized in the Russian Church, though a language no longer of the lips but only of the missal, so the Latin of the Church continued to live, but at the altar and in the seminary. As a language it acquired a hieratic quality which it had not quite possessed before the Reformation. In 1500 a man would have been more likely to assume that the liturgy should be in Latin because the liturgy should be in the highest prose that was available, and Latin was that highest form. In 1650 a defender of Latin in the Counter-Reformation would have been more likely to declare that Latin was the sacred language of the liturgy.

CATHOLIC SCHOLARSHIP

Catholic scholarship in the age of the Counter-Reformation was much hampered by the control of the press. The condemnation of Galileo in 1633 is but the most notorious of a long succession of decisions by cautious conservatives against bold and original minds. But scholarship everywhere was much hampered by censorship. The pile of books condemned by Protestant censors reached as high towards heaven as those condemned by Catholic censors. The defenders of orthodoxy were slow to realize that where they once cut manuscripts to pieces, the printed book was bound to escape their clumsy scissors. Pope Urban VIII and his advisers who condemned Galileo (it has been said by Giorgio de Santillana) were not so much oppressors as the first bewildered casualties of the scientific age.

Repressive machinery is sometimes more vexatious by its clumsiness than by its violence. Merchants who wanted trade in Protestant countries found the requisite papers tedious to obtain. The desks of those responsible for the censorship were piled high with books awaiting licences, and the trials of Italian authors during part of the second half of the sixteenth century would have been laughable had they not been unendurable. The rules were difficult enough to enforce. There must be no laudatory mention of heretical persons, no manuscript must be followed against the readings of the Vulgate, and the censors were sometimes unlearned persons unfit to examine the books of the learned and therefore likely to resort to delay, the characteristic device of the inefficient and uncertain. Among the worst delays were the textbooks for schools and universities, urgently needed for teaching purposes but important for the censors to approve.

The standard of editing found in sixteenth-century Rome was not the standard of seventeenth-century France. An edition of St Ambrose was prepared by the future Sixtus V. It corrected all the Scriptural quotations to the text of the Vulgate, altered the text, transposed words, changed the order of the paragraphs, inserted ceremonial detail which the saint unaccountably omitted, clarified obscurities and suppressed eccentricities. The extension of these bureaucratic methods to the rest of the Church would have destroyed Catholic scholarship.

The oddest thing about the reforming censorship of the Counter-Reformation was its attitude to morality. Books which attacked the clergy or stank of heresy were repressed ruthlessly. Books which were obscene did not suffer quite the same fate. The *Decameron* of Boccaccio underwent a whole series of bowdlerizing editions during the course of the sixteenth century. The authorities at first put it upon the Index, among other obscene publications, but works which were just as obscene were allowed to be published freely, and the *Decameron* had become classical in Italian literature. In a country rich in vernacular poetry, it was one of the few masterpieces in vernacular prose. Cosimo de' Medici of Florence asked Pope Pius V if Rome would publish an expurgated edition. This edition appeared in 1573, prefaced by a *motu proprio* from Pope Gregory XIII, an authority from the supreme court of the Inquisition, another authority from the Inquisitor-General of Florence, and privileges from the kings of France and Spain, the dukes of Tuscany and Ferrara, and other heads of states. It is an extraordinary edition. The passages redolent of heresy were removed – for example, a sentence reflecting on the efficacy of good works; so were the passages where monks or priests were mocked or represented as guilty of criminal acts. Every time the censors met a clergyman in these situations they changed him to a layman. They left the obscenities in print, but protected the reputation of priests.

The effect of repression should not be exaggerated. Latini refused to put his name to an edition of Cyprian because the censors insisted upon changes which he could not accept. Luis de León, lecturing at Salamanca, declared that the Vulgate edition contained many errors, though not in faith and morals, and was imprisoned for five years. When released, he began his lecture with the words: 'As I was saying last time . . .' The words have been inscribed on the pedestal of his statue, and are the fairest expression of the tranquil integrity of mind among threatened students. Catholic scholars suffered, but remained scholars.

Gregory XIII (Pope 1572–85) revived a shadow of the Renaissance patronage of scholarship. He protected the greatest Catholic exegete of the day, Juan Maldonado, from obscurantist enemies, and brought him to Rome to work upon a new edition of the Septuagint. In 1578 labourers quarrying two miles outside the city found apertures which led to extensive rediscovery of the Roman catacombs, most of which, apart from the sepulchral chambers beneath churches, were forgotten and largely filled with rubble. During the next fifty years the range of underground galleries was excavated and the inscriptions collected by Roman archaeologists. In 1584 the Pope set up a printing press for Oriental literature, which began with an Arabic translation of the Gospels. He caused proper care to be taken of the collections in the Vatican library. In 1580 he published a new text of the code of canon law. The court of Rome displayed a signal triumph of reason and astronomical science when Gregory reformed the calendar. He consulted the universities, and the Sorbonne authorities replied that a change of calendar would confess the ancient church to have been in error on the subject of Easter, and therefore weaken the basis of authority in the Church. In 1582 the Pope suppressed the old calendar and made 5 October into 15 October. It was accepted almost at once in the Catholic states, which thus achieved a more scientific accuracy, while the benighted Protestant countries continued to suffer under the old calendar.* They would not change their year at the decree of a pope, and sought error in the Roman mathematics. It was observed that violent storms raged over Germany during the ten days which the Pope had removed. The new calendar was adopted by Protestant Switzerland in 1700–1, by England as late as 1752, by Sweden in 1753; and among the Eastern Orthodox people the Bulgarians were the first to accept it, during the 1914–18 war.

* Germany being divided in religion, the two systems of dating henceforth existed side by side, causing embarrassment at imperial meetings and in the imperial law court.

In one especial area of study the polemics of the Reformation age laid the basis for scholarly advance; the study of history. It was impossible for Catholic to argue with Protestant except upon the ground of historical inquiry, for there was no other common ground. The Reformation appealed to the Bible, the Counter-Reformation to the Bible as understood by an infallible Church. The common ground for argument, therefore, lay in the history of the Church, whether that history supported the idea of an infallible Church, whether the practices of the Protestants or the definitions of the Council of Trent could find support in the history of the Christian centuries. Each side appealed to history in support of its interpretation, and this was a study where signal advances were possible. Between 1559 and 1574 the Lutheran Flacius Illyricus and his collaborators published the Magdeburg *Centuries*, the first serious and scholarly survey of the history of the Church, tracing with zeal and care the slow corruption of the Church from New Testament times into the Middle Ages. Flacius had to be answered, and could only be answered, by better scholarship. In 1568 the founder of the Oratory, Philip Neri, charged his Oratorian Caesar Baronius with the task of answering Flacius and the Centuriators. Baronius published his *Annals* in twelve folio volumes from 1588 to 1607, the year of his death. The *Annals* were as biased as the *Centuries*, and as inaccurate, though inaccurate in different places. But they were indispensable to later students, because Baronius, unlike Flacius, used the archives and manuscripts of the Vatican library, where he was librarian from 1597. The *Annals* sought to show, partly on the basis of documents not yet known to be spurious, that the practices or beliefs alleged by Flacius to be corruptions were in truth found from the earliest times of the Christian Church. He satisfied and reassured a public anxious that modern historical criticism had shaken the evidence for early legends, and preserved the popular notions of antiquity in a picturesque haze.

The study of history, however partial, cannot exist without sooner or later breeding truth and impartiality. Already in the earlier half of the seventeenth century French Catholic scholars were embarking upon those scholarly inquiries which by the end of the century made the French Benedictines of St Maur the first to be worthy of the modern title of critical historians. In 1606 the Belgian Jesuit Herbert Rosweyde obtained leave to be free of all teaching and to devote himself to scholarship. In furtherance of the pious ideals of the Counter-Reformation he planned a great collection of the lives of the saints, but these lives were to be edited and published in accordance with the critical standards of modern historical study. He had other tasks, including a defence of Baronius against his most formidable Protestant critic, and died in 1629 with the work barely begun; and even in what had been done, he never quite lost sight of the rule that the chief object of historical study is to controvert Protestants. In achievement and critical skill he had passed far beyond Baronius; and his vast plan was taken up by another Jesuit, John van Bolland (died 1665), who ransacked the libraries of the monasteries, and who founded that eminent society of Bollandists which took his name and which still continues to profit the world with its erudition.

The new historical learning was turned to its weightiest use in controversy by another Jesuit, Robert Bellarmine (died 1621). His *Disputations against the Heretics of Our Time*, in three large volumes (1586–93), were the most systematic and cogent defence of the Counter-Reformation against the Reformation. Pope Gregory XIII helped to found at Rome a professorship of Controversy to instruct the young German or English priests in Rome, and Bellarmine was named to be the first occupant. He took the new historical equipment of the age into a calm and magisterial system, far above the lively repartees of a John Eck, and was afraid of no argument, not seeking to solve problems with turns of phrase or specious appeals, not abusive of personalities, yet in most areas of the battle as uncompromising as any of the more acrimonious warriors.

The canon of the Bible, the inspired nature of the Vulgate, the necessity for an infallible Church to interpret the Scriptures, the authority of tradition, the doctrines of transubstantiation and of the eucharistic sacrifice, the inerrancy of the Pope's decrees – the whole complex of definitions half-formulated at Trent and believed by the Protestants to be indefensible – found a defender who set 'the errors of the heretics' side by side with the teaching of 'Catholic divines' and then sought to prove on grounds of history and reason that the heretics had no standing whatever. The Protestants could not despise him. They turned against him their heaviest artillery.

In the same epoch when English Reform acquired intellectual self-confidence with Richard Hooker, the Counter-Reformation lost the slickness and abusiveness which betrayed a sense of insecurity, and displayed in Bellarmine its recovery of assurance.

THE POLITICAL COUNTER-REFORMATION

The name of Counter-Reformation is loosely applied not only to the movement for Catholic reform, but to a movement distinct from reform, the political revival of the Catholic powers of Europe and the rising fear, at the end of the sixteenth century and after, that they would yet succeed in crushing the Protestant states and reimposing Catholicism by force.

The beginning of this movement is to be dated from the peace between France and Spain arranged at Cateau-Cambrésis in 1559, and the outbreak of religious and civil war in France soon afterwards. For France was thereby removed for the time from the European balance of power. In the early and weak years of the Lutheran states, the Protestants were saved from destruction by the existence of Catholic France, whose political needs they admirably served. As late as 1551 Pope Julius III called wildly for a war against the French, so mischievously allied with Protestants and Turks. From 1562 to 1598 France was in epidemic anarchy, and after 1598 was recuperating. Not until 1629 was a French army again able to intervene decisively in external European politics and thereby swing back the balance of power once again towards the Protestants. The political Counter-Reformation may be dated from 1562 to 1629, and coincides with the weakness of divided France. It depended upon a free hand for the foreign policies of the Habsburg powers in Spain and Austria and Italy.

The coming of Protestantism helped to divide France, Germany, Switzerland, Ireland. The Catholic kings perceived, or thought they perceived, that Protestantism and popular movements were allied, that their political authority was dependent upon the union of Catholic Church and State and the suppression of heresy. During the second half of the sixteenth century, encouraged by Pope Pius V and his successors, the league of Catholic kings began to take the appearance of a political alliance for the defence of the Church and perhaps for the destruction of Protestantism. The most powerful and most Catholic of these kings was Philip II of Spain. Devout, determined, austere, spending long hours upon his knees before statues of saints, living in his Escorial rather as a monastery than as a palace, ruling the Church of Spain as tyrannically as Henry VIII ruled the Church of England, identifying heresy with treason to the established authorities, wealthy with the gold of Peru, he governed Spain and the Netherlands, South Italy and Sicily, Sardinia, Milan, all the Spanish colonies in the Americas, and after 1580 Portugal and all the Portuguese colonies in the Indies. In 1599, the year after Philip died, Thomas Campanella published an absurd book, *De Monarchia Hispanica*, to prove or predict that Spain was destined to succeed to the Holy Roman Empire, and would at last unite France and Spain and Italy into a great power which would force the Protestants to submission. The dream was not visionary. Victory in one of three campaigns would have brought success near. If the Armada had beaten the English warships; or if Alva had beaten resistance in Holland; or if the Catholic League had beaten Henry of Navarre, the Protestants would have been insecure. The dream was not confined to the fantasies of academics. Pope Sixtus V encircled the world with vast insubstantial alliances, imagining that he would conquer the Turks with his galleys, recapture Jerusalem, and destroy the Protestants with a league of Catholic princes. He excommunicated Henry of Navarre, like a Pope of the high Middle Ages, and talked of sending a papal army to help the Spaniards in France against the Huguenots. There was question of papal support for the Poles in an attack upon the Russians, a hope of Catholic restoration upon the Baltic coast and a scheme to invade Algiers from Italy. It was easy to represent all wars against non-Catholic states, from whatever motive, as crusades; and like the conquistadors in America, the Spanish soldier believed himself to be serving God and his king. In the Brussels portrait by Antonio Moro, the Duke of Alva is painted wearing a crucifix over the armour upon his breast. At Alva's side in 1572 rode the Archbishop of Cologne, with pistols in his holsters.

The dream came nearest to fulfilment in Germany.

In 1562 it looked as though the great Catholic states of south Germany, Bavaria and Austria, upon which the cause mainly rested, might follow north Germany into Protestantism. Many Austrian priests and monasteries were already administering the sacrament in both kinds, and some were altering the liturgy, dropping prayers for the dead, and treating their concubines as legal wives. Probably two thirds of the population of Austria were already Protestant in sympathy, and where there had once been an absurd superfluity of clergy, now one priest was having to serve four parishes. In Bavaria a diet met at Ingolstadt in

1563 to discuss a proposal to legalize the Augsburg Confession; and though the proposal was rejected, the diet approved the gift of the chalice to the laity, the legalizing of clerical marriage, and the use of the German language at baptisms.

In the lands of south Germany, where the old abuses already prevailed enough, the power of the Reformation to the north meant the further loosening of ecclesiastical discipline. Reform of corrupt and secularized canonries and monasteries was long overdue, and now the word Reform had become associated with heresy and mob rule. The conservative resistance to Protestants was not in these circumstances far removed from resistance to every kind of reform or change, however salutary. 'I know one cathedral church,' wrote John Eck to Cardinal Contarini in 1540, 'where only three out of fifty-four canons are priests.' Eck found a cathedral where neither the bishop nor the dean had been ordained to the priesthood. When, just across the border to the north, marriage was permitted to clergy, the unmarried priests, long accustomed to keep concubines, hankered after a legalization of their women into wives and their children into legal and honourable heirs. Several eminent German bishops argued in 1561 that the only solution of Germany's problem was the permission for priests to marry, under conditions. Duke Albert V of Bavaria informed the Council of Trent that he could hardly keep Bavaria in allegiance to the Holy See unless the chalice and clerical marriage were allowed. In April 1564 Pope Pius IV sent a brief to many of the German Catholic bishops, sanctioning the gift of communion in both kinds to laymen who wished to receive it. Under these conditions the Protestants were still making progress.

Between 1565 and 1585 it is possible to discern a change in morale. The Protestants became less certain of themselves, the Catholics more self-confident. The decline in Protestant hopes and expectations was partly due to the new and tougher Catholic policy pursued by rulers like Albert of Bavaria. But even more it arose from a measure of recognition that the Reformation, though its truth and necessity were not doubted, had not succeeded in what at the first flush of enthusiasm it had been expected to do. 'We imagined that a golden century was in store for us,' said the Calvinist pastor Scultet when he visited Wittenberg in 1591. 'The enemy,' wrote the Heidelberg pastor Boquin in 1576, 'seemed at last disposed of, when lo, he raised a new army and entrenched himself in his stronghold.' A part of this sense of disillusionment arose from the Protestant divisions. The weightiest states of Protestant Germany were Lutheran, and yet during these years the Reformed polity and teaching, which some Lutherans feared almost as they feared Rome, was making strides in Germany. The University of Wittenberg was declining while the Jesuit University of Ingolstadt was rising. Another element of disillusionment was the inevitable reaction among all reformers after a wave of reform has spent its first force; the character and intelligence of the human race are unexpectedly resistant to all attempts to reform them, and even in a state of better discipline men and women are often tenacious of superstition, evil custom, and lax morality. The Counter-Reformation was finding the same, for all that Trent and new orders could do. An eminent hammer of the Protestants as late as the end of the century, Wolf Dietrich von Raittenau, Archbishop of Salzburg 1587-1612, was notorious for his expensive concubine, his three sons and seven daughters. But despite the many exceptions, the Catholic reformers steadily improved standards everywhere, and there was no longer the glaring contrast between the 'Reformed' and the 'unreformed'. The Catholic who contended for reform as the only way to resist Reform was proved right by the event.

The altered strength of the respective parties may be illustrated from Graz, from Cologne, and from Poland.

Graz

In 1570 the inhabitants of Graz were almost all Protestants; there were said to be about twenty Catholic communicants in the city. In 1573 Archduke Charles founded and endowed at Graz a Jesuit college, but he was still bound to allow freedom of religion and of education to the Protestants, and promised them this freedom at the Diet of Brück in 1578. He began, however, to employ only Catholic cooks in his court and to raise Italians and Bavarians to high positions. In 1581 the evangelical pastors were expelled from the city and replaced by priests, the citizens of Graz were forbidden to attend the city school, which was Protestant, and in 1585–6 the Jesuit college was raised to the rank of a university, with the avowed purpose of maintaining the purity of the Catholic faith and destroying heresy. The archduke then felt strong enough to allow citizenship only to Catholics. He died in 1590, exacting from his successor, who was twelve years old, a vow to maintain the Catholic faith. During the minority the Protestants flourished again. It was untruly said that at Easter 1596 the young duke was the only citizen of Graz to receive the sacrament in accordance with the Catholic faith. But when Ferdinand reached his majority, the tide turned again. He is reported to have said: 'I would rather rule a country ruined than a country damned.' In 1598 he expelled from Graz all Protestant pastors and schoolmasters. In 1599 he closed all Protestant churches and chapels, and local resistance to the decree was crushed by force. In 1628 he compelled 800 Protestant members of the upper class to leave the country.

Cologne

The Peace of Augsburg was politically successful. From 1555 to 1605 both sides appealed to it as the foundation of German law upon religious division. Wise rulers upon either side would countenance no breach of it, even if that breach were to the advantage of their own side, lest Germany be plunged again into confusion. It must not be thought that the German peasant was always free from devastation and campaigning troops during these years of 'peace'. But the campaigns were always local and continued the ancient German practice.

Nevertheless, the Peace of Augsburg suffered from two main defects. It made no provision in two important directions: the status of the Calvinists and the status of the ecclesiastical territories.

Being a treaty between Catholics and Lutherans, it did not mention the Zwinglians or Calvinists, whose presence the Lutherans regretted almost as warmly as the Catholics. Therefore the Calvinist princes and cities had no legal right to exist in Germany. But this was absurd, for Zwinglian and Calvinist princes and cities did exist in Germany, and in increasing strength. Yet in theory they had no status in the imperial courts, and the Lutherans, clinging to the authority of the Peace of Augsburg, often sided with the Emperor and the Catholic territories against them.

The second defect of the Peace was the absence of effective legal provision if a prince-bishop turned Protestant. It is true that (see p. 146) there had been added to the peace terms the regulation known as the Ecclesiastical Reservation; but the regulation had never been accepted as legal by the Protestants. The Ecclesiastical Reservation declared that a prelate who became a Protestant had thereby resigned his ecclesiastical office. It aimed at securing that no further bishoprics should be secularized and appropriated as Protestant lands.

A clause which one side believed to be valid and the other side believed to be invalid could only be a source of strife. And its working depended in fact upon the local strength of the contending parties. With the complaisance of the Emperor Ferdinand I it failed to prevent great sees like Magdeburg and Halberstadt from becoming Protestant territories. Eleven years before the Peace, Hermann von Wied, Archbishop of Cologne, turned Protestant and attempted to secure the territory of the prince and bishopric as a principality. He was deposed by the armies of the Emperor Charles V, and his intentions frustrated. But if the bishop who became a Protestant were an Elector, other considerations besides ecclesiastical law entered in. If one more Elector turned Protestant, the Protestants would secure a majority in the electoral body and would probably elect a Protestant to be Holy Roman Emperor at the next vacancy.

In 1582 the then Archbishop of Cologne, Gebhard Truchsess, wanted to marry a nun, become a Protestant, and secularize his territory. His Catholic rival, Duke Ernest of Bavaria, was not at all reformed, and was already the bishop of three other sees, a drunkard, and the owner of a concubine. To the dismay of the Protestants, the Catholics invoked the Ecclesiastical Reservation, and the Lutherans withheld their support, partly because they feared Truchsess to be friendly to the Calvinists. He was driven from his see by Spanish and Bavarian troops, and the Bavarian prince was installed as his successor.

The existence of the prince-bishoprics, where the bishop was temporal sovereign as well as spiritual, assisted the cause of the Counter-Reformation as soon as general Catholic power was strong enough to give them political support. Great Catholic bishops were ruling territories where the population was largely Protestant, and so long as the balance of power in Germany lay with the north, the Protestants continued to be immune and to spread. It is a sign of the changing balance that bishops were beginning to take forcible action. In 1595 the Bishop of Bamberg ordered the mass or exile, and though the edict was opposed by the nobles, the cathedral chapter, and the neighbouring lords, on the whole it was executed. In 1596 Theodore von Fürstenberg, the Bishop of Paderborn, imprisoned all the priests of his diocese who administered the communion in both kinds. He then had to face the nobles, who began to drive off his cattle and horses, and the city, which elected a demagogue and had to be suppressed. Thus in command, the bishop lavishly endowed a college for the Jesuits and published the edict ordering the mass or exile. The continuous history of the Roman Catholic tradition in the Rhineland, which on grounds of geography might have been expected to be universally Protestant, is due partly to the Spanish armies in the Netherlands and partly to the success of the Counter-Reformation in holding and utilizing the great prince-bishoprics. For all its legal uncertainty, the Ecclesiastical Reservation was a momentous clause.

Poland

The tide began to turn in Poland after Stephen Báthory was elected king in 1575. He protected the Protestants and the Catholics equally during his reign, and was himself a moderate; but the tide was running in favour of the see of Rome throughout eastern Europe, and by the end of his reign there were 360 Jesuits in Poland. His successor Sigismund III (1587–1632) was a vehement Catholic. The successful introduction of the Gregorian calendar, which is one test of the progress of the Counter-Reformation, was accompanied by the receiving of the decrees of the Council of Trent. He would confer no office upon a Protestant, and under his encouragement Catholic nobles evicted Protestants from their estates, Catholic law courts ruled the recovery of parish churches, even in towns where the population was Protestant, and forced the Lutheran service into the town hall. Almost all the higher education was in the hands of the Jesuits. In 1607–8 the Protestant lords were rash enough to join a revolt of the discontented, including some Catholics and some Orthodox; and the suppression of the revolt meant the final victory of the Roman Catholic Church in Poland. No mixed marriages were legally recognized unless they were performed by the parish priest, and the parish priests refused to perform them. As early as 1598 the papal nuncio said: 'A short time ago, it might have been feared that heresy would entirely supersede Catholicism in Poland. Now Catholicism is bearing heresy to its grave.'

The Jesuits

Political Catholicism was becoming more aggressive with self-confidence. We may register the change by observing the declining international reputation of the Jesuits. The Jesuits had not come into the world with the notoriety which they later achieved; and when the heroism of their members in the Indies and the Americas is considered, it might be thought odd that their name should have acquired so evil an odour. In an order which expanded so rapidly, there was inevitably a proportion of regrettable men, but probably no higher a proportion than in any other order, and at their best, in a Francis Xavier, they added lustre to the name of Christian.

They began with the simple reputation of strictness, and their first unpopularity was the honourable disrepute of a sincere puritan. The name Jesuit was first used in Germany, like the name Methodist in Georgian England, as a synonym for severe. 'The young women,' said Hermann Weinsberg of Cologne, 'are good Jesuits; they go to church first thing in the morning, and fast a great deal.' If it was said that 'so-and-so is too much of a Jesuit', it meant that he was leading a life unreasonably strict for a layman.

But within the Church the old rivalry of orders found a new focus. Franciscan and Dominican looked askance at this new body, which claimed to be an order of religious yet lived in the world and was loaded with exceptional privilege. When they encountered them in Spain, Japan, the Indies, the Curia of Rome, the different methods and atmosphere bred constant misunderstanding and repeated controversy. In 1577 an eccentric Dominican declared that he crossed himself whenever he met a Jesuit. The Franciscans of Ingolstadt in 1583 called the Jesuits there 'the scourge of the monks'. It was thought that Bellarmine

might have been elected Pope in 1605 but for the impossibility of electing a Jesuit. As the leading propagators of the
faith they came to be associated in the mind of the Protestants with the spearhead of the political peril which they
were facing. The England of Queen Elizabeth was mortally
afraid of subversion by Catholic plots with Spanish aid,
and associated Jesuits with the foreign attempts to encourage
treason – upon Edmund Campion the judgement of England
was wrong, upon Robert Parsons it was right. A religious
order engaged in all the work of the world, they were known
to have the ear of several Catholic sovereigns; some were
rightly believed to be encouraging the Catholic league and
its campaigns in France, others were believed to be advising
the Emperor of Germany or the Duke of Bavaria. Canisius
tried to keep them away from courts and palaces; the
Jesuit General issued an order against mixing in German
affairs of state. But affairs of state were unavoidable. And
so the reputation grew. Small boys in the streets of Augsburg
in 1582 ran after a group of Jesuits shouting *Jesuswider!*
(Antijesus). In parts of Germany at this date they were
dubbed 'the black horsemen of the Pope'. In 1593 was
published at Frankfurt a *History of the Society of Jesus,* by an
ex-associate and hater of the society, Elias Hasenmüller, in
which the stories have begun to gather; and thereafter the
legends grew to overwhelming proportions – the Jesuits
intoxicated men into steam when they administered the
Spiritual Exercises; they were masters in impregnating
saucepans and salt-cellars with poisons; they made a
fabulous fortune in the Reductions of Paraguay or the trade
with Japan; they taught that any lie was justifiable if the
end served the purpose of the Church. The myth of gold in
the Reductions had to be investigated by a commission in
1640, and again in 1657, to prove it false. The Oxford
English Dictionary dates in 1640 the first occurrence of the
word *Jesuit* to mean treacherous.

Thus their reputation was achieved between 1575 and
1640. It was achieved partly because they could not, or

would not, avoid the politics of the crusade (and the politics even of a crusade are not likely to be clean), and partly because it was a barometer registering the success of the political Counter-Reformation and the fears and passions which that success engendered.

The Thirty Years War

The more aggressive the attitude, the more risk of a crusade, and soon the German Protestants began to fear that they could be secure only if they mobilized a league of arms.

In the free city of Donauwörth in south Germany the Protestants were far more numerous, but Catholic worship was permitted. Despite the order of the magistrates, who feared riots, the Benedictine abbot insisted (April 1606) upon sending a ceremonial procession through the streets, and the procession was attacked by a mob on its return journey. In 1607 Maximilian of Bavaria, with an imperial commission, occupied Donauwörth and treated it as a conquered city, annexing it to Bavaria, installing Jesuits in the church, and making it forcibly Catholic. It seemed a blatant transgression of the Peace of Augsburg, and the Protestants could no longer rely on that treaty for their protection. In 1608 the Protestant states formed the Evangelical Union to defend Protestant states attacked in contravention of the Peace of Augsburg. It was primarily Calvinist, though with French support, had the Elector Palatine at its head, and did not include the chief Lutheran state, Saxony. One alliance leads to a rival alliance and in 1609 was formed the Catholic League, headed by Maximilian of Bavaria. The two sides were arming.

On 13 May 1618 the Protestant nobles of Bohemia, whose king, Ferdinand, was ruler of Austria and Holy Roman Emperor, threw the imperial commissioners from the windows of the castle at Prague, drove the Jesuits out of the country, and revolted against Austria. They offered the crown to the Elector Palatine, Frederick V, and

Frederick's acceptance precipitated the Thirty Years War. A Calvinist ruler in Bohemia would have tilted the balance of power throughout Europe.

The Thirty Years War was a religious war only until 1635. It was at first a war of Calvinists against Catholics, for Saxony and some other Lutheran states stood aloof, believing the Elector Palatine's action to be foolish and illegal. At the decisive battle of White Mountain the imperial troops advanced with the cry '*St Mary!*', and a church of St Mary of the Victory was built in Rome. By 1620 Frederick had been driven out of Bohemia, and by 1623 out of the Palatinate. But the war was prolonged because the success of the Imperial arms was so overwhelming as to bring other states into action against it – Denmark (1625–9), Sweden under Gustavus Adolphus till his death in 1632 and then under the chancellor Oxenstierna, Saxony (1631–5), and above all Catholic France under Richelieu. After 1635 the war was no longer in any real sense a religious war, but a modern European war dependent on rivalry between revived France and imperial Germany.

Sixty-five years before, France and Poland had been divided between Catholic and Protestant, south Germany was wavering, and the political hope of the Papacy rested upon Spain. By 1628, Spain was much weaker, but France had recovered its Roman Catholic status and hedged the Huguenots into an impotent minority, Poland had turned decisively to Rome and eschewed Protestantism, and now the war carried the triumph northwards in Germany. In 1620–27 Bohemia, for so long Hussite and Protestant, was made forcibly Catholic by Austrian armies, the Protestants were deprived of civil rights, the university of Prague was given to the Jesuits, and some 30,000 Protestant families were expelled. This was the most signal and permanent triumph of the Counter-Reformation, and was accompanied by similar measures elsewhere in the imperial lands, especially in Austria. In 1628 it looked as though the forcible conversion of Protestant Germany would proceed much further. Bavarian troops expelled the Lutherans and Calvinists from power in the Palatinate and confiscated from the library of Heidelberg a treasure of books and manuscripts, most of which are still in the Vatican library. The imperial army under Wallenstein conquered north Germany to the Baltic coast, except 'neutral' Saxony and Brandenburg, and enforced the Edict of Restitution, which is rightly regarded as the highest moment of the political Counter-Reformation.

The Edict of Restitution (1629) declared that all ecclesiastical lands alienated by the Protestants since 1552 must be restored, and that the Calvinists must be excluded from all rights of the Empire. Not only would the Protestants lose those great bishoprics, like Magdeburg and Halberstadt and Bremen, which they had absorbed since 1552. The Electors of Saxony and Brandenburg had acquired much ecclesiastical property since 1552, and the Elector of Brandenburg was a Calvinist. If the Edict had been fully enforced, German Protestantism would have been prostrate.

It was saved, first because of the genius of the Swedish king, Gustavus Adolphus, who believed himself called of God to save the Protestants and Swedish power in the Baltic; and then because European powers entered, to abolish the crusade and reintroduce the politics of balance of power. If the Edict had been fully enforced, the power of the German Emperor would have been intolerable to Spain, to France, to Bavaria. The war ceased to be a religious war. It was necessary to France and Sweden that the Protestant states of Germany be made secure.

The terms of the Peace of Westphalia in 1648 established the religious lines of modern European states. It was a recovery for the Protestant sovereigns, a blow to the political axioms of the Counter-Reformation. It re-established the Peace of Augsburg of 1555, with the momentous addition that its protection was now extended to the Reformed as well as to the Catholic and to the Lutheran. A compromise was reached over the ecclesiastical lands, whereby the lands of bishoprics held by Protestants on 1 January 1624 were to remain Protestant; and this was sufficient to recognize finally the Protestant secularization of the great sees like Magdeburg, Bremen, and Halberstadt. The imperial court was to be composed of Protestants and Catholics in equal numbers. Except in the hereditary Habsburg dominions, all states were to tolerate the minority of the other religion, if it had existed before 1624; and the property of those exiled for religious reasons might not be confiscated. France gained Alsace (except Strasbourg), much of which was Protestant. The United Provinces of the Protestant Netherlands and of Switzerland were recognized as states. The Elector Palatine recovered his lower Palatinate and the electoral dignity, but the Duke of Bavaria was allowed to keep the upper Palatinate and the electoral dignity (hence the number of electors rose from seven to eight). Of all the gains of 1628, the Catholic cause was left with (1) Bohemia, (2) a fully Catholicized Austria, (3) the upper Palatinate under Bavaria, (4) parts of Alsace, under France, (5) the recognition by the Protestants that the south German bishoprics were secure. In return the Protestants gained Catholic recognition that their chief secularizations were legal, recognition of the Dutch republic, recognition that Germans might legally be Calvinist, and a substantial measure of toleration for Protestants inside Catholic territories in return for a substantial measure of toleration for Catholics inside Protestant territories.

Recognized by the German Catholic powers, indeed, but not by the Pope. The Papacy had not been conspicuous in the German crusade. Once again the Pope's political character as an Italian prince had interfered with his ardour for religious victory. Since the age of the Saxon Ottos in the tenth century, the Popes had seen the predominance of a single great power in Europe as a threat to Italy and therefore to their temporal security. Even when they were intent upon resisting Protestants, they never forgot this principle of policy. Pope Urban VIII (1623–44) welcomed the Edict of Restitution; but like the French he realized that an emperor so supreme in Germany would soon be an emperor supreme in Italy, and he therefore encouraged France and Cardinal Richelieu – who needed no encouragement – to that policy which at last saved the German Protestants. He refused to condemn the alliance of the French with the Protestants, and in 1632, replying to the imperial ambassador who wanted him to declare the war a crusade, said coldly that the war was not a war of religion, but related to matters of state. On the one hand he was demanding the full restoration of Catholicism in Germany, on the other he feared the political consequences of that restoration and therefore sought to impede it.

It might therefore have been expected that Urban's successor, Pope Innocent X (1644–55) would have been at once vexed and relieved by the terms of the Peace of Westphalia; vexed by the concessions to the Protestants, and relieved by the recovery of a balance of power in Germany. Innocent gave every sign of being vexed, no sign of being relieved. His legate Chigi protested against the terms of the treaty, and in the Brief *Zelo domus dei* he solemnly declared the anti-Catholic clauses of the treaty to be invalid. If the Reformation had done anything, it had rendered useless this old-fashioned kind of papal intervention in the political necessities of nations.

9

The Conquistadors

CATHOLIC Europe, while engaged in reforming and defending itself, was carrying Christianity into the Americas and Indies. Between 1493 and 1620 Spanish and Portuguese missionaries changed the Christian map of the globe.

In 1492 Columbus sailed for the New World, and in 1493 Spain was already in diplomatic conflict with Portugal over the new territories. The two governments appealed to the Pope to arbitrate between them; an instance of those papal exercises of international authority so familiar to the Middle Ages and rendered so obsolete by the events of the sixteenth century. On 3/4 May 1493 Pope Alexander VI (Borgia) conferred upon Spain the right of possession over all islands and lands now discovered or to be discovered, provided that they were not already occupied by a Christian power, and confirmed an earlier grant to Portugal of the coasts of Africa. A line was drawn from the North Pole to the South, running 100 Spanish leagues to the west of the most westerly island in the Azores. All that was east of the line was given to Portugal, all that was west to Spain. Subsequently the diplomats, by the Treaty of Tordesillas in 1494, rearranged this boundary line 270 leagues further to the west, and so Brazil was to become Portuguese instead of Spanish. The grants were made only on condition that the Europeans should propagate the Christian faith among the native inhabitants.

Thereafter the colonists began to settle, and the churches to be planted, throughout the coasts of the Americas and Indies. The Portuguese founded settlements along the coasts of West Africa and the Congo and Angola, in India and Ceylon, with Goa (1510) as their headquarters, in Brazil and St Helena and Socotra and Mozambique; in Hormuz in the Persian Gulf, in the Malay Archipelago and Macao (1555) off the coast of China; and even where they could not colonize, as in Japan, their trading settlements gathered little churches. The Spanish conquered Mexico and Peru and the West Indies and established settlements in Colombia and Panama and along the Spanish Main, with outposts in California, New Mexico, Chile, and the River Plate and its hinterland.

In the Far East alone, they came into rivalry with the Portuguese. Since Magellan proved in 1522 that the world was round, a new line was needed on the other side of the world to correspond with the dividing line in the Atlantic, and the calculations needed for discovering this line were complex. The Spanish claimed that the true line, making a Portuguese hemisphere and a Spanish hemisphere, ran by Malacca near modern Singapore. The Portuguese claimed that it ran out in the Pacific to the east of the Philippines. The Portuguese were right; but the dispute allowed the Far East to be divided, leaving the Moluccas to Portugal, with their communications westward through Malacca and Goa; the Philippines, named after Philip II, to Spain, with their communications eastward through Mexico. The dispute was to have a fatal consequence in the Christian history of Japan.

THE AMERICAS

To civilize and to evangelize were believed to be one. From the first, bishoprics and convents were founded and endowed. Soon schools were built, and in 1544 the first university of the New World, that of Mexico, to be followed before 1600 by the universities of Lima, San Domingo, and Bogotá. The first see in the Americas was that of San Domingo in 1511, and there were fifteen more by 1582, including Cuba, Mexico, Lima, Quito, Santiago, Bogotá, and Buenos Aires.

The Christian expansion into the Spanish Americas

resembled the Carolingian missionary expansion into Germany seven hundred years before, in that the soldier was mightier than the preacher. Missionaries, often devoted missionaries, accompanied the conquerors and established churches and schools in their wake. But, far from the control of the central government, Spanish adventurers were not easily restrained if they were of a mind to rob and kill. Some of them inherited a measure of that Spanish crusading zeal which created the nation during the long years of fighting against the Moors. Cortés, the conqueror of Mexico, unscrupulous and debauched though he might be, had crusading ardour in him, was devoted to the Virgin Mary and always kept a statuette of her upon his person, said his prayers and attended mass daily, carried a cross upon one flag and upon the other flag the arms of Castile and a picture of the Virgin. These expeditions are in one aspect the authentic successors of the medieval crusade (already obsolescent against the Turks), and must be judged in a crusading context. We see the same fanaticism, the same nobility, superstition, opportunity for feats of arms and for plunder, and withal the opening of new lands to Christianity – but with the two ominous differences, first that the opposing tribes were weak and unwarlike, and secondly that the fight lay at a greater distance from the control of a just and effective government. Cortés sent the citizens of Cholula in Mexico a demand that they should recognize his authority and accept the Christian faith; but hearing a rumour that they were preparing to massacre the Spaniards, and fearful because of his tiny numbers, he invited the leading Cholulans to the sacred square of the temple, where his troops were encamped, and there, at a signal from a musket, he murdered more than 3,000 of them, the killing taking more than two hours.

At evening on 16 November 1532, the Inca Atahualpa came in his litter into the great square at Cajamarca, with some 5,000 followers, to meet Pizarro and the Spaniards. Father Vicente stepped forward and explained to him the

Christian faith, and demanded that the Inca accept it and become the vassal of the Emperor. The Inca asked for his authority, and the friar proffered a copy of the breviary. Atahualpa looked at it and threw it angrily upon the ground. The friar ran to Pizarro and demanded vengeance, promising absolution. The Spaniards, concealed in the buildings round the square, poured out and slaughtered several thousands of the Peruvians, at the cost of a single wound, to Pizarro himself from one of his own men, as he warded off an attack upon Atahualpa. Several months later Atahualpa was strangled after a judicial murder trial, the penalty of burning alive being commuted because, while the faggots were being piled round his stake, he allowed himself to be baptized.

The scum of the Spanish army did not immediately instruct the Mexicans or the Peruvians in the beauty of the Christian faith. 'Is that person a Christian?' asked a puzzled convert in Manila, when he saw Spaniards misbehaving. 'Why, then, does he not observe the commandments?'

The orders of friars were as much in need of reform as other medieval institutions at the beginning of the sixteenth century. Their record in the Americas for the next hundred years demonstrated that the patient had risen from his bed of sickness. The endeavours of Franciscan and Dominican in the New World are too little known. Almost all the best work was done by those two orders of friars, and by the Augustinians and later the Jesuits, who arrived in Peru in 1568 and in Mexico in 1572.

We must not underestimate the decision necessary to cross the seas. There was no home leave, and the voyages were not yet secure. Out of 376 Jesuits who sailed for China between 1581 and 1712, 127 died in transit. In the history of the missions it is important that the work attracted two kinds of men; at one end those of heroism and decisiveness, at the other those who had failed in Europe. None was more persistent in defending the Indians than the Dominican Bartholomew de Las Casas.

LAS CASAS (1474–1566)

Las Casas, whose father sailed as a seaman with Columbus, witnessed the worst excesses in the territories and the horrors in the system of slave labour. The first priest to be ordained in the New World (1510), he is said to have sung his first mass at a ceremony where the collection plate was filled with rough pieces of American gold and the celebrant could not use wine because no fresh supply had arrived from Spain. Admiring the Dominican protest against the colonist, he joined the order, and soon became the leading protector of the native inhabitants. With a wiry constitution and an inexhaustible energy, he travelled up and down the coast and among the islands, observing, protesting, complaining, organizing, running the gauntlet of hostility and sometimes of as much danger from his compatriots as from the Indians, crossing the Atlantic fourteen times in the effort to secure adequate legal remedies from the imperial government, hated both by the colonial realists and by the merchant houses, receiving aid from the crown that was always well-intentioned but too rarely efficacious. He constantly hampered and thwarted his cause by a utopian idealism and a tendency to bleat. But, despite the tiresome quality that marked his persistence, despite his failure to care for the African slave immigrant as he cared for his Indians, despite his unwisdom and lack of balance, he was one of the most remarkable men of the Reformation age. There are moments in Christian history when to be immoderate is necessary, if justice is to be done. For more than forty years Las Casas reminded the Spaniards at the top of his voice that the Indians, his children, were human beings and to be treated as human beings. If his practical endeavours were often ineffectual, he secured the backing first of Cardinal Ximenes and then of the Emperor Charles V, and received a guarantee under the 'New Laws' of 1542 that Spanish and Indian were equal before the law.

Was there moral justification for the conquests in the Americas? Opponents of Las Casas, like the Spanish theologian Sepulveda, argued thus. Pope Alexander VI, in the Bull of 1493, gave the Spanish a sovereignty over the Americas and instructed them to convert the Indians to the Catholic faith. He who wills the end must will the means. It is fanciful to suppose that Indians will be converted unless they are first subjected to Spanish rule and a settled government. The Indians are a backward people, of low intelligence and in some ways nearer to animals than men. ('The Spanish', said Sepulveda, 'are as much above the Indians as man is above the ape.') They are guilty of gross crimes like human sacrifice, idolatry, and sodomy. As every citizen has a duty to repress crime wherever he sees it and is able to stop it, so it is the duty of the Spanish to stop these barbarities, and therefore their wars of conquest are righteous wars. The Israelites had no legitimate sovereignty when they invaded the Promised Land, but they were justified in their invasion by crimes of the Canaanites. Though the conduct of the Israelites in Canaan is no model for the Spanish in America, it suggests at least that the Spanish are right to establish rule over the Indian in order to afford opportunity to the preachers of the Gospel. War is not to convert men but to make them submit; and when they are subjects of Spain, the preachers will be able to preach and then the Indians will learn that the Christian religion is peaceable and opposed to the excesses of a conquering soldiery. St Augustine understood the text *Compel them to come in* to justify the use of force in preparing men for conversion.

This defence of Christian imperialism was repellent to Las Casas. He knew the Indian to be a human being, a child perhaps but still a human being. He believed that Pizarro was nearer a brute than the Inca whom he had conquered. He thought that without the elementary rights of a human being no one could be truly moral, that the idea of a Christian congregation demanded a worldly polity wherein the sanctity of the family and the rights of property were duly safeguarded, and that the one hope for Spanish America lay in giving the native inhabitants the rights possessed by the inhabitants of Castile.

It was therefore necessary to maintain that the kingship of heathen kings is legitimate, that the property of heathens is to be respected, that heathenism is no just pretext for conquest, and that the crimes committed by Indians are to be punished by Indian laws and offer no excuse for the assault of European armies. The Spanish have a duty, laid upon them by the Pope, to convert the native tribes. But the only true, the only workable method is that which the Church has approved, the way of reasoning and gentle persuasion, added to the example of a Christian way of life. The suzerainty over America is not given to enable the Spanish king to pillage and to exploit, but to ensure the rule of justice and of peace, and thereby assist the spread of the Gospel. Though the text *Compel them to come in* has been quoted in favour of forcible conversion, the true compulsion is inward only, the irresistible conviction of the soul.

At a staged debate before the court of Spain in 1550, Las Casas and Sepulveda argued the question passionately. To read their debates is to see old and new ideas jostling for place – the holy war of the crusader, the moral right of ownership over ill-used or little-used land, the right of persecution and of tolerance, the scholastic doctrine of the heathen – but, above all, the defenders of the Indians, Las Casas and his successors, should be honoured among the earliest originators of what was later to be called international law.

Las Casas contended that war on a plea of Christian mission was anti-Christian and led to the rejection of the Christian religion. The warriors replied that they were but protecting missionaries and removing obstacles to preaching. Las Casas denounced the plea as a mere excuse for robbery, and, where not an excuse, a violation of the law of charity. The only way to convert is by peaceful preaching of the Word, and by an example of holy living. He wrote a treatise to prove this, but it remained unprinted till 1941, and therefore the credit for the first modern theory of evangelism fell to a Jesuit, Joseph Acosta, who had served among the Indians in Peru, and who in 1584 published a famous little book *On the Preaching of the Gospel among the Savages*, the first systematic treatment of missionary theory. It considers among much else the nature of military 'protection', mass baptism, instruction, and indigenous priesthood.

It is to the credit of the Popes of the Counter-Reformation that they steadily condemned the doctrine of slavery for the Indians.

Despite all these idealists, the Spanish clergy in America (and the Portuguese in Brazil and Africa) were not for the most part perturbed by the condition of slavery or serfdom under which lived so many of their flocks.

By 1541 the Spanish government achieved a measure of control over the settlements, and a series of viceroys, many of them excellent governors, attempted to remedy the worst consequences of the conquest. The Council of the Indies controlled all appointments, ecclesiastical as well as civil. Its power over the Church in the colonies was as absolute as that of King Henry VIII over the Church of England. The viceroy was entrusted with the duty, not only of secular administration, but of building churches, organizing dioceses, and educating the natives. Money and endowments were poured into the work, and nothing is more evocative of the secular-religious nature of the conquest than the wide squares of Spanish-American cities dominated by a magnificent and baroque cathedral. In 1569 the Inquisition, as a further agent in royal control, was established in the New World. Of the great ecclesiastics, the most eminent was Turibio, Archbishop of Lima 1580–1606, known as the apostle of Peru. In 1583 he held a council which passed laws to defend the liberties of Indians and Negroes, he educated them, translated textbooks including the catechism into the Quichua language, and travelled perpetually among the tribes. In 1594 he wrote to Philip II that he had already confirmed 500,000 people. He was sainted in 1726.

The Indians were ready and eager to accept the Christian faith. The difficulty was that they were equally ready to abandon it. The missionaries normally baptized after very short preparation. It was odd that a papal Bull, by Paul III in 1537, was necessary to declare that Indians were capable of receiving baptism.

Felix de Viler, who arrived in the Congo in 1647, said that in four years they baptized more than 600,000 adults. Between 1524 and 1531 the Franciscans baptized more than a million Mexicans. Peter of Ghent, in a letter from Mexico dated 27 June 1529, talks of 14,000 baptisms a day. The catechumenate, the long discipline of preparation for baptism, had flourished in the fourth and fifth century, and was not revived until the mission fields of the nineteenth century. The Spanish missionaries expected that the neophyte should profess his understanding of the simplest truths. The catechism was instruction for everyone, adults as well as children, but after baptism not before. In 1541 they were requiring of the Indians of New Galicia that before baptism they should believe in one God, creator of heaven and earth, and of man as soul and body, in original sin, the divinity of Christ, heaven and hell, good and bad angels, and that they should profess themselves subjects of the Pope and the Emperor. After baptism they must learn answers and recite them publicly in church on Sundays and holy days.

The practice of mass baptism left the same natural effects as the mass conversions of northern Europe in the early Middle Ages: the persistence of magic, superstition, and ignorance. At one city Cortés left the strictest instructions that the inhabitants were to worship the Christian God, and were also to care for one of his horses, which was lame. The inhabitants faithfully obeyed his behest. They fed the horse on fruit and flowers until it died; but their confused minds supposed that the horse and the Christian God were the same, and they were later found by two Franciscan missionaries to have made an image of the horse and to be worshipping it, believing that it was the god of the thunder and lightning. To this day there are primitive peoples in the mountains of Mexico, with a cult of old gods, where the Christian priest takes but a lowly rank among the village sorcerers.

But it is rash to attribute every superstitition of the New World to survival of ancient religions. Even superstitions may be, and have been, exported from Europe.

The problem of language was at first grave, and the Indians loved to come to confession. For many years confessions were allowed to be heard through interpreters, a practice at last forbidden by a Council of Lima in 1567, though lasting in Brazil till 1580–90. Slowly the Indian languages were studied, grammars composed, catechisms and mass books printed.

The medieval inheritance was shown not only by the mass baptisms but by the reluctance to admit to holy communion. In Brazil the Jesuits admitted selected Indians of the villages to Easter communion for the first time in 1573. From 1574 they were allowed to communicate a little more frequently, and a very few, after undergoing examination, to communicate once a month. The Franciscans in Mexico encouraged Indians to communicate more freely. The mass, and all the liturgical year, were surrounded with the maximum of ceremonial, a gala of processions and feast-days, a solemn and pictorial rejoicing at baptisms or marriages. When Manila received the news that the Pope had beatified Ignatius Loyola (1609), a life-size statue of Ignatius was installed above the high altar of the Jesuit church and covered with jewellery, fireworks were exploded from the church tower, a literary competition was held, the students paraded on horseback, and a dancing group from St Michael's parish performed a ballet, staggering into the arena as halt and maimed and blind, falling on their knees and crying to Blessed Ignatius, and then leaping to their feet into a sword dance. All over the Indies there were groups of penitents and flagellants, and the Indians were gathered in pious confraternities of the Holy Sacrament or of Our Lady. Marriage gave endless trouble, because Indian tribes were often polygamous and Rome needed to give dispensations in some complex human situations. The ideals of higher education for Indians limped dismally into practice. The great viceroy of Peru, Francisco de Toledo, began to build at Lima a college to educate the children of chiefs, but when he returned to Spain the building stopped, and colleges founded later admitted none but young Spaniards.

The Spaniards, even the idealists, thought the Indians to be but children, and adopted a policy of keeping them in tutelage. The missionaries loved their peoples, but sometimes like a possessive parent who will not risk their growing up. They found it hard to imagine that an Indian could ever become a priest. In Mexico some progressive missionaries, led by the Franciscans and the bishop John de Zumárraga, planned a native clergy, and as early as 1536 founded a college in a suburb of Mexico City restricted to Indians and intended to train priests. The college succeeded in educating Mexicans, but produced not one Mexican priest. The Spanish laity thought the idea of a Mexican priest to be repugnant, the Dominicans disliked the college, and slowly it fell into such decay as to be effectively suppressed near the end of the century. The first native Mexican to be priested was perhaps Nicolas del Puerto, who became Bishop of Oaxaca in 1679. It came late indeed. The first Indian priests in Chile were ordained in 1794, the first in Paraguay after 1768, the first in the Philippines after 1725. There was no native clergy during almost the whole of the colonial period of America.

THE REDUCTIONS

The Indians of the Americas were peoples not then capable of meeting Europeans upon equal terms. The consequent difficulty of creating a Christian polity out of two utterly different peoples, the difficulty of preventing the settler from ill-treating or depraving the aboriginal, forced experiments which were a Catholic form of the later Indian reservations in the United States or the protectorates within modern South Africa.

Las Casas attempted to create a model multi-racial settlement at Puerto Rico and it ended in war between Indian and Spaniard. Slowly it became a policy, especially among the Franciscans and Augustinians, to organize Indian Christian villages where children would be educated and the people protected from each other and from the colonists. The Jesuits in Brazil soon adopted the method.

It had the obvious inconvenience that friars and priests became responsible for miniature governments; they had to perform the functions of magistrates, order a flogging, administer an exchequer, perhaps command a little force of militia. The moral theologians of Manila were required to determine in 1630 whether a missionary priest, as leader of his community, could organize an ambush against raiders. (Answer, yes: a measure of lawful self-defence.) Francis Borgia, the aristocrat who was General of the Jesuits 1565-72, advised that these functions should not be undertaken; in 1597 the General Claudius Aquaviva attempted more forcibly to remedy the system. But the system was irremediable. The Indians trusted the religious as they trusted no one else among the settlers; and if just government and proper evangelism were to be achieved, there was no alternative.

It had the further inconvenience that the Indians, separated from the main development of Mexican or Peruvian life, were never prepared to face the rigours and competition of an adult world; and the modern political problems of Mexico, for example, have stemmed partly from the difficulty of integrating the Indian into the national life. But this inconvenience the Spanish missionaries could not have foreseen.

The most successful attempts at a native reservation were the Reductions of Paraguay, among the tribe of Guaranis. Franciscan and Jesuit missionaries worked in Paraguay (that is, the area of modern Paraguay round Asunción) between 1583 and 1605. In 1605 a second band of Jesuits arrived at Asunción. They first obtained independence of the colonial government by having their settlement placed directly under the king of Spain. They created some thirty 'Reductions', estates with a central church, a hospital, a convent, and a school where the best children were taught Spanish and even Latin. Here the Indians were educated in a little world kept away from white corruptions, with a regular discipline of church-going and communion in property. All the members of every community attended mass and vespers daily, hymns were used at work, there was daily catechism for the children. There was a working day of eight hours; orchestral music and the theatre and sport were encouraged. In at least one of the early Reductions everyone was taught the multiplication table by having to recite it in church after mass on Sunday. They needed to defend the settlements against land grabbers and slave traders, who destroyed several of the Reductions, killed or enslaved thousands of Indians, and drove the Fathers to lead an exodus of 15,000 through the jungle. The Jesuits applied for, and at last obtained, the right to train the Indians in arms, and thenceforth private armies preserved these Indian farming societies from contamination.*

It must not be supposed that most Indians in South or Central America were in reservations. Most of them were in 'colonial' parishes, with ordinary clergy as pastors, a not very reformed but transplanted version of the churches of Spain and Portugal. In Quito of the seventeenth century it was estimated that the clerical population was as numer-

* For their later destruction, see *The Pelican History of the Church*, Vol. 4, pp. 189–90. Ruins of their great churches are still to be seen in remote areas.

ous as the laity. The medieval Church prolonged its existence overseas, while Europe was engaged in modernizing it.

THE PORTUGUESE

While the Spanish were at work in the Americas, the Portuguese were moving eastward. Their progress is traceable by the foundation of new sees: Madeira 1514; Cape Verde 1532; Goa, which became the seat of the viceroy in the far eastern empire, 1533, and an archbishopric from 1558; Malacca 1557; Macao on the Chinese coast 1576; Mozambique on the East African coast 1612. Their missions travelled to Sofala in East Africa, up the Zambezi to Tete, up the Congo, into Ethiopia; the Jesuit Benedict de Goes crossed the Khyber pass disguised as an Armenian merchant and journeyed through Afghanistan and over the Hindu-kush into Chinese Turkestan, to die at Suchow in China. The Portuguese missions had many deficiencies, but they lacked neither courage nor enterprise. They were less conscious of a colour bar than other Europeans.

The Portuguese in the East were facing a different problem. They were weaker than the Spanish, and were meeting civilizations and religions far stronger than those of Inca and Aztec.

The size of the task was not at first understood. In some places in the East the pace of conversion was as rapid as in the Americas. In the Philippines the Spaniards achieved the outstanding success of all the eastern missions: 400,000 converts by 1585, about two million by 1620. Manila was founded in 1571, had a bishop from 1579, an archbishop from 1595, a Dominican university from 1619. The Filipinos became the single Catholic nation of the Far East. It was natural that expectations everywhere should be sanguine.

When Francis Xavier on 7 April 1541 embarked at Lisbon for the Indies, with three companions, he had authority from the king of Portugal as well as the Pope. He was the Pope's vicar for all the coasts of the Indian ocean, and he possessed the king's credence for his mission and an order from the king that all Portuguese officials were to support him with every means at their disposal.

An aristocrat of charm and nobility, and yet of extreme simplicity and directness of character, he might have seemed likely to be a fashionable guide of princely souls or the grateful instructor of a south German court. From Goa, where he found a bishop, a cathedral, convents, and numerous churches already flourishing, he moved to Travancore, thence to Malacca and the Malay peninsula, thence to Amboina, and back to Travancore. In 1549 he sailed from Goa to Japan, accredited with letters to the sovereign. After preaching in the streets or disputing with the monks for two years, he determined to convert China as a preliminary to converting Japan. To secure the requisite authority he returned to Goa. But he found it difficult to get further than Singapore, tried to smuggle himself into Canton, and died on the Chinese coast near Macao late in 1552.

He was a man of sudden decisions or insights or enthusiasms, always eager to be penetrating new ground and converting unknown tribes and undergoing danger for his faith. He mastered none of the numerous languages which he encountered, he settled nowhere, he wandered onward with sudden half-chivalrous resolutions. 'All things to all men' was a motto familiar to Ignatius's missionaries; and Xavier above all others, selfless and open and sympathetic in his outlook upon human beings, rapidly felt himself at home and at ease among Hindus or Muslims or Japanese.

He followed the method of mass conversion. He utilized the secular means of coercion placed at his disposal by Portuguese officials, appealed to the king when he thought them to be failing in their duty. He practised mass baptism, like the Spaniards in the Americas. On the fishers' coast near Cape Comorin he wandered from village to village accompanied by his interpreters. He would gather the villagers together by ringing a handbell, and recite the creed and the Lord's Prayer, the Ten Commandments, and the Hail Mary, which had already been translated into Tamil. When the audience, after a few days or weeks, had sufficiently learnt the words and professed their belief in the articles of the creed, he baptized them, and went on baptizing until his hands sank with exhaustion. He would leave behind catechists to baptize and to marry and to remind the converts every Sunday of the creed which they professed. He tried also to leave schools behind him, and wherever possible European priests. Though these efforts at pastoral care could not remedy the defects of this method of evangelism, others followed where he had opened the door. It was extraordinary that a single man should have succeeded in opening so many doors.

In the East the evangelists confronted a task of which the American missions knew nothing – the great religions. The Jesuits, who in 1579 went to the court of the Great Mogul, Akbar, found that their Christian worship was acceptable in the temple which he had built at Fatehpur-Sikri, but they must share the building with Parsees, Hindus, Jains, and Buddhists. The normal and traditional attitude of the Christian was that the idols must be hewn down. An alleged tooth of the Buddha was brought to Goa in 1560, and though a bankrupt government wanted to accept an offer of £100,000 from a rajah, the archbishop stepped in to destroy the relic. The Spaniards in America and in the Philippines followed the principle that all the old religions must be destroyed as being heathen, that thus the new might enter in all its purity. The Bishop of Manila in the Philippines forced the Chinese converts to cut off their queues and wear their hair like the Spaniards, as a visible sign that they were freed from heathenish customs. 'I longed,' wrote the Jesuit Vilela in 1571, after he had seen the worshippers dancing at the Shinto shrine of Kasuga in Japan, 'I longed to have had a second Elijah there to do what he did to the priests of Baal.'

But in the religious circumstances of India and China,

this Hebraic and exclusive tradition within Christendom began for the first time to be challenged or modified. When tolerance and eclecticism were virtues among the Hindus, when holiness and the ascetic life was valued by Hindu or Buddhist, some Christian missionaries began to acquire a new respect for these religions, and a new distaste for the hewing methods as a hindrance to true evangelism. Even Xavier modified his earlier ideas of throwing down the idols.

This gentleness towards the customs or beliefs of non-Christians, a gentleness usually disliked and controverted by the Dominicans, was carried to its limit by the Jesuits.

In the Americas and the Philippines most of the Spanish acted as though there was nothing whatever in the old religions of the inhabitants whereon they might build to expound the Christian faith. In 1531 Bishop Zumárraga wrote from Mexico that they had destroyed more than 500 temples and 20,000 idols. Father Bernardino de Sahagún made a profound anthropological study of the tribes, a study which is necessary evidence for that vanished society. But Sahagún was not popular with his colleagues; his volumes were suppressed and published only in modern times, and he had no successor. The appearance of human sacrifices and crude repellent cults made missionaries see the primitive approximations to Christian truth rather as demonic parodies. Spanish experience of tribal religion in America afforded no basis for the encounter, now imminent, between Christianity and Hinduism, between Christianity and Buddhism.

The immediate problem with the Eastern religions concerned language, the terms used to expound Christian doctrine. The Christian teacher would be more intelligible if he used the terms parallel in the other religion, but he ran the risk of misleading his hearers by taking a word out of a non-Christian system with all its erroneous connotations. Xavier at once met the problem. In Japan he first translated *God* by its Buddhist equivalent *Dainichi*, and only after some months discovered that this was a disastrous translation and substituted the Portuguese *Deos*, which was orthodox but unintelligible to the Japanese.

As the other religions became better known, the question of practice became crucial. The Spanish had hardly been troubled; they discouraged all old practices, and turned their converts, not only into Christians, but into Spaniards. The Portuguese tried the same policy in Goa. The original Portuguese catechism for India translated the question 'Do you want to become a Christian?' as 'Do you want to join the caste of the Europeans?' But the policy was soon found impossible, and their missionaries must therefore decide which of the social customs of Japanese, Chinese, or Indian were merely social and civil, which were religious but capable of a Christian meaning, and which were incompatible with receiving baptism.

In China reverence for ancestors and in India caste was integral to the social system. The Jesuits in China contended that the reverence for ancestors was a social, not a religious act, or that if religious, it was hardly different from Catholic prayers for the dead. They wished the Chinese to regard Christianity, not as a replacement, not as a new religion, but as the highest fulfilment of their finest aspirations. But to their opponents the Jesuits appeared to be merely lax. In 1631 a Franciscan and a Dominican from the Spanish zone of Manila travelled (illegally, from the Portuguese viewpoint) to Peking and found that to translate the word *mass* the Jesuit catechism used the character *tsi*, which was the Chinese description of the ceremonies of ancestor-worship. One night they went in disguise to such a ceremony, observed Chinese Christians participating, and were scandalized at what they saw. So began the quarrel of 'the rites', which plagued the eastern missions for a century and more.

The Jesuit responsible for this remarkable venture in Peking was Matthew Ricci. He mastered classical Chinese, dressed himself in the garb of a mandarin, studied Chinese science, presented Christianity as the fulfilment of Confucianism, and was ready to allow the traditional cult of ancestors. In 1599 he founded the first Catholic Church at Nanking. In 1601 he had an audience at Peking of the Emperor Wan-Li and demonstrated to him a clock which chimed the hours. The Emperor was astonished, and gave Ricci a pension. It was characteristic of this method of evangelism that Ricci should draw an excellent map of the world, with China in the centre, but with a cross and texts of Scripture in the blank spaces. His evangelism was as far apart as possible from the decisive proclamations of the Spaniards in Mexico. He spent weary hours over cups of tea, discoursing with intelligent visitors on problems of science and philosophy. When he died in 1610 there was a Christian congregation in Peking, and some 2,000 baptized persons scattered through China.

After Ricci's death, and a temporary anti-Christian reaction, the mission was continued by Father Adam Schall, who was in China from 1622 to 1666, and made himself necessary to the court by a method developed out of a plan of Ricci's. The Chinese calendar, upon which lucky and unlucky days depended, was based upon accurate astronomy. Schall mastered astronomy, and by showing the inexactitude of the reigning Muslim astronomers, became indispensable and was elevated to be director of the Chinese observatory and a Minister of State for mathematics. He composed many text books of Chinese arithmetic and geometry and constructed a foundry to make cannon. His ancestors were solemnly ennobled, he was given the title of Master of the Mysteries of Heaven, and some Chinese called Christianity 'the religion of the great Schall'. His relations with his colleagues were not always happy, partly because he was quick-tempered and would not suffer fools, and still more because it was doubted whether a Jesuit ought to be a Minister of State and responsible, however indirectly, for deciding unlucky days. Before his end, he was sentenced to death in a reaction, but not executed; his friend and successor, Father Verbiest, was elevated to the board of mathematics and constructed (and in stole and surplice, dedicated) cannon of a type superior to any known to the Chinese, and with the name of a Christian saint engraved upon each.* The Jesuit influence became more purely scientific and less religious; and it may reasonably be doubted whether Ricci's successors had discovered how to reconcile the absolute claims of their religion with the proper sympathy for Chinese religion and culture. Ricci's methods, however, were not vain. By 1650 Christian congregations were scattered through the main Chinese cities. But by then not a single Chinese had been made priest.

Japan looked like becoming a field of missionary triumph like the Philippines. 'In ten years,' wrote a sanguine missionary in 1577, 'all Japan will be Christian if we have enough missionaries.' In 1579 Jesuit missionaries were able to found a new town, Nagasaki, to be a home for Christian converts, and claimed that there were already 100,000 Japanese converts; in 1587 they claimed 200,000 converts with 240 churches, two Jesuit colleges, and a school for young nobles. Japan had no settled government but an anarchy of feudal barons, or *daimyos*, and Christian *daimyos* protected the young Church. Though the Japanese regarded the Europeans as barbarians from the south, they were interested in the mechanical arts of Europe and still more in the Portuguese trade through Macao, of which the Jesuit missionaries, despite the nervous protests of their home authorities, took charge.

The rapid expansion of Christian faith was halted abruptly. Unlike the American chiefs, the Japanese barons were not impotent, and at their elbow they had Buddhist and Shinto priests ready to stimulate resistance. Between 1580 and 1614 three warlords established an effective central authority in Japan. For a time the new central government

---

* The calendar as revised by Verbiest lasted, in substance and popular usage, until the changes of this century in China.

saw the Christians as a useful aid in resisting the pretensions of Buddhist priests. Then the local Christian *daimyos* began to be the sole surviving obstacle to absolute government. The Portuguese trade with Macao, which rendered the Jesuits so useful to non-Christian rulers, suffered a rude shock when Dutch ships began to arrive, and a still ruder shock when the Spaniards in the Philippines, claiming a right under the old papal division of the world, landed Franciscan missionaries in Japan. It was known, even in Japan, that Spanish missionaries went hand in hand with Spanish conquerors. The Jesuit Father Alonso Sánchez drafted (1586) an evangelistic scheme for the invasion and military conquest of China, and the Bishop of Manila told King Philip II that 'Not even Julius Caesar nor Alexander the Great ever had an opportunity such as this; and on the spiritual plane, nothing greater was ever projected since the time of the apostles.' In 1596 the pilot of a Spanish galleon, wrecked upon the Japanese coast, is alleged to have told one of the ruler's counsellors that the missionaries had greatly helped the Spanish conquests. In these circumstances the ruler began to look upon the missionaries as Queen Elizabeth of England regarded the Jesuits, as the spearhead of Spanish invasion. Various edicts and a few crucifixions marked the change of policy. In 1614 the ruler Ieyasu issued an edict which accused the missionaries of treason and of trying to overthrow true doctrine, and expelled them from Japan.

Then began a persecution unparalleled in Christian history. Between 1614 and 1646 4,045 martyrs are proven, some by the sword or stake, others by slow boiling in a cauldron, others by hanging upside down over a pit full of ordure, with an incision in the head to allow the blood to flow and thus the sufferer to remain alive for several days. From 1627 suspects were forced to muddy with their feet a picture of Christ or the Virgin. From 1623, in many districts, everyone had to present an annual paper in a temple or before a magistrate to certify that he belonged to one of the

Buddhist sects. In 1637–8 a large number of Christians joined a peasant rebellion of Shimabara; in the ensuing massacre, everyone who declared himself not to be a Christian was given his life, and the rest, men, women, and children, were killed – to the number of 37,000, according to a contemporary estimate.

A decree of 1638 closed the country to foreigners. In 1642 eight Jesuits landed secretly, but were at once discovered and killed after terrible torture. Ten more were tried in 1643 and seem to have abandoned their faith under the torture of the pit. The persecution continued sporadically throughout the century. The opening of the modern archives has shown that 486 Christians at Bungo were executed or died in prison between 1660 and 1691. In 1614 there had been about 300,000 Christians in Japan; in 1697 there were few indeed.

In recorded Christian history no destruction of a church has been more spectacular or calamitous.

The example of Ricci's method of evangelism was followed with resounding success by two Jesuits, Alexander de Rhodes in Indochina and Robert de Nobili in South India.

From 1606 Nobili conducted a mission at Madurai. He had himself taught by a Sannyasi, a penitent of the Brahman caste, dressed himself in the saffron robe of the Brahman ascetic, shaved his head and wore earrings, lived as a hermit in a turf hut upon a vegetarian diet. The Brahmans began to admire him as a holy man, and ended by recognizing him as one of themselves. He wrote in the Tamil language works in which the Hindu wisdom and the Christian were brought into harmony. He composed Christian poems which resembled the ancient Vedic hymns. He allowed his Brahman converts to continue wearing the sacred thread and to celebrate certain Hindu feasts; in the school which he opened, he allowed pagan rites to be continued and he respected Hindu prejudices over caste; he allowed no outcaste to touch his person, and if he needed to administer the sacrament to a member of an inferior caste, he proffered the Host at the end of a little stick. It is not surprising that some of his fellow Europeans were shocked, and a long succession of denunciations went back to Rome. In 1618 he was brought before the court of the Archbishop of Goa, and astounded the court by appearing in the garb of a Brahman ascetic. 'The case of the Malabar rites' was referred to Rome. In 1623 Rome refused to condemn Nobili, 'till further information was available', and he continued to extend this unusual and successful evangelism until there were twenty-six Brahman converts among the 4,000 Christians of Madurai.*

The King of Spain and the King of Portugal controlled the missionary churches even more absolutely than the King of Spain controlled his church at home. This control had been sanctioned by the Pope in a Bull (*Universalis Ecclesiae*) of 1508, and was invaluable in the early organizing of the far-flung and sometimes anarchic churches. As the churches matured, it became a rigid framework which shackled the missionary effort. But only in the seventeenth century was Rome able to intervene more directly in the mission field, and then because the political powers of Spain and Portugal were weakening. Towards the end of the sixteenth century Rome created a commission of cardinals to determine missionary questions, and in 1622 Pope Gregory XV elevated this into the Sacred Congregation of Propaganda for the direction of missionary endeavour. Propaganda at first suffered the usual difficulties with the established authority of the Spanish and Portuguese kings. A bishop sent by Rome to China was thrown by a storm upon the Philippine coast and sent back by the Spaniards across the Pacific, thus involuntarily circumnavigating the globe. It was an important sign, both of the political weakness of Portugal and of the growing ability of Rome to interfere in the mission field, when the Jesuit Alexander de

* See also *The Pelican History of the Church*, Vol. 4, pp. 190–92; and Vol. 6, chapter 6.

Rhodes, wanting to develop his mission in Indochina, secured what he wanted from Rome and not from Madrid or Lisbon. But the extreme political weakness of Portugal in the middle of the seventeenth century destroyed the driving force of Catholic missions in the east, and proved that Pope Alexander Borgia had been rash to entrust half the world to so diminutive a power. The early reports sent to Propaganda show that the Counter-Reformation had hardly touched some of the dioceses of America or the East Indies.

The Portuguese in the East were not so slow to encourage a native priesthood as the Spaniards in the West. The son of an African chief of the Congo was consecrated a bishop as early as 1518, after training in Portugal. Ricci pressed for Chinese priests, and was bitterly disappointed at not getting them, but in China there was the special difficulty of infant marriage. In Japan and in India there were ordinations, the first in Japan as early as 1601. A Brahman named Matthew de Castro was refused ordination by the Archbishop of Goa. He went in person to Rome, and after a course of theology was ordained priest and sent back to Goa. He was received with abuse and disbelief, and despite the police escaped again to Rome. In 1637 Rome consecrated him a bishop, and he sailed to serve Idalcan, near Goa but outside Portuguese control. The Archbishop of Goa refused to help him, declared him suspended, and imprisoned Indians whom he too rapidly ordained priest. He left again for Rome, was in 1645 nominated as vicar apostolic in Ethiopia, failed to reach the country, retired to Rome, and was ordered back to Ethiopia. He was not the man to seek martyrdom, and went instead to the Great Mogul at Agra. Returning again to Rome, he lived for nineteen more years as an adviser on Indian affairs to Propaganda.

This fate of the first Indian bishop was not encouraging to those who were clamouring for an Indian clergy. But Rome was undaunted, and sent out two of his nephews to India as vicars apostolic.

About 180 Indian priests were counted at Goa itself in the year 1656. The quality was by no means high, and the Portuguese government was still prejudiced against them, but the obstacles to an indigenous clergy had been overcome for ever.

Thus were laid the foundations of new churches in America and Asia, and Catholic Europe called a new world of faith into being.

In this age the divisions of Christendom hardly penetrated the missions. On the rare occasions when they were exported across the seas, they were difficult to distinguish from political or commercial rivalry. A Spanish commander butchered 200 French Huguenots on a Florida beach, but the butchery was as much because they were French as because they were Huguenots. In Japan, English and Dutch rivalry with the Portuguese contributed to the calamity which overwhelmed the infant Church. In North America, French Catholic settlements in Canada (New France) excluded Huguenots by law, but the law was not enforced rigidly. The rise of English and Dutch maritime power during the seventeenth century carried European politics into the remote seas, and with it the antipathy of Protestant and Catholic. The Dutch founded Batavia in 1619, captured Malacca in 1641, and conquered Ceylon by 1658. They and the English stepped into the vacuum left by declining Portugal, with calamitous consequences for the Catholic missionaries. The bells stolen by Dutch raiders from the Catholic church in Puerto Rico were brought to be hung in the Dutch church at New Amsterdam (later New York). But for the most part the globe was still big enough for all.

To meet the great religions of Asia with sympathy, as so many of the Jesuits met them, was bound sooner or later to affect Christian thinking. The effect was delayed until the age of the Reformation was past and the age of Reason had begun, and then the momentous questions had to be reconsidered – how revealed law was related to natural law, how Christian ethics were distinguished from natural ethics, whether there might be said to be a partial 'revelation' given to men who are not Christians. These main questions, with which Asia faced the Christian Church, were hardly asked during the Reformation epoch. Matthew Ricci in Peking began to see that the long history of the Chinese demanded a revision of the chronology of the Old Testament. But the intelligence of Europe was barely touched until the second half of the seventeenth century. As late as 1681 Bossuet could write his *Discourse of Universal History* without going outside the Mediterranean and European world.

Some of the questions which perplexed lively minds in the sixteenth century proved to be minor in a later perspective. The discovery of chocolate forced the theologians to determine whether, for the rules of fasting, it was a food or a liquid; but soon it was suspected of being inimical to chastity, and at last its consumption by some religious orders was forbidden. Father Alonso Sánchez, travelling from the Philippines to Macao, tried to celebrate the mass of St Athanasius (2 May) on his arrival, and was astonished to find that the churches of Macao were celebrating the mass of the invention of the Holy Cross (3 May) and yet that neither had mistaken the calendar. These newly discovered tribes of the Americas must be descended from Adam, indeed, from Noah, in accordance with Holy Writ. If all animals descended from the beasts of the ark, how had they crossed the oceans to the Indies? Perhaps, thought the Jesuit Acosta, we may yet find a land bridge whereby men and animals can pass from Europe or Africa to the Americas, either in the Arctic or the Antarctic regions (for he dismissed the legend of Atlantis as absurd). But what of the animals in America which have no counterpart in Europe? If they came from the ark upon Mount Ararat, why were there no such species in Europe? Since all beasts came from the ark, we must postulate that some species found that habitat most suitable to their way of life and deserted the other regions or perished in them. Acosta was anxious that, despite the voyages round the world, men should not despise those ancient fathers or doctors of the Church who upon insufficient data supposed the earth to be flat.

10

The Eastern Orthodox Church

THE oldest of the divided Churches of Christendom was experiencing the long agony of hostile rule. By 1526 the Turks completed the conquest of the Balkans, the Aegean, the Crimea, Belgrade, two thirds of Hungary. Most of the members of the Church known to itself as Holy Orthodox were now under alien domination.

THE CRUSADING SPIRIT

The crusading spirit was not dead in the west, but was not lively enough to overcome the practical difficulties of launching a crusade. Idealists and politicians clamoured for a crusade against the Turk. On 14 March 1518 Pope Leo X walked barefoot from St Peter's to the Minerva and sat through a largely inaudible sermon proclaiming the holy war. Throughout the century his successors talked and planned to the same end. The Emperor Charles V thought that the highest of political aims was the capture of Constantinople, and King Francis I of France, when negotiating for the imperial crown, said that if successful he would be in Constantinople within three years or dead. Even a century later Father Joseph the Capuchin, Richelieu's Grey Eminence, wrote an interminable poem called *The Turciad* to cry the holy war against Islam.

These large aspirations corresponded to little enough in the realm of the practicable. The European powers were more frightened of each other than of the Turk. A certain scepticism began to appear; Erasmus asked cynically whether if a crusade were successful the Pope would be likely to govern the east better than the Turk. Even the most idealistic of crusades needed the backing of commercial incentive, and now half Europe was beginning to look westward instead of eastward, to the Americas or the Cape and India. If a Spaniard wanted a crusade, he looked to Cortés and Mexico, to Pizarro and Peru. And with the Spaniard rising in Europe, a crusade without Spanish help was doomed.

The western powers attained the nearest point to a crusade against the Turk in the year 1571, and nothing so near to a crusade was ever seen again in the history of Europe. The Sultan was known to be about to attack Cyprus, which Venice ruled. Pope Pius V, an idealist oblivious of political obstacles, devoted medieval efforts to raising a league of Christian powers, and made even the Venetians nervous whether Spanish power in the east would not hurt them more than the loss of Cyprus. It is a measure of the Pope's prestige and stature that he succeeded in fitting out a naval expedition of Spanish, Venetian, Papal, and Italian troops under the command of Don John of Austria. At the battle of Lepanto, off the western coast of Greece, the Turkish fleet was shattered, and western naval power in the Mediterranean was thereby preserved. But it was the last of the western crusading alliances. The victory failed to recover Cyprus or to contain the Turkish arms. The Christian league collapsed. Pius V died seven months after the battle, and the opportunity became an anachronism. The crusading ideal burnt itself out in plundering raids by the Spaniards, or the Florentines, or the Knights of St John from Malta, upon the coasts of the Turkish Empire.

THE CHURCH UNDER THE TURKS

The Eastern Orthodox Church cannot be said to have flourished under Turkish rule. Its wealth had been confiscated, its educated men had fled westward, it had lost the long-accustomed direct rule of a Christian sovereign, its peasants were subjected to a crushing burden of taxation, including many male children to Mohammedan religion and service. The impoverished cities and villages struggled to pay their priests and repair their churches, and in many areas, especially the countryside of Asia Minor, the churches decayed and not seldom were abandoned. Destitute Christian peasants were not reluctant to send their children to the janissaries to be educated as Mohammedan troops. The Christian decline is apparent from the existence of prelates with high-sounding titles but with hardly any flocks, like the metropolitan of Pisidia, who became a mere dependant of Constantinople. Like certain of their contemporaries at the Vatican, the ancient name became in practice that of a titular bishop *in partibus infidelium*.

There were exceptions to the general poverty. Prominent places of pilgrimage, like Jerusalem and Sinai, continued, though guardedly, to flourish. Some officials or churches in Jerusalem or Constantinople still received pensions or indirect aid from the west, from the Pope or the king of Spain. In Constantinople, the trading communities of wealthy Venetians or Genoese and the embassies of western powers formed another indirect support for the Orthodox churches of Constantinople. The trade of the capital was often conducted by Greek merchants, and although it was necessary to be a Moslem to hold one of the highest offices of state (we hear of occasional exceptions even to this rule, as when a Christian commanded an army of the Sultan upon the plains of Hungary) Christians were much used as contractors, ship-builders, or cannon-founders, and thereby accumulated useful fortunes. About 1570 one Greek of ancient family, Michael Cantacuzene, achieved such eminence organizing the Turkish trade in Russian furs that the Patriarch was accustomed to call upon him weekly, perhaps to consult him, perhaps to receive instructions. At least the clergy in the cities could live, and their churches be maintained. Marauders always seemed to find plenty of church plate as booty. But the general impression is the burden of poverty. We know of several begging expeditions from Constantinople to the west, to Moscow, or to the Balkan principalities.

The Sultan, like his Byzantine predecessors, preferred to control the election of the Patriarch of Constantinople. The Sultan normally sold the see, or (we ought to say) exacted high fees for entry upon the office. In this he was doing no more than the Protestant Queen Elizabeth or some Catholic sovereigns of France and Spain, though in Constantinople the price was higher. The fee to the Sultan at election of the patriarch was nothing in 1453 but rose quickly after 1466 and was 3,000 ducats in 1537. The annual tribute rose from 500 ducats to 4,100.* The rising price was caused less by direct exaction than by the readiness of contending factions to offer higher sums to the government and outbid their rivals. In 1555 the Patriarch Joasaph II, with extraordinary skill, succeeded in getting the election fee reduced, and was later deposed, ironically enough, on a charge of simony, if the chronicler is to be believed. In addition, powerful Greek laymen exacted substantial fees for their services with the government on behalf of the Church. Michael Cantacuzene is said to have exacted many ducats for his services at the election of the Patriarch Metrophanes (1565). Though the blood of martyrs may be the seed of the Church, persecution and the rule of a contemptuous government afford new and splendid opportunities to ecclesiastical vice.

The Sultan removed the Patriarch at his inclination, and the seat was never comfortable. The line of Orthodox bishops had its martyrs under the Turk. Though two arch-

* Lest we blame the sultans overmuch, let us record that the most Protestant sovereign Queen Elizabeth of England kept the see of Oxford vacant for twenty-one years because she wished to pocket the revenues; that the most Catholic sovereign Philip II of Spain kept the archbishop of Toledo in prison for many years for similar reasons; and that the Mohammedan governors of Erevan in Persia were not only putting up the chief Armenian see to auction but torturing the bishops if enough money was not forthcoming. Governments have adopted a variety of devices for taxing the offerings of the faithful.

bishops of Canterbury between 1550 and 1650 ended their lives by execution, a prudent man, offered the choice between Canterbury and Constantinople, would not have chosen Constantinople.

The danger was less commonly physical than moral. For the Turks were usually tolerant, at least of the Orthodox. Even the fees exacted were rather typical of the venality of the court than a sign of religious hostility. From time to time a zealous sultan or mufti would declare that it was the duty of the Turks to exterminate all the Christians; and the bloodthirsty Selim I, who is extolled by a Turkish historian for his humanity in forbidding the roasting of condemned persons over a slow fire, is said to have been restrained with difficulty from killing Christians; but these statements were rather metaphysical than practical. The Turks exacted their tribute of children for Turkish instruction and use. They normally commandeered at least one church in every conquered town and transformed it into a mosque, and they might commandeer more if the city was big – at Constantinople itself they appropriated at least eight other churches beside the great St Sophia. In 1537 the Turkish muezzins in Constantinople declared that according to Moslem law all Christian churches in a conquered city must be destroyed, and that Constantinople was a conquered city. The Patriarch embraced with lamentations the image of the Virgin in Our Lady Pammacaristos, his cathedral since the loss of St Sophia, consulted the Grand Vizier and the legal authorities, distributed presents, and hired an ancient witness named Mustapha who said that he was 102 years old, had fought at the siege of Constantinople, and could testify that the city had not been *conquered* but had *surrendered*. The lawyers accepted the plea, and the passing of the danger was celebrated with litanies and thanksgivings. The project of a general massacre of Christians was revived in 1595, on the news of the sack of Patras by a Spanish fleet, and again in 1646, but it was never implemented. The device was profitable to the Turks and doubtless was intended to be profitable, for these proposals were not in harmony with Turkish practice and policy.

Except for the sacking of churches, with every other building, at the capture of many cities, the Turks destroyed few churches. They preferred churches to be secluded, ordered the removal of the tall cross on the dome of Pammacaristos, visible afar from land and sea, and thereby lowered the morale of the Orthodox in the city. In 1586 they expelled the Christians from Pammacaristos, and from 1601 to 1924 the Patriarch was perforce content with the smaller church of St George. But churches were rarely disturbed unless, as in some parts of Asia Minor, there were no Christians left to maintain them. If a mosque converted from a church were later found to be unwanted, the Christians were permitted to buy it back, as happened at Larnaka in Cyprus. At Damascus the great church was divided, oddly and perhaps uniquely, between the two religions. The communities of monks upon Mount Athos seem to have suffered little from the Turkish conquest, and in 1542 the Patriarch Jeremiah was able to found the great new house of Stavronikita. The monastery of St Catherine on Mount Sinai, doubtless for reasons of political prudence, allowed a Moslem chapel to be built within the precincts, but was otherwise little disturbed except by the heavy pressure of taxation. Where funds were available, it was easy to repair and decorate churches, though this was liable to be a delicate undertaking, for one Patriarch was removed (1502) on a plea of new construction without authority. Movement of bishops was not especially restricted, and the Patriarchs of Antioch, Alexandria, and Jerusalem were able to join in synods at Constantinople without difficulty.

In the Greek lands, the Balkans, and the young Russian principalities, the Orthodox Church was still the church of the people. In Crete, Euboea, and parts of Albania the Moslem advance meant the conversion of Christians to Islam. On state occasions, as at the circumcision of the heir of Murad III in 1582, numbers of Christians were displayed abjuring their religion. But almost everywhere in Europe Islam remained the religion of a ruling minority. The ancient Christian liturgy and the sacramental structure still permeated the lives of the impoverished and oppressed peoples. Salonica remained strongly Greek, with twenty churches and four monasteries against six mosques. About 1570 Sofia had thirteen mosques, but the metropolitan controlled some 300 churches and two church schools.

How powerful were the Greek mysteries may be seen in their impact upon the simpler Moslem. Though the noblest of Byzantine churches, St Sophia, had been given minarets and converted into a mosque, Christians continued to visit the holy places there, and Turks joined with them in their reverence for the doors made from the wood of the ark or for the holy well covered with a stone from the well of Bethlehem. Sometimes the Turks imposed their own tradition upon the building, by means of that slow growth of knowledge evident to everyone familiar with professional guides to ancient buildings. The dome, it was said, fell upon the day when the Prophet was born, and could not be rebuilt until the holy Mohammedan Khidr appeared and instructed the builders to make mortar compounded of sand from Mecca, water from the well Zem-zem, and saliva of the Prophet. At Salonica the grave of St Demetrius, though in the building converted into a mosque, continued to be the goal of Christian pilgrimage and soon of Mohammedan pilgrimage. There is good evidence of Turks being secretly baptized in the hope of healing cures or other benefits, possibly among them Sultan Murad III himself (1585), and of Turks wearing amulets containing texts from the preface of St John's Gospel as well as from the Koran. Selim II is said to have supplied oil for six silver lamps before an icon at Xeropotamou on Mount Athos, because he believed the saints to have helped him. He was friendly to the Christians, and allowed the restoration or building of churches more freely. There is evidence of simple Christians consulting the muezzin as well as the priest when in need.

The mingling of beliefs and superstitions easily arose when Christian women became members of a Turkish harem. Yet few facts testify so vigorously to the strength and continuity of the Orthodox tradition under its discouragements. The Christian priests might be poor and simple villagers, peasants among their flocks, but their office continued to be respected; Orthodox women crossed themselves when they passed the Patriarch's door and its guard of two janissaries. The sense of age-long tradition persisted as strongly as ever, or more strongly, as it became identified with the existence and the nationality of a subject people.

The Sultan's law courts strengthened the ecclesiastical authority of the Patriarch over the Greek church. The Turks treated the Orthodox as a subject nation with its local laws, and regarded the Patriarch of Constantinople as its representative.

During the sixteenth century the Patriarch was already beginning to acquire certain judicial functions for settling disputes among the Greeks. In the hierarchy itself, the Turkish government continually strengthened patriarchal authority over other bishops and metropolitans within the empire. By 1576 the Patriarch achieved a power, in elevating or deposing bishops, more effective than that of any of his predecessors since the foundation of the see. It was normally Turkish policy to bring the newly overrun churches into subjection to the capital. In the Balkan territories this was liable to exceptions, for local policy or the influence of friendly viziers allowed a measure of autonomy to the Serbian archbishop of Pec and the Bulgarian archbishop of Ochrida. But the ecclesiastical authority of Constantinople, despite the internal troubles of the city, was being strengthened throughout this age, to reach its height in the eighteenth century.

THE ORTHODOX AND THE LATIN CHURCH

The attitude of the Orthodox towards Rome had not weakened. They felt as antipathetic towards its pretensions

as ever. In Hungary and Poland the land was part Orthodox and part Catholic, and the struggle helped to keep alive
the old bitterness. Nevertheless, a wave of Latin theological
influence spread, almost unobserved, through the Greek
Church.

The influence of Latin theology was no novelty in the
East. Since the age of the Crusades the partial isolation of
the Byzantine tradition was modified by knowledge of
western ways and western thought, and by attraction or
repulsion towards them. After 1204, with Latins installed
for a time in Constantinople and cities like Venice dominating the Levant, the communications at times became close.
And though these communications were hindered by the
Mongol invasions and the new aggressiveness of the Otto-
man Turks, the very weakness of Constantinople, its desperate political need of western help against the Turks,
made the hundred years before 1453 a time of close association between the Greek Church and the Italians.

The fall of Constantinople to the Turks in 1453 did not
break this association. In the sixteenth century many of the
best young men of Orthodoxy came to pursue their studies
in Italy, at a university like Padua, since they were unable
to receive an equivalent education under the Turks.
And so the Turkish invasion, and then Turkish rule,
created the conditions for an indelible change among the
Easterns. The Orthodox never ceased to be themselves,
never ceased to treasure their own liturgy and their traditional modes of life and expression; but now they learnt –
or some of them learnt – to express their uppermost forms
of doctrine with the aid of methods and language drawn
from the Latin schoolmen. Orthodox theologians accepted
the tradition of the seven sacraments (or mysteries), no more
nor less, and were more inquiring than their predecessors
about modes of the Real Presence; in short, asked themselves theological questions unfamiliar to the older tradition; and some Western answers to these questions slowly
passed into the tradition and became part of it. The

incorporation of the word *transubstantiation* into some Eastern thought is a famous example.

Latin language began to penetrate Eastern theology during the last centuries of the Middle Ages. But now, in Orthodox Poland and even in western Russia, some theological education was given in Latin. At Kiev, Roman Catholic textbooks were used to train Orthodox students. In 1569 the Ukraine was incorporated politically with Poland and Lithuania; and in 1596, by the union of Brest-Litovsk, the Church of the province became united to Rome. Between 1596 and 1620, when an Orthodox hierarchy was restored, the metropolitans of Kiev were Uniate members of the Roman Catholic Church. The theological tradition of Orthodoxy, in appearance and in reality so static and conservative, was little by little being affected.

The Turks regarded the Roman Catholics in the east as a dissenting minority and discouraged them. There were many Latin Christians in the ex-Venetian islands of the Aegean, in Bosnia and Serbia and Albania, even some surviving in Trebizond. It was safer for Latin communities to allow it to be assumed by the Turkish governors that they were Eastern Orthodox. It was in the Turks' interest to appear as the protector of the Orthodox against western evangelism, though the Greeks only succeeded in persuading the government to make Latin proselytism illegal as late as 1728. From time to time one of the Popes pursued the traditional plans for reunion with the East, and an apostolic delegate conferred politely but fruitlessly with the Patriarch of Constantinople. There were Uniate communities, subject to Rome, in the Lebanon, Syria, and Palestine. A Greek College was established in Rome, but failed to flourish. In 1576 Rome sent into the Levant 12,000 copies of a Greek translation of the Roman catechism and 12,000 copies of the decrees of the Council of Trent, but we cannot imagine who perused them. In 1583 the Pope established in Constantinople a small Jesuit house, with three fathers and two lay brothers, and three years later every member had died of the plague. It was reopened in 1609 under the protection of the French embassy.

THE ORTHODOX AND THE PROTESTANTS

Under these circumstances the tensions of the reforming west were found to touch, however superficially, the east.

It was natural for the Protestants to be interested in the Orthodox. Luther's studies into the past history of the Christian east helped to convince him that the claims of Rome were to be resisted. Protestants, especially among the Lutherans, sometimes thought it possible to establish friendly relations with the eastern sees. Greek students in the west passed beyond Padua and Venice to hear lectures at Tübingen, where the Lutheran Martin Kraus taught the possibility of uniting the Greek Church with the Evangelical. In 1559 a Lutheran friend of Melanchthon took the trouble to translate the Augsburg Confession into Greek. A diplomatic chaplain named Stephen Gerlach offered this Greek translation to the Patriarch of Constantinople, Jeremiah II, and hoped that he would see the doctrinal agreement of the two Churches even while their ceremonial was so manifestly different. The Patriarch replied by a statement of the points wherein the Churches were not agreed, and by a courteous suggestion that the Lutherans should accept the teaching of the Orthodox Church and join it. The Patriarch's statement slipped by mischance into the hands of a Roman Catholic priest of Poland, who published it to prove the vanity of the Lutheran hopes of an alliance; and the Patriarch had the pleasure or the trial of being congratulated by Pope Gregory XIII upon his noble answer to the schismatics.

LUCARIS (1572–1638)

Cyril Lucaris was a Greek who knew much of western ways, for he studied at the universities of Venice and Padua, could read and write Italian and Latin with ease, and served as an Orthodox controversialist and teacher in Poland. This service in Poland transformed his outlook. Seeking to defend Orthodoxy against Rome, he found allies in the Protestants, who in those days were still powerful in Poland. Lucaris was ready to go a long way with the Protestants for the sake of unity. And it appears that he was sincerely persuaded that some of their doctrines were true.

In 1602 he became Patriarch of Alexandria; in 1620, to the pleasure of the Protestant ambassadors in Constantinople and the horror of their Catholic colleagues, he became Patriarch of Constantinople itself. He entered into cordial relations with the Archbishop of Canterbury and other eminent Protestants. He presented the Archbishop with an Arabic manuscript of the Pentateuch, and the king of England with the great *Codex Alexandrinus* of the Bible. He sent his ablest young priests to study at Oxford and Helmstedt and Geneva. He found that it pained him to conform outwardly in the liturgy to the invocation of saints. Through the Dutch ambassador he allowed to be printed at Geneva his *Confession of Faith*, which resounded with the language of Calvin and caused the Protestants to acclaim the agreement in faith between the Orthodox Church and themselves. He taught that the Church was subject to the Scripture, and could err; predestination to life irrespective of good works; justification by faith; two sacraments of the Gospel; and a Reformed doctrine of the Eucharist. It was no common sensation in Europe to find the head of the Orthodox churches publishing a quasi-Protestant confession of faith. And after being the plaything and sometimes the organizer of intrigue among the rival diplomats of the city, Lucaris was strangled by order of the Sultan in 1638 and his body was thrown into the Bosporus. His *Confession* was condemned by two synods shortly afterwards. It is a sign of the powerful ties between the eastern and the western churches that Peter Mogila, the chief Orthodox refuter of Lucaris, drew much of his material from Roman Catholic sources like the

catechism of the Jesuit Peter Canisius, and first published
it in Latin.

In 1672 the great Orthodox synod of Jerusalem formally
condemned the errors of the Protestant heretics.

There was no natural sympathy between the Orthodox
and the Protestants. When Tsar Ivan the Terrible captured
Kochenhausen in Livonia in 1577, he found a Lutheran
pastor in the high street and engaged in friendly discussion
upon theology – friendly, until the Lutheran compared
Luther with St Paul, when Ivan cut him over the head with
his riding-whip and rode off, with the cry: 'To the devil
with thee and thy Luther!' However antipathetic the
Orthodox might be to Rome, the language and ethos and
doctrine of the Protestants always seemed strange, odd, un-
traditional, erroneous.

It is still a fact of great moment in Christian history that
the Orthodox Church, despite these various influences,
should have missed both the Reformation and the Counter-
Reformation. Though we may not speculate profitably upon
the might-have-beens of history, we may at least affirm that
the chains of Turkish rule made it possible to avoid these
two forces, so dynamic and so transforming.

MOSCOW

The continuing strength of the Orthodox Church can be
seen not only in its hold upon the Balkans, but in its steady
expansion northwards and eastwards.

The Russians always looked to Constantinople, received
their faith from the south, felt themselves to participate in
Christendom by means of their Slavonic Orthodoxy.

By 1505 Russia had been created by Ivan III the Great
out of the little principalities of the great plains. He married
Sophia, the niece of the last Roman Emperor of Constantinople, and looked upon himself as the heir to the Christian
heritage of East Rome. He took for the Russian arms the
double-headed eagle of the Byzantines. These notions were

powerful in the formation of Russian tradition and autocracy. We find a monk named Philotheos writing to the Tsar
between 1505 and 1533: 'Two Romes have now fallen, and
the third one, our Moscow, yet standeth; and a fourth one
there shall never be . . . In all the world thou alone art the
Christian Tsar.' The climax of this mode of thinking was the
creation in 1589 of the Patriarchate of Moscow. Jeremiah II
of Constantinople travelled to Moscow in search of alms;
and in return for munificent generosity he consecrated a
nominee of the Tsar to be the first Patriarch of Moscow,
taking rank after Jerusalem.

The Russian principality was now the sole country where
the Orthodox Church was established and not under Mohammedan rule. As early as 1576 an intelligent Venetian
observed the political possibilities when the ruler of Moscow
professed the same religion as the peoples of Bulgaria,
Serbia, Bosnia, Morea, and Greece, and at a word could
summon Turkish subjects to a crusade of liberation. But this
was clever prophecy. Russia had to pass through much
anarchy and civil war before it could exert effective political
power in eastern Europe, and without that there could be
no protection or liberation of the Orthodox peoples. For the
time, communication was restricted mainly to almsgiving or
to Russian pilgrims passing through Constantinople towards
Jerusalem, and to the growing Russian interest in Mount
Athos.

With Russian expansion went the Orthodox faith. In a
vast country of few towns, the monasteries colonized the
wilderness and became the owners of great tracts of agrarian
land. The growth of monastic colonies was continuing
through the sixteenth century. Here, almost alone in Christendom, the primitive ideals of the old Egyptian solitaries
continued to be renewed among the forests, while the bigger
communities established remote parishes and built churches
for the peasants. Cyril of Novoyezersk walked barefoot upon
pilgrimage and lived upon pine bark, roots, and grass,
spending twenty years among the wild beasts before he

decided in 1517 to build himself a cell and stay at Bielo-zersk. Nowhere else in the Europe of 1517 might this fresh-ness be found, so reminiscent of early Celtic Ireland. *The Praise of Folly* by Erasmus, sophisticated satire on dilapi-dated monks, published six years before, is a world away.

Part Three

THE REFORMATION AND THE LIFE OF THE CHURCH

11

Divided Christendom

THE Western Church was irremediably divided from the Eastern Orthodox Church since the capture of Constantinople by the crusaders in 1204. An obvious consequence of the Reformation was the further splintering of western Christianity. This disunity was made possible by that decline in the idea of Christendom, through the rise of national sovereignties, which was not a result but a cause of Protestant success. Western Christendom, being ready for secular division, was open to religious division. The Protestant revolt, and the stern answer of the Counter-Reformation, not only split the Church but hardened the antagonisms of political division.

The wars of religion were only about religion in a restricted sense. The Dutch cities were fighting for their independence and their trade against imperial and Spanish control and taxation, the Spanish to repress their rebellious subjects. None of the great expeditions, not even the Spanish Armada against England, was a crusading expedition in the idealistic sense of Pope Urban II's first crusade against the Holy Land. If we call them the wars of religion, we do not thereby mean that Catholics were seeking to kill Protestants solely because they were Protestants, or Protestants seeking to kill Catholics because they were Catholics. 'Take out of the Catholic army,' said Montaigne once, 'all the soldiers whose motive is not pure zeal for religion or patriotism or loyalty to the sovereign, and you would not be left with enough men to form a company.' One of the nearest approaches was the massacre of St Bartholomew at Paris in 1572, when Catholic bands murdered thousands of Huguenots in their beds. But that massacre was ordered by Queen

Catherine de' Medici, into whose mind and heart religious motives hardly seem to have entered.

Men might be divided by fear for their pockets, or fear of tyranny, or fear of greed, by those suspicions which always divide the human race. With Europe split into religious camps, the difference of religion was a deep motive for fear and for political disunity. When it is asserted, therefore, that the wars of religion were not wars of religion in the sense of pure crusades, it is not being asserted that fear of persecution, or hostility to alleged heresy, were never present or potent in the minds of the warriors. They were often present, and the religious motive was the most compelling motive in the mind of individuals or groups. In the seventeenth century a few men began to be cynical about the motive. John Selden said that religion must be put forward as the motive for fighting because it was the only motive which touched the interest of the lowest equally with the highest. During the sixteenth century such sophistication was hardly found.

By 1648 the religious map of Western Europe, as it would persist for 300 years, had taken shape. In the north the Protestants were in control – Lutheran churches in Sweden, Norway, Denmark, Iceland, the northern and central states of Germany; Calvinist or Reformed churches in Scotland, the Netherlands, Hesse, the Palatinate, and a few of the western German states. In the south the Catholics were in control – Spain, Italy, Austria, Bavaria, and elsewhere in southern Germany. And across Europe ran a belt of disputed states in which victory was not yet clear: Ireland, where the Roman Catholic Church struggled to maintain its grip against a Reformation spreading under the political aegis of England; England, where the Calvinists were still striving, with Scottish and Dutch support, to establish a Calvinist polity against a more conservative, or less conservative, mode of reform; France, where after nearly forty years of war the Huguenots had established the legal right to exist but commanded the allegiance only of a large minority in the population; Switzerland, where the advance of Calvinist and Reformed had been stayed and where the revival of the Counter-Reformation, supported from Milan, sustained the traditional allegiance of the Catholic cantons; and some of the middle states of central Germany.

Was there any notion of one Christian Church surviving these divisions of passion, nationalism, political suspicion, and religious controversy?

Little enough. Fear trampled upon charity. A Dutch prelate wrote a poetic panegyric to glorify the assassin of William the Silent. Catholic antagonists of John Knox circulated scandalous and baseless rumours about his birth, ancestry, and character. Protestant divines spread scandalous and untrue gossip about the birth of the Jesuit Robert Parsons, and when Parsons's brother John, a loyal Anglican clergyman, rebutted the charge with vehemence, it was bruited that John Parsons must be sympathetic towards the papists. These controversies were not conducted with clean hands.

It was not easy for traditional divinity to find room inside the Church for those divided from it, whether by their faith or their discipline. Orthodox Roman Catholics believed that outside the visible church there was no salvation and that to be a member of the visible church it was necessary to be subject to the Pope of Rome. A man cannot be saved without the true and complete faith; and he cannot believe the true and complete faith unless he believes the word of the infallible Church. Orthodox Calvinism believed that outside the visible church there was no salvation and that a Christian must be a member of a congregation where the Word was purely preached and the sacraments rightly administered; and since they could attribute neither of these virtues to the Roman Catholic Church, they found it not easy to see how a Roman Catholic could in a true sense be a member of the Church of Christ.

The intolerable rigidities of logic were softened by the

skill or charity or eccentricity of thinkers upon either side. There were still old-fashioned minds which impracticably idealized the medieval theory of one Christian Empire, but now looked to find an Empire which could peacefully house within its borders the three main groups of Christians, the Catholic, the Lutheran, and the Reformed. Henry IV of France even thought of a Council of Europe to administer its troubles, to plan a general disarmament among Christian nations whether Protestant or Catholic, to control a Christian-European army, and to restrict wars to campaigns against the Turk. King James VI of Scotland wrote a poem – or constructed verses – to celebrate the great victory over the Turks at Lepanto, and only a few among the Scots were critical that he celebrated a Catholic victory. In 1608 Stephen Pannonius of Belgrade imagined a great European empire from Holland to Greece and from England to Poland, based upon toleration of all Trinitarian Christians.

It was impossible for the barriers not to be lowered in a world where the humanist spirit was powerful and a middle class was ever growing in numbers and in education. The profit motive knew no barrier in religious division. The book trade crossed the frontiers, wherever censorships were inefficient. Protestant musicians composed masses and motets for Catholic churches; Catholic musicians arranged choral melodies for Protestant churches. Learning knew no boundaries, unless it were theological learning. The Reformation, or the national and religious divisions of Christendom, delayed the arrival of an international amity of scholarship. Scholars rarely laboured with the patronage of their government unless their scholarship could be observed to be useful, and to be useful was generally to be effective in controversy. But humane inquiry transcended these discouragements. After the Edict of Nantes, we find in France a genuine fraternity of scholars, transcending the religious division, encouraged by the Catholic court and the Huguenot minister Sully, and gathered round the historian de Thou and the classical scholar Isaac Casaubon.

Skilful divines softened the hard edges of dogmatism. On the Roman side, a long line of thinkers, and they of high reputation, sought to find some place for the man who – to put it thus – would have been a Catholic had his external circumstances been different. Cardinal Bellarmine hinted at a comparison between the sincere Protestant and the catechumen who died before his preparation for baptism could be completed; and others made a more explicit comparison between the faith of a simple, ill-instructed heretic and the faith of a child. There might therefore be persons, even among the Protestant bodies, who adhered in their soul, by some mysterious means, to the Catholic Church. It cannot, however, be claimed that these more liberal admissions were prominently offered to Protestants during the age of the Reformation.

Upon the Protestant side, there was a wider division in opinion. Reformed churchmen felt the breach from Rome to be an irreparable rending of a garment, the cutting out of a motheaten patch of the cloth and the renewal or cleansing of the remainder. They transformed the appearance and atmosphere of their churches, they found a strange or repellent or unintelligible atmosphere when they entered a Catholic church, they had little sense of continuity with the Christian past of the Middle Ages. When they looked into history for their Christian predecessors, they found them, not in the main stream of the tradition, but in the little persecuted groups of medieval Christendom – Hussites and Wycliffites and Waldensians. When they looked to the rock whence they were hewn, they looked to the Bible, and they expected to find half-hidden, secret traces of Biblical religion even amidst the corruptions of the fifteenth century. They recognized not at all that the Church of the Counter-Reformation bore a resemblance to the Church whence they had sprung. Those who meditated upon the Book of Revelation, and compared its forebodings with the signs of the times, saw in the Pope of Rome the Scarlet Woman, or the Beast, Antichrist sitting upon the throne destined for another.

Calvin himself admitted the Roman Catholic Church to possess the 'traces' of the true Church. The building had collapsed, but there amidst rubble the seeing eye might still discern the authentic foundations. Most Reformed divines were ready to distinguish between the authorities of the Roman Church and its members. They confessed that by God's mercy Roman Catholics might be saved, but it was as individuals, as a remnant, as fish taken out of the sea, as Elijah and the band of true prophets among the prophets of Baal, a remnant saved out of the Roman Church and in spite of the Roman Church, not saved through its ministry and its sacraments; sharing in the true Church although and not because they were members of that visible communion.

The Lutherans were ready to go further. They, like the Reformed, distinguished between the authorities of the Roman Church and its members. But they had a stronger sense of their continuity with the Church of the medieval centuries. They had altered the appearances of their churches little; their worshippers had less sense of strangeness upon entering a Roman Catholic church; they retained the mass and the sacrament of confession, and were conservative in their ceremonial. Luther and Melanchthon always believed and taught that they had cleansed the old Church of impurities. When they looked back to the Church of the fifteenth century and before, they found their predecessors in the main stream of medieval tradition, in an Aquinas, an Occam, a Duns Scotus. Men were saved within the Church of Rome in spite of the Pope but not in spite of the visible Church. Within that Church they were baptized, and heard the Bible read, and received the holy sacrament, and believed in the true Presence, and shared in Christ's priesthood.

The English divines, from Hooker onwards, carried the recognition no further, but sometimes they expressed it in even stronger language by freely allowing a continuity between the Church of the medieval centuries and the contemporary Church of Rome. 'With Rome,' wrote Hooker, 'we dare not communicate concerning sundry her gross and grievous abominations, yet touching those main parts of Christian truth wherein they constantly still persist, we gladly acknowledge them to be of the family of Jesus Christ.' 'You know,' wrote John Donne to a friend, 'I never fettered nor imprisoned the word Religion, not . . . immuring it in a Rome, or a Wittenberg, or a Geneva; they are all virtual beams of one Sun . . . They are not so contrary as the North and South Poles.'

Each side, therefore, confessed with a stammer that the other side contained members of the true Church. The Roman Catholics and the Reformed thought that those persons were truly Christians, in spite of their participation in the corrupt or heretical body; the Lutheran and the Anglican that they were truly Christian, in part at least because heresies or corruptions could not deprive fragments of the Roman Catholic Church of the features of a true Church.

An occasional divine would be bold enough to map a pattern whereby Catholic and Protestant might yet be brought to agree. The most celebrated of these was George Cassander (died 1566), a Flemish teacher at Cologne, where the atmosphere was often more eirenic than in some other cities of the Rhineland. He was a Catholic humanist, an admirer of Erasmus and a friend of Protestants, a man with a tolerant mind. And he formulated an idea, of which hints may be found in the schoolmen and more explicit formulations in a peaceable thinker like Melanchthon, but which had not yet been thrown into the front of the religious argument and was now destined to a long history; the idea of *fundamental articles*. The principles were enunciated in the admirable-sounding and famous phrase (probably of the sixteen-twenties): 'In essentials, unity; in inessentials, liberty; in everything, charity.' But these programmes were academic, smelling of the study, and the phrase still left undiscovered how 'essentials' were to be determined.

The only country where discussions of this sort looked for

a moment as though they might be fertile was Sweden. King John III of Sweden studied Cassander and other divines of Christian reunion, and married a Roman Catholic wife. His new order of 1571 allowed the use of Latin psalms and prayers and made public provision for confession, excommunication, and public penance. The Archbishop of Uppsala, Laurentius Petri Gothus, was likewise a student of the ancient Fathers, and after assenting to seventeen articles – including prayers for the dead, the veneration of saints, and the restoration of monastic life – was consecrated with mitre, crosier, ring, and chrism. Some of the old convents were reopened. In 1576 the King drafted a still more Romanized liturgy, 'The Red Book of Sweden', caused a Diet of 1577 to accept it, and attempted to force it upon the country. In 1577 the Jesuit Antony Possevinus appeared in Sweden and persuaded the King to accept the Council of Trent without waiting for concessions. The King made the profession of faith and received communion in the Roman manner. Bishop Olafsson of Linkoeping was deposed for calling the Pope Antichrist. Luther's catechism was removed in favour of that of Canisius, and the Jesuits were admitted. But the King continued to insist upon the cup for the laity, the use of Swedish in the liturgy, the marriage of the clergy, and the acceptance of the legal changes of the Reformation. The Pope refused further concession. The Roman Catholic Queen Catharine died in 1583; the Jesuits were expelled; and John, after taking a little glance at the Orthodox, accepted the conservative tradition of the Swedish Reformation. On his death the crown came to Sigismund, the King of Poland, who was a Roman Catholic. John's brother Charles prevented Sigismund from gaining power, a synod at Uppsala formally accepted the Augsburg Confession as the standard of faith, the use of the Red Book was forbidden, Luther's catechism was 'restored, and a simplified version of the 1571 Ordinance made the standard of worship. There was no further hope for ideas like those of Cassander.

The barriers of Christendom were crossed, though not frequently, by books.* Protestant divines of the seventeenth century learnt much, and not only by repulsion, from Jesuit divines of Spain. Hooker learnt from St Thomas Aquinas. Teachers and students at Oxford and Cambridge between 1600 and 1640 were reading Bellarmine and schoolmen of the Counter-Reformation. The puritan John Preston used to read the *Summa* of Aquinas in the barber's chair; when his hair fell upon the page he would blow it off and continue reading. The historians crossed the borders, and great editions of documents were used without regard to their origins. An author of a manuscript in the library of St John's College, Cambridge, recommends the student of history to Cardinal Baronius as of much advantage, 'but take heed how you trust him'. Izaak Walton tells a story, embellished with circumstantial and apocryphal detail, that Pope Clement VIII read with admiration and indeed reverence the first book by Hooker. Cardinal Bellarmine is said to have kept a portrait of the puritan William Whitaker in his library, and to have pointed it out to visitors as that of 'the most learned heretic that ever I read'. Cardinal Barberini is said to have recommended the *De Veritate* by Hugo Grotius and always to have kept it by him.

More conservative Protestants, Lutheran or Anglican, continued to use medieval books of devotion, or even those of the Counter-Reformation. As Catholics were ready to use Lutheran hymns, Lutherans were not afraid of using Catholic literature to nourish or instruct their piety. Isaac Basire sent his fiancée a copy of the *Introduction to the Devout Life* by

* Books sometimes crossed the frontier because they were not recognized. An edition of Melanchthon's *Commonplaces* was printed at Venice and read with applause at Rome, until a Franciscan detected the author and the edition was burnt. A Book of Hours was published at Paris with some appended prayers said to have been composed by Calvin. Bucer's commentary upon the Psalms is said to have been popular among Catholics until the author became known. 'So,' smiled Scaliger in reporting freaks of this kind, 'we regard not what is said, but who says it.'

Francis de Sales, thinking that it would help her soul, first marking with a cross in the margin the passages where caution was needed – 'else, all is safe'.* *The Imitation of Christ* received several English translations, and there were Protestant editions of the Spanish devotional writer Luis of Granada: here is a writer of the Counter-Reformation whom a Protestant editor dares to call matchless, a spiritual captain. Protestant editors changed certain phrases to make them palatable to their readers – a monk became 'a religious man', priest became 'minister', the saints became 'the holy and ancient fathers', St Francis of Assisi became 'a certain holy man', St Thomas became 'the great schoolman Aquinas'. But if it is complained that the author is a papist, it is replied, in the words of one Protestant translator: 'Shall not the corn be reaped because there's cockle in the field? Shall not the rose be plucked because it grows on a briar?' Spanish books poured into Protestant libraries. John Donne looked along his shelves in 1623 and saw more Spanish authors than those of any other nation. The most surprising use is that of the *Book of Resolution*, by the Jesuit Robert Parsons, feared and hated by the English as a plotter. An Anglican minister named Bunny bowdlerized the book under the patronage of the Archbishop of York, and we even hear of a minister reading it aloud in his church. 'Mr Bunny,' grumbled Parsons, 'makes me speak like a good minister of England'. Stout Protestants were not ashamed of using Latin books of piety.

A fair bulk of divinity, and a stream of devotional writing, succeeded in crossing the chasms, and testifying, though in a whisper, to the continued existence of Christendom. Charity, whipped and bleeding, limped up the ladder into the ark.

---

* Laud burnt 1,100 or 1,200 copies of the *Introduction* in 1637, an unusual holocaust of a devotional book. There were special circumstances: the archbishop's chaplain licensed a bowdlerized edition, and the printer and translator reinstated the censored passages before printing.

12

The Decline of Ecclesiastical Power

THE Church of 1600, considered as an organization able to exercise pressure upon governments, possessed less effective power than the Church of 1500.

We must beware of exaggerating. In 1500 the lay powers had already achieved a measure of immunity from ecclesiastical sanctions; in 1600 ecclesiastical sanctions were still exceedingly effective. Royal power in the state was advanced, not created, by the Reformation. Nor was royal power advanced uniformly. In some states, like Scotland, the king who once struggled to keep his head amidst baronial bishops now struggled amidst popularly supported preachers. Wherever a Calvinist or near-Calvinist polity prevailed, the secular government was not stronger than before, but still weak in relation to the Church. The preacher Andrew Melville was able with impunity to call King James VI of Scotland to his face 'God's silly vassal'.

Consider the excommunications launched from the See of Rome. It is sometimes supposed that the Reformation rendered these fulminations as futile and as unheard as the shouts of a man standing upon the brink of a waterfall. By abstracting half Europe from the Pope's jurisdiction, the Reformation prevented the see of Rome from undertaking those practical measures which once had lent weight to its rebukes, and left the excommunication to lean only upon the wobbly staff of a dubious moral prestige. But ever since Pope Boniface VIII had been kidnapped in the fatal day at Anagni two centuries before, the Pope walked delicately amid the sovereigns of Europe. If he wished to excommunicate the Queen of Naples, it was useful only if at the same moment some adventurer wished to occupy that territory.

If he laid an interdict upon the city of Venice, it was useful only if Milan for secular reasons wished to attack Venice. And the weapon had continued to be used on bizarre occasions, as when Pope Urban VI, besieged in the castle at Nocera, appeared at a window three times a day, with bell, book, and candle, solemnly and absurdly to excommunicate the besiegers.

The excommunications of the Reformation were often as vain – Luther in 1521, or Henry VIII. But with the rising moral prestige of the reformed Papacy, excommunication was not trivial. In 1570 Pope Pius V excommunicated Queen Elizabeth of England. The Bull wrecked the prospects of Roman Catholics in England, and in later perspective was bitterly regretted. Its effects, or non-effects, were sometimes used later to persuade the Pope not to excommunicate another monarch. But the Bull was not insignificant. It caused some Roman Catholics in England to sympathize with conspiracy and to believe the queen to be an unlawful sovereign. The English government was not contemptuous, for it replied with the most savage penal legislation of any Protestant state during that age. In 1573 Cardinal Charles Borromeo excommunicated the powerful Spanish governor of Milan, and nobles and working men refused to walk with him or doff their hats. Twenty years later, King Henry IV of France was struggling for the throne against the armies of the Catholic league. The Pope put Henry under an excommunication, and wished to prevent him from gaining the sovereignty of France. The excommunication was not potent enough to frustrate the king, but was potent enough to delay his success by a few years. The thunders of the reformed Popes were treated more seriously than those of the Renaissance Popes. They were strong enough, not to gain their ends, but to cause anguish to faithful Catholics. Thenceforth the weapon began to gather a coat of charitable mould in the cellars of the Vatican, to be refurbished every Maundy Thursday in the solemn Bull of General Excommunications, ever becoming more like an antique rite and less like the rhadamanthine judgement that once had stricken kings to their knees.

EXCOMMUNICATION AND CHURCH DISCIPLINE

If the papal excommunications were inefficient, that was not because excommunication was outmoded. On the contrary; the pastoral discipline of the clergy, of which the ultimate sanction must always be excommunication, became if anything more effective during the sixteenth century. Ecclesiastical discipline was more powerful in 1600 because it had been made effective by the new sovereign states. It was the secular authority alone which could reform the Church adequately. And where, as in the Papal States, the discipline was exercised by the clergy, they exercised it in their capacity as secular rulers.

In all the states of Europe the greater excommunication continued to carry penalties in this world as well as the next. In England, for example, the excommunicated had no status in a law court, could not prosecute if his goods were removed, could not give evidence, could not be married, could not receive Christian burial, and if he remained excommunicated for forty days was arrested and imprisoned by a writ issued by the bishop to the sheriff under his episcopal seal, certifying the contempt of the party towards Holy Church. Luther denounced it as a punishment of earthly and not heavenly power, and believed that it should simply be a form of local and pastoral discipline at the discretion of the minister and his flock. But the old excommunication possessed a useful side to those who were intent upon policing the country, and in Lutheran churches the legal aspect continued to dominate the pastoral. In England the same legal predominance may be found. The ban was used not so much as a pastoral discipline in the true sense, but as one mode of securing obedience to ecclesiastical law. Its victims regarded it no longer as a judgement of God but only as a judgement of the magistrate. It was still used to enforce such parts of the law as the payment of tithes, or to compel appearance in the ecclesiastical court. As lately as 1812 an English woman was imprisoned for contempt of court under a writ *de excommunicato capiendo*, a proceeding which at last shocked Parliament into abolishing the use of excommunication in such a matter and providing some other penalty.

In the Reformed as in the medieval churches, the congregation was subject to a moral discipline for acts which were not precisely crimes against the state. Here is a typical item chosen at random from the parish registers of a city church in London, St Botolph's Aldgate (spelling modernized):

Memorandum that William Erishe who was excommunicated for the non-payment of the parson's dues and yet presumed to be married to his wife before that he was according to the canonical law absolved wherefore the said William Erishe did stand in the church in time of a sermon and did ask both God and the people forgiveness for the said offence according to the judgement of Mr Dr Stanhope. This penance was done the 15th day of December in anno 1583.

Mr Erishe also had to pay the preacher a fee for his sermon. At St Paul's Cross in Elizabethan London, a row of penitents in white sheets and carrying tapers was not uncommon in time of sermon. All over Europe penitents continued to stand in white sheets, and in the disciplinary system of Scotland or parts of Germany they might have also to stand in 'the jugs', an iron collar fixed to a pillar in the church. One of the last persons to be compelled to do penance in an English church was the village fiddler of Fen Ditton, in the year 1849.

Since the penalties in the ecclesiastical courts were not only a mode of moral discipline in the church but a useful way of policing the people (the distinction between the two laws being not easy to determine), secular governments resisted the right of the clergy to excommunicate and thereby inflict secular penalties without reference to their magistrates. The argument lay between the Papacy and the Calvinists upon the one side, and all governments, supported by Lutheran and Anglican and Zwinglian theologians, upon the other. The word Erastian has come to symbolize a wrongful interference by the State in the affairs of the Church. So far from teaching that the State might interfere in the private concerns of the Church, Erastus* taught that the Church must not interfere with the proper concerns of the secular authorities and that secular penalties might be inflicted only at the will of a secular court. And everywhere in Europe his view was to prevail, though the old 'delivery to the secular arm for punishment' lingered long in Spain and Italy, and curious survivals might be found in Protestant countries.

The age of the Reformation saw the courts increase in effectiveness, an improved machine in organizing that moral discipline which the age demanded. There came to be a point where the courts of the State were now so much more efficient and commanded so much more of the public confidence than formerly that a system of church courts was no longer needed, and it slowly withered away except for the internal needs of church life and the moral discipline of the clergy. Punishment after excommunication had been appropriate to a simpler age, had helped to bind a rougher society. The greater excommunications died away in the seventeenth century because men trusted the strong arms of secular justice.

SANCTUARY

We see the same process happening to the right of sanctuary. In an earlier age of blood feud and of limping justice, the provision of sanctuaries was needed so that the accused might shelter his head until a fair trial could be secured. The idea of sanctuary is not specially Christian. But in a Christian world of sacred places, men in trouble were soon fleeing to the altar, and the Roman Emperors had regulated

* For Erastus, see pp. 149–50.

the practice. In the later Middle Ages it became a way of evading justice. In some notorious cases, like the church of St Martin-le-Grand in London in the early fifteenth century, a group of men living in a public sanctuary became little more than a band of brigands issuing forth from an immune fastness. It was much used by more harmless folk; the sanctuary register of St John at Beverley shows that nearly 500 people took refuge there in the sixty years before 1538. Most governments of the later Middle Ages, including the Popes, attempted to abridge the right.

The more powerful states of the sixteenth century were not prepared to tolerate the archaism. In 1539 the French government, by the ordinance of Villers-Cotterets, abolished the right of sanctuary in civil matters and drastically limited it in criminal cases. In 1540 King Henry VIII of England halved the number of sanctuaries and excluded from sanctuary persons guilty of murder, rape, highway robbery, burglary, arson, or sacrilege. The right was not abolished in England until 1624, and even after that certain privileges were claimed in Durham and Chester, as palatine counties, until 1697. All the Protestant countries abolished the right during the course of their reformation, some more slowly than others; in Scotland, though the right in its old form was early swept away, Holyrood Park survived as a theoretical sanctuary for debtors until the year 1880. In Roman Catholic countries the right was restricted, especially by Pope Gregory XIV, who in 1591 withdrew it from assassins, heretics, traitors, brigands, and robbers of churches. But it became a matter of principle to maintain it, chiefly as a sign of ecclesiastical independence, despite the manifest inconveniences which it often caused. (In a church in the duchy of Baden in 1770 it cost 1,173 florins to provide a guard for a man who was accused of stealing a shirt and a pair of shoes.) A few enclosed areas, especially the Temple at Paris, survived in France till the revolution of 1789. It was abolished in Silesia in 1743, in Tuscany in 1769, and in the Catholic German states at the beginning of the nineteenth century. Vestiges may still be found in Catholic countries. The concordat of 1929 between Mussolini and the Pope, which still regulates Italy, provides that secular officials shall not exercise their functions in a church without giving previous notice to the ecclesiastical authorities.

Like the penalties carried by excommunication, the right of sanctuary was appropriate to a simpler world. The efficiency of public justice made it obsolete.

BENEFIT OF CLERGY

In the early days of the Christian Roman Empire, and in the barbarian kingdoms, certain exemptions had been granted to the clergy. They received the right to be tried in their own judicial system, the ecclesiastical courts. The extension of this exemption, before the end of the Middle Ages, not only to the clergy proper but to anyone who could plead minor orders though he lived as a layman, almost to anyone who could show himself able to read, rendered the exemptions one of the weaknesses of medieval government. Medieval sovereigns did what they could to limit its force. No effective state could tolerate the system, and the new monarchs, like Henry VII of England, made inroads upon it before the Reformation.

The Protestant countries abolished it in their several ways. The Papacy attempted to maintain it, as it was seeking to maintain all the ancient exemptions. But Catholic sovereigns, by their various methods, secured almost as efficient a control over the exemptions as Protestant sovereigns. Some Lutheran countries continued for a time to exempt pastors from the normal jurisdiction of the secular courts and treated the consistory as a kind of spiritual court for the purpose. The Swedish Charter of 1611 provided that no priest could be tried unless his case was first investigated by the bishop and the chapter. In England a statute of 1513 excluded from benefit those guilty of petty treason, murder, robbery of holy places, highway robbery, and the burning of houses or of barns where grain was stored, and took away the privilege from men who were not truly in holy orders. The statute led to controversy and was not at once efficient, but in the Reformation of Henry VIII a series of statutes swept away the old rights and it looked as though benefit of clergy would vanish as rapidly in England as in Scotland. Even until 1576 the clergy could escape for the first offence if they were able to collect compurgators to swear to their innocence before the ecclesiastical court. But in 1576 Elizabeth's government abolished compurgation. It is one of those unpredictable survivals in the English Reformation that (nominal) benefit was not finally abolished until 1827.

THE CLERGY AS OFFICERS OF STATE

It had been natural, before the Reformation, for the greatest offices of state to be filled by high ecclesiastics; partly because more of the clergy than of the laity possessed the requisite education; partly because effective administration in the state must include effective administration in the Church; partly because the stipends of secular officials were paid without loss to the royal treasury if they were paid out of Church endowments; and partly because the public stature of churchmen made them obvious choices as the sovereign's advisers.

The old habit whereby a Cardinal like Wolsey was the king's chief minister persisted in Catholic countries into the eighteenth century. It is enough to mention Cardinals Richelieu and Mazarin as the rulers of France during the middle of the seventeenth century. The old prince-bishoprics of the Rhineland continued their sovereign status, under the protection of the German Emperor, until the Napoleonic era. But even in Catholic countries there was more opportunity for the lay minister. Government was becoming more complex and needed growing numbers of civil servants educated in the schools of the Renaissance. Public opinion demanded that bishops should reside upon their sees, and was not so tolerant of bishops who never saw their dioceses because they were serving the king.

In the Protestant countries the process was less gradual. The sovereigns achieved more legal power over the ecclesiastical corporation and did not need high ecclesiastics to govern. The fierce Protestant enmity to ignorance, and the diversion of ancient endowments, enabled the education of the laity to leap ahead in Protestant countries. The pastoral ideals of ministry were hostile to the bishop or cleric who drew the stipend of the Church and performed the work of the State. In many Lutheran states bishops or pastors continued sometimes to serve the prince in secular capacities. In Sweden no one in holy orders was admitted to membership of Parliament. Elsewhere representatives of the ministry continued to be members of the national council where such existed; as in England the bishops continued to sit as of ancient right in the House of Lords, and it was thought proper, until the eighteen-forties or eighteen-fifties, that clergy should be magistrates and justices of the peace. The early Stuart kings, in their unskilful contest with Parliament and their attempt to assert the royal prerogative, came nearer than other Protestant sovereigns to reviving medieval habits. From 1621 to 1625 Bishop Williams of Lincoln was Lord Keeper, the first for seventy years. From 1635 Archbishop Laud of Canterbury was sitting in the Commission for the Treasury and the Committee of the Privy Council for Foreign Affairs. From 1636 to 1641 Bishop Juxon of London held the office of Lord Treasurer, the first cleric to do so since the reign of King Henry VII, and soon afterwards was made a Lord of the Admiralty. From 1635 to 1639 Archbishop Spottiswoode of St Andrews was Lord Chancellor of Scotland. It cannot be said that this experiment was successful. On the one hand we find Archbishop Laud, who held strong opinions on all questions which engaged his attention but whose financial acumen was not equal to the force of his character, giving bad advice upon a monopoly in soap. Upon the other we find the clergy identified with political strife and their pastoral endeavours suspect. The Reformation gave the Protestant clergy something of the same painful but healthy fillip which the Italian Revolution of 1860–70 gave to a reluctant Papacy by freeing it from the age-long incubus of the Papal States.

THE DIVERSION OF ENDOWMENTS

The Church as a corporation was poorer in 1600 than in 1500. Lay hands – royal or municipal treasurers, nobles or squires or civil servants – pocketed a substantial fraction of the endowments which early medieval piety had bestowed.

In some Protestant countries the need of the State for church money was a motive in the State's support of the Reformation. Some endowments looked to be, and were, used wastefully. It was true that in every country in Europe the needs of a more effective administration combined with the eroding of money value, through the inflation during the century, to render governments even more liable to bankruptcy than governments usually are, and therefore made them eye idle resources with appetite.

Sweden adopted a Lutheran Reform principally on the ground that the country was bankrupt, that the State could not exist without a larger revenue, that the revenue could be found only if the church lands contributed more, and (since canon law made church property inalienable) that the authority of Rome must be thrown off if the revenue was to be found.

King Henry VIII of England, though also possessing a more intimate motive for his desire to throw off Roman authority, was assured by his agent Thomas Cromwell that he could enrich the kingdom with the spoils of the monasteries. The Lutheran envoy Myconius, who came hopefully to engage in theological negotiations with the English divines, was afterwards hostile to the king. 'King Henry's sole concern was the income of the Church. He stripped the gold and silver from the tombs of the saints ... and robbed the Church of its estates ... That was the Gospel that Henry wanted.' The irritation of the Lutheran is pardonable, for there was some truth in his words.

The largest transfers of property were the confiscations of monastic lands. In Lutheran and Calvinist countries, with certain exceptions like Sweden, where shadows of cathedral chapters survived, the endowments of bishops and chapters went by the same road, into the ownership of the government, princely or municipal. As with the monasteries, the governments often used part of the episcopal endowments to ecclesiastical ends. But we ought not to overestimate the loss to the Church. As late as 1580, when the Counter-Reformation in Germany was advancing in power and zeal, all the Catholic canons of the cathedral at Trèves were lay aristocrats living in the country upon their fat prebends – there was not a priest among them. If the endowments of such a corporation were confiscated when a state was made Protestant, there was a chance that some at least of the endowment might go to education or to pastoral endeavour. If none of it went to these proper destinations, the confiscation was merely the transfer of property from one set of nobles to another – except that the new set acquired an undoubted right to bequeath the property to legitimate children and were consequently alienating it, probably for ever, from its intended destination.

To secure a part of the old endowments for the Church, Protestants sometimes had to compromise with the old legal and Catholic terms under which the endowments were administered. In Lutheran Germany we hear of the tonsure, even of celibacy or Catholic episcopal consecration, being accepted by Lutheran clergy as a mode of retaining the legal right to old endowments. The classic instance of this type of compromise with necessity was Scotland, where the bulk of church lands was episcopal. There seemed to be no prospect of securing any part of these lands for the clergy unless clergymen legally occupied the old episcopal sees with their rights of property. The ministry were at first paid an inadequate stipend of only a tax of one third upon all benefices, a system which shows how much had gone into the pockets of the Scottish lords. In 1572, with the approval of Knox, 'bishops' were instituted, primarily for the purpose of securing some part of the old episcopal revenues. Posterity has known them as 'tulchan' bishops, a tulchan being a dummy calf designed to lure a cow to give more milk; the charge being that they were channels through which more church revenues could be diverted to the crown and the lords. Whatever this record, which in the state of modern knowledge is uncertain, they were designed for the opposite purpose, to prevent the government from swallowing all.

While the English preserved bishops, the episcopal lands were not therefore exempt from contributing to the national treasury. Queen Elizabeth once told Bishop Edwin Sandys that she would never impair any bishopric. Few sovereigns of the Reformation were as successful as Elizabeth of England in bullying the bishops into making leases, exchanges, and other bargains at terms advantageous to the crown and disadvantageous to the see. In 1559 Parliament gave her an ominous Act called the *Act for Exchanging Bishops' Lands*, whereby on any vacancy she could take into her hands some of the temporalities of the see, in return for impropriated parsonages and tithes. Thus, we are told by Strype, the queen and her courtiers had a fair opportunity to pick and choose what episcopal houses, lands, and revenues they pleased, and in lieu they made over parsonages burdened with decayed chancels, or ruinous houses, or pensions for maintaining vicars or curates. Several sees were kept vacant for long years while the government drew the revenues, and the refugee King of Portugal was nicknamed the Bishop of Ely because he was supported from the income of the see. Richard Fletcher, Bishop-elect of London, was imprisoned in his own house to compel him to accept the nefarious bargain which the queen proposed. Most of the payments were made at the vacancy and election; and therefore, upon the death of Archbishop Parker of Canterbury in 1575, a cynical courtier proposed that all the bishops should be moved simultaneously to other sees (except Bangor, St Asaph, and St David's, 'to stand still, because they be but poor and in Wales'), and drafted a plan whereby this might be done 'without just cause of much offence' to the bishops. The dilapidation continued throughout the reign and was only halted under King James I. No bishop after the English Reformation could afford to do what William of Wykeham had done, found colleges like St Mary at Winchester and New College at Oxford.

'The temporality seek to make the clergy beggars,' wrote Whitgift, then Master of Trinity College in Cambridge, to Bishop Cox of Ely in 1575, 'that we may depend upon them.' Probably he was attributing to the laity, whose concern was their purses, a more far-reaching purpose than they possessed. But the effect is undeniable. The great lords of the Church, once the equals or superiors of the great lords of the State, were becoming more dependent upon them, and this through successful plunder.

THE PARISH CHURCHES

The Reformation had no wish to diminish the status of parish churches. On the contrary, the congregation and its church must be elevated as the strong home of religious life, where the Word was truly preached and the sacraments duly administered. Though predatory lords succeeded in laying their hands upon money from benefices, the plunder was less open and the need and utility of the parish more evident.* The allocation, especially in parts of Germany and Switzerland, and for a brief time in Cromwellian England, of episcopal or cathedral money to parochial ends substantially strengthened the parishes.

* Usually less open. But Gustavus Vasa of Sweden resumed 13,700 manors, of which nearly half were supporting the clergy of parishes, a calamitous act for parochial life.

The poor curate in the country parish was living on a pittance in 1600. His plight had been equal in 1500, and in the meantime the purchasing power of money had fallen to a fraction of its old value, in the great inflation during the century. On paper, therefore, his stipend was raised substantially during the century, though his standard of living remained much the same. It was more difficult to provide adequate stipends for men of distinction, because reforming ideals restricted the piling up of pluralities which had normally been used to reward able servants of the Church or state. It was as difficult as ever to find the money for the repair of churches. It was much more difficult to finance the building of a mighty cathedral. The fifteenth century, and the first quarter of the sixteenth, was a great age for the building of churches. The Elizabethan age was a great age for building mansions in the country. A walk round the aisles of almost any of the old cathedrals of England is enough to persuade the thoughtful person of the difference between the possibilities of 1500 and the possibilities of 1600. When Archbishop Laud wished to restore St Paul's Cathedral during the sixteen-thirties, he was forced to lead a national movement to find enough money.

Those comparative difficulties of the church treasury were no doubt due, in part, to the decline in the value of money, as much as to the appropriations of the laity.

The Reformation was a revolution, and revolutions are always destructive. The transfer of power from an old authority to a new authority, even if accomplished without civil war, is not accomplished without a loosening of the bands of authority and of public allegiance, an opportunity for mobs, for what John Knox used to call *the rascal multitude*. But looting and civil war must have accounted for only a small fraction of the loss of the art treasures of medieval Europe. Some noble churches fell into ruins because they were monastic churches now without purpose. Many chantry chapels were allowed to fall into ruin, even within a great and still used church, their purpose and the money for their maintenance being gone. Relics or alleged relics of saints were thrown upon rubbish heaps, but many were saved by reverent hands and collected into new treasure houses in southern Europe, like the treasury of relics at Sâo Roque in Portugal; and this was to a lesser extent true even of vestments. The old woodwork would be removed and cut down, in some country districts to be used for fuel and in others to board a ruined church; but some of it was saved.

It is an extraordinary fact that we find more of medieval art and architecture in countries which became Protestant than in countries which remained Catholic at the Reformation. This rule is liable to much exception, but in general it is the hand, not of the looter, but of the restorer which is chiefly responsible for pulling down. The baroque movement swept southern Europe in the sixteenth and seventeenth century, transforming the medieval churches. The baroque movement came likewise, though more slowly, into the countries of the north, creating the great churches, from St Paul's Cathedral in London downwards, and incidentally destroying more traces of the medieval art and architecture than the Protestant Reformation had attempted. The least conservative of congregations are those which have most money, the most conservative those which have least money. In the southern baroque countries, the Church still possessed much land and endowments, and its ecclesiastics could afford to build with magnificence. In many Protestant countries the comparative loosening of old endowments in the Reformation, partly through the action of the governments and partly through the inflation of the sixteenth century, meant that most Protestant congregations had enough to do to keep in repair the old churches which they inherited. They preserved the ancient jewels, not because they loved them, but because they could not buy new and could but keep the old.

The loss of furnishing was severe. We can trace it in the records of a city church in London, St Botolph's Aldgate. It began as early as 1547, soon after the death of King Henry

VIII. The congregation was glad and eager to have the service in English, but the curate resented the disappearance of Latin, and refused to say or sing the psalms with the new English books. The congregation appealed to the Lord Mayor to remove the curate, and on 6 October a new curate used the English language to conduct four weddings. There was no use for the old service books, and on 14 November they were sold for eighteen shillings. The same purchaser bought five mass books, nine passionaries, and various other liturgical books, some torn and of no value, for the sum of fifteen shillings. During the following twelve months they also sold the remains of a stock of wax to a chandler for forty shillings, and the vestments – altar cloths embroidered with pictures of Christ and angels and apostles and Our Lady with birds of gold, two copes of velvet garnished with flowers of gold. Most of the vestments went to a tailor in Cornhill, and at the sale the parish entertained the buyers with beer at a cost of sixpence. In 1551 the vestry determined to sell the bells and part of the church plate in order to buy houses near the church for the curate and the clerk. But some of the congregation refused consent to the sale of bells, and so there was difficulty in raising money to buy the houses. They were still debating tenancies when a royal commission stepped in, appropriated the money 'for the King's use', and gave the parish in return a receipt and an acknowledgement that the money was in safe custody. Two years later Queen Mary came to the throne, and the vestry was buying candlesticks, cross, chalice, corporal, censer, cruets, cope, incense, a mass book. Though a benefactor gave them vestments, the prices show that the new were inferior to the old in quality.

The medieval Church was too rich for the health of Church or State. This proposition commands our intellectual assent as a generalized, abstract statement. But remove it from the general and consider it in the particular; and anyone who contemplates the vestry of St Botolph's brooding over the royal receipt for the money with which they had planned to buy houses for the curate and the clerk, may be pardoned a sigh of melancholy.

Money is power, and the Church was less powerful in 1600 than in 1500. If its moral authority increased with reform, its political power diminished; and some idealists would think that the diminution of political power was necessary to the increase of moral authority. Those medieval thinkers who attributed the ills of the Church to its establishment by Constantine, and saw in its money bags the root of all the evils of Christendom, would not have been displeased if they had seen the consequences of the Reformation.

THE GODLY PRINCE AND CHRISTIAN DOCTRINE

The dogma that kings rule by divine right was common ground to everyone who used his Bible. How far a citizen might engage in resistance and rebellion, and under what conditions, if any, a king might lose the allegiance of his subjects by his tyranny, were widely and urgently canvassed; but the doctrine that the secular power is of God was common to everyone. It was common ground also (except among some of the little groups, Anabaptist or Brownist) that the ruler possesses a duty to the morality and the religion of his subjects. As in the Middle Ages, he must establish and defend the true, protect the ministers of orthodox religion, repel the corrupt and the heretical.

Does he who defends truth and repels error determine what is true and what is false? No one held this before the age of Hobbes in the middle seventeenth century, and it was agreed that there existed a body of truth in the world which the State received from the Bible and the Church.

But Protestantism could not hold absolutely that in establishing religion the State must simply obey the ecclesiastical authorities, the Pope or the hierarchy. For the hierarchy, when brought to the test of the Bible, could be seen to have erred. There could be no freedom for

Biblical truth unless the State stepped in to lift from it the repressions of the past. Asked under what authority the State interferes, Luther compared it to the duty of the neighbours to bring buckets and put out the fire in a burning house. They need neither warrant nor permission, they see a need and must fly there with whatever aid they can bring.

As the ideas of sovereignty of the State were examined by the political theorists, it appeared that the right of the ecclesiastical authorities to bind the whole people without the consent of the secular sovereign could not be tolerated. Rome continued to demand that the canon law, and the decrees of Popes and Councils which created it, must be binding upon all men (so that, for example, it must be an offence liable to secular penalty if a priest married). The Calvinists continued to demand that the legislating authority in the Church should be the consistory, and that the secular State had a duty to execute the decrees of the consistory (so that, for example, if the consistory found a girl guilty of fornication it was the duty of the secular arm to punish her). But even in the Catholic and Calvinist countries governments could not accept these absolute claims and hope to remain governments. The Catholic kings of Spain and France and Austria sought in various ways to limit the legal effectiveness of papal intervention in their countries. The Calvinist governments of Geneva or Scotland or Holland sought, sooner or later, to restrict the legal compulsion of the consistory's decrees. And wherever men took their ideas from Wittenberg or Zurich or Canterbury, they repudiated an independent power in the consistory (or its equivalent, like Convocation in England) and held that it derived its effective jurisdiction from the secular sovereign.

Let us be clear what was being asserted in denying independence to the consistory. They were not denying that the ecclesiastical authorities may consider points of doctrine or ceremonies or ecclesiastical practice. They were denying that the decisions of the ecclesiastical authorities could have the force of law without the assent and decree of the secular sovereign. They were asserting that only the secular sovereign can make a law which is binding upon the people. Perhaps the ecclesiastical authority might declare that anti-Trinitarian heretics should be burnt, or adulterers whipped through the streets. The sovereign is not thereby held bound to burn or to whip. Nor is he exempt from the duty of examining the ecclesiastical advice before he gives it legal force. He must consider the welfare and expediency of his subjects, and no other authority can exempt him from this God-given duty, even when the most solemn truths of the Christian faith are at stake.

It is therefore impossible, according to this theory, that the Christian sovereign of a Christian state should not consider doctrine. The Church authorities declare that some kinds of teaching are erroneous, vicious, or immoral and must therefore be banned by law. Since the sovereign must enforce the ban, he cannot avoid the responsibility of seeing that this teaching is in truth erroneous or immoral. It is certain (so they held) that the sovereign's moral duty includes the duty of allowing only true worship in his territory, the duty of repressing blasphemy, immorality, and idolatry. For the most part it is obvious what is blasphemy and idolatry. Where it is not obvious the sovereign must consult the godly and learned ministers. But no plea that this law concerns spiritual matters can exempt the sovereign from his final responsibility of deciding the law to be good for the State and the people.

What must be taught in the pulpits? Or rather, since you cannot compel the positive, what must be forbidden in the pulpits? The Protestant ministers say that transubstantiation is erroneous and must not be taught in a Scriptural church. If this is to be legally effective, the sovereign must ban by law the teaching of transubstantiation. Then he is bound, with whatever advice he can muster, to enter even the land of theology.

Doughty controversialists from Rome or Geneva abused

this idea as 'Caesaro-papist'. They ridiculed the defence which appealed to Byzantine precedents or illustrated the necessity of secular power in religion by the examples of Constantine or Justinian. The power of the Byzantine emperor in religious matters had been less extensive or absolute than popular history supposed. And, in theory, the power of the Protestant sovereign in religion was equally restricted. He could command nothing contrary to the Word of God. If he made a law contrary to the Word of God, he must be disobeyed. And for this reason his power is narrower in the sacred realm than in the secular. For the Scriptures have laid down more in the sacred realm. The sovereign cannot command what God has forbidden or forbid what God has commanded. It is impossible for him to ban the teaching of a Pauline Gospel, or the due administration of the sacraments – of course not physically impossible, but if he does so he is acting as a non-Christian tyrant and is to be disobeyed. (Whether he should be *resisted* was another question; most of this school held that he should not.) He cannot make new articles of faith or institute new sacraments. He cannot legalize marriage between two men, or between babies, or between mothers and their sons. These are immutable laws which the sovereign may not touch.

Probably the most clear-headed and intelligent statement of this theory is found in a book by the Dutch Arminian Hugo Grotius *On the Sovereign's Power in Religion*, published posthumously in 1647. But substantially the same theory is found throughout non-Calvinist and non-Anabaptist Protestantism, some of the best writing being found in the English theorists of King James I. It was easy to abuse the theory as Caesaro-papist and Erastian. But as long as the unity of the Church and State was believed to be necessary to the State, and as long as a toleration was believed to be impossible, it was a defensible theory. For the alternative appeared to be laws made by Pope or by presbytery, binding upon all the people without the assent of the secular sovereign, who thereby ceased to be sovereign. Europe was learning not to suffer interference with the laws. Advice from the Church was one thing, compulsion another.

The reasoning of this theory had important consequences.

In its more extreme manifestations it led Protestant thinkers to push far the right of the sovereign to intervene in the spiritual realm. The momentous change in the Reformation idea of the State appeared to be a legal change – the subjection of clerical legislation to the secular. Therefore it was widely held in Lutheran Germany that all the jurisdiction of the medieval bishop passed to the secular sovereign. In England, asked in 1540 whether the apostles made bishops from their apostolic authority or only from necessity because there was no Christian sovereign to make them, Archbishop Cranmer of Canterbury replied hesitantly that the jurisdiction of the bishop was derived from the sovereign just as was that of the Lord Chancellor. The king needed ministers for the different spheres of the realm, some civil and some ecclesiastical. But Cranmer's theory was extreme, and the later English Erastians would probably not have gone so far.

It was never contended that the king could control Word or Sacraments. In this he was subject, like everyone else, to the Word. Grotius and others departed from the crude simplicity of Cranmer by making an important distinction: the Christian pastor, *qua* minister of Word and Sacrament, of course derived his authority from Christ – it was *qua* officer of the State that he derived his jurisdiction from the sovereign. For it was agreed that in a rightly ordered State the pastor must in a manner be an officer of the society. He was supervising the morals of the people, he was dealing in wills and births and marriages and deaths, he was responsible for the education of the children. It was inevitable that he should be an officer of the State, and as such his jurisdiction must be derived from the sovereign, or the sovereign would not be sovereign.

The sovereign therefore has a rightful authority in

promulgating doctrine, in deciding what may or may not be preached. The question is whether his doctrine is in accordance with the Word of God, and the same question must be asked of a declaration of doctrine by pope or presbytery or anyone else. If the godly and learned pastors of the state are opposed to the prince's doctrine, it is probable that he is acting tyrannically in promulgating it.

It was a saying in Germany that 'the Duke of Cleves is a Pope in his duchy'. The more extreme forms of practice to which the theory was put rode roughshod over the authority of the pastors.

In 1588 Duke John of Zweibrücken changed from being a strict Lutheran to being a Philippist, and in commanding his subjects to conform is reported to have said: 'Rulers have the Spirit of God, and according as God is pleased from time to time to enlighten the mind of the ruler, his subjects must be ready to follow the Spirit, which blows where it lists.' I note such extreme claims only as eccentric. But the practical consequence could be more extreme than the theory. King Charles I, to the distress even of his most loyal supporters among the clergy, issued not merely royal injunctions for the conduct of service but canons, or what he called canons, for the Scottish Church. The first clause of Article 20 in the Thirty-Nine Articles of the Church of England was added by royal authority without at first receiving any approval from the English Convocations. A theorist of the school like Hugo Grotius would have seen nothing improper in these actions, with the single condition that the sovereign decreed nothing contrary to the Word of God.

The supremacy of the sovereign appeared to be necessary to the non-Calvinist theory of Church and State. It was a little easier to hold, in sympathy though not in reason, if sovereignty was believed to reside in a single individual. The more intelligent theorists like Grotius or Selden perceived that there was no difference between the responsibility of a king and that of an oligarchy or a popular assembly. If a law concerning religion was to be enforced, the popular assembly could not evade the task of considering whether it was a good law, could not shelve its responsibility upon any body of clergy or assembly of the Church. But some churchmen felt a qualm about admitting the sovereignty over religion of a popular assembly. When the English Parliament of 1625 was summoned to Oxford, they met in the Divinity Schools, and the Speaker sat in or near the place where the Regius Professor of Divinity usually lectured; and the Laudian clergy had a legend that this first gave Parliament the idea that it could determine religious doctrines. There was a feeling that this particular exercise of sovereignty was less suitable to an assembly of elected laymen than to one anointed of God to the crown.

The sovereignty of the godly princes affected the Church in one way which a liberal posterity would confess to be an unqualified good. If the prince secured a sufficient agreement in religion to prevent strife, he did not usually wish to pry into men's souls. It is a rule, liable to some important exceptions, that the non-Calvinist and the non-Catholic states allowed a wider liberty in doctrine than did the Calvinist or the Catholic. Compare the breadth of the English Thirty-Nine Articles of 1571 with the Calvinist Westminster Confession. When Archbishop Whitgift of Canterbury found that the Thirty-Nine Articles were too broad to avert academic dispute, he attempted to add new articles, the Lambeth Articles of 1595, precisely defining the doctrine of predestination. Lord Burghley, on hearing of them, told the Archbishop that the matter was too mysterious for his own understanding, and the indignant Queen required the Archbishop to withdraw them. Grotius held a restraint in religious definition to be a virtue in any sovereign. Even if he and his Church believe a doctrine to be true, it may not be right to enforce it. 'It is dangerous' – Grotius used the old saw movingly – 'to speak the truth about God.' *Dogmata definienda sunt paucissima.*

TOLERATION

The Reformation made a toleration possible. It began with no such intention. The states and Churches of a divided Europe found in the end that they must tolerate or die.

From the first the Protestant atmosphere was a little less unfriendly to nonconformity. Themselves dissenters from an established tradition, they looked with a little more hesitation upon the suppression of dissent. Luther began with an almost tolerant attitude, and lost it when he observed the anarchy that followed religious freedom and when Melanchthon's clear head pronounced decisively for religious repression. The Protestant states did not question that teachers of disapproved doctrines should be prevented from preaching. Nor did they question that the state should use laws to encourage men and women in their church-going. In Anglican England and Lutheran Germany, Reformed Holland or Catholic Spain, the citizens were alike liable to penalties if they failed for no good reason to attend the worship of their parish churches. The main Christian tradition still believed that, as it was good to suppress a preacher who persuaded the congregation that adultery was right, so it was good to suppress a preacher who persuaded them to be atheists or to think the baptism of infants a mockery. The morals of the people and the religious opinions of the people were not two things but one.

It would be an anachronism to suppose that all sensible Protestants ought to have perceived how wrong was persecution of religious opinion. On the contrary, the immense majority of sensible Christian divines agreed that doctrinal error should normally be punished by civil penalties. This majority was composed, not only of disciplinarians like Calvin and his consistorians or Pope Pius V and his inquisitors, but of humane scholars like Melanchthon or gentle devotional Catholics like St Francis de Sales.

In 1553 Michael Servetus was executed at Geneva for his anti-trinitarian heresy. And though the leading Protestant divines supported Calvin's view that the execution had been more than justified, there was enough of an outcry to make further defence desirable, and in the next year Beza published his book *Whether Heretics Should be Punished by the Civil Magistrate?* It was written in an irritable moment and not devoid of abusive passages, but it ably represents contemporary opinion. Here are its main arguments. The magistrate was concerned with the morals of his people – the proposition seemed to the sixteenth century to be a platitude which only madmen would dispute. And if it is true, as Beza once admitted, that a few men may be bad in their private life and good in their public duty, they are so exceptional that they can afford no rule to the magistrate's function.

It is said that Christ was gentle, and taught the Christian to offer the other cheek, and to be merciful and charitable. But why do not the critics of penalties for heresy therefore agree that the magistrate should refrain from punishing murderers? It is the truest charity to protect a flock of sheep from a marauding wolf, not to leave them defenceless. The question then is not whether the magistrate should punish evil, but whether heresy is an evil like theft. It cannot be denied that its influence upon the moral life of a community is as destructive as theft.

It is said that the heretic is a sincere man, obeying his conscience. If a pacifist goes round the besieged city exhorting the garrison to lay down their arms, do you plead that he is obeying his conscience and therefore exempt him from penalty? In the same way, it is said that you cannot compel men to faith, you can only persuade. Of course. Penalties for heresy are not designed to compel the heretic to faith. They are designed to prevent the little ones from being led astray, to protect the sheep from the wolves, to preserve the community and thereby to exclude injury to God's glory. It is mere calumny that we want to spread Christian faith by force. The authorities of a university dismiss from office a professor whom all sane men agree to be teaching what is untrue. Is such a dismissal to be called cruelty?

It is clear that the state does protect, and ought to protect, true religion. And most critics of persecution admit the fact, since they allow that extreme cases – atheists or blasphemers – ought to be penalized. The question remains, if any penalty is permissible, whether the penalty of death can be declared not permissible. In this question we not only have to encounter cranks, but good and intelligent men who argue that if death is exacted there is no chance of penitence.

We must first lay it down that cruelty, and rashness, are to be excluded. We are to remember that no one can be forced into faith, and that Christians are to be gentle and merciful. But we are also to remember that our first duty is to the sheep. It is evident that heretical teaching (look at the Anabaptists at Münster) is as grave a crime as many for which the punishment is death. To say that we ought not to inflict the death penalty for this is to challenge capital punishment for any offence whatsoever – and this no one is prepared to do. Indeed it is more than arguable that this crime is graver than any, since it destroys men's souls, while murder destroys their bodies, and is a direct offence against God's majesty.

Beza's argument shows that, at least among the Protestants, weighty opinion was beginning to move, not against penalties for religion, but against the death penalty for heresy. After 1600, persons were rarely executed on this charge. But the opinion that the magistrates must ensure only one religion in a state survived for much longer.

The case for penalties rested upon two premises: first that the truth was known by all sensible men, and secondly that the state could not exist if more than one religion were widely accepted within it. Toleration was not to become established until both these assumptions were proved by events to be erroneous.

Meanwhile the occasional surreptitious liberty possible here and there among the European churches – at Basle, for example, in one or two towns of Poland, and later in the century among the Dutch – allowed theorists of an original mind to print demands for a wider toleration and to attempt to base that demand upon sound reasoning. They had often been influenced by Anabaptist thought, or by others among the radical groups who contended that, as Christ's kingdom is not of this world, the magistrate has nothing whatsoever to do with religion.

Sebastian Castellio (Castalio, a Latinized version of Chatillon) fled to Geneva for refuge, but was refused ordination there because Calvin suspected his orthodoxy. He retired to Basle, where after a few years of poverty he became professor of Greek. He was tried for his various heresies, even at Basle, but died in 1563 still suspect. He was shocked at the execution of Servetus, and was moved to publish the most important manifesto of the sixteenth century in favour of toleration, *Whether Heretics Are To Be Persecuted?* Beza rightly regarded Castellio as his most imperative opponent. The book was a mosaic of quotations, and Castellio was the editor; but some of the most pointed quotations came from authors otherwise unknown, and the 'editor' seems to have composed them for the purpose.

The arguments of Castellio are unimportant. Indeed he has few to set against the coherence of Calvin or Beza. This is no reasoned study in political thought but a simple cry of the Christian heart and Christian conscience. What sort of a person was Christ? And how are Christians, who should be his imitators, behaving to each other?

'O Christ, creator and king of the world, dost thou see? Art thou become quite other than thyself, so cruel, so contrary to thyself? When thou didst live upon earth, none was more gentle, more merciful, more patient of wrong. . . . Men scourged thee, spat upon thee, mocked thee, crowned thee with thorns, crucified thee among thieves and thou didst pray for them who did this wrong. Art thou now so changed? . . . If thou, O Christ, hast commanded these executions and tortures, what hast thou left for the devil to do?'

Castellio's cry of the conscience depends upon the assumption, which Beza could not share, that truth is difficult to find. Do we know who are the true heretics? Christ and his apostles were killed as heretics. Can we be sure that we are not likewise killing good and innocent men? If you are asked to define heresy, how will you do it, when there is such a variety of Christian doctrines in the world? 'I have carefully examined what the word *heretic* means', he wrote, 'and I cannot make it mean more than this, a heretic is a man with whom you disagree.'

Even to Castellio it appeared obvious that the state might exact penalties for blasphemy and false teaching of an extreme kind. But force, he thought, is a poor weapon for defending truth. 'To kill a man is not to defend a doctrine, but to kill a man.'

Castellio's book was the most influential publication in favour of toleration. It was quoted again and again by those who clamoured for toleration, at first an occasional voice here and there, but, as the seventeenth century passed its first quarter, a swelling chorus of voices.

Christendom continued to believe that a state could neither prosper nor survive if more than one religion were permitted among its citizens. How could a Protestant citizen be loyal to a Catholic sovereign, or vice versa? The experience of every day confirmed the opinion.

Nevertheless, the Reformation moved Christian minds to the most important step towards a widespread belief in the right to be tolerated. It made this advance because it established in Europe the rival confessions of Catholic and Protestant; and in some states one of the two confessions failed to capture the whole of the state. Men believed that a state could not survive with two public religions among its citizens. What happened if the force of circumstances, or of evangelistic zeal, or of political decision, erected a state with a large minority of citizens not of the dominant religion?

In Spain and Portugal and Italy among Catholic countries, and in Scotland and the Netherlands and Scandinavia among Protestant countries, there was no problem. The Reformation either triumphed totally or failed totally. The vast majority of the citizens of these countries were of one religion. It was true that in the north-east of Scotland Catholics survived, protected by the Huntly family, that in the north-west of Italy a few Waldensians survived in close alliance with Calvinist Switzerland, and that in the southern lands of the independent Netherlands there were many inarticulate peasants who retained their Catholicism like their neighbours and brothers over the border in the Catholic Netherlands of Spain. But these tiny or powerless minorities could be disregarded. If a Protestant pastor began to preach in Spain, he was punished. If a Catholic priest began to celebrate mass in Scotland, he was punished. From these countries new ideas upon toleration would not appear. The ablest defence of persecution during the seventeenth century came from the Scottish Presbyterian Samuel Rutherford (*A Free Disputation against Pretended Liberty of Conscience*, 1649). In Italy Pope Gregory XVI condemned liberty of conscience to be 'madness', as late as 1832. The countries with a great majority of one faith were not those which moved most rapidly towards tolerance.

But in Germany, in France, in Poland, and in England the Reformation failed to triumph so absolutely as Protestantism triumphed in Scotland or Catholicism in Spain. In those countries divines continued to worry over the problem, and Catholic and Protestant divines made momentous admissions. If we pose the question as the schools posed it, we ask with the Protestants whether, since the mass is idolatry, it is not always a sin to tolerate idolatry? And we ask with the Catholics whether, since heresy is an evil, it is not always a sin in a Catholic prince if he tolerates heretics in his territory? Many thinkers replied in the affirmative: Yes, in all circumstances it is a grave sin to tolerate idolatry or heresy.

But others felt this rigorous conclusion to be offensive. Martin Becanus (a Dutchman by origin), a Jesuit professor in Germany who died in 1624, held that this conclusion proceeded more from zeal than from reason. Suppose that the heretics are too numerous to be suppressed: it will then be more calamitous to Catholicism if the prince seeks to suppress them than if he tolerates them. Alternatively, even if the prince could successfully destroy the heretics, he might think that more good might be achieved by mercy, that if the Protestants were tolerated the Catholics would become more fervent, more self-denying, more faithful in their religion, and better missionaries for their faith. Under such conditions there may be many circumstances (almost, one might think, most) when it would be better to tolerate than to burn.

It is clear how the Edict of Nantes and the consequences of divided France and divided Germany had begun to liberalize the thinking of the schools. The Lutheran Gerhard expressed it succinctly in his *Loci Theologici* of 1619 (Book 27). If a kingdom is united, toleration is wrong. If it is divided, then the ruler must put up with the divisions. It is better to have a state disunited in religion than no state at all. It was a Frenchman, President Jeannin, who said that peace with two religions was better than a war which had none.

The main Christian case for toleration therefore rested, not upon principle, but upon expediency. None of the thinkers of the Catholic, Lutheran, or Reformed traditions passed beyond the idea of expediency. But we ought not to underestimate the weight of this admission. The strength of the case for religious repression rested upon the agreement between a religious doctrine (the moral duty of the magistrate) and a political assumption (no state can survive if divided in religion). Becanus and Gerhard and their like destroyed this agreement by admitting that states like France may exist though divided in religion, and may exist only if the division is permitted to continue. The French *politiques* of 1570 saw with infallible clarity that expediency was no support for persecution. And once this prop was removed, it was easy to re-examine the nature of the magistrates' moral duty. Statesmen who began by admitting that repression was inexpedient might end in asking how far it could ever be a moral obligation. Castellio's cry of the Christian conscience was slowly coming into its kingdom.

13

Ministry and Worship

THE Reformation and Counter-Reformation may not
always have achieved what reformers wanted, but they
raised the standards of the Christian ministry, whether
priestly or pastoral. And if the adage *like priest like people*
has force, that achievement was powerful in public and
private life.

It is not right to see the contrast between pre-Reformation and post-Reformation in black and white. *The Imitation
of Christ*, written early in the fifteenth century, is enough to
recall the lofty and profound piety to be found in the later
Middle Ages, the power of the medieval Christian ideal
which helped to create the Reformation. There is plenty of
evidence from 1600 that the Christian ministry could be as
worldly or as depraved as it sometimes was in 1400. A few
Roman cardinals continued to amass a fortune by decidedly
old-fashioned methods. At the end of 1596 forty French
bishoprics were still held by laymen. Meiler Magrath, the
Protestant Archbishop of Cashel in Ireland, though not
invariably sober, was bishop of three other Irish sees and
controlled, in person or through his numerous children, a
large number of benefices (rumour in London said seventy).
It was not difficult throughout the Reformation to find
exceptions. But, in general, there was less graft, less corruption, less illegality, less non-residence, less simony, and there
was more teaching, more preaching, more pastoral care,
better education, better understanding of the faith by laymen and their ministers, less worldliness and more fervour
among pastors or priests, less superstition and more
religion, less arid intellectualism, and a more Biblical
apprehension.

The ideals of the Reformation and the Counter-Reformation sharply divide into an ideal dominantly priestly and an ideal dominantly pastoral. It was not likely that the more decisive conservatives would abandon the notion that the supreme and ultimate act of the Christian minister was the celebration of the mass; while the Reformers, reacting against salvation by forms or by ritual, saw the sacraments as one part, though a momentous and indispensable part, of a total ministry to the people, wherein the supreme and ultimate act was the exposition of the Word of God. In the one the altar, in the other the pulpit, was the focus of the church.

But this crude antithesis was liable to much exception. Some Catholics of the right always wished to give prominence to the pulpit and the sermon. The Lutherans retained the altar as an altar; and though English parish churches, before the unsuccessful reforms of Archbishop Laud, usually followed the Swiss mode of turning the altar into a holy table, most English cathedrals retained the altar until the civil wars of 1642–8. In parts of Protestant England and Germany and Switzerland and Scotland there was more and better preaching and instruction in 1600 than in 1500. But this was also true of Milan and of other cities in the Counter-Reformation, especially where the Jesuits or Dominicans were powerful. In some parts of the Catholic Church, especially in Southern Italy and parts of France and Germany, the pastoral office was as silent as ever. Western Christendom was struggling, and not vainly, to raise its pastoral and moral standard, but untidily, as circumstances offered or men responded.

In the later Middle Ages were published several useful handbooks or guides to clerical and pastoral duty. If we compare these with similar handbooks from the end of the sixteenth century, whether Protestant or Catholic, we observe a certain change of atmosphere. The medieval handbooks are somewhat more liturgical, a mixture of pastoral duty and conduct in church or the sacristy, they are more

emphatic upon the exact performance of external rites.
Turn the page of history for 200 years, and now the handbooks are more emphatic upon the necessity that words shall
not be repeated parrot-fashion, that exact ritual shall be
sacramental of an inward reverence of the heart. They are
designed for a more educated ministry, a ministry which
preaches constantly, where the pulpit is the pastor's joy and
throne, a ministry which ever sucks at the study of the Bible
and the Fathers. The Counter-Reformation handbooks
share these common qualities with those of the Protestant.
The Protestant books usually contain a new, unprece-
dented section upon the wife and children and household
as the pattern of village family life, even the orchard and
poultry and pigs. The Counter-Reformation books attach
an equal weight to the pulpit and to inward sincerity, an
equal weight to learning and education, though there is less
stress upon Biblical study and more stress upon theological
knowledge and Church history. Here the minister is pictured as more of a 'professional' in no bad sense, more of an
ecclesiastic, there are longer and more precise lists of the
doctrines which he must inculcate, there is more urgency
that Biblical exposition shall conform to that of the Church.
If we compare the Protestant pastor in George Herbert's
A Priest to the Temple (written about 1632, near Salisbury)
with the Catholic priest in Charles Borromeo's *Instructions
to Pastors* (written at Milan, soon after 1565) Herbert's pastor
is conceived as more sociable than the Italian, less separated
from the people; he is among them as a friend as well as a
director of souls, he receives them at his table. Borromeo's
pastor is to refuse every possible invitation from the laity to
dinner or supper. There is something more vehement in
Borromeo's ideal, an ardour more fervent than that in the
quiet, humane, gentle, devoted Herbert. While this last
contrast points to something in the characters of the two
men, it may yet be taken to illustrate a certain antithesis
between the pastor of the Reformation and the pastor of the
Counter-Reformation.

THE MARRIAGE OF CLERGY

Legal marriage was the greatest single change affecting the status of the Protestant clergy. Though the habit varied from country to country and even from diocese to diocese, many priests of the old dispensation, from Pope Alexander VI downwards, possessed concubines. Some parishes preferred it, and it was not unknown for Catholic patrons to refuse to appoint a priest unless he had a woman. One highly regarded French curé tranquilly noted in his book the regular birth of his bastards. In 1476 the chapter at Brunswick ordered the canons and vicars, not to put away their concubines, but to keep them somewhere else than in the cathedral close. In Scotland between 1548 and 1556 two illegitimate children of clergymen were legitimized for every five children of laymen, an astonishing ratio when the respective numbers are remembered. To turn the mistress into an honourable wife, to turn the bastards into honourable children, was the momentous single gift bestowed upon the clergy by Protestantism. Apart from higher considerations it was said that, before his marriage to Catherine von Bora, Luther's bed had not been made for a year.

The Popes of the Counter-Reformation were subjected to a certain pressure to permit marriage. From 1400 a few conservative reformers, including Erasmus, pleaded for it, and justified the plea by the example of the Eastern Orthodox Church. Catholic states with a strong Protestant minority repeatedly asked that it might be conceded, and reasoned Bavarian and Austrian appeals were presented to the Council of Trent in 1562. French bishops even suggested that if celibacy were to be preserved, only elderly men should be henceforth ordained. The choice, it was said cynically, was between few clergy and married clergy. The Pope exempted members of certain military orders from the rule of celibacy, for the sake of avoiding scandal.

The Council of Trent was uncompromising. In November

1563 it pronounced anathema upon all who asserted that clerics, monks, or nuns could contract a valid marriage, and upon all who asserted that it was not better to live the celibate than the married life. But it was not quite so uncompromising as it looked, for it left open the question whether a married man might be ordained.

It took many years for the decrees of Trent to be effective. A French nobleman who in 1583 was resisting the publication in France of the decrees of Trent used the argument that in Italy no one paid the slightest attention to the decrees reforming the morals of the clergy. Provincial councils continually and half-hopelessly reiterated the decrees. All that the Archbishop of Salzburg dared to achieve, as late as 1616, was a decree that priests should remove their concubines to a distance of six miles and should not have their children living openly with them except by special leave. One practical measure of assistance, introduced from the middle of the sixteenth century and made compulsory in 1614, was the confessional box. But slowly the custom of cohabitation was discouraged, slowly the custom of genuine celibacy became more familiar. Whether because of better discipline, or because of zeal in the movement for reform, or because the general standard of decency was rising, the evidence of the seventeenth century is very different from that of the sixteenth. If the decrees of Trent and the Counter-Reformation failed to prevent concubines, they stamped out the expectation that wives might be allowed and the complacency that mistresses were venial or respectable.

Among the Protestants, the marriage of clergy began with an air of bravado and was quickly the most natural thing in the world. A few priests began to marry while Luther was in the Wartburg, and in 1523 Luther preached a sermon in favour of marriage at the wedding of the former vicar of the Austin Friars, his friend Wenceslas Link. In 1525 Luther invited his friends to supper and without warning married Catherine von Bora in their presence. One by one the

Protestant states legalized the marriage of their pastors. Calvin, though he never remarried after the death of his wife, encouraged his friends and colleagues to marry for the good of the Church.

It was not easy for the laity, who are more conservative of custom than the clergy, to adjust themselves to the change. Several of Luther's close friends were offended at his marriage. Lawyers are more conservative than most laymen, and as late as 1536 the Wittenberg lawyers were holding, to Luther's disgust, that the children of priests were illegitimate. Some people could not bring themselves, at first, to receive communion at the hands of married priests, and even midwives were known to refuse to attend their wives in childbirth. Queen Elizabeth of England always preferred unmarried bishops, and caused wives to be ejected from the precincts of colleges and cathedrals. 'Her Majesty,' wrote Cecil to the Archbishop of Canterbury in 1561, 'continueth very evil affected to the state of matrimony in the clergy.' We may be sure that others besides the queen found it odd to receive the parson's wife into company. Early in her reign there was a brawl on a ferry boat crossing the Severn because passengers jeered at two wives of parsons. Even the unmarried Archbishop Laud once gave offence by rashly saying that other things being equal he would prefer to appoint an unmarried candidate. In England Elizabeth never renewed the Act of Edward VI legalizing clerical marriage, allowing it rather as an indulgence than a right; it was formally renewed only under James I.

Nor was it easy for the clergy to choose suitable wives. Sometimes the old concubine easily became the new wife, and country clergy on a tiny stipend might in any case, as was said, have to marry a chambermaid. The authorities tried to prevent unsuitable marriages. The Archbishop of Uppsala exacted an oath from his clergy that they would not marry without the consent of the bishop and chapter. Queen Elizabeth ordered that the minister

must win for his lady the approval of the bishop of the
diocese and two magistrates and the consent of her master
and mistress 'where she serveth', and this order was enforced in the courts.

But all was quickly natural. A questionnaire sent out in
October 1561 showed that half the clergy in the archdeaconry of London were already married. Within a generation
nearly everyone was acting as though the habit was immemorial. Under Archbishop Laud, we are told by a
Laudian writer, the clergy were held in such esteem that
the gentry thought none of their daughters to be better
disposed than such as they 'lodged in the arms' of a parson.
Not everyone agreed. As late as 1610, at King's Sutton in
Northamptonshire, a man and his wife were in trouble for
abusing the minister's wife and saying 'the world was never
merry since priests were married'. And a legend persisted
into the middle of that century that the offspring of priests
were unlucky in their lives – despite numerous examples
already of boys of the parsonage who rose to high office
in Church and State.

In judging the Reformation, it will not do to forget the
burden that poured from so many consciences or the true
and honourable homes and families which thus became
possible.

THE SOCIAL STATUS OF THE CLERGY

The gentry of Elizabethan and Stuart England sometimes
grumbled that the bishops were raised from the dust, men of
low condition. But the Reformation made less difference to
their social status and origins than might have been expected. The medieval Church always opened the doors to
able men, and the Protestant Churches continued to do so.
Of the five Protestant archbishops of Canterbury between
1575 and 1645, two were the sons of prosperous cloth
workers, one the son of a farmer, one the son of a wealthy
merchant, and only one whose father might have been

described, in the language of the day, as 'gentleman'. But aristocrats had no monopoly of greatness before the Reformation. Of the seven archbishops of Canterbury, between 1414 and 1532, five were of ordinary birth, the sons of yeomen or country squires, and only two were of the highest rank, one (Bourchier) being descended through his Plantagenet mother from King Edward III. Reginald Pole, archbishop from 1556–8, was likewise of the highest rank.

Something comparable is observable in the men who became Popes. Of five Popes between 1471 and 1521, three were of the highest rank, one (Leo X) being the son of Lorenzo the Magnificent of Florence; one was the family of a Genoese senator; and the fifth (Sixtus IV) came from nowhere. Of five popes between 1559 and 1591, two were of humble extraction, one of a middle-class bankrupt, one of a minor aristocrat, and one of a good family from Bologna. We may not generalize from such observations as these. I use them only as illustrations that, though humble men often rose to rule in the medieval church, the Reformation and Counter-Reformation opened the doors wider, partly because the new world of the Renaissance opened other doors to the younger sons of aristocrats, and partly because society as a whole was broadening its base.

The poorest of the inferior clergy lived not far from subsistence level before the Reformation, and they lived not far from subsistence level after it. They were partly protected from the inflation by tithe, although the richest of the new sources of wealth were impossible to tithe. The social situation of the parochial clergy as a whole did not alter significantly between 1500 and 1600, in an absolute sense. But their situation altered in relation to the laity. For the laity were becoming wealthier, while the parochial clergy were remaining where they were. In Protestant churches a double standard of clergy, though often crossed, became common – the distinction between the city clergy and the country clergy. The city clergy were highly educated, married to the daughters of gentry or even of the nobility, socially esteemed, receiving a reasonable income. The city pastor of Wittenberg in 1529 received 200 gulden, and later 300 gulden and fifty bushels of corn, whereas we hear of country pastors on a stipend of twenty gulden. The country clergy were often of peasant origin, married to peasants, dominated by the squire or lay patron, receiving a subsistence wage and supplementing it by secular occupation – usually in 'farming', for pigs and sheep were often part of the stock which they took over with the vicarage.

In Germany, though the pastor's wage might be desperately low, he had certain advantages in that it was normally exempt from taxation and carried the right to brew ale freely, and (for example in Saxony after 1527) the congregation was bound to maintain and repair the vicarage.

The clergy came nearest to destitution in some parts of Germany, where there were clerical beggars in Protestant churches as once there had been in medieval churches. German pastors sometimes undertook secular occupations in order to live. One was a tanner and weaver, another a linen worker, a third a vendor of butter and cheese. Knipstro said that when he was a deacon at St Mary in Stralsund he was only saved from begging by his wife's sewing. Most country clergy in Germany were smallholders with a few pigs and cattle, and so survived. Many English clergy likewise maintained themselves as small farmers. It is a famous though suspect story how Richard Hooker was found by his old pupils reading the *Odes* of Horace while he tended his 'small allotment of sheep in a common field'. The vicar of Liddington in Rutlandshire made his living as an assistant to a thatcher of houses; Mr Mills of Badeley was a coal-miner; we know of a blacksmith, a rope-maker, and several other trades in the English ministry. If these were ills, they were not ills of the Reformation but ills which it failed to remedy. Throughout Christendom authority continued to frown on any occupation but the cultivation of glebe and teaching or lecturing.

The rising wealth of the laity, compared with the static incomes of the clergy, did not encourage parents to send their children into the ministry. When (about 1625) George Herbert told a court friend that he intended to take orders, the friend tried to deter him, saying that it was 'too mean an employment, and too much below his birth and the excellent abilities and endowments of his mind'. And Herbert replied that 'though the iniquity of the late times have made clergymen meanly valued, and the sacred name of priest contemptible; yet will I labour to make it honourable . . .'

We know the fathers of ninety-five pastors in the state of Oldenburg in north Germany, with these professions or occupations: fifty-five pastors, sixteen peasants, two soldiers, seven shopkeepers, one teacher of Latin, six vergers or sextons, six burgomasters or aldermen, two noblemen.

It has been loosely calculated that half the clergy of Sweden during the seventeenth century came from clerical homes. The profession (so now to call it) could become almost hereditary. Benedict Carpzov, a stiff Lutheran theologian who died in 1624, was succeeded by four generations, each of whom became a doctor of divinity, the fifth of the series dying in 1803. Melanchthon's friend John Fabricius, who was pastor at Nuremberg, was succeeded by four generations, of whom two were also pastors at Nuremberg.

The country pastor was a little more dependent than his predecessors upon the lay lords and gentry. The country pastors of the late medieval church were dependent, but often upon ecclesiastical personages like abbots and absentee bishops. The Protestant country pastor was more dependent upon the gentry. In Germany of the Thirty Years War we hear of chaplains to gentlemen acting also as their butlers and waiters, but these were conditions of war. It could hardly help making the inferior clergy less ready to censor their lords' vices. In Germany some pastors carried deference so far in the seventeenth century that they allowed the gentry to receive the sacrament separately, or even used a different and more polite formula in the administration of the sacrament to noblemen. In Denmark King Christian III had to pass a law of 1551 that the children of ministers should not be treated as the serfs of patrons.

But the dependent clergy of the impoverished countryside never had been able to rebuke eminent vice in their lords; and if the Reformers had not succeeded in improving the social lot of the clergy, they were slowly and painfully raising the standards of education. More and more clergy received an education at a school and university. The respect which was not gained by wealth was slowly being gained by learning. Both Reformation and Counter-Reformation succeeded in creating a learned ministry. The divine of the German university, the pastor of the great city church, received a sufficient stipend and was often held in high regard, as was his Dutch or English or Scottish equivalent. In the German cities he took public precedence over the senators. The German pastor Valentine Andreae, who died in 1654, possessed a select library, some rare manuscripts, a _Virgin_ painted by Albrecht Dürer and a _Conversion of St Paul_ by Holbein. In England ministers engaged upon those studies which would ultimately gain the English clergy the reputation of _stupor mundi_ for learning. Far more clergy of 1630 than of today possessed at least a smattering of the Hebrew language as well as the Greek. The English lawyer John Selden, no mean critic of the clergy for their morals and their politics, said: 'All confess there never was a more learned clergy. No man taxes them with ignorance.'

All the main Protestant churches struggled to make a university degree a necessary qualification for ordination. They all found practical difficulty in coming near their goal. A conference at Leipzig in 1544 laid down this rule, and it was the first of many such decisions. Weimar in 1550 established an easier examination for country clergy, and they must pass the more difficult examination if they moved to the town.

We know how Melanchthon conducted the examination before ordination at Wittenberg in 1549–55. It was primarily concerned with orthodoxy, not with devotion. The ordinand must understand the differences between Protestant and Roman Catholic teaching, and the Biblical grounds of Protestant teaching. Melanchthon asked questions on ethics and church history, and hard questions on dogmatics, and unlike himself he could be fierce in *viva voce* examinations. The examination was usually held in Latin, and might last an hour. Inevitably many candidates learned, not the divinity of the university, but Melanchthon's textbooks. At Stettin in 1545 the failed candidates were ordered to be kept in the poorhouse and instructed further. In 1552 Melanchthon published an *Examination of Ordinands*, devised to help examiners as well as candidates, and this was soon taken into official church orders. At Wittenberg the examination ended with a short address reminding the ordinands of the importance of their office. Luther's liturgy of ordination contained a simple vow to watch over the people for whom Christ died, and to live, and cause wife and children to live, in a Christian manner.

Everywhere in Europe, Catholic or Protestant, there was more of an examination before ordination. And ordained clergy were sometimes compelled to courses of theological study. In 1586 the Archdeacon of Colchester prescribed the study of certain books, ordered incumbents to compose specimen sermons under a tutor, and required a certificate of performance at his next visitation. We can trace the rising number of clerical graduates. In 1573 the Bishop of Lincoln ordained as priests twenty-five men of whom eight were graduates. In 1583 he ordained thirty-two of whom twenty-two were graduates. In 1585 there were 399 graduate clergy in the Lincoln diocese; in 1603 there were 646.

SERMONS

A higher education for the clergy was imperative, because more was expected of them as preachers and teachers.

Stricter Protestants maintained that on Sunday two services with sermons were obligatory. But they were often unsuccessful in getting the habit established. In not every parish church would the countrymen have heard a sermon, at either or both of their services.

There were two different answers to the problem of staffing the country parishes. One was to lower the standard of ordination below the ideal of an educated ministry, and allow the men thus ordained to preach; and there were constant complaints, especially upon the Continent, that cobblers and mechanics and other incompetent persons were making their unintelligible or unedifying noises in the pulpit. The practice was defended because it was held better for an ignorant man than no man to expound the Word of God, provided that ignorant man be a man of his Bible and of faith. Archbishop Matthew Parker of Canterbury began by ordaining too many people too suddenly, with the laudable desire to fill the parishes, but he soon repented and changed his policy. The alternative was to keep a tight hand upon preaching, limit the right of preaching to the reasonably qualified, and force the country parishes to be content with the service and an officially published homily uttered by the reader. About 1620 the village church of Eaton Constantine in Shropshire was served by four readers in succession. Each of them was the village schoolmaster, all four were ignorant, and two were immoral. They read common prayer on Sundays and holy days, were not allowed to preach sermons, taught in the school and tippled on weekdays, whipped the boys when drunk, and were dismissed. In the villages round there were a dozen ancient clergy, about eighty years old, none of them preachers, most of them living scandalous lives. Nearby there were three or four churches served by able and devoted men. But if anyone went from his own parish to hear their sermons, he was despised in his village as a zealot, under the name of 'puritan'.

A visitation of the Archdeaconry of Norfolk in 1597

shows that there were eighty-eight churches with only four sermons in the year, eight churches with no sermons at all.

The endeavour to remedy the old ignorance of clergy as of people was not the work of a few years. But something was accomplished. In the later sixteenth century, the miners of the Harz mountains were capable of using abstruse terms of theology, doubtless without understanding. If we may judge from the printed sermons of 1600 and after, the congregation was capable of a more theological apprehension than most congregations of the twentieth century. The sermon would not be likely to be mealy-mouthed, would not avoid controversy, and might fasten directly upon the sins of members of the congregation. More frequently than would later be the custom, it would be directed at rebels against the sovereign, or the papists, schismatics, or Anabaptists, and on those occasions words would not be minced. Between 1621 and 1631 the poet John Donne was preaching from the pulpit of St Paul's Cathedral in London some of the fairest and deepest sermons of the Reformation and of all the Christian centuries. They cannot have been easy to follow, in any age of the Church. It was a common belief among the Protestants that the preacher should always include in his sermon something above the heads of the congregation, to lead their minds to reach upwards. Even when allowance is made for this belief, Donne expected a high standard of Biblical and theological knowledge in his congregation and, to judge by the profit which some of his hearers claimed to have derived, he found it.

In the cities, unlike the country, sermons were frequent. An exposition of the Scripture was believed to be needed at every act of worship, if it could be had. In a little town like Torgau there were five weekday services with sermons. Strasbourg had sermons every morning and evening at the cathedral, and four times a week in several other churches. The total could mount, both for preachers and for people. In the city of Rostock the total number of sermons preached during the calendar year 1640 was calculated at 1,500.

Some Lutheran critics held that it was overdone, that a surfeit was harmful to preachers and people. 'In this city,' said Herberger of Fraustadt, 'we preachers preach ourselves to death.' In England Lancelot Andrewes summed up his objection in the epigram that when he preached twice a day he prated once. But the appetite for sermons was avid. Chaderton once preached for two hours, and then said that he would stop as he was trying their patience; but there were cries of 'For God's sake, go on! We beg you, go on!' And he continued for another hour.

The churches of the sixteenth century acquired a new article of furniture, the hour-glass by the pulpit. These were rare before the Reformation, and became common in English parish churches during the reign of Elizabeth. Many sensible men regarded an hour as the limit which their congregation should be asked to bear, though on special occasions like Lutheran funerals sermons of three hours were not unknown. Calvin rebuked Farel for preaching long and tedious sermons. Cranmer advised Latimer not to preach for more than an hour and a half, lest the king grow weary. Most church orders demanded the full hour, at least on Sundays. But printed sermons prove that there were many shorter. The humane Melanchthon thought that half an hour was enough, as the ear is the first of the senses to tire. Half-hour glasses are known; and the makers, not always accurate, sometimes erred in favour of the congregation. There is a surviving hour-glass which unwaveringly completes its hour in forty-eight minutes.

The Sunday morning service was usually succeeded by a catechism or class, often attended by adults as well as children. Even ruling princes were known to attend the catechism in Lutheran Germany. The exercise slowly faded in importance during the seventeenth century as schooling improved and it became more appropriate to the classroom than to the church. The century from 1550 to 1650 witnessed a vast extension of the knowledge of the Bible among the Protestant laity. The advance was slow and uneven. William Bradford, who was born at Austerfield in South Yorkshire in 1590, remembered that the villagers of his boyhood were totally ignorant of the Bible. But evidence on the other side is so plentiful that two instances suffice. It was Sunday when the Marquis of Montrose stayed at Keith in 1650 as prisoner, on his journey to the scaffold. The minister preached a sermon against him, from the text about Agag and the Amalekites. He said: 'Rail on, Rabshakeh!', and turned his back upon the preacher. At Cupar church in 1652 crowds gathered to hear a debate between a Presbyterian and an Independent from the English army. Subjects? Original sin, predestination, forms of worship.

CHURCH BUILDING

The new importance of preaching required a different structure for the building, and a loftier or more central pulpit. In 1575 was built a great church at the Jesuit headquarters in Rome, the Gesù; a militant, elevated house of preaching. The Protestants built few churches, partly because they were afflicted with the ruins of endowed foundations, and partly because the absence of means dilapidated some churches* and gave the parishioners a hard task to maintain others. The first church built for Lutheran worship, the castle chapel at Torgau (1543), had a simple altar and no chancel. The church of St Paul's

---

* Some of the most dilapidated churches in Elizabethan England were those where the rector had formerly been a monastic house and therefore the duty of repairing the chancel now fell to the queen. The queen's officers were signally careless about paying for the repair of chancels. Other troubles of the transition arose from ancient customs in villages. At Fuyston the monastery of St Robert at Knaresborough had always supplied a buckram covering for the altar. The parishioners naturally expected the queen to supply the buckram, and the table was left bare.

Covent Garden, built in 1631, consisted of a simple rectangle with a portico. Among the Reformed, the greatest
new building was the Huguenot temple at Charenton (1623),
designed as a simple rectangle, with two tiers of galleries,
to hold 5,000 people, a preaching house and little more.*
But much was done within the framework of the older
churches, as a visit to the ancient churches of Edinburgh or
Amsterdam shows. Sometimes the old nave would be used
for preaching, the old chancel for the sacrament. The pulpit
rose higher, and by 1648 the first embryos of the great three-
decker were appearing. Even in some Lutheran churches
Reformed influence caused the pulpit to become dominant,
in front of the altar as at Lauenburg (1615) or almost on
top of the altar as at the palace church at Schmalkald
(1590), an arrangement which became common in Hesse
and Thuringia, despite the disapproval of strict Lutherans.

In Elizabethan and Jacobean England, there was controversy between the Prayer Book men, who, knowing it to
be impossible to find a good preacher in every parish, contended for the read service as a true vehicle of worship, and
the Puritans, who contended that in every service the
Scripture must be expounded. Thus the reading desk made
its appearance as a necessary article of church furniture,
normally facing the congregation with the back of the
reader towards the east. It was made obligatory on all English churches by the canons of 1604. A few English churches
(Leighton Bromswold in Huntingdonshire under George
Herbert, Little Gidding under Nicholas Ferrar) had two
pulpits of equal height, one for the reader and the other
for the preacher, to show that prayer and preaching were of
equal honour.

CLERICAL DRESS

The Lutheran pastor wore his long black gown in the
streets. Calvin is represented in some contemporary wood-

* The Charenton temple was destroyed by Louis XIV in 1685.

cuts in doublet and breeches, and most Reformed pastors eschewed any dress that might distinguish them from the laity. The Lutheran ruff round the neck began as a secular innovation of which some clergy disapproved, but soon became liturgical and grew larger and larger until by the middle of the seventeenth century it had become the 'millstone ruff'.* Visitation orders restrained display in clerical dress – we hear of measures against German pastors who wore coloured cloth or upturned toes on their shoes, or who cut their beards like soldiers.

Lutheran congregations resented clergy who appeared at altar or in pulpit as laymen in coloured coats, and church orders soon regarded this as an abuse to be repressed. Zwingli began to preach in a black gown during the autumn of 1523, and on the afternoon of 9 October 1524 Luther preached in a black gown, whereas at the morning service he had preached in the friar's habit and cowl. But, though the gown spread rapidly among the Reformed, the Lutheran churches varied in speed of change. In Augsburg they took a solemn resolution not to listen to a preacher who was wearing a cope, and Württemberg forbade it in 1536. But in the north vestments, and especially the surplice, lasted much longer. The surplice was abolished in Nuremberg only in 1810.

In England, dress became one of the arguments between puritan and episcopalian – the surplice in church, and whether the clergy were rightly distinguished by any mark of dress in the streets. The puritan divine Dr Reynolds caused a stir by appearing in a turkey gown at the Hampton Court Conference of 1604. The English Canons of 1604 insisted that English ministers, like the Lutheran, wear their black academic gown in the streets, and their surplice in the church. Under Cromwell the puritan Vice-Chancellor of

* The ruff has survived in certain Lutheran churches to this day, especially in north Germany. The modern clerical collar owes its remote origins to an attempt by the austere of the later Counter-Reformation to prevent priests from wearing large ruffs like the laity and to restrict them to simple collars.

Oxford University is said to have given offence by appearing in a cocked hat and Spanish leather boots.

THE INTERIOR OF THE CHURCH

A Protestant minister, standing in his English pulpit about the year 1600, would find much similar to the old church – the stone stoup to the side of the door, the font in its old place, the open nave with stools and a few benches, the men still sitting on one side and the women on the other, the magnate's pew (somewhat enlarged now; there were perhaps one or two new private pews), the floor strewn with rushes and straw, for this village vestry had not yet been able to afford what was done in some other village churches, the covering of the floor of the church with flagstones. (As late as the eighteenth century there were some country churches with a bare floor.) One corner of the church might be a heap of earth, but he was used to men being buried inside the building. Some of the older people still bowed towards the altar on entry, though countrywomen mistook this for a curtsy to the minister. The church, in comparison with the same church seventy years before, would give him a sense of coolness, of absence of clutter, of bareness and nakedness. Though the oak screen still divided the chancel from the church, the rood loft above it had disappeared, the statues to the left and right likewise, the pictures which hung on the walls had been removed, and the frescoes which, in their newest glow, had given the body of the church a sense of rosiness and warmth, but in dilapidation distracted the mind and made the church seem tawdry, were concealed beneath a cool whitewash. The organ, if the old church had an organ, was not to be seen. He would probably have seen the Royal Arms, though their display was not compulsory by law, and the Ten Commandments inscribed upon the wall. The overwhelming impression must have been change from dark to light, cosiness to austerity, clutter to bareness. And how the soul responded would depend on its taste and temperament as well as its wont.

Much depended upon the village and its parsons and its tradition; but the behaviour of the worshippers would probably be a little more solemn than of old, a little more reverent, a little less uninhibitedly natural. There were still the clerk and the dog-whipper, and probably there was whispering and some strolling about; but less business would be transacted, few bargains would be made, the nave would have a little less of the feeling of an open and secular meeting-place for gossip and affairs, the centre of village secular life. It will not do to exaggerate the change, but some change towards solemnity would already have been evident. In part change was due to different moral habits, new conceptions of good behaviour and decency, and in part it was due to the new liturgies, with their attempt to make the worshippers an active congregation. The medieval village congregation must have been mainly passive in the art of worship. When the bells rang at solemn moments, they turned to the altar, or knelt, or offered their little ejaculations of prayer. But for the most part the services were done rather for them than by them, the worship of the priest or priests at the altar which they attended and heard. And being comparatively passive, except at high moments of the service, many of them continued meanwhile with what interested them and their neighbours. Though Protestant squires were still known to transact business from their pews, the new liturgies were beginning to make demands even upon the squires.

In the Middle Ages the church had been the sole public building possessed by many communities. Without a hall of meeting, townsmen or villagers habitually used the church for business, for a law court, a market, a school, a promenade, a feast. Judged by a later standard, much irreverence would have been observed in churches, from horse-dealing to women gossiping over shopping baskets. In southern Europe the tradition has not quite died; even in a Protestant church like St Paul's Cathedral, surrounded by a teeming population, it persisted till the nineteenth century. Whatever the faults of this conduct, the people had felt the church to be their own, had literally taken their daily chores into it, had regarded it as a natural place for meeting friends as well as a supernatural place for meeting God.

The changing habits of the sixteenth century are hard to trace. We hear of Protestant transepts still used for storing ammunition, of German peasants using the church as a cool cellar for their beer, of a Protestant chancel used as the parish library, of parsons storing their tithe of wool in the belfry, of theatrical performances (for a time) in German churches, of a disused country church filled with hay; local meetings, coroner's inquests, the overseers of the poor, sometimes an ecclesiastical court would use it, and the school until there was a schoolroom. The first elected legislature to meet in America, that of Virginia in 1619, met in the choir of the church at Jamestown. Something of the older atmosphere was maintained because the clergy were in one aspect officials of local government. They administered the Elizabethan poor law with their church-wardens, were responsible for collecting the rates and keeping the registers in Sweden, were everywhere in charge of such education as existed, were liable to be asked by the government to preach against women's broad-brimmed hats or insolent modern fashions, or required to arrange a search for recusants by members of the vestry. As with the Ninety-five Theses, the church door or porch continued to be the place to pin public notices. As the clergy were public officers, they sometimes included public notices with the banns, like citing the creditors of a bankrupt. The Saxon church order of 1580 and the English canons of 1604 forbid such secular notices, but convenience continued to triumph over reverence. Archbishop Laud attempted with his usual energy to render the canon effective, and summoned Bishop Goodman of Gloucester before the High

Commission because he allowed the judges to hold quarter sessions in a church. In 1571 Archbishop Grindal of York needed to order that no dinners be held in church or dances in the churchyard, and that no pedlars should display their wares in the church porch during service time. As early as 1599 an intelligent and not unsympathetic English traveller upon the Continent, Edwin Sandys, was surprised by the talking and laughter and inattention during Roman Catholic services.

We shall not be going far astray if we think of the church as becoming, within the consciousness of the community, less like a market place or town hall and more like a school; a building necessary to the community, where men and women performed a particular function and received a particular gift, and where they still met to gossip naturally, but a building conceived to be more set apart, as though the old sanctuary was extending its dominion and territory down the nave towards the west door.

The logical end to this swing of opinion against secular uses for the church was to close the building except at the times of service. Country churches had often been locked before; it was no novelty to lock churches. About 1600 the feeling grew that the building ought to be set apart for divine worship, and this could be achieved only if it was shut at other times. The Sebaldus church at Nuremberg was closed, though not finally, in 1603. In 1616 the chief pastor of Zurich, Breitinger, advised the city council to close the minster, on the ground that traders were still using it to transact business and children were playing and dirtying the seats. I know no trace of any feeling that Protestant churches should be open so that individuals might use them for private prayer. Once they had been encouraged to enter and study the great lectern Bibles; but now there were pocket Bibles. The proper place for private prayer was believed to be the home and the family.

Protestant discipline demanded a higher standard of attention and outward reverence at services. In the Reformed churches the elders, in the English church the churchwardens, had the duty of repressing ill-behaviour, walking, talking, going out into the porch in the middle of service, arriving late. From towards the end of the sixteenth century beadles were provided and were armed with sticks to walk round the congregation and check any form of irreverent behaviour. But so long as an element of compulsion entered the motives for going to church, the behaviour of mere conformists was not likely to be devotional. Beadles could prevent noise, they could not create an atmosphere of prayer.

The alternative to gossip and misbehaviour, no longer permitted, was sleep. Beadles were instructed to wake sleepers, but still there were those who slept. It was evidently becoming common when Gerhard, in a funeral panegyric upon Major, felt it right to say that no one had ever seen the great man sleeping in church. Andrewes was consulted by a scrupulous soul who had been told in a sermon that sleeping was a sign of reprobation, and who for all his struggles still fell asleep; and advised him that it was a fault of the body, not of the mind, and that he should eat more sparingly upon Sunday before service. At one service at Boston in Lincolnshire an observer claimed to have seen half the congregation asleep. At Geneva in Calvin's time Jacques Pichard went to sleep early in the sermon, awoke uncomfortably with a pain in his leg, and disturbed the congregation and preacher by shuffling with his feet and calling his neighbour a baboon.

We hear of these exceptions because now they mattered more. The due solemnity of worship must be observed. One consequence was the exclusion of very young children, and therefore of their mothers. The Irish canons of 1634 directed the churchwardens to warn people not to bring children who could not be kept quiet in their seats, and in 1616 the Kirk Session at Perth directed the beadle with his red staff to remove 'greeting bairns'.

So long as penalties could be exacted for not going to

church, an ideal reverence could not be expected. When Paul Gerhardt, writer of great hymns, arrived at Wittenberg in 1628, he found that if he said his prayers in the castle chapel where Luther had nailed his Theses he was disturbed by students swearing, drinking, and brawling. The English liturgy ordered kneeling, not only at the reception of the sacrament; but in a large congregation few seem to have knelt, and the reason was not so much puritan feeling as old custom, a straw floor, and the absence of hassocks. King Henry III of France, poor wastrel, frolicked all through the mass with his puppy. On the other hand, especially from the Calvinist countries, there are reliable descriptions of the close attention and solemn demeanour which marked public services.

One custom from the past seemed an irreverence to posterity but not to most contemporaries – the wearing of hats by men in church. They were doffed for prayer and of course for sacrament, but there are many pictures of congregations listening hatted to a sermon. It became one of the differences between the Laudian and puritan, for the Laudians tried to remove hats. In parts of Switzerland the wearing of hats continued to the nineteenth century.

SURVIVALS

In Protestant lands countrymen often continued their old customs. They still crossed themselves as they came into church, or bowed to the holy table, unless they were vehemently instructed to the contrary; and even in Reformed countries they did not always receive such instruction, or heed it when they received it. Their curate might be indifferent to these matters, or contemptible in the sight of his flock. Immemorial rites, baptized or created by the medieval Church, originating in the mists of a simple people's imagination, sometimes inherited from a pre-Christian era, were not eradicated by reformation. The great bell of Shrove Tuesday, called the Pancake Bell, which once had

summoned the people to confession, continued to ring out
in the rustic belfries, its reason forgotten, until it was
believed to be a signal for the housewife to begin her frying.
Peasants still celebrated Passion Sunday with peas and
beans, or Easter Day with eggs, boys still collected willows
on Palm Sunday though the palm procession was now
disused or forbidden. Visitations found old people telling
their beads by the graves of their dead, or curtsying to
crosses, or making a detour to pass a cross on their right
hand, or giving offence to their neighbours by making the
sign of the cross upon their breasts (but in some Lutheran
churches the sign of the cross was still encouraged). The
ringing of bells was still believed to avert lightning, and
pastors expostulated against the baptism of bells or the
burning of consecrated incense against thunderstorms.
German villagers forced reluctant pastors to ring the bells
against storms, and at Kümmersbruck the people were
convinced of the physical necessity because the storm
destroyed buildings on the first occasion when they failed
to ring the bells. Even good Protestants could not be
stopped from saying 'God have mercy on his soul', and
many inscriptions of *ora pro nobis* were left unharmed.

In Lutheran countries the new mass, though simpler,
was little changed from the old. Melanchthon once advised
a pastor to alter as little as possible for the sake of his
congregation. Though the Lutheran mass changed over the
years, it changed slowly. In various churches there were
lights, vestments, Latin for parts of the service, altars,
choirs, liturgical singing, bowing and kneeling, crucifix,
images, and embroidery. At Frankfurt pre-Reformation
missals were still in use at the end of the sixteenth century.
From 1536, when the Reformed pastor Wolfgang Musculus
attended the Lutheran service at Eisenach, to 1653 when
the puritan English ambassador to Sweden attended the
cathedral at Skara, there is a continual record of the shock
felt by men of the Reformed tradition when they saw the
Lutheran liturgies. As late as 1635 an attempt to remove

Latin from the service at Hamburg was accused of being Calvinist.

In Reformed countries a few people grumbled that the churches were like barns, that there was nothing in them to curtsy to. At Battle in Sussex the congregation was reported in 1569 to leave the church if the preacher denounced the Pope, and the people there were still using their beads. Poor Mother Waterhouse complained in 1566 that Satan would not allow her to pray in English, but kept thrusting the Latin prayers into her mind. A citizen of Geneva grumbled that the singing of metrical psalms reminded him of the old singing of priests and gave him a headache. There was a pastor at Geneva who had formerly been a monk, and was criticized for holding his hands in a monkish manner.

It was not to be expected that changes so radical could fail to disturb or confuse the generation of worshippers who witnessed them.

On the other hand, there is limited evidence of confusion and discontent. The protests in favour of tradition were few. Most protests came from those who wished to carry change still further, and considered that the survivals of old liturgy, old customs, or old ornaments, were too reminiscent of popery not to be eradicated. To understand the impact of the Reformation upon the ordinary congregation, it is necessary to realize that superstitions associated with the mass had given some instructed persons a sense of repulsion towards it, a repulsion so strong that it was almost physical. It has been said that the attitude of John Knox towards the mass is explicable only if, during the years when he attended mass, he found no numinous quality whatsoever, observed nothing in it to lead the soul heavenward, associated it only with the false worship of an idol. To many educated men the simplified, Biblical, vernacular liturgy came with a liberating, cleansing sensation of the heart, as though the ecclesiastical stables were now swept through by the clear water of divine truth. Like converts, they so acclaimed the power of the new as no longer to see goodness in the old, and preferred to dismiss every trace of it from mind and sight.

SUNDAY

Closely connected with the desire for order and reverence in services was the desire for a more solemn observance of Sunday. Though Sunday had been a day of worship, it had also been a day of plays and May-games, football, feasts, and wakes; cock-fighting, hawking, hunting, dice, bowls, bear-baiting, and church ales – which were the contemporary mode of raising money for church repairs, barrels of strong beer sold in the church or the churchyard to the public, the profits to church funds. The Lutherans were not rigorous about Sunday. They protested against habitual work or preparations for market, but Cassel held its annual fair and market at Epiphany, Küstrin held it on Septuagesima. Landgrave George of Darmstadt moved all fairs that fell on a Sunday to a weekday, but he was exceptional.

Without committing the excesses popularly known as sabbatarianism (which became a badge of the puritan party in England after 1585), moderate Protestants preferred not to associate either work or many games with Sunday. The number of illicit children begotten from village maidens in the May-games was high. In the feast of the 'lords of misrule', which continued to the end of the reign of Elizabeth, the hotheads of the parish would appear in church in fantastic clothes, with scarves, ribbons, and laces, with hobby horses and dragons, pipes and drums, jingling bells and making procession round the church while the rest of the congregation stood upon the benches to see and laugh. But it was easy to point out unusual abuses. Sunday sport and church ales were defended by many English clergy, and not only by Archbishop Laud, though it was because they helped the funds of the church as well as for their harmless good cheer.

The medieval borough and the medieval diocese had

sought to repress misconduct; for example, to see that Sunday was kept holy. Legislation to achieve a grave Sunday was not new to the Protestants; they inherited it, as they inherited civic endeavours to make the community attend service upon Sunday. But the Reformation so transformed Sunday that by the middle of the seventeenth century the Sunday of Reformed countries had acquired a tone and atmosphere different from that of Roman Catholic countries. Even in England, where the consistory never achieved legal authority, where the court consistently favoured a Sunday on which masques or plays or even jousts were permitted after time of service, and where King James I and King Charles I issued and re-issued *The Book of Sports* (1618, reissued 1633) to prevent an excess of interference with harmless games on Sunday, the public Sunday even of the Restoration maintained a sobriety which might in later years have been known as Victorian. And this was achieved although the Swiss Reformers abolished at a stroke all the holy days apart from Sunday, leaving only Sunday and the summer weekday evenings as a time for games and public recreation. The shops were closed (exceptions being permitted for milk and often for meat), markets and fairs removed from Sunday, the baiting of bears and bulls suppressed, the taverns shut during the time of service, and gaming suppressed. As late as 1662 a very poor cobbler in London, being brought a pair of shoes late on Saturday night, worked at them till after midnight, and rose early next morning in order to escape observation; a disagreeable neighbour nevertheless observed him and laid an information, and he paid the penalty of imprisonment and hard labour in beating hemp. From the later Elizabethan age onwards licences were often issued to keepers of taverns on the condition that they should sell nothing during the time of divine service, except in emergency, on penalty of losing their licence; sometimes it was made a condition that they should turn everyone out of the tavern when the last bell began to ring for morning prayer.

By comparison with this sobering of atmosphere, what is known as the sabbatarian controversy was less significant. The question was whether the Mosaic regulations about the Sabbath applied in any manner to the Christian Sunday. Those who contended that they did so apply refused to countenance any games whatever on Sunday, whereas their opponents allowed games *not in time of service*, provided they were harmless, on the ground that physical recreation was good for the people. In England sabbatarian controversy was started by the book of a puritan named Nicholas Bound, called *The True Doctrine of the Sabbath*, published in 1595. It was caught into the controversy between the Stuart crown and the half-puritan Parliament. The debate became acrimonious because of the absurd exaggerations on the Mosaic side, like those of the preacher in Somerset who said that to play bowls on the sabbath was as great a sin as to kill a man, and because of the unwisdom of the crown in making it a test of obedience. But in itself it was less important than the steady growth of Sunday quiet and sobriety. Two Acts of Parliament (1625 and 1627) forbade parishioners to meet for sport outside their own parish, made bearbaiting, bull-baiting, and plays illegal on Sundays, and forbade waggoners, carriers, and drovers to drive their vehicles or herds on Sundays and butchers to kill or sell meat. The substance of these Acts was renewed in England by an Act of 1677.

MUSIC

The greatest liturgical innovation of the Reformation was the congregational hymn. Familiar to the monks, and not unknown to the laity of the later Middle Ages, the hymn or metrical psalm became the main vehicle of congregational praise and the most powerful of devotional forces within the Protestant churches.

In Lutheran Germany the hymn would be one of the great new hymns, written by Luther or his colleagues and often set to old and familiar folk tunes. But in England, as in all the Reformed countries, hymns were only permitted if they were Scriptural, that is if they were Psalms. The Psalms so hauntingly translated by Miles Coverdale were sung only in the cathedrals, or churches with special and trained choirs, to the new settings which were not yet known under the name of (single) Anglican chants. In the village church the words of Coverdale were read by priest and clerk, and were not yet evocative to the ordinary worshipper. But it was otherwise with the hymn at the beginning and end. These were the metrical Psalms, in the translation of Sternhold and Hopkins.

It must not be thought that congregations took without hesitation to the singing of hymns or metrical Psalms. As late as 1640 four out of the eleven churches in Zurich had no congregational singing, and in Lutheran Sweden such singing was rare until the seventeenth century. The incumbents of English country parishes found it hard to persuade their congregations to sing, especially because they were slow to learn the words, and some could not read. In the years before 1640 a habit grew whereby the reader recited a verse of the Psalm, and then the whole congregation, thus informed of the words, sang the verse. The Westminster Assembly of 1643 recommended that this practice be followed in all churches. Though it was probably the best that could be done, it must have resulted in an odd and staccato mode of musical continuity.

It is a far cry, in every age, from the music of the village church to the music of the cathedral or the city church with trained choir. The dissolution of the monasteries struck a grave blow at the musical profession, from which it recovered slowly.

Every reformer or Reformer agreed that the old music was too elaborate and ought to be simplified. The destruction of the meaning of the words by the convolutions of the composers had at times reached a pitch of absurdity and extravagance comparable to that of the later caricatures of grand opera. 'Modern church music,' Erasmus had written, 'is so composed that the congregation cannot understand a word.' The puritan strand in Christianity, evoked or encouraged by Reformation and by Counter-Reformation, suspected music as it suspected useless ornaments in a church. Catholic musicians were at one time afraid that the Council of Trent would record so ruinous a decree against music in churches that their profession would face a disaster comparable with the calamity which was befalling it in the Protestant lands. The need to readjust minds and compositions to a revolution in taste and liturgy, though less overpowering among the Catholics, was still a pressing need. The Church cried for simplicity; and the problem for both Catholic and Protestant, was how to be simple without being bald and dull. In Palestrina, or in Orlando Gibbons among the Protestants, it could be seen that in simplicity was the supreme art, and out of such simplicity rose some of the loveliest of church music.

Melanchthon believed in sacred music as one of the fairest vehicles of Christian worship. Luther said that he would be at peace with no one who condemned music, for it is a gift not of man but of God. 'If I travel in your company,' wrote George Herbert in an apostrophe to church music, 'you know the way to heaven's door.' Herbert, whose chief recreation was music, is said to have ridden from his country parish twice a week to hear the cathedral music in Salisbury, though the evidence does not suggest a high standard in the Salisbury choir of his day. In England cathedral music laboured for many years under suspicion. Even Dr John Hacket, pleading for the survival of cathedrals before the Long Parliament, could make no plea for the music, and admitted that what was intended for devotion vanished away into quavers and airs.

The musicians of the cathedrals were confronted with the demand for new music to accompany the vernacular, and the names of Marbeck and Tallis (to take England alone) show how the challenge was met. The musical tradition of the old world was slow to die, and composers like Byrd preferred the old religion and its music, and wrote in the new manner out of necessity. The Wanley manuscript at the Bodleian Library, dating from early in the reign of Edward VI, contains settings for the morning and evening canticles, a number of anthems, and ten different settings for the office of holy communion. And in England, as the most conservative of the Protestant countries after north Germany and Scandinavia, the old tradition of music for the glory of God was continued, at first under something of a cloud, but established during the reign of Elizabeth and before the end of the century accepted by many churchmen as a true and beautiful aid to the worship of the church. The greatest musical achievement of English Reformed worship, the Anglican chant, is not common until early in the seventeenth century, almost always in its single form. The double chant became common only after 1700. Until the Commonwealth it was customary in cathedrals to intone not merely the versicles and responses, but the lessons, in order that the people might hear. One other glory of new English music during the reign of Elizabeth was the anthem, historically derived from the old motet.

The Council of Trent made regulations for the control of music in churches, to encourage simplicity and the use of plain chant. But the quest for simplicity did not prevent the creation of the new kind of musical performance, the oratorio, under the impulse of St Philip Neri, who used dramatic and musical representations with sermons as a means of attracting the crowds. The first oratorio proper is of the first years of the seventeenth century. And the new mood of the seventeenth century was more sophisticated and lavish. The baroque spirit reacted against the simplicity of the earlier Counter-Reformation. It was the Church triumphant and magnificent which must now be represented, its worship celebrated by priests in ornamented vesture beneath the domes of the new architecture, the walls rich with pictures, the monuments with statues, the organs sounding their solemn harmony. The processions were more elaborate, marching to the trumpets of military bands and carrying banners and torches, with floats and statues upon wheels. It was a mood of superabundance, of decorated excess to overwhelm the feelings. In 1639 we hear of an Italian cathedral with ten organs, besides several lutes and violins, so that the high services must have given the impression of a mingling of concertos with massed choirs. Organ recitals became common in Italy. We hear of an audience of 30,000 listening to a recital of Frescobaldi (1608) in St Peter's at Rome. Many of the Italian violin concertos were written for performances in churches, especially at the elevation of the Host. It has been said that the most stupendous of the baroque masses was that written by Orazio Benevoli for the consecration of Salzburg cathedral in 1628. The tranquillity of the old music was going, and there was an open quest for passion, emotion, pathos, poetry, excitement. Medieval music was the music of the cloister. Baroque music was music coming out into the world.

Reformed churches would not permit organs. Why they should have objected to the organ is not at first easy to see. It filled the church with ornamental and non-Scriptural sound, it stood for that dominance of the choir and passiveness of the congregation which they were seeking to remedy, it represented in their minds an instrument of the elaboration and clutter which their cleansing stream of simplicity was washing away. Though Luther had not much liked organs, they survived in many Lutheran churches, and thus, by making possible the combination of congregation and choir and organ, founded one of the chief glories of Protestant church music, the chorale.

But in Calvinist countries, except Holland where excellent organs survived, they preferred to have no organs. There a large number of organs were removed or sold, a large number of musicians were unemployed. There is a story of the organist of the people's church at Zurich weeping as he watched the axes smashing his great organ. But the destruction of organs has been overdrawn, for few were broken by mob violence. Many were sold to taverns or the wealthy, or their components were dismantled and sold, or they stood idle until the moths rotted them. At Worcester Cathedral the pipes made dishes for the prebendaries, the case became a bedstead. An unusual example, because we can follow the details of it in the city records, was the handsome organ of the church of Rive in the Geneva of Calvin's time. In 1544 it was found to be in the way, and someone proposed that it be moved into the greater space of St Peter's church. Calvin said that the move might give rise to scandal, and the council resolved to put it up to auction. Those responsible for the sale found the trumpet stop was missing and one of the bellows was broken, and they therefore paid for its repair in preparation for the sale. Nevertheless no purchaser appeared, and since it must be moved from Rive, it was agreed, in spite of Calvin, that it should be housed in St Peter's, where it apparently stood, deteriorating, for fifteen years. In 1562 the council at last resolved to melt the metal of the pipes, and allowed the hospital to use what it needed for its utensils.

In England the Laudians restored organs to several cathedrals and parish churches. James I and VI installed an organ in the chapel of Holyrood, but the craftsman in charge said that he had been better treated when a prisoner of the Turk. All the English organs were sold or demolished again in 1644. In the Reformed village church there was no organ. Nor was there often, as yet, the fiddler or the flautist in the gallery. There was only the unadorned singing of the congregation in unison, circling round a limited store of tunes, often led by the parish clerk; despised by Shadwell as 'a company of peasants praising God with doleful untuneable hoarse voices', but doubtless as acceptable in heaven as a majestic oratorio.

STAINED GLASS WINDOWS

Just as severe Protestants objected to musical instruments in church but not outside it, they did not object to art provided that it was not obtrusive in church. Though puritans removed the pictures from churches, they might hang the fairest of paintings in their private apartments. In Switzerland the art of stained glass, ejected from the churches, was adopted by homes, and the Swiss workers soon led Europe in their artistic skill. In a few great cathedrals (King's College Cambridge, Exeter, and York are among the most famous in England), and in a few country churches where the squire was sympathetic or no one bothered to intervene, the old glass was allowed to survive. Some stained glass fell or was broken, for Renaissance glass was more fragile and thin than the Decorated glass, and the quest for pictorial art led to a dangerous attempt to leave windows with as little leading as possible. During the Laudian period in England, Flemish artists (especially the brothers Abraham and Bernard Van Linge) left notable examples of their art, the best being in some of the colleges of Oxford University. But the church must be light, the walls must be white, and stained glass was believed by most Protestants to be unfitting and distracting in worship. Destruction in England, except for the first unruly breakages of 1559 and the more systematic smashing during the Civil War, was haphazard. Glass was better plain, but it was expensive to replace. The stained glass was often allowed to remain until it fell or was broken, and when the window required mending, it was filled with plain glass. Much depended upon the parson, the churchwardens, the squire, and the wealth of the parish. There was an illuminating case in 1629. The church of St Edmund's at Salisbury had retained its coloured windows. One, which was dilapidated and badly cracked, represented God the Father as a little old man in a red and blue coat, with a pouch by his side. Another showed him creating sun and moon with a pair of compasses. On others he was making the various plants and animals and man, and in the last window he was represented as sitting and resting in an elbow-chair. Simple members of the congregation were known to bow to the window as they passed to their seats. Henry Sherfield, M. P. for Salisbury, saw a woman do it, was shocked, and brought a motion to the next vestry meeting that the windows be replaced by plain glass. Though the motion was carried, the bishop intervened and nothing was done. Vexed at the delay, Sherfield got possession of the key from the sexton's wife, locked himself in the church, climbed on a seat and smashed the window with a stick, overbalancing with the force of the blow. Bishop Laud being in power, he was fined £500. There must have been similar but immune coups while Laud was not in power.

For the rest, art like music was 'secularized' in northern Europe during the age of the Reformation; not because the artists were less godly than before (the contrary is often true) but because the churches had ceased to be the patrons and employers of the artist, who was now working to beautify the houses of rich laymen.

14

Conclusion

CHRISTENDOM had grieved that the lords, lay and ecclesiastical, should prosper mightily upon the ill-gotten goods of the Church. Now the lay lords prospered so mightily that the goods were no longer the goods of the Church. If the Church had possessed too much wealth, this at least had been willingly reformed.

The critics in the Renaissance were painfully conscious of a clash between the Bible and the modern Church. Half the western Church chose the modern Church as the key to understanding the Bible, the other half chose the Bible as the judge of the modern Church. Western Christendom was divided, and hopeless of unity. The division of the west into Protestant and Roman Catholic was made permanent as the two rivers, sprung from one source, deepened their own channels of doctrine and devotion. The religious painting of Rembrandt penetrates the inwardness of Scriptural story in terms of contemporary life in Holland, it is painting for the family and the ordinary home, it breathes the spirit of the northern Reformation. The religious painting of El Greco breathes the spirit of the Spanish Reformation, portraying men not of this world, reaching upward to the holiness of heaven, set apart in the spirit, still the painting of a cloister, but of a cloister which has beckoned the world within its gates. Different streams of devotion, as they flow, may lead religious men apart in a subtle but no less momentous way than the hard dogmatic negatives of anathema.

Christendom had been distressed that so many clergy should live illegally with women. Half of the western Church admitted the legality of wives, the other half was struggling, not unsuccessfully, to make a celibate clergy.

Christendom had grieved at the ignorance of the clergy and the consequent ignorance of the people. Though you cannot remedy ignorance by changing the clothes of the clergyman or the posture of the worshipper, the pastoral vehemence of the age was directed to instruction, and with the aid of the printer was steadily raising the standards of priest, of pastor, and of people.

Christendom had discovered that an efficient modern state was incompatible with the immunities of the Church and the canon law. Everywhere those immunities were abolished or restricted.

Christendom had been tragically conscious of the gulf between the Christian ethic and the practice of the people. The Reformation was incapable of curing lust, pride, greed, oppression. The new security of life in the state, and the improved system of secular justice, were as potent as sermons in civilizing the people. But the general standards of moral habit, the tone of manners and customs, had been elevated.

Family prayers were far more common, knowledge of the Bible widespread and often deep, behaviour in churches more reverent outwardly; the psalms had become songs of the people, devotional literature and poetry had flourished. One summit of the devotional writing of the Reformation was *Pilgrim's Progress* – singing the praise of sovereign grace, tracing the growth of the Christian character, directed not to the professional but to the simplest heart that served in the fields or kitchen.

Christendom had grieved at the neglect of the parish for the sake of all else in the Church, from religious orders to bureaucracy. The Reformation diverted energies, and some endowments, to sustain the pastor and his people.

Medieval Christianity had been rich and varied, but it had been like a church where the furniture is cluttered, the altar obscured, and the corners undusted. The Reformation age, amid grievous destruction, swept away the clutter, pursued simplicity of vision, and directed the gaze of the worshipper towards that which truly mattered. After Luther it was not possible for either Protestant or Catholic to imitate some of the old ways of neglecting God's grace and sovereignty. So far as the Protest consisted in Luther's cry that salvation was not by ritual – not by the outward act, not by the pardoner, the pilgrimage, or the moving Madonna – the Protest was triumphant. The Ninety-five Theses once nailed upon the door at Wittenberg intended no revolution, but the essence of what they demanded was achieved, and not only in Protestantism.

By 1650 the centre of theological interest had shifted from justification by faith. To Luther and his generation this was the one thing necessary. It was a clamant need to prophesy against religion by works, salvation by ritual and external acts; they had to cry for the religion of the heart and will. In 1650 they still needed to cry for the religion of the heart and will, but not more vehemently than is necessary in every age of Church history. The chief need now appeared to be morality, the chief problem of theology the course and growth of the good life. The theological controversy which dominated the French Church of the seventeenth century was directed to the allegedly lax moral teaching of the Jesuits. The puritans made a study of 'casuistry', cases of conscience; and English episcopalian divines like Jeremy Taylor carried it further. The earnestness engendered by the Reformation epoch thrust morality into the centre, not as a substitute for, but as a consequence of, faith. And thus justification by faith alone, though still cardinal in Protestantism, was receding a little into the background of interest. It was accepted, or it was not. There were other matters now to argue.

In truth, the world was a little weary of the dogmatic arguments which accompanied the wars of Christendom. Away with the clangour; let us recover charity and generosity, let us reduce the essentials to the minimum and try to find common ground with opponents. At the Treaty of Westphalia in 1648 Christendom heaved a sigh of relief, and turned to seek intellectual as well as political peace.

In the England of 1660, the word *Reformation* had acquired an ill odour. For two centuries and more it had been a glorious or wistful word, a word of hope and idealism. The word enshrined the high endeavours of medieval sanctity, gazing backward towards a golden and simple age. Now at last the word lost its halo of idealism. It was associated with zealotry, with destruction, with discontent. It had begun to be a harassing word, encouraging the captious who would not leave good alone, stimulating the fanatical critic. We begin to hear of a world worried by reformation, reformed and ruined, reformed to the ground.

The main work, many supposed, had been done. It was time to remember how imperfect every human institution must be, to beware of bedevilling the sober pastoral care of the churches by insatiable cries for change or by swivelling the eyes to see formalism or idolatry where the reasonable man sees customs innocuous or edifying –

> As if religion were intended
> For nothing else but to be mended. (*Hudibras, 1663*)

Christendom was entering a new age, with other interests and inspirations from those of the sixteenth century. The world, they thought, had change enough. The time had come to preserve, to rest, to salvage, to see what sobriety and reason would do.

It turned out, however, that in its different way reason would be as revolutionary as the cry for reform.

Suggestions for Further Reading

GENERAL

FOR a fuller reading list, refer to the select bibliography in my *The History of the Church*, published by the Historical Association (Helps for Students of History, no. 66). For documents, H. A. Oberman, *Fore-runners of the Reformation*, 1967; H. J. Hillerbrand, *The Reformation in its Own Words*, 1964; B. J. Kidd, *Documents Illustrative of the Continental Reformation*, 1911.

PART ONE: THE PROTEST

1: The Cry for Reformation

For general background, good chapters in *New Cambridge Modern History*, vol. 1. Denys Hay, *The Italian Renaissance*, 1961, for the south. J. Huizinga, *The Waning of the Middle Ages*, 1924 (Penguin Books, 1965), for the north. R. H. Bainton, *Erasmus of Christendom*, 1970. H. Maynard Smith, *Pre-Reformation England*, 1938, is a good and sympathetic study of English religion on the eve. R. W. Chambers, *Thomas More*, 1935 (Penguin Books, 1963).

For reference, E. G. Léonard, *A History of Protestantism*, Eng. trans., 2 vols., 1966–7.

2: Luther

The works of Luther are being published in English translation in America in 55 volumes, 1955 onwards. Good selections in the Library of Christian Classics, vols. xv–xviii; and vol. xix on Melanchthon and Bucer.

Biographies of Luther: Popular but excellent, R. Bainton, *Here I Stand!*, 1951. E. G. Rupp, *The Progress of Luther to the Diet of Worms 1521*, a very readable and scholarly account of the young Luther. Fuller in R. H. Fife, *The Revolt of Martin Luther*, 1957. R. Stupperich, *Melanchthon*, Eng. trans., 1966. For political background: (e.g.) K. Brandi, *The Emperor Charles V*, Eng. trans. 1939. Catholic view in J. Lortz, *The Reformation in Germany*, Eng. trans. 2 vols, 1963.

3: Calvin

Several good translations of the *Institutes*. Outline biography of Zwingli by J. H. Rilliet, Eng. trans. 1964. A fuller biography of Bucer by H. Eells, 1931. Of Calvin by R. N. Carew Hunt, 1933. Best general modern study of Calvin by F. Wendel, Eng. trans. 1963. J. T. McNeill, *The History and Character of Calvinism*, 1954, is a useful survey.

4: The Reformation in England to 1559

Documents in G. R. Elton, *The Tudor Constitution*, 1960. Smaller selection in H. Gee and W. J. Hardy, *Documents Illustrative of English Church History*, *1896*.

Distinguished study in A. G. Dickens, *The English Reformation*, revised ed. (paperback) 1967. Fundamental on suppression of the monasteries, M. D. Knowles, *The Religious Orders in England*, vol. iii, 1959. For helpful summary with different view, G. W. O. Woodward, *The Dissolution of the Monasteries*, paperback, 1966.

Among biographies, consult especially those of Ridley and Cranmer by J. Ridley (1957, 1962) and those of Tyndale, Foxe, and Coverdale (1937, 1940, 1953) by J. F. Mozley. For the Prayer Books, F. Procter and W. H. Frere, *A New History of the Book of Common Prayer*, 3rd ed. 1905 (still in print). *Henry VIII*, by J. J. Scarisbrick, 1968.

5: The Growth of Reformed Protestantism

For background, McNeill (see under chapter 3). P. McNair, *Peter Martyr in Italy*, 1967.

For the French, outlines in J. E. Neale, *The Age of Catherine de' Medici*, 1943. Or A. J. Grant, *The Huguenots*, Home University Library, 1934. R. M. Kingdon, *Geneva and the Coming of the Wars of Religion in France*, 1956.

For the Germans, T. M. Parker in *New Cambridge Modern History*, vol. 3 (1968).

For the Swedish Reformation, M. Roberts, *The Early Vasas*, 1968.

For the Dutch, P. Geyl, *The Revolt of the Netherlands*, 2nd ed. 1958. Biography of William the Silent by C. V. Wedgwood, 1944.

For Scotland, outline in J. H. S. Burleigh, *A Church History of Scotland*, 1960. Important monograph in G. Donaldson, *The Scottish Reformation*, 1960. *Life of Knox* by J. Ridley, 1968. Good modernized edition of the chief source, Knox's own history, by W. C. Dickinson, 1950. Narrative in G. Donaldson, *From James V to James VII*, 1965.

For puritanism: W. Haller, *The Rise of Puritanism*, 1938, paperback, best general survey. Christopher Hill, *Society and Puritanism in Pre-Revolutionary England*, 1964. P. Collinson, *The Elizabethan Puritan Movement*, 1967. For their worship, Horton Davies, *The Worship of the English Puritans*, 1948. For their relation to art generally, P. Scholes, *The Puritans and Music*, 1934. For the theatre, see (e.g.) the account in E. K. Chambers, *The Elizabethan Stage*, 1923.

For the Bible, see *Cambridge History of the English Bible*, vol. 2 (1963), ed. S. L. Greenslade.

6: *The Radicals of the Reformation*

General survey in G. H. Williams, *The Radical Reformation*, 1962. Select documents in *Spiritual and Anabaptist Writers*, ed. G. H. Williams and A. M. Mergal in Library of Christian Classics, vol. xxv. Good short introduction by E. A. Payne in *New Cambridge Modern History*, vol. 2, chapter 4. The Mennonite Encyclopaedia has many valuable articles. E. G. Rupp, *Patterns of Reformation*, 1969.

For Socinians, general survey in E. M. Wilbur, *A History of Unitarianism, Socinianism and its Antecedents*, 1945.

For early English Baptists, E. A. Payne, *The Free Church Tradition in the Life of England*, 2nd ed. 1952, outline. Fundamental study in C. Burrage, *The Early English Dissenters*, 1912. For the English radicals, G. F. Nuttall, *The Holy Spirit in Puritan Faith and Experience*, 1946. For the radicals in America, P. Miller, *Orthodoxy in Massachusetts 1630–1650*, 1933.

7: *The Assault upon Calvinism*

Izaak Walton's *Lives* are an important and easily accessible source for the whole anti-Calvinist movement in England; many editions. Many corrections to his life of Hooker in C. J. Sisson, *The Judicious Marriage of Mr Hooker*, 1940. Good general introduction to Hooker in F. Paget, *An Introduction to the Fifth Book of Hooker's Treatise . . .*, 1907.

For Arminius: A. W. Harrison, *The Beginnings of Arminianism*, 1926. P. Geyl, *The Netherlands in the Seventeenth Century*, part i, 1961.

For the Laudians: biography of Laud by H. R. Trevor-Roper, 2nd ed. 1962. Of Andrewes, P. A. Welsby, 1958. For the Laudians after Laud's death, R. S. Bosher, *The Making of the Restoration Settlement*, 1951.

For the Church under Cromwell: W. A. Shaw, *A History of the English Church 1640–1660*, 1900. G. F. Nuttall, *Visible Saints; The Congregational Way 1640–1660*, 1957.

For the Quakers: the best edition of Fox's journal, 1952. And see W. C. Braithwaite, *The Beginnings of Quakerism*, new ed. 1955.

PART TWO: THE COUNTER-REFORMATION
8: *The Counter-Reformation*

General surveys in P. Janelle, *The Catholic Reformation*, 1949, and B. J. Kidd, *The Counter-Reformation 1550–1600*, 1933. H. O. Evennett, *The Spirit of the Counter-Reformation*, 1968. Best general study of Jesuits by H. Boehmer. Of the Capuchins by Father Cuthbert, 1928. Good survey of the new religious orders by H. O. Evennett in *New Cambridge Modern History*, vol. 2, chapter 9. Very readable narratives of early Jesuits in J. Brodrick, *The Origin of the Jesuits*, 1940, and *The Progress of the Jesuits*, 1947.

The first sessions of the Council of Trent are studied afresh and profoundly by H. Jedin, *History of the Council of Trent*, vols. 1–2, Eng. trans. 1957 and 1961. The last session, briefly, in H. Jedin, *Crisis and Closure of the Council of Trent*, Eng. trans. 1967.

For the Popes of the Counter-Reformation the big history by L. Pastor (Eng. tr.) is indispensable.

For the recusants in England, useful outline in E. I. Watkin, *Roman Catholicism in England*, Home Univ. Library, 1957. Best general account in A. O. Meyer, *England and the Catholic Church under Elizabeth*, Eng. tr. 1916. Or P. Hughes, *Rome and the Counter-Reformation in England*, 1942.

9: The Conquistadors

General for Americas in R. B. Merriman, *The Rise of the Spanish Empire*, 4 vols., 1918–34. Good study of Las Casas etc. in L. U. Hanke, *The Spanish Struggle for Justice in the Conquest of America*, 1960. Popular English biographies of Ricci and Nobili by V. Cronin. Important, C. R. Boxer, *The Christian Century in Japan 1549–1650*, corrected ed. 1967. C. R. Boxer, *Race Relations in the Portuguese Colonial Empire, 1415–1825*, 1963. R. Ricard, *The Spiritual Conquest of Mexico*, Eng. trans. 1966.

10: The Eastern Orthodox Church

General survey in D. Attwater, *The Christian Churches of the East*, 2 vols., 1947–8. S. Runciman, *The Great Church in Captivity*, 1968. P. Miliukov, *Outlines of Russian Culture*, vol. i, *Religion and the Church*, 1942.

PART THREE: THE REFORMATION
AND THE LIFE OF THE CHURCH

Useful survey of European disunity in R. Rouse and S. C. Neill (ed.), *A History of the Ecumenical Movement 1517–1948*, 1954.

For the life of the ordinary clergy the best book (for England) is C. Hill, *Economic Problems of the Church from Archbishop Whitgift to the Long Parliament*, 1956. And A. T. Hart, *The Country Clergy in Elizabethan and Stuart Times 1558–1660*, 1958.

On toleration etc.: general in J. W. Allen, *A History of Political Thought in the Sixteenth Century*, 1928 (paperback). The best study of the European problem of toleration is J. Lecler, *Toleration and the Reformation*, Eng. trans., 2 vols., 1960. R. H. Bainton's *The Travail of Religious Liberty*, 1951, approaches the subject through nine short biographies.

Excellent introduction to the history of church furniture in J. C. Cox, *English Church Fittings*, 1923; or the same author's *Pulpits, Lecterns, Organs*, 1915. Good survey in G. W. O. Addleshaw and F. Etchells, *The Architectural Setting of Anglican Worship*, 1948.

For music, P. Le Huray, *Music and the Reformation in England*, 1967. *New Oxford History of Music*, iv (ed. G. Abraham): *The Age of Humanism, 1540–1630*, 1968.

Index

Clement VIII, Pope, 165, 167, 373

Clergy, marriage of, 409–12;
social status of, 412–17

Clerical dress, 422–4

Cochlaeus, 73

Colet, John, 31

Coligny, Admiral, 155, 156, 158, 162, 163

Columbus, Christopher, 24, 321, 325

Commonwealth, the, 240, 292, 437

Communion, holy, 58, 59, 65, 77–8, 84, 88, 90, 117, 118, 120, 121, 122, 131, 132, 137, 144, 155, 161, 166, 196, 205, 206, 213, 230, 257, 274, 277, 278, 289, 293, 294, 295, 298, 305, 307, 308, 310, 359, 370, 372, 411, 437

Condé, Prince de, 158, 160, 162, 163

Condren, *see* De Condren

Congregationalism, 208, 209–10, 229–30, 239, 240, 247

Conquistadors, 307, 321–47

Constance, Council of, 20, 50, 55, 103, 266

Constantine, Emperor, 16, 19–20, 391, 394

Contarini, Cardinal, 267, 268, 269, 271, 308

Cornish rebels of 1549, 122

Cortés, Hernando, 323, 329, 349

Cosimo de Medici, 271, 301

Cosin, John, 227, 228, 246

Counter-Reformation, 63, 174, 176, 219, 251–362 *passim*, 365, 367, 373, 374, 406, 407, 408, 409, 410, 413, 416, 423, 436, 437–8

Counter-Reformation devotion, 23, 293–8, 385

Coverdale, Miles, 113, 114, 120, 123, 133, 435

Cox, Richard, 133

Cranmer, Thomas, 101, 103, 114–17, 118, 120, 121, 122, 123, 125–6, 131, 132, 223, 225, 230, 247, 284, 395, 420

Crépy, Peace of, 141, 273–4

Crespin, Jean, 175

Cromwell, Oliver, 187, 236, 238, 239, 246, 423

Cromwell, Thomas, 100–101, 104, 105, 109, 110, 113, 114, 115, 116, 223, 384

Cujus regio ejus religio, principle of, 143, 173

Curwen, Hugh, 134

Cyprus, 349, 353

Cyril of Novoyezersk, 361–2

Da Bascio, Matteo, 254

D'Albret, Jeanne, 164

D'Amboise, Cardinal, 27–8

D'Andelot, 158

Daniel of Volterra, 271

Day, Bishop, 120

De Azevedo, Inácio, 273

De Bérulle, Pierre, 294–5

De Castro, Matthew, 344

De Condren, Charles, 295

De Goes, Benedict, 334

De la Roche, Alain, 23

Del Puerto, Nicolas, 331

Denmark, 24, 25, 97, 113, 137, 317, 416

De Nobili, Robert, 342–3

De Rhodes, Alexander, 342, 343–4

De Sahagun, Bernardino, 337

De Sales, Francis, 294, 297–8, 374, 398

De Thou, 368

De Toledo, Francisco, 331

De Viler, Felix, 329

Directory of Public Worship, 235, 244

Dispensations, 13, 40, 41, 53, 99